James Holland is a historian, writer and broadcaster. The author of the bestselling *Fortress Malta*, *Battle of Britain* and *Dam Busters*, he has also written nine works of historical fiction, five of which feature Jack Tanner, a soldier of the Second World War.

Also a TV historian, he features on programmes shown around the world and has presented and written a large number of documentaries, both series and stand-alone films. With Dan Snow, he has co-founded the online WWII oral-history project WarGen.org, and is also Chairman and Programme Director of the Chalk Valley History Festival. He is a Fellow of the Royal Historical Society. Many of his own WWII interviews can be found at www.griffonmerlin.com. On Twitter he is @james1940

Holland is currently writing *Normandy '44*, to be published in 2019 to mark the 75th anniversary of the D-Day landings.

www.penguinbooks.co.uk

Praise for James Holland:

'James Holland is the best of the new generation of WW2 historians.'
Sebastian Faulks

'Holland is good on the mechanics of warfare and gives a thrilling blow-by-blow account of the fighting, which will please military buffs. But it is the voices of the fighting men that lift this book above the level of a simple battle narrative. Holland has a good ear for the telling reminiscences that authenticate the dialogue of so many war films of the time.'
The Times

'The always excellent James Holland tells a tale of heroism and grit to match any in the annals of war.'
Mail on Sunday

'A first-rate popular history of a fascinating and neglected battle . . . James Holland is a master of spinning narrative military history from accounts of men and women who were there.'
BBC History Magazine

'Holland has something new to say. Every page is alive with a level of excitement and enthusiasm. Here is a perspective that turns on its head what I thought I understood – filled with insight and detail.'
Neil Oliver

By *James Holland*

Non-fiction
FORTRESS MALTA
TOGETHER WE STAND
HEROES
ITALY'S SORROW
THE BATTLE OF BRITAIN
DAM BUSTERS
AN ENGLISHMAN AT WAR
BURMA '44
BIG WEEK

THE WAR IN THE WEST
Volume I: Germany Ascendant 1939–1941
THE WAR IN THE WEST
Volume II: The Allies Fight Back 1941–1943
RAF100: THE OFFICIAL STORY

Ladybird Experts
BLITZKRIEG
THE BATTLE OF BRITAIN
THE BATTLE OF THE ATLANTIC
THE DESERT WAR

Fiction
THE BURNING BLUE
A PAIR OF SILVER WINGS
THE ODIN MISSION
DARKEST HOUR
BLOOD OF HONOUR
HELLFIRE
DEVIL'S PACT

For more information on James Holland and his books,
see his website at www.griffonmerlin.com

Big Week

The Biggest Air Battle
of World War II

James Holland

CORGI BOOKS

TRANSWORLD PUBLISHERS
61–63 Uxbridge Road, London W5 5SA
www.penguin.co.uk

Transworld is part of the Penguin Random House group of companies
whose addresses can be found at global.penguinrandomhouse.com

First published in Great Britain in 2018 by Bantam Press
an imprint of Transworld Publishers
Corgi edition published 2019

A CIP catalogue record for this book
is available from the British Library.

ISBN
9780552173506

Typeset in 11.5/14pt Minion Pro by Jouve (UK), Milton Keynes
Printed and bound in Great Britain by Clays Ltd, Elcograf S.p.A.

Penguin Random House is committed to a sustainable
future for our business, our readers and our planet. This book
is made from Forest Stewardship Council® certified paper.

1 3 5 7 9 10 8 6 4 2

For James Petrie

Contents

List of Maps and Diagrams   x
Principal Personalities   xxvii

Prologue: Dogfight over Germany   1

Part I: Crisis
1   For the Love of Flying   13
2   Flying for the Reich   30
3   Black Thursday   47
4   America's Bomber Men   70
5   Learning the Hard Way   88
6   The Defence of the Reich   107
7   The Nub of the Matter   132
8   In the Bleak Midwinter   145
9   Mustang   160
10   New Arrivals   188

Part II: The Turning Point
11   Fighter Boys   215
12   Change at the Top   234
13   Berlin   254
14   Spaatz and Doolittle Take Charge   269
15   Thirty Against One   286
16   Dicing with Death   301
17   Little Friends   315
18   Waiting for a Gap in the Weather   327

Part III: Big Week

19	Saturday, 19 February 1944	345
20	Sunday, 20 February 1944	365
21	Monday, 21 February 1944	390
22	Tuesday, 22 February 1944	414
23	Thursday, 24 February 1944	428
24	Friday, 25 February 1944	446

Postscript — 463

Glossary — 481
Appendices — 483
Timeline — 485
Notes — 491
Selected Sources — 507
Acknowledgements — 519
Picture Acknowledgements — 523
Index — 527

List of Maps and Diagrams

The Aircraft: Allied Bombers, Allied Fighters and
   Luftwaffe Fighters — xi
RAF Bomber Command Bases — xv
US Eighth Air Force Bases — xvi
German Day- and Night-fighter Units — xviii
Targets and Fighter Ranges — xx
Defence of the Reich Structure — xxii
US Combat Box Formations — xxiii
Boeing B-17G Flying Fortress — xxiv
P-51B Mustang — xxv

THE AIRCRAFT
ALLIED: BOMBERS

Boeing B-17G Flying Fortress

Crew: 10
Engines: 4 x 1,200 h.p. Wright R-1820
Wingspan: 103 ft 9 in (31.5 m)
Length: 74 ft 9 in (23 m)
Max Speed: 287 m.p.h. (462 km/h)
Cruising Speed: 180–185 m.p.h. (257 km/h)
Service Ceiling: 35,000 ft (10,668 m)
Armament: 13 x .50 (13 mm)-calibre machine guns
Bomb Load: 6,000 lb (2,724 kg)

Handley Page Halifax III

Crew: 7
Engines: 4 x 1,650 h.p. Bristol Hercules XVI radials or Rolls-Royce Merlin XX
Wingspan: 104 ft 2 in (31 m)
Length: 71 ft 7 in (22 m)
Max Speed: 282 m.p.h. (454 km/h)
Cruising Speed: 220 m.p.h. (354 km/h)
Service Ceiling: 24,000 ft (7,315 m)
Armament: 8 x .303 Browning machine guns
Bomb Load: 13,000 lb (5,897 kg)

Avro Lancaster

Crew: 7
Engines: 4 x 1,460 h.p. Rolls-Royce Merlin
Wingspan: 102 ft (31 m)
Length: 69 ft 4 in (21 m)
Max Speed: 287 m.p.h. (462 km/h)
Cruising Speed: 220 m.p.h.
Service Ceiling: 24,500 ft
Armament: 8 x .303 Browning machine guns
Bomb Load: 14,000 lb (6,350 kg) or 22,000 lb (9,979 kg with modification)

Consolidated B-24 Liberator

Crew: 10
Engines: 4 x 1,200 h.p. Pratt & Witney R-1830
Wingspan: 110 ft (33.5 m)
Length: 67 ft 2 in (20.4 m)
Max Speed: 290 m.p.h. (467 km/h)
Cruising Speed: 215 m.p.h. (346 km/h)
Service Ceiling: 28,000 ft (8,534 m)
Armament: 10 x .50 (13 mm)-calibre machine guns
Bomb Load: 8,000 lb (3,629 kg)

ALLIED: FIGHTERS

Lockheed P-38 Lightning

Crew: 1 Pilot
Engines: 2 x Allison 1,600 h.p. V-1710
Wingspan: 52 ft (15.8 m)
Length: 37 ft 10 in (11.6 m)
Max Speed: 414 m.p.h. (666 km/h)
Service Ceiling: 44,000 ft (13,411 m)
Armament: 1 x Hispano M2 .78 in (20 mm) cannon, 4 x .50 (13 mm)-calibre M2 Browning machine guns, 4 x M10 4.5-in (114 mm) rocket launchers

North American P-51B Mustang

Crew: 1 Pilot
Engine: Packard Merlin V-1650 (Rolls-Royce Merlin 61 under licence)
Wingspan: 37 ft 0.5 in (11.3 m)
Length: 32 ft 2.5 in (9.8 m)
Max Speed: 440 m.p.h. (708 km/h)
Service Ceiling: 41,900 ft (12,770 m)
Armament: 4 x .50 (13 mm)-calibre M2 Browning machine guns

Supermarine Spitfire Mk IX

Crew: 1 Pilot
Engine: Rolls-Royce 1,720 h.p. Merlin 66
Wingspan: 32 ft 6 in (9.9 m)
Length: 31 ft 1 in (9.5 m)
Max Speed: 408 m.p.h. (657 km/h)
Service Ceiling: 42,500 ft (12,954 m)
Armament: 2 x Oerlikon .78 in (20 mm) cannons and 2 x .50 (13 mm) M2 Browning machine guns

Republic P-47 Thunderbolt

Crew: 1 Pilot
Engine: Pratt & Witney 2,000 h.p. R-2800 radial
Wingspan: 40 ft 9 in (12.5 m)
Length: 36 ft 1 ft (11m)
Max Speed: 433 m.p.h. (697 km/h)
Service Ceiling: 43,000 ft (13,106 m)
Armament: 8 x .50 (13 mm)-calibre M2 Browning machine guns

LUFTWAFFE: FIGHTERS

Focke-Wulf 190 A-8

Crew: 1 Pilot
Engine: 1 x 1,677 h.p. BMW 801 radial
Wingspan: 34 ft 5 in (10.5 m)
Length: 29 ft 5 in (9 m)
Max Speed: 408 m.p.h. (657 km/h)
Service Ceiling: 37,430 ft (11,408 m)
Armament: 2 x .50 (13 mm) MG 131 machine guns and 4 x .78 in (20 mm) MG 151 cannons

Junkers 88 G-1 Night-fighter

Crew: 3
Engines: 2 x 1,677 h.p. BMW 801 G-2
Wingspan: 65 ft 10 in (20 m)
Length: 50 ft 9 in (15.5 m)
Max Speed: 342 m.p.h. (550 km/h)
Service Ceiling: 32,480 ft (9,900 m)
Armament: 4 x .78 in (20 mm) MG 151 cannons, 2 x .50 (13 mm) MG 131 cannons and 1 or 2 x MG 151 *Schräge Musik* cannons

Messerschmitt 109G

Crew: 1 Pilot
Engine: Daimler-Benz DB605A-1
Wingspan: 32 ft 6 in (9.9 m)
Length: 29 ft 7 in (9 m)
Max Speed: 398 m.p.h. (640.5 km/h)
Service Ceiling: 39,370 ft (12,000 m)
Armament: 2 x .5 in (13 mm) MG 131 machine guns and 1 x .78 in (20 mm) MG 151 cannon

Messerschmitt 110F

Crew: 2 (3 for night-fighter versions)
Engines: 2 x 1,475 h.p. Daimler-Benz 605B
Wingspan: 53 ft 4 in (16.3 m)
Length: 40 ft 6 in (12.3 m)
Max Speed: 370 m.p.h. (595 km/h)
Service Ceiling: 36,000 ft (10,970 m)
Armament: 2 x .78 in (20 mm) MG 151 cannons & 2 x 1.2 in (30 mm) MK 108 cannons

Messerschmitt 210

Crew: 2
Engines: 2 x 1,332 h.p. Daimler-Benz DB601F
Wingspan: 53 ft 7 in (16.3 m)
Length: 37 ft (11.3 m)
Max Speed: 350 m.p.h. (563 km/h)
Service Ceiling: 29,200 ft (8,900 m)
Armament: 2 x .78 in (20 mm) MG 151cannons, 2 x .3 in (7.92 mm) MG 17 machine guns and 2 x .50 (13 mm) MG131 machine guns

RAF BOMBER COMMAND BASES

6 GROUP

4 GROUP

1 GROUP

5 GROUP

8 GROUP

3 GROUP

100 GROUP

Middlesbrough
Middleton St George
Croft
Leeming
Skipton-on-Swale
Wombleton
Dishforth
Topcliffe
Tholthorpe
Linton-on-Ouse
East Moor
Driffield
Allerton
Full Sutton
Lissett
Marston Moor
York
Pocklington
Leconfield
Rufforth
Melbourne
Elvington
Holme
Riccall
Breighton
Hull
Burn
North Killingholme
Snaith
Sandtoft
Elsham Wolds
Kirmington
Lindholme
Blyton
Grimsby
Sheffield
Bawtry
Hemswell
Ludford Magna
Binbrook
Kelstern
Faldingworth
Wickenby
Wigsley
Skellingthorpe
East Kirkby
Waddington
Woodhall Spa
Swinderby
Coningsby
Winthorpe
Nottingham
Syerston
Langar

North Creake
Little Snoring
Oulton
Great Massingham
Foulsham
Swannington
West Raynham
Bylaugh Hall
Leicester
Downham Market
Methwold
Birmingham
Upwood
Mepal
Feltwell
Warboys
Witchford
Mildenhall
Wyton
Waterbeach
Graveley
Huntingdon
Oakington
Tuddenham
Exning
Little Staughton
Gransden
Chedburgh
Tempsford
Lodge
Stradishall
Felixstowe
Wratting Common

Great Yarmouth
Lowestoft

N

0   50 km
0   50 miles

North Sea

The Wash

ENGLAND

London

High Wycombe

KEY

◼ Main towns   ☐ Headquarters

HEADQUARTERS

🔺 RAF Bomber Group   ▲ RAF Airfield

UNIT AREAS

High Wycombe: HQ RAF Bomber Command and 8th US Force

US EIGHTH AIR FORCE BASES

KEY

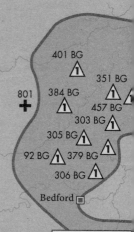

①	1st US Bomber Division
②	2nd US Bomber Division
③	3rd US Bomber Division
—	Bomber division boundary
◼	Main towns
☐	Headquarters
✚	Special Operations (Carpetbaggers)

HEAVY BOMBARDMENT GROUPS

34. Mendlesham, B-24
44. Shipdham, B-24
91. Bassingbourn, B-17
92. Podington, B-17
93. Hardwick, B-24
94. Bury St Edmunds, B-17
95. Horham, B-17
96. Snetterton Heath, B-17
100. Thorpe Abbotts, B-17
303. Molesworth, B-17
305. Chelveston, B-17
306. Thurleigh, B-17
351. Polebrook, B-17
379. Kimbolton, B-17
381. Ridgewell, B-17
384. Grafton Underwood, B-17
385. Great Ashfield, B-17
388. Knettishall, B-17
389. Hethel, B-24
390. Framlingham, B-17

392. Wendling, B-24
398. Nuthampstead, B-17
401. Deenethorpe, B-17
445. Tibenham, B-24
446. Bungay, B-24
447. Rattlesden, B-17
448. Seething, B-24
452. Deopham Green, B-17
453. Old Buckenham, B-24
457. Glatton, B-17
458. Horsham St Faith, B-24
466. Attlebridge, B-24
467. Rackheath, B-24
486. Sudbury, B-24
487. Lavenham, B-24
489. Halesworth, B-24
490. Eye, B-24
491. Metfield, B-24
492. North Pickenham, B-24
493. Debach, B-24

HEADQUARTERS

Bushy Park: HQ, United States Strategic Air Forces in Europe (USSTAF). Code name: *Widewing*
High Wycombe: HQ Eighth AF. Code name: *Pinetree*
Bushey Hall: HQ, Eighth AF Fighter Command

401 BG ①
351 BG ①
801 ✚
384 BG ①
457 BG ①
303 BG ①
305 BG ①
92 BG ① 379 BG ①
306 BG ①

Bedford ◼

1st U BOMBER DIVISION

☐ High Wycombe

Bushey Hall ☐

London ○

Bushy Park ☐

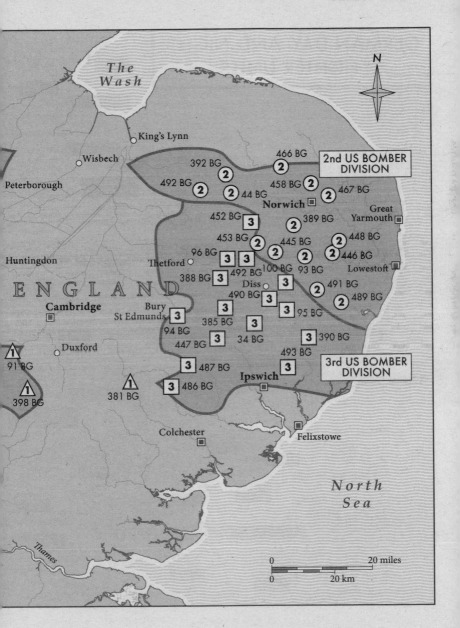

The Wash

King's Lynn

Wisbech

Peterborough

392 BG ②

492 BG ②   ② 44 BG

466 BG ②

2nd US BOMBER DIVISION

458 BG ②   ② 467 BG

Norwich ▣

452 BG ③

② 389 BG

Great Yarmouth ▣

453 BG ②

445 BG ②   ② 448 BG

Huntingdon

96 BG ③ ③

③

② 446 BG

Thetford ○

492 BG ②   100 BG ③   93 BG ②   Lowestoft ▣

ENGLAND

388 BG ③   Diss ○

② 491 BG

490 BG ③   ② 489 BG

Cambridge ▣   Bury St Edmunds ③

③ 95 BG

385 BG ③

34 BG ③

94 BG ③

447 BG ③

393 BG ③   390 BG ③

Duxford ○

⚠ 91 BG

487 BG ③

Ipswich ▣

3rd US BOMBER DIVISION

⚠ 398 BG

⚠ 381 BG

486 BG ③

Colchester ▣

Felixstowe ▣

North Sea

Thames

0 — 20 miles
0 — 20 km

N

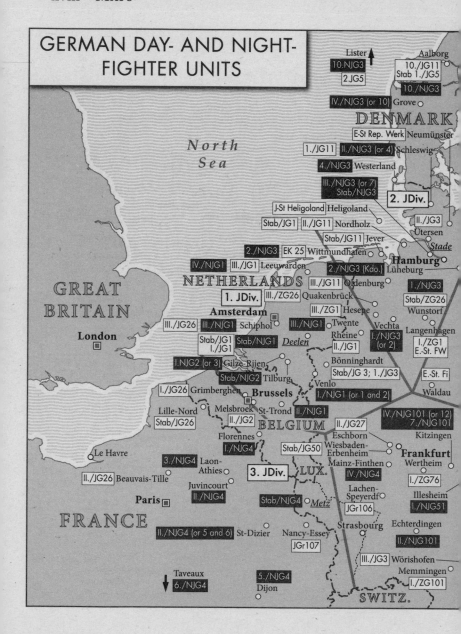

GERMAN DAY- AND NIGHT-FIGHTER UNITS

TARGETS AND FIGHTER RANGES

GREAT
BRITAIN

East
Anglia

London

	RANGE (miles/km)	*With drop tanks*	Date
A1	175/282	none (P-47C)	May 1943
A2	230/370	none (P-47D)	June 1943
A3	340/547	75-gallon belly	July 1943
A4	375/603	108-gallon belly	August 1943
A5	425/684	150-gallon belly	February 1944
A6	475/764	2 x 108-gallon wing	February 1944
B1	520/837	none	November 1943
B2	585/941	2 x 108-gallon wing	February 1944
C1	475/764	none	January 1944
C2	650/1,046	2 x 75-gallon wing	March 1944
C3	850/1,368	2 x 108-gallon wing	March 1944

KEY

Air base

Original targets

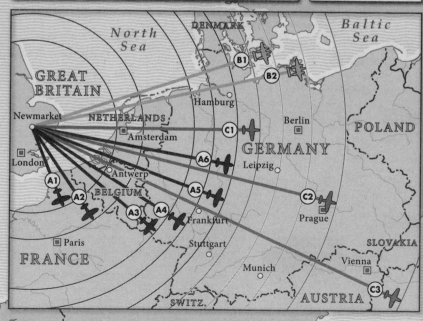

DEFENCE OF THE REICH STRUCTURE

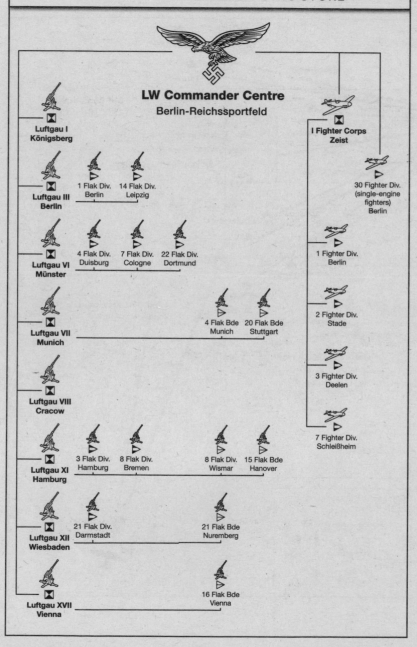

LW Commander Centre
Berlin-Reichssportfeld

Luftgau I
Königsberg

Luftgau III
Berlin

1 Flak Div.
Berlin

14 Flak Div.
Leipzig

Luftgau VI
Münster

4 Flak Div.
Duisburg

7 Flak Div.
Cologne

22 Flak Div.
Dortmund

Luftgau VII
Munich

4 Flak Bde
Munich

20 Flak Bde
Stuttgart

Luftgau VIII
Cracow

Luftgau XI
Hamburg

3 Flak Div.
Hamburg

8 Flak Div.
Bremen

8 Flak Div.
Wismar

15 Flak Bde
Hanover

Luftgau XII
Wiesbaden

21 Flak Div.
Darmstadt

21 Flak Bde
Nuremberg

Luftgau XVII
Vienna

16 Flak Bde
Vienna

I Fighter Corps
Zeist

30 Fighter Div.
(single-engine
fighters)
Berlin

1 Fighter Div.
Berlin

2 Fighter Div.
Stade

3 Fighter Div.
Deelen

7 Fighter Div.
Schleißheim

US COMBAT BOX FORMATIONS

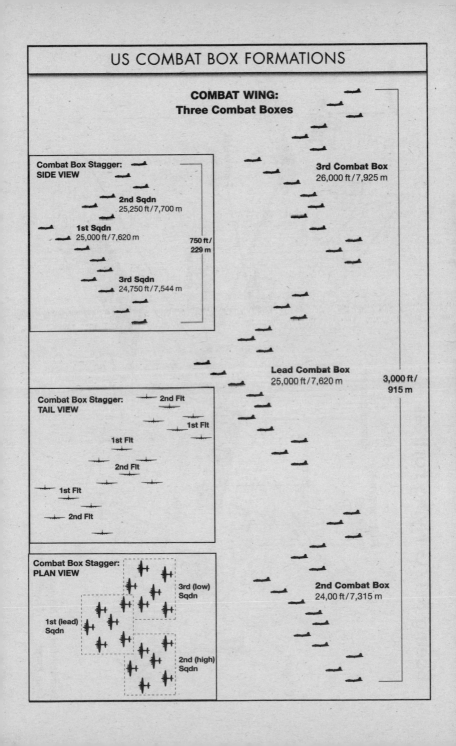

COMBAT WING:
Three Combat Boxes

3rd Combat Box
26,000 ft / 7,925 m

Combat Box Stagger:
SIDE VIEW

2nd Sqdn
25,250 ft / 7,700 m

1st Sqdn
25,000 ft / 7,620 m

750 ft /
229 m

3rd Sqdn
24,750 ft / 7,544 m

Lead Combat Box
25,000 ft / 7,620 m

3,000 ft /
915 m

Combat Box Stagger:
TAIL VIEW

2nd Flt

1st Flt

1st Flt

2nd Flt

1st Flt

2nd Flt

Combat Box Stagger:
PLAN VIEW

3rd (low)
Sqdn

1st (lead)
Sqdn

2nd (high)
Sqdn

2nd Combat Box
24,00 ft / 7,315 m

Boeing B-17G Flying Fortress

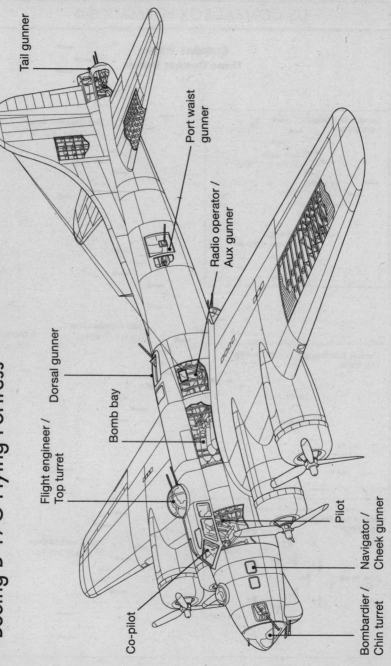

Tail gunner

Port waist gunner

Radio operator / Aux gunner

Dorsal gunner

Flight engineer / Top turret

Bomb bay

Pilot

Co-pilot

Navigator / Cheek gunner

Bombardier / Chin turret

P-51B Mustang

Radio transmitter /
receiver

Pilot

Oxygen tanks

.50-calibre
machine gun (x 4)

V -1650 Packard-
built Rolls-Royce
Merlin engine

Auxillary fuel
'drop' tank

PRINCIPAL PERSONALITIES

(ranks at February 1944)

Americans

Lieutenant Clarence 'Bud' Anderson
Pilot, 363rd Fighter Squadron, 357th Fighter Group (P-51).

Major-General Frederick Anderson
Commanding officer, VIII Bomber Command, US Eighth Air Force.

General Henry 'Hap' Arnold
Commander-in-chief, United States Army Air Forces.

Captain Duane 'Bee' Beeson
Pilot, 334th Fighter Squadron, 4th Fighter Group, VIII Fighter Command, US Eighth Air Force (P-47 and P-51).

Lieutenant-Colonel Don Blakeslee
Commanding officer, 4th Fighter Group (P-47 and P-51).

Major-General Jimmy Doolittle
Commanding officer, Eighth Air Force.

Lieutenant-General Ira Eaker
Commanding officer, Eighth Air Force, then Mediterranean Allied Air Forces.

Major Francis 'Gabby' Gabreski
Pilot, 61st Fighter Squadron, 56th Fighter Group, VIII Fighter Command, US Eighth Air Force (P-47).

Captain Don Gentile
Pilot, 336th Fighter Squadron, 4th Fighter Group, VIII Fighter Command, US Eighth Air Force (P-47 & P-51).

Sergeant Larry 'Goldie' Goldstein
Radio operator, 563rd Bomb Squadron, 388th Bomb Group, VIII Bomber Command, US Eighth Air Force (B-17).

Lieutenant Bob Hughes
Pilot, 351st Bomb Squadron, 100th Bomb Group, VIII Bomber Command, US Eighth Air Force (B-17).

Lieutenant Bob Johnson
Pilot, 61st Fighter Squadron,
56th Fighter Group, VIII
Fighter Command, US Eighth
Air Force (P-47).

Lieutenant James Keeffe
Co-pilot, 566th Bomb
Squadron, 389th Bomb Group,
VIII Bomber Command, US
Eighth Air Force (B-24).

Major-General Bill Kepner
Commanding officer, VIII
Fighter Command, US Eighth
Air Force.

Lieutenant William R. Lawley
Pilot, 364th Bomb Squadron,
305th Bomb Group, VIII
Bomber Command, US Eighth
Air Force (B-17).

Sergeant Hugh 'Mac' McGinty
Tail gunner, 524th Bomb
Squadron, 379th Bomb Group,
VIII Bomber Command,
US Eighth AF (B-17).

**Lieutenant J. Kemp
McLaughlin**
Pilot, 326th Bomb Squadron,
92nd Bomb Group, VIII
Bomber Command, US Eighth
AF (B-17).

Sergeant John Robinson
Waist gunner, 703rd Bomb
Squadron, 445th Bomb Group,
VIII Bomber Command,
US Eighth AF (B-24).

**Lieutenant-General Carl
'Tooey' Spaatz**
Commanding officer, United
States Strategic Air Forces in
Europe.

Major Jimmy Stewart
703rd Bomb Squadron, 445th
Bomb Group, 2nd Division,
VIII Bomber Command,
US Eighth AF (B-24).

**Lieutenant Robert 'Sully'
Sullivan**
Navigator, 32nd Bomb
Squadron, 301st Bomb Group,
US Fifteenth Air Force (B-17).

**Lieutenant T. Michael
Sullivan**
Bombardier, 429th Bomb
Squadron, 2nd Bomb Group,
US Fifteenth Air Force (B-17).

Captain Dick Turner
Pilot, 356th Fighter Squadron,
354th Fighter Group, VIII
Fighter Command, US Eighth
Air Force (P-51).

British

Squadron Leader Gordon Carter
Navigator, 35 Squadron, Pathfinder Force, RAF Bomber Command (Halifax).

Air Marshal Sir Arthur Harris
Commander-in-chief, RAF Bomber Command.

Air Chief Marshal Sir Charles Portal
Chief of the Air Staff.

Flight Lieutenant Russell 'Rusty' Waughman
Pilot, 101 Squadron, 5 Group, RAF Bomber Command (Lancaster).

Canadian

Flight Lieutenant Bill Byers
Pilot, 429 'Bison' Squadron, 6 Group, RAF Bomber Command (Halifax).

German

Margarete Dos
Red Cross nurse living and working in Berlin.

Generalmajor Adolf Galland
General der Jagdflieger.

Reichsmarschall Hermann Göring
Commander-in-chief, Luftwaffe.

Oberst Hans-Joachim 'Hajo' Herrmann
Inspector of Night-fighters, CO 30 Jagddivision, *Wilde Sau* (FW190).

Oberleutnant Wilhelm 'Wim' Johnen
5/Nachtjagdgeschwader 5 (Me110).

Leutnant Heinz Knoke
5/Jagdgeschwader 11 (Me109).

Feldmarschall Erhard Milch
Deputy commander, Luftwaffe.

Generalmajor Josef 'Beppo' Schmid
Commanding officer, 1 Jagddivision.

Prologue
Dogfight over Germany

AROUND 3.30 P.M., SUNDAY, 10 October 1943. Forty-nine P-47 Thunderbolts were speeding towards an already ferocious aerial battle. Ahead and below, more than 130 B-17 Flying Fortresses were attempting to drop bombs on the marshalling yards at Münster in north-west Germany. Over the target, puffs of flak – heavy anti-aircraft fire – were bursting all around them in dark smudges of smoke. But the bombers were strung out over around 6 miles and the tight formations of those still heading to the target were being harried and shot at by large numbers of enemy fighters, as were those that had already dropped their loads and were now turning westwards for their bases in England. Tracer from machine guns arced across the sky, and bombers were falling out of their tight formations, trailing flame and smoke, others disintegrating mid-air.

This was a long trip for the Thunderbolts, single-engine fighters that could fly this far, some 50 miles into Germany, only with the addition of auxiliary fuel tanks. These were now jettisoned, making each of the P-47s suddenly and dramatically faster and more manoeuvrable once the extra weight and cause of drag had gone. Then someone

shouted, 'Forty bandits! Seven o'clock to the bombers,
same level! Shaker Three, out!' In his Thunderbolt, Lieutenant Robert 'Bob' Johnson knew they had the perfect
'bounce' – that is, a surprise dive on the enemy with the
advantage of height: at some 30,000 feet they were easily
8,000 feet above the melee and had manoeuvred across
the sky so that the sun was behind them. The P-47s were
being led by Major Dave Schilling of the 62nd Fighter
Squadron; Johnson was part of the 61st. Each squadron
flew with sixteen pilots and planes, and these two, along
with the 63rd FS, made up the 56th Fighter Group.
'Zemke's Wolfpack' they were known as after their brilliant group commander, Colonel Hubert 'Hub' Zemke.
They were the leading fighter group in the US Eighth Air
Force, with more enemy planes shot down than any other.
Johnson was proud of that. They all were, and now it
looked as if they would soon be adding to that tally.

As Schilling and the men of the 62nd FS peeled off and
dived, Johnson followed, catching a glint of the sun on his
wingtip as he flipped the big 7-ton 'Jug' over and pushed
the stick forward. The needle on the air speed indicator
soared, while Johnson felt himself pushed deeper back
into his seat, the g-forces pulling across his skin.

For long months since arriving in England in April that
year, Johnson had been a wingman, playing second fiddle
and watching the back of his buddy, but now he was the
lead in his pair, and Bill Grosvenor was watching his tail.
A wingman was 75 per cent of a lead pilot's eyes, Johnson
reckoned. A good wingman meant the lead could get on
with the job of shooting down the enemy, knowing he did
not have to spend half his time protecting his own tail.
Johnson realized this was about as good as he could ever

hope for: the advantage of height, speed and surprise, and with someone to protect him for a change rather than the other way around.

A little way ahead, another pilot was opening fire on a Focke-Wulf 190. Smoke was already streaming from the German's wings. Bullets – little beads of tracer – arced and spat across the sky. A second FW190, presumably a wingman, swept in, already too late to protect his leader. Johnson saw him, pressed down on the starboard rudder and with his left hand opened the throttle wider, then with his right pushed the stick slightly over so that his Thunderbolt turned towards the German fighter. He had him in his sights, but fleetingly only, because his enemy knew he was too late to save his comrade but not himself and so, flicking over, he dived earthwards.

Johnson glanced around – where the hell was Grosvenor? – and saw the sky full of turning, swirling planes. Abandoning the FW190, he pulled up and, swivelling his head frantically, could suddenly see no Thunderbolts at all but plenty of Germans. *Got to hit 'em*, he thought, *take them off the bombers*. Away to his left, a Messerschmitt 110 twin-engine fighter, with two Focke-Wulfs, all three in a long, shallow dive towards the bombers and waiting for the Me110 to get in range to fire its rockets. If those hit a bomber it was all over. A B-17 could take a hell of a beating, but it had no answer to a rocket – a 90lb projectile full of high explosive that could create a hole 30 yards wide.

Got to break them, get in there fast, Johnson told himself. A kick on the rudder pedal, open the throttle and the Thunderbolt sped towards the enemy planes, Johnson bringing his gunsight on to one of the Focke-Wulfs. Both the 190 pilots saw him and pulled their fighters up into steep climbs. *To hell with them.* Johnson now lined up the 110, big and increasingly filling his sights. Spotting him, the German pilot tried to evade, twisting and turning, but the two-engine *Zerstörer* – 'Destroyer' – was not agile enough and, by using the rudder, Johnson was able to press his gun button and rake the Messerschmitt from side to side. The Me110's rear canopy disintegrated in a spray of Perspex and metal, then the navigator-gunner flung up his arms and collapsed.

There were hits all over the stricken enemy fighter. Desperately, the pilot tried to get away, then flipped the plane hard to port. Johnson slammed his foot down on the rudder, eased back the stick, then rolled, his Thunderbolt responding smoothly and cleanly like the thoroughbred she was when handled by such an experienced pilot. Now the Messerschmitt filled his sights once more. Finger on the gun button, the shudder from a short burst, and eight lines of smoking, bright tracer as the bullets of the big .50-calibre machine guns converged and tore the 110 apart. Johnson sped past, so close that his Thunderbolt shook from the violence of the explosion. Bits of debris clanged sharply against his own airframe as he hurtled through the mass of flame, smoke and obliterated enemy aircraft.

Stick back, throttle forward and a surge of power as he climbed up out of the fray to where he could see more clearly the air battle that was now raging. There was space behind him and to his right, but no sign of Bill Grosvenor. German fighters filled his view, some firing rockets towards the bombers. All around him he saw FW190s, Me109s and 110s, and the newer upgraded twin-engine Messerschmitt, the 210, and even some Junkers 88 twin-engine bombers. Repeatedly they were attacking the bomber stream, diving in and stabbing at them, swirling around the vast formation like angry wasps. Johnson watched their cannons and machine guns sparkle, then suddenly he saw a large leap of flame as another rocket was launched. There was a bigger flame in the sky too: a bomber plunging earthwards, spinning grotesquely. Parachutes blossomed – that was something – half-spheres of white against the vivid blue, the streaks of smoke and flash of flame and luminescent dots of tracer. Fighter planes everywhere, but, curiously, none seemed to have spotted Johnson in his big Jug.

Now he saw three Focke-Wulfs diving down hard towards the rear of the bombers, several thousand feet below. Johnson realized he was the only friendly fighter between them and the Flying Fortresses, so he pulled the stick to his left, put his foot down on the port rudder, flicked the Thunderbolt over and dived down like a banshee. His closing speed was over 700 m.p.h., which made it difficult to score any hits, but he hoped he could ruin their attack and protect the Fortresses.

He spotted one of the Focke-Wulfs climbing steeply and turning towards him. *These boys want to fight!* Johnson thought to himself. Keeping a close watch on that 190 out of the corner of his eye, he continued to dive towards the lead Focke-Wulf, convinced the German now turning towards him could not possibly hit him. He pushed the stick further forward. The speed and g-forces were immense as he dived ever more steeply: 80 degrees, 90 and then the vertical. Still he pushed the stick forward until the fighter dipped under the vertical so that he was starting to loop upside down as he readied himself to open fire on the lead 190. The angle of his dive meant he was hurtling towards the enemy plane at 90 degrees: the 190 streaking towards the bombers and he in his P-47 diving in from above. Despite the speed, his mind was clear. Carefully, he increased the lead, aiming off so that the Focke-Wulf and his bullets would converge. A squeeze of the trigger, then that familiar judder of the aircraft as the machine guns fired. White flashes peppered the 190, little stabs of orange as they struck. The cockpit shattered, then a sudden flash, an intense glare, as the fuel tanks burst and erupted into flames.

A loud crack and Johnson's plane jarred. He felt the hit. The climbing third Focke-Wulf, guns still twinkling. A cannon shell tore into the tail of the P-47, snapping a rudder cable. The Thunderbolt rolled. A blinding flash just ahead and the lead Focke-Wulf exploded, flame and matter flung outwards. Johnson gripped the stick through the debris, but the Thunderbolt was slow to respond. Then at last the nose began to turn and the big fighter climbed once more. As the speed dropped, Johnson pushed the stick forward and regained level flight.

But no respite. Ahead, slightly to his port, a grey Me110 sped towards him, guns winking. Streaks of tracer and smoke rushed harmlessly past. Johnson kicked on the rudder – a slight yaw was all that was needed and the Me110 would be kill number three – but the rudder did not respond. *No rudder!* A rocket flashed towards him just above his head. Johnson ducked involuntarily, then pushed open the throttle and climbed once more until he had reached 30,000 feet and some kind of safety. Far below the air battle had shifted, slipping away, fighters still swirling around the bombers like hornets, but little dots now.

Johnson flew on, straight and level, trying to gauge just

how bad his situation was. One rudder cable snapped, gaping holes in his tail and fuselage. It wasn't good. The stricken Thunderbolt might be managing to fly now, but he knew at any moment it could easily slip out of control and into a spin, or worse, from which he would not be able to recover. That realization was enough. Pulling back the canopy, he released his belt and shoulder straps and readied himself to jump.

Wind slapped hard as he began to climb on to the seat. But he was a long way up and there below was Germany. Nazi Germany. Enemy territory. Perhaps, he thought, it would be better at least to try to reach one of the unoccupied countries. Then he remembered how a couple of months earlier one of his fellow pilots had nursed a Thunderbolt home successfully. That Jug had been in a worse state than his. Using one arm to pull the broken rudder cable, he did nothing more than gather a length of wire, but then thought of the rudder trim tabs and – *yes!* – they responded. It wasn't much, but by working the stick and using his ailerons and the rudder trim he was able gradually to bring the Thunderbolt around so that he was heading west in the direction of home. He was now flying back over the air battle as it continued to drift westwards, bombers and fighters still swirling around the sky. Johnson began to feel scared; there were too many aircraft with black crosses and he was in a crippled plane that needed careful nursing home and nothing more. On the other hand, just below him and utterly oblivious of Johnson and his Thunderbolt above, was a Focke-Wulf, flying straight and level. It was hard to imagine a juicier target, ripe for the plucking. And because Johnson was just twenty-three years old and because his job was to shoot down Germans, he dropped the nose, opened the throttle and began to dive towards him.

Another Thunderbolt now dropped in front of him, cutting in on his prey, then opened fire at close range and blew the 190 out of the sky before continuing with his dive, on the lookout for other targets.

Johnson, recognizing it was time to quit while he was still just ahead, pulled back on the stick and climbed up to safety again, then began calling for help on the RT. A pilot named 'Hydro' Ginn responded – from the 62nd, not Johnson's 61st Fighter Squadron, although in Zemke's 56th Fighter Group everyone knew everyone pretty much.

'Bob, we have you in sight,' he heard Ginn say over his headphones. Johnson looked around and saw three of them heading towards him in a shallow dive.

'Come, escort me,' Johnson replied. 'I got a little problem here and I don't know when I am going to have to bail out.'

He was still flying all out. 'Bob, for God's sake,' said Ginn, 'cut that thing back.'

Doing as Ginn suggested, he pulled back on the throttle and was relieved to be joined by fellow P-47s on either side.

'To hell with walking out,' he told them. 'I am going to fly!'

On the way home they were bounced by two German fighters. Johnson's protectors saw them early, climbed up to meet them and the would-be attackers rolled away. Without those friends, he would have been dead meat.

At last they neared the English coast, but Johnson was still not home and dry. Over England lay a heavy cloud mass, dense, low and through which nothing could be seen. For twenty minutes they descended slowly in a wide spiral, hoping they might spot a break in the cloud. And then, as if by magic, the gap they needed appeared and below them lay their airfield. Hydro Ginn was the first to land, but Johnson's buddy Ralph kept circling, warning the control tower to get the fire engine and ambulance ready. Now came the moment of truth: Johnson flew towards the runway, low and still at around 120 m.p.h., using the trim tabs to steady the big Thunderbolt. Suddenly the ground was rushing towards him. *Easy does it!* One wheel then a second hit the ground heavily, too fast, but Johnson slammed on the brakes, the port rudder cable taut in his hand.

Slowing now, and eventually the big Jug came to a halt. Power off, then Ralph Johnson's Thunderbolt pulled up alongside, but fog was closing in. As he clambered out and jumped down from the wing, Johnson was conscious that he had had the luckiest of escapes. Then came exhilaration: two kills, which his gun cameras would soon confirm. That made five to his name in all and made him an ace – the fifth American pilot in the European theatre to achieve that coveted accolade. 'It was,' he noted later, 'a great and auspicious moment for me.'

Bob Johnson had been one of some 216 Thunderbolts dispatched in waves that day to protect the bombers. That was five fighter groups, and between them they had shot down twenty enemy aircraft for the loss of just one of their own – a good ratio. Even so, the raid had cost VIII Bomber Command another 326 casualties, of whom 306 were still missing in action. Of the fourteen Flying Fortresses from the 100th Bomb Group, for example, just one had made it back. That was a truly devastating level of losses. One hundred and twenty men from that single bomb group and one airfield alone had gone. Such casualties were not sustainable. Not sustainable at all. Men like Bob Johnson were doing a great job – they were besting the enemy when they caught up with them – but they were not protection enough. Not yet at any rate. But it was the fighters, not the bombers, that held the key: to wrest back the initiative from the Luftwaffe, they needed many more and better fighter aircraft than those of the enemy, flown by pilots with greater skill and experience and employing superior tactics, and, perhaps most important of all, with greater range.

But in the dark days and nights of the autumn of 1943, bringing these six criteria together still seemed a long way off.

PART I

Crisis

CHAPTER 1

For the Love of Flying

B Y OCTOBER 1943, BRITAIN had been in the war for just over four years and the United States for almost two. For Britain, the war had brought a number of defeats, from the terrible shock of the collapse of France at the hands of Germany in 1940, to the catastrophic loss of Singapore, Malaya and Burma to the Japanese in early 1942. Yet there had been some notable triumphs too. The emphatic defensive victory in the Battle of Britain in the summer of 1940 had changed the entire course of the war, forcing Hitler to fight a long and attritional war Germany could not afford, and to turn east into the Soviet Union in June 1941 far earlier than ever originally intended. It was a gamble that had failed: the Soviet Union had not collapsed and Germany, increasingly short of vital resources, had been forced to fight a war on multiple fronts, an eventuality Hitler and his commanders had been so desperate to avoid from the outset.

Then there had been the Allied victory in the Battle of the Atlantic, which, in the circumstances of the wider war, had so far proved the most important theatre of all, for without access to the world's sea lanes – and specifically the Atlantic because all global shipping passed through that ocean en route to Britain – neither Britain nor the United States would be able to fight Germany, nor the United Kingdom take on Japan either. Britain, quite sensibly, had poured a huge amount of effort into winning this all-important clash at sea. In terms of the number of ships being built and in vital technological advances, as well as in the strikes scored against the Kriegsmarine, the German Navy, by as early as May 1941 Britain had reached a point where she was no longer going to lose that particular battle. Two years later, in May 1943, the U-boats, the biggest threat to Allied shipping, had been emphatically defeated. This meant that not only were the sea lanes largely clear, but that the Allies could now properly plan the road to final victory because they now knew how much shipping they could expect to reach Britain safely from around the world.

Then there had also been the victory in North Africa, fought first with the successful harnessing of her Dominions and Empire – and the Free French – and later, in Tunisia, with the help of new coalition partners the United States, whose troops had landed in Northwest Africa in November 1942. Yet while America had entered the war only in December 1941 following the Japanese attack on Pearl Harbor, the USA had been helping Britain long before that. With the fall of France, President Franklin D. Roosevelt had quietly begun to ready America for war. Her tiny pre-war army began to expand, her minuscule air corps rapidly increased and became the biggest focus of the exponential growth in defence spending, and her navy vastly enlarged. Isolationism, so ingrained in 1939, gradually began to slip into the shadows as America's burgeoning commercial home industry was turned over to armaments production. By December 1941, the USA had certainly become, as Roosevelt had pledged, an arsenal of democracy, but the journey there had begun back in the summer of 1940, eighteen months before formally entering the war. And as with Britain's war effort, America's journey to become the world's leading armaments manufacturer had been a long and rocky one with plenty of lows as well as highs along the way.

Air power, however, had been central to both Britain's and America's military growth, and a key part of their strategy. 'Steel not flesh' was the mantra; both nations were determined to use modern technology and mechanization to limit the number of their young men who actually had to fight at the coalface of war. Compared with Nazi Germany or the USSR, for example, with their enormous armies and already monstrous casualty lists, this was proving a remarkably successful and efficient strategy. Air power had halted German ambitions in 1940, had helped win the Battle of the Atlantic and had saved the British Eighth Army in the summer of 1942 as it had fallen back in retreat to the Alamein line in Egypt; Allied air power had also made a massive contribution to the victory in North Africa and, more recently, to the successful conquest of Sicily. Yet in terms of the strategic air campaign against Germany – that is, the bomber war – it was only since March 1943, just half a year earlier, that the commander-in-chief of RAF Bomber Command, Air Marshal Sir Arthur Harris, had been able to launch his all-out air assault on Germany, and only in the past couple of months, a year on from its first operations from Britain, that the US Eighth Air Force had accumulated enough bombers and fighters to make a significant contribution to this effort to bludgeon Germany from the air.

Now, though, other constraints were emerging, and not least the weather. Already, summer had become a distant memory. The days were shortening and the skies darkening with what seemed like incessant low cloud and rain. It was largely down to the weather, for example, that between 1 and 10 October 1943, the pilots of the 56th Fighter Group had flown just three operational missions.

On the other hand, such light combat flying was good news for these fighter boys and for the future prospects of VIII Fighter Command. Without question, American fighter pilots were given a far better chance of survival than any other of the world's air combatants. They began their flying training in the wide open skies of Florida, Texas, Arizona and elsewhere – parts of the United States where the sun invariably shone, cloud cover was mostly minimal and which enabled them to begin their flying careers with a consistency and intensity that was just what was needed. It was true that Canadians, Australians, South Africans and many embryonic RAF pilots were also able to make the most of peaceful clear blue skies through training schemes in the US and in British Dominion countries, but few were sent to operational units with as many hours in their logbooks as US fighter pilots. A British fighter pilot by 1943 might have around two hundred hours' flying by the time he joined his squadron; a US fighter pilot would have more like three hundred.

Entire fighter groups were being formed in the US and, like Bob Johnson and others, had trained and then headed overseas to England together. What's more, a number of them had already learned to fly long before joining the

United States Army Air Forces (USAAF). Bob Johnson was a case in point. Born and raised in Lawton, Oklahoma, he was the son of a motor mechanic and so grew up around engines and automobiles. When he was eight, his father took him to see a travelling barnstorming team, after which he became determined to fly. By the age of eleven he was working for a cabinetmaker when not at school and saving up to learn to fly. A year later, having saved enough, he began flying lessons and, incredibly, soloed after less than six hours' flying time. Later, while still at college, he joined the Civilian Pilot Training Program and managed to notch up over a hundred hours in his logbook before the start of his sophomore year. By the time he joined the Army Air Forces in the summer of 1941, he already had hundreds of hours under his belt. In the United States – even as it emerged from the Depression – it was possible to be the teenage son of a car mechanic and still learn to fly privately.

Once arrived in Britain, American fighter pilots had plentiful supplies of high-octane aviation fuel and, with just one operational mission every few days, plenty of time to hone their skills further. New pilots arriving to join the 56th FG, for example, were now entering an increasingly combat-experienced outfit. A rookie would arrive with a pretty good feel for his aircraft and with already decent flying skills; standards were high and it was all too easy to get washed out, as Major Francis 'Gabby' Gabreski, Bob Johnson's flight commander, had discovered during his training.

The son of first-generation Polish immigrants from Oil City, Pennsylvania, Gabreski began flying lessons while at Notre Dame University, but much to his dismay, and in sharp contrast with Bob Johnson, quickly discovered he lacked any kind of natural aptitude. After around six hours' instruction he ran out of money, but then the Army Air Corps – as it had been at the time – recruiting team turned up on campus. Aware that Poland had already been consumed by Nazi Germany and the Soviets, Gabreski decided to do his bit to help and so joined up. The trouble was, as his flying training began, he struggled to overcome his heavy-handedness and was soon put up for an elimination flight. This was his final chance to prove himself; thankfully, he managed to scrape through and was given a second chance. He was lucky, as few others were given that opportunity, and by March 1941 he had accrued more than 200 hours in his logbook.

From there he was posted to Hawaii, where he had plenty of time to increase his flying hours further. After surviving the attack on Pearl Harbor in December 1941, life seemed a bit monotonous. It was all very well practising, but he wanted to get involved in the war, and with his Polish roots he was keen to get over to Europe to fight the Nazis. Aware of the Polish squadrons now in the RAF, he began wondering whether he might transfer to one of them and put in a request to do so.

Much to his surprise, his application was taken seriously and he was sent halfway around the world to England with instructions to report to the embryonic Eighth Air Force Headquarters at Bushy Park in southwest London. After flying the full raft of Eighth Air Force aircraft, albeit with no specific role, he finally got his transfer to 315 Polish Squadron in the RAF. Nearly two years after being awarded his wings in the US, Gabreski flew his first combat mission in January 1943. A month after that, he was posted out of the RAF and back into the USAAF, to join the 56th Fighter Group, initially based at Kings Cliffe, a satellite of RAF Wittering in Cambridgeshire. 'Remember, my friend,' Tadeusz Andersz, a fellow pilot at 315 Squadron told him before he left, 'don't shoot until you're close enough to make a sure kill.'

It was good advice, and when Gabreski reported for duty to Colonel Hub Zemke, the CO of the 56th, this pilot who had so nearly dropped out of training had been transformed. He still had a lot to learn about combat flying, but he had so many flying hours in his logbook, he no longer had to think too much about the actual flying part – that was pretty much second nature – and could focus on the combat element instead. What's more, he'd been able to learn from hugely experienced pilots like Tadeusz Andersz and took that with him to the 56th.

Gabreski was assigned to the 61st Fighter Squadron and given command of 'B' Flight. Each fighter group had three squadrons, rather like an RAF wing or a Luftwaffe fighter *Gruppe*. An American squadron, however, was much larger than either the German or British equivalent, with around forty aircraft and a similar number of pilots. This was roughly four times the size of a Luftwaffe *Staffel* and almost double the size of an RAF squadron. Admittedly, American fighter pilots joining VIII Fighter Command were generally flying longer combat sorties than their opposite numbers, but they were still flying a fraction of the number of sorties expected of Luftwaffe pilots. Rarely would an American fighter pilot fly on operations on two consecutive days, and often only once or twice a week. As it was, the 56th FG's pilots did not fly operationally until

13 April – in other words, a further six weeks' training after their arrival in England. Gabreski, for one, was not even on the roster to fly that mission; only sixteen out of the forty flew – that is, two flights of eight. Nor was he assigned to fly two days later on the 56th's next mission. He finally flew on 17 April and then a harmless 'rodeo' – a fighter mission using bombers as bait – to the Belgian coast. They saw nothing.

Gabreski found the slow start frustrating, but in every regard this nurturing of fighter pilots was a better deal for them than the approach of the Luftwaffe General Staff to their German counterparts. Combat flying was incredibly exhausting, both physically and mentally, so the fewer the combat missions, the fresher the pilots remained and the further their store of courage was likely to go. It also meant, of course, that there was more time to practise and hone skills, and to build up flying hours, which in turn meant their chances of survival in combat were greater.

By the autumn of 1943, Gabreski had become Bob Johnson's squadron commander in the 61st and had two Focke-Wulf 190s shot down to his name. He was, by this time, a fine pilot and, more to the point, a highly trained and skilful *fighter* pilot who was able to throw his P-47 around the sky to the maximum of its capabilities and had a wealth of experience that he could pass on. He was also part of an outfit that was growing in confidence and ability, and was about as physically fit for the task in hand as was possible. This meant that when rookie pilots arrived, once in the close and convivial environment of the squadron and group, there was ample opportunity to listen and to feed off the more experienced pilots like Gabreski and Bob Johnson. They could practise dogfighting, iron out gunnery skills and build up hours in their logbooks. There was time for them to improve. Even when first made operational, they were very unlikely to be sent on a long trip. Rather, it would be a 'milk run' to northern France, where the chances of meeting many enemy were slight and where they could get a feel for operational life without undue risk. This gave the growing US fighter force in England an increasingly large advantage over the enemy.

Men like Bob Johnson might have arrived in England with some eight hundred hours in their logbooks, but there were also a number of American fighter pilots who had already been here in England flying and fighting the Luftwaffe long before the United States had even entered the war and who, when the Eighth Air Force was first considering how to build a fighter arm, were therefore on hand with a great deal of combat experience on which to draw – a huge asset for the new formation.

The 4th Fighter Group lived down the road from the 56th at Debden, a former RAF fighter base during the Battle of Britain. South of Cambridge, and just a few miles from the north Essex market town of Saffron Walden, it was a well-equipped base complete with distinctive RAF-style brick mess buildings, officers' quarters, hangars, workshops and ammunition and fuel stores. Many of the men of the 4th had been based there for more than two years already, as the core of them had earlier flown for the RAF, first in squadrons throughout RAF Fighter Command and then in a wing of three 'Eagle' squadrons made up entirely of American pilots. It was fair to say the men of the 4th thought of themselves as a cut above any other American fighter group in the Eighth, or any other air force for that matter.

Executive officer of the 4th – that is, deputy commander –
was Lieutenant-Colonel Don Blakeslee, already something
of a legendary figure within VIII Fighter Command.
Handsome, square-jawed and with pale blue eyes, he was a
6-foot, square-shouldered bull of a man, decidedly tribal
and someone never known to beat about the bush. A
superb pilot but a notoriously bad marksman, what he
lacked in shooting prowess he more than made up for in
his innate ability to lead others. He was gruff, bluff and
never shy about swearing, but others were drawn to him
and his magnetic personality that oozed confidence and
self-belief.

He also loved flying and had done ever since he was a
boy watching the Cleveland Air Races near where he lived
at Fairport Harbor, Ohio. With money he saved from
working at the Diamond Alkali Company, he and a friend
bought a Piper J-3, which they flew as much as they could.
In 1940, however, his friend managed to crash and write it
off, and they had neither the insurance nor the funds to
get another. Blakeslee didn't want to stop flying, however,
so took himself to Canada and joined the Royal Canadian
Air Force, having assured his mother he was being taken
on as an instructor and would never go into combat.

After training in Canada, he reached England in May
1941. Although the first all-American Eagle Squadron
had already been formed within RAF Fighter Command,
Blakeslee was posted to 401 Squadron at Biggin Hill, to
the south of London in Kent. After two hundred hours of
operational flying he was told he was being taken off ops
and would have a recuperative stint as an instructor.
Blakeslee was not interested in that at all, so applied to
join 133 Squadron, one of the Eagle squadrons, which was

then based at Great Sampford, a satellite airfield to Debden in Essex.

By the summer of 1942, a number of the Eagle originals were eligible to be rotated back home to the US and that included the CO of 133, Carroll 'Red' McColpin. However, on an escort mission to France, their Spitfires got held up by excessively strong headwinds and eleven out of the twelve flying were lost, while the twelfth crash-landed back in England. This left a skeleton squadron, shaken to its core and with absolutely no *esprit de corps*; Blakeslee was charged with picking them up and leading them as their new CO. His approach, on his first evening in charge, was to forgo any speeches but instead to stand on the bar in the mess and announce that drinks were on him. 'He was a great believer in the RAF tradition of hard drinking and high living,' noted Jim Goodson, who joined 133 Squadron at that time and who also became a mainstay of the 4th Fighter Group, 'and never permitting either of them to interfere with constant readiness to fly, and fly well, at any time.' At well after one in the morning, by which time the pilots were mostly semi-conscious, Blakeslee announced they all needed to be ready to fly at 6 a.m.

It was usual for fighter planes to take off in pairs or, at a push, in fours, but that next morning Blakeslee ordered them to take off together – all sixteen of them – in formation. After the spontaneous gasp of horror, Blakeslee yelled at them to move and they all headed out to their waiting Spitfires. And somehow, they all managed to do exactly as he had demanded. 'Tighten up!' yelled Blakeslee. 'Let's show these bastards!'

The bastards in question were the other Eagle squadrons at nearby Debden, and sure enough, before most of the 133 Squadron pilots had had a chance to think too much about what was happening, they were flying in perfect formation at 500 feet. And right over Debden. By the time they landed, everyone was talking excitedly, with a palpable, breathless pride. 'That evening,' added Goodson, 'Blakeslee wasn't the only 133 pilot with the belligerent swagger.'

Soon after, the Eagle squadrons were transferred into the US Army Air Forces – specifically the Eighth – and were given new squadron numbers: 133 Squadron became 336th Fighter Squadron in the newly formed 4th Fighter Group, and the old RAF rondels were scrubbed out and repainted with USAAF stars.

Blakeslee had been happy to keep his Spitfires and was none too amused when, the following April, he was told they would be re-equipping with P-47 Thunderbolts. On 15 April 1943, he was leading the squadron on a 'ramrod' – fighter escort for a bombing mission – over Belgium when they spotted a couple of FW190s. The German pilots dived out of the way and the squadron followed from a height of around 20,000 feet. By the time Blakeslee pulled out and blew one of the Focke-Wulfs to pieces, he was at just 500 feet and almost flying into Ostend. It was, however, the first recorded victory ever in a P-47 and it was entirely appropriate that this victory had been achieved by a 4th Fighter Group pilot and by Blakeslee in particular.

Back at base, Goodson, who before the mission had tried to persuade Blakeslee of its virtues, said to him, 'I told you the Jug could out-dive them!'

'Well, it damn well ought to be able to dive,' Blakeslee growled, 'it sure as hell can't climb.'

Not long after, Blakeslee was made excutive officer of

the entire Fighter Group, although only on the condition he could keep flying – and that meant combat flying. 'We love fighting,' he once said. 'Fighting is a grand sport.' He continued to love drinking too. When the mess secretary complained that the pilots were smashing too many glasses, Blakeslee replied, 'Good show. Shows their spirit.'

Although Blakeslee's personal score was gradually mounting, he never painted swastikas on his fighter plane like most others, nor did he get much better at shooting. 'Hell, I can't hit the side of a barn,' he told a reporter. 'There's no sport in it for a guy who can shoot straight. The sport comes when somebody like me has to pull up behind 'em and start shooting to find out where the bullets are going.' In a dogfight, he was everywhere – twisting, climbing, rolling, bellowing and blinding. Blakeslee swore like a trooper. But first with the 336th FS and then with the 4th Fighter Group, he was venerated as a fighting air leader par excellence – so much so that by the autumn of 1943 his fame had spread throughout the Eighth Air Force.

In many ways, Blakeslee was the embodiment of the spirit of the 4th, but he was far from unique in possessing an obsessive love of flying combined with stubborn single-mindedness and an unshakeable thirst for adventure. Being both single-minded and stubbornly determined were also most certainly attributes that could be applied to Captain Duane 'Bee' Beeson. From Boise, Idaho, 22-year-old Beeson had decided to become a lawyer and so had sold magazines and newspapers until he had saved up enough money to hitch-hike to Oakland, California, where he took a job as a hotel clerk while attending law classes. Then came the war and he decided to forgo a legal career to become a pilot instead and do his bit in the fight against Nazi Germany. Since there was no opportunity for him to join the US Army Air Corps at this time, he, like Blakeslee, went to Canada and joined the Royal Canadian Air Force instead.

Beeson was a young man with a fastidious attention to detail and, if he was going to do something, he did it properly. He regarded flying as something of a science, applied himself to the task in hand with zeal and, as had been his intention from the outset, by the summer of 1942 he was in England and a fighter pilot in the RAF. 'In the RAF,' wrote the 4th's public relations officer, 'he was always spoiling to go out and kill Germans, having picked up an unaccountable Hun phobia somewhere along the line.'

Beeson had barely joined the Eagle squadrons before they were transferred to the Eighth and became the 4th Fighter Group. From the outset, he applied himself to getting ever better as a fighter pilot. At Debden, he built his own gunnery gadget to help him practise deflection shooting – aiming ahead so that his bullets and an enemy plane would converge. Very few pilots mastered this, but those who did had a massive edge because it allowed them to attack at an angle rather than just from directly behind. Beeson, who was a small, slight fellow with the face of a boy younger than his twenty-two years, also made a point of carefully studying the legendary fighter pilots who had gone before and working hard to put theory into practice. It was perhaps not surprising, then, that on 8 October 1943 he became the group's first ace when he shot down two Me109s to bring his score to six.

Don Gentile, on the other hand, was another who was utterly obsessed with flying and who had, like Bob Johnson, decided at a very early age that it was going to become his life. 'I can't remember the time when airplanes were not part of my life,' he said, 'and can't remember ever wanting anything so much as to fly one. Once I had started I had to keep flying.' From Piqua, Ohio, Gentile – known to his pals in the group as 'Gentle' – was the son of Italian immigrants; he had a lean face and dark, decidedly Italian good looks. As a boy, he assiduously saved up for flying lessons and then, having earned some more by working as a waiter at his father's club, he bought – without his parents' authority – a beaten-up old plane for $300. Someone – Gentile never found out who – rang his mother and said, 'Your son bought himself a death trap.' So it proved when the plane was checked over, but by then it was too late: the purchase had been made. 'Okay,' Gentile's father told him, 'You've learned a lesson. You've got $300 worth of experience now.' Gentile eventually wore down his parents, however, and when he was seventeen his father bought him a $450 Aerosport biplane.

Gentile was a naturally gifted pilot, but like many teenagers he believed himself immortal and developed an unhealthy lust for speed. That biplane got him into a lot of trouble, because he liked nothing more than flying low over the town, the church, the school and buzzing the people below. He was still at high school when Hitler invaded Poland in September 1939 and immediately he realized it was a war that he had to get into as a pilot. His parents wanted him to go to Ohio State University on a football scholarship – he'd never paid much attention to his academic subjects – and a university education would have helped him get into the Army Air Corps. Gentile, however, had learned that the RAF was taking young American pilots like himself, so he joined up, trained in

Canada, got his wings with an 'above average' qualifica-
tion, then shipped to England to join 133 Eagle Squadron.

On joining the Eagles, Gentile quickly realized how
much he still had to learn. 'Flying an airplane is only a
part of fighting with one,' he said, 'and most of the other
part a man has to learn from his fellow soldiers, and from
the enemy.' That was certainly true. He soon understood
he had been very fortunate to reach the front line at a time
when there was comparatively little operational flying
and so was able to learn the ropes steadily and from others
who already had a great deal of experience. His first few
operational sorties were bewildering, but he learned, and
slowly but surely his confidence grew. On 19 August 1942,
during the air battle over the ill-fated Dieppe Raid, he had
shot down first a Ju88 and then a Focke-Wulf. He also discovered he had superb twenty-ten vision. 'Twenty-twenty
is perfect,' he said, 'but twenty-ten is better than perfect . . . that half-second or one-second advantage it gives
you over your enemy in picking the black speck of him out
of a scud in the sky or the flecked-up greys, blues or blinding, bleached-out yellow is the difference, other things
being equal, between killing or being killed.'

By October 1943, Captain Don Gentile was a flight
commander in the 336th Fighter Squadron and had some
fifteen months of operational flying under his belt. Many
of the 4th's pilots were similarly experienced, yet Gentile
knew he was still not the finished article and had much
still to learn. He had become a flight commander only at
the end of September when the previous commander,
Captain Spike Miley, had finished his tour and headed
home. Before he left, Miley had taken Gentile to one side
and said, 'All right, you're red hot and it's natural you

should want to be a fire-cracker over here. But you've got boys following you now who have things to learn before they get red hot. They're going to follow you wherever you take them. Remember that whenever you take them anywhere. It's not only your brains that are going to get knocked out, but the brains of the kids who are depending on you.' It was good advice, and Gentile knew it. He was determined he was going to look after the men in his charge and help them develop.

By the autumn of 1943, VIII Fighter Command was turning itself into a very impressive organization. It had highly motivated pilots of increasing skill and experience, and fine aircraft with which to fight. The weeks ahead promised them an opportunity to hone their skills yet further. In fact, the only missing ingredient was an aircraft that could take them deep into enemy territory. Although the pilots and aircrew knew little about new technological developments, the powers that be were working on it. When that conundrum was successfully resolved, VIII Fighter Command was going to prove itself a truly formidable outfit.

CHAPTER 2

Flying for the Reich

In SHARP CONTRAST to the Americans, the Luftwaffe's fighter arm was increasingly short of training, fuel and even aircraft that could keep pace with the Allies' latest fighters. Like all aspects of Germany's war effort, the air force was feeling the pinch, and badly so. No part of the Wehrmacht – the German Armed Forces – had been so overused and, frankly, under-appreciated. The Luftwaffe had come into being in 1935 and had emerged as a symbol of the new military dynamism of the Third Reich, with glistening new fighter aircraft, bombers and dive-bombers. Its pilots were Nazi pin-ups and during the early years of the war the Luftwaffe had led the way: screaming Stuka dive-bombers and lithe, feline, deadly Messerschmitt 109s had been among the primary symbols of the so-called Blitzkrieg, bringing a new brand of shock and awe as they swept over their enemies.

The Luftwaffe had been expected to continue this dominance and crush the RAF in the summer of 1940, then hammer British cities throughout that winter and the spring of 1941. It also had to spearhead the attacks on Malta, in the Balkans, against Greece and then against the Soviet Union. There had been no let-up. More and more was expected of the pilots and aircrew, with no defined regulations about tours of duty or even regular rest of any kind. Meanwhile, production of aircraft, despite Germany's head start over other nations in the 1930s, had slowed and then become mired in bureaucracy and the hubris of many of the leading designers and manufacturers. The air force had also been forced to play second fiddle to the army when it came to allocations, while when things went wrong, as had been happening for the past two years, the Luftwaffe had often received the blame. The blazing spearhead had become the scapegoat.

Up until the summer of 1943, the Luftwaffe had maintained its presence over the front line wherever its ground forces were in action, which in the summer months of that year had been the Eastern Front and the Mediterranean. In early July, the army had launched Operation ZITADELLE to close off the Kursk salient in the Soviet Union, but even before that battle began, many of the air forces had already been transferred to the Mediterranean. The Eastern Front might have been where the bulk of the army's divisions were fighting, but it was the Mediterranean where much of the Luftwaffe was operating. This had been catastrophic for them. Between June and September, the Luftwaffe had lost 704 aircraft over the Eastern Front but a staggering 3,502 in the Mediterranean, most of them in a vain effort to save Sicily and keep Italy in the war. This kind of effort simply could not be maintained and with RAF Bomber Command attacking German cities by night, and now with the American heavy bomber force increasingly attacking by day, the focus for the Luftwaffe had to be the defence of the Reich.

At this stage of the war there was absolutely no doubt about the outcome. This had been clear to the Allies back in January 1943 when the American and British Chiefs of Staff as well as President Roosevelt and Winston Churchill, the Prime Minister, had met at Casablanca to plan for victory in Europe. At the time, the Germans were suffering a terrible reverse on the Eastern Front, while it was expected the British and Americans would secure all of North Africa by May, in what was their first joint land campaign since the USA's entry into the war.

So far, 1943 had proved the optimism of Casablanca had not been misplaced. In February, at Stalingrad on the Eastern Front, the German Sixth Army had been surrounded and annihilated, a defeat that had prompted deep shock at home. Twenty months after Hitler's great gamble to invade the Soviet Union in June 1941, its failure had been dramatically laid bare. Then, in May, as predicted at Casablanca, the joint German–Italian forces in North Africa had been forced to surrender with the loss of even more men than at Stalingrad and considerably more aircraft, tanks and other materiel. That had been swiftly followed by ZITADELLE and the Germans' last counter-attack in the east; a few days later had come the invasion of Sicily – the first Allied land attack on European soil – and by mid-August the island had fallen. By the end of July Hitler's fellow dictator and ally, Benito Mussolini, had been overthrown. On 8 September, Italy signed an armistice and the following day Allied forces landed at Salerno, just south of Naples.

Germany simply could not compete with the industrial output, technological advances and vast global reach of the Allies, nor with the immense reserves of manpower and burgeoning war industry of the Soviet Union. By the autumn of 1943, Germany was short of just about everything, but especially of manpower, food and oil, the three requirements needed above anything else for a long attritional war.

The Nazi leadership continued to cling to the belief that wonder weapons would come to their rescue, but this was a vain hope; their atomic programme, such as it was, had been taken off any priority list and, in any case, was riven by the kind of rivalries and splintering of effort that was all too common within the Third Reich. Instead, hope rested with their missile programme – the V1 and V2, both currently still in development – with new-generation submarines and advances in airframes and jet power. The V1s and V2s, although brilliant technological breakthroughs, lacked any kind of accuracy, while the Type XXI U-boats had been developed far too late to be decisive. Finally, new jet engines had been hurried and were not as good or advanced as those now being developed in Britain. In other words, despite the fantasies of Hitler, none of these developments had the slightest chance of turning the war in the favour of the Germans.

However, Hitler's expectations for the Luftwaffe remained enormously high. German aircraft production – and that of fighters especially – might have been on the rise, but there could be no escaping other shortages and, of those, fuel was the one that was hurting the Luftwaffe the most. There was simply not enough of that precious fluid for training or even for practising. Training was being cut and pilots were being sent to front-line units with only 150 hours or fewer in their logbooks – around half the hours of an American. Even once attached to an operational unit there was little opportunity for pilots to build up their skill levels or add hours to the logbooks outside operational flights.

Luftwaffe fighter pilots were expected to operate at an intensity that was utterly unsustainable. They would often be required to take off, meet the enemy, land back down, then, after refuelling and rearming, take to the skies again. There was no 24-hour pass each week and 48-hour pass every three weeks as there had been in RAF Fighter Command during the Battle of Britain. German fighter pilots were expected to keep flying. On and on, relentlessly. More often than not, the only way out of this cycle of endless operational flying was by getting shot down and wounded or, more likely, by being killed.

This rather undermined the inherent advantage of flying over home soil, where the distances flown tended to be less and where if a pilot was shot down and bailed out safely, he could return to the action right away. Furthermore, because German fighter pilots did not know when they would be attacked, they had to be on standby all the time, which, in turn, meant there were fewer opportunities for practice. American and British fighter pilots, in contrast, with their plentiful supplies of fuel and aircraft could practise pretty much whenever they liked, weather permitting.

Unsurprisingly, the rate of attrition in Luftwaffe squadrons was horrendous, and not just in new pilots. The Luftwaffe were treating their prized asset – the pilots – with the same lack of due care that both the Luftstreitkräfte and Royal Flying Corps had demonstrated in the First World War. It hadn't done either side much good then and it wasn't doing the Luftwaffe any favours now. But it could not be helped – not unless Germany brought the war to a swift end. Every nation is always bound to defend its homeland above all, and with Allied bombers pounding Germany's cities there was an imperative that the Luftwaffe meet this threat as forcefully as they possibly could.

One of those flying almost daily in defence of the Reich was Leutnant Heinz Knoke, just twenty-two years old and an ace nearly four times over, with nineteen confirmed enemy aircraft shot down. Like the Pied Piper, he was from Hamelin, a small country town lying underneath much of the air battle that raged in the skies. Knoke had begun the war full of patriotic zeal and admiration for the Führer. When still only seventeen, he had gone for a pleasure flight at a public air display and there and then had determined to become a pilot. During the last, long summer before the war he had applied to join the Luftwaffe and had been accepted; a year later, in August 1940, as the Battle of Britain raged, he had finally been awarded his wings and been posted to fighters. More training followed; in those far-off, heady days the Luftwaffe still had the luxury of training its pilots properly without cutting corners, so not until just before Christmas 1940 was Knoke finally posted to his operational unit, Jagdgeschwader – Fighter Wing – 52.

More than two and a half years later he was still combat flying and now a hardened veteran. He was married too – young men like Knoke were old beyond their years; a boyish pilot grew up fast and, as for many in wartime, with the future so uncertain it paid to take the chance of love and happiness while he could. In his case, he had been taking cover in an air-raid shelter in Berlin on a brief foray into town while stationed at Döberitz, just outside the city. After giving up his seat to a 'strikingly attractive' girl, he had struck up a conversation. She was called Lilo and to begin with she had been reserved and even cool, but eventually his perseverance had paid off. On 24 March 1941, his twentieth birthday, he had asked her to marry him.

This would not have pleased the Luftwaffe's General der Jagdflieger – General of Fighters – Adolf Galland, who took a dim view of his pilots getting married. He was happy for them to sleep around and sow their wild oats, but he thought it a mistake to allow them to settle down; he wanted them thinking about flying, not worrying about wives back at home. 'Better wait until the war is over,' was the response of Leutnant Öhlschläger, Knoke's senior squadron officer, echoing Galland's sentiments.

'But the war may drag on for thirty years,' Knoke confided in his diary. 'In any case, I do not want to wait so long before learning all about love.' Galland, who had never been shy with the ladies, would have argued that the one did not at all depend upon the other, but Knoke was of a more traditional nature. Promising they would be wed as soon as he was able, he and Lilo were parted in May that year when Knoke was posted first to France and then, in June, to the Eastern Front for the invasion of the Soviet Union. A couple of months later he was posted west once more and granted both a brief leave and permission to marry his Lilo. A short registry office ceremony on 28 August was the best they could manage. The following day he was back with his squadron and flying once more.

Over the next two years this still extremely young man had continued flying. Relentlessly, come rain, come shine. During this excessively prolonged stint of front-line combat flying, he had developed the technique of dropping a single bomb on top of American bomber formations – literally, a hit-or-miss technique – which had prompted a personal call from Reichsmarschall Göring himself. He had also been given responsibility for training new NCO pilots arriving to join the fighter group and then had been placed in command of his own *Staffel*. He had lost his best friend and fellow pilot, Dieter Gerhard, and many other comrades beside, and had had more close shaves of his own than he cared to remember. Youthful exuberance had given way to weary resignation. Skill and experience helped a great deal, but Knoke had learned to accept that luck played a huge part. Ultimately, it was a numbers game in which the more one flew, the greater the chance one's luck would run out.

He had thought it had done so on 17 August 1943, when the US Eighth Air Force's bombers first hit the ball-bearing plant at Schweinfurt, some 100 miles east of Frankfurt and deep inside Germany. The Americans had lost sixty aircraft on that mission alone, but the Luftwaffe fighter force had suffered too. That day, and now flying with 5/JG11, Knoke had shot a Fortress down in flames, but had been hit in turn. His engine had been set alight, but he had managed to put out the fire and had been on the point of bailing out when instead he had decided to try to nurse his stricken aircraft back to base. He had crash-landed at 100 m.p.h., smashed through three wooden fences, bounced into the air, then finally come to a halt. Apart from light shrapnel wounds to his upper right arm, he had survived intact. A miracle.

Not quite six weeks later, on 27 September, he had been shot up again. On standby at 10.30 a.m., fifteen minutes later he had been checking over his brand-new 'Gustav' – a Messerschmitt 109G that had been polished up to brilliance by his ground crew. Ten minutes after that, the squadron had been scrambled and he was off, albeit sluggishly, as they had all been equipped with auxiliary fuel tanks and rockets under the wings, and the extra weight and drag held them back.

At 10,000 feet they had emerged out of the cloud base and spotted the Fortresses on a parallel course above them. Climbing to 20,000 feet, the *Staffel* had jettisoned their drop tanks – external fuel tanks – on Knoke's orders, then dived down and head-on as the bomber formation began to split. At 2,000 feet distance, Knoke had fired his rockets and been amazed to see the warheads register a direct hit on a Fortress. The bomber exploded in a giant ball of flame; Knoke had never seen anything like it. Bits of debris began fluttering downwards as he flew on, climbing out of the fray and spotting first some twin-engine P-38 Lightnings and then some Thunderbolts. Cursing, and diving down towards them, he had then seen a lone Fortress with an equally lone Me109 on its tail, which he recognized as his friend and wingman Obergefreiter Peter Reinhard's plane. Behind Reinhard, though, were some Thunderbolts. Warning his wingman to wake up, Knoke had hurtled after the Thunderbolts, opened fire on the nearest and saw that one of them had burst into flames too – his second kill of the day. Then suddenly three more Thunderbolts were on his tail. Pushing forward on the stick, he had dived for the cloud, but it was too late: his engine was on fire once again. This time, though, there could be no nursing it back. Pushing back the canopy, he had unclipped his leads, kicked the stick forward and dropped out in a great somersault, then remembered to pull the ripcord.

A moment later, the harness had cut into his shoulders and he jolted as the billowing parachute put the brakes on his descent. He felt as though he were standing on air and, as he drifted down, the air swooshing in the great white awning above, he had found himself rather enjoying the experience and marvelling at what a wonderful invention the parachute was. He touched down at 11.26 a.m., only thirty-one minutes after taking off.

Since he had come down not far from Jever, on the North Sea coast just to the west of Wilhelmshaven, where he was now based, he had soon been back at the airfield and facing the disappointment of his ground crew over losing the new plane. Worse news followed, however. In Knoke's squadron alone – only nine men strong that morning – Unteroffizier Rudolf Dölling had been killed and two more shot down, one of whom, Jonny Fest, had been wounded. The fourth *Staffel* had also lost two killed and one badly wounded, while the 5/JG11 had lost nine out of twelve, all killed, and the remaining three crash-landed or bailed out. 'The heavy casualties on our side,' Knoke noted, 'are to be explained by the fact that nobody had anticipated an encounter with the enemy fighters. We were taken completely by surprise.' It was a clear demonstration of what the Allies could achieve when their bombers were supported by modern fighters in plentiful numbers – on this occasion some 262 Thunderbolts had been dispatched, including fifty-one from the 56th Fighter Group.

Knoke might have wondered how he had managed to stay alive when so many of his colleagues had not, but he was to test his luck still further just a couple of weeks later. On Monday, 4 October, the Eighth Air Force launched a major strike into Germany to hit targets around Frankfurt and Saarbrücken. The weather was good over central Germany that day, so Knoke sensed they would soon be in action. Sitting by the hangars that morning, he had been cursing the amount of paperwork he was expected to do and listening to music over the loudspeaker, when suddenly the music faded and a voice called out, 'Attention all squadrons! Attention all squadrons! Stand by for take-off!' Mechanics began running towards the aircraft, the pilots following. Up on to the wing, then hoisting himself into the cockpit, with its low-slung bucket seat. Safety harness on, manual checks, canopy hanging open to one side on its hinges. Unteroffizier Alfred Arndt, his ground chief, passed Knoke the ground telephone extension. Hauptmann Sprecht was on the line. The Americans were approaching over the North Sea coast. Knoke and the rest of the group were to make a frontal attack in close formation. Just after 9.30 a.m., one *Staffel* after another took off, then wheeled to the left until all were airborne and they could begin their climb together.

At 22,000 feet Knoke noticed the contrails from their aircraft and saw his breath freeze on the oxygen mask he wore; he had to slap his legs to keep himself warm. Soon after, they spotted the enemy bombers. As many as four hundred, Knoke reckoned. The *Jagdgeschwader* now turned towards the American planes and a few minutes later they were tearing into them, flying head-on, guns blazing and tracer arcing across the sky. Knoke aimed for a B-24 Liberator, opened fire when he had come as close as he dared, then involuntarily ducked as he sped past, beneath the nose and right through the formation, before pulling back on the stick and climbing up in a left-hand turn. Watching his Liberator, he saw it pull away from the rest of the formation, exposing itself. Knoke turned towards it, flying beneath it, then pulling back and letting rip at its belly. Moments later it was gushing flames and eight men jumped, parachutes mushrooming. He now drew up alongside, less than 100 feet away, and saw the great holes torn by his cannons. Then suddenly the dorsal turret flashed and bullets were hitting him. Knoke could scarcely believe it – how could anyone still be alive in that burning crate? And yet someone was, and now his own aircraft was on fire.

Once again, he had to bail out, dropping clear of the stricken Messerschmitt, his parachute blossoming. Below were several others. 'This is one time,' he noted later, 'the Americans and I go bathing together.' Hitting the water, he was stunned by how cold it was and, after releasing his harness, he was immediately hit by a wave that knocked him backwards and left him gasping. Fortunately, he was able both to inflate his life jacket and grab his half-inflated dinghy and scramble into it, despite the swell. Catching his breath, he emptied his packet of dye and watched it spread across the water around him creating a patch of yellowish-green. Much of the North Sea was dominated and controlled by the Royal Navy, but fortunately he had come down in German waters and fairly near the coast.

Certain that his comrades had seen him float down, Knoke was confident he would be rescued, and so he was. Not long after, a Focke-Wulf seaplane flew over. He waved like mad and saw the crew circle low, then wave and drop a larger, more sturdy rubber dinghy. It was no easy matter either reaching it or clambering from one to the other, especially with the relentless waves crashing around him, but eventually he made it, slumping down in exhaustion. For perhaps two hours more, he lay there, bobbing up and down on the swell, until finally a launch approached and he was pulled aboard. He had survived yet again.

Those first ten days of October saw three big raids deep into Germany by the Eighth Air Force. On the 8th, their target was Bremen. Inevitably, Knoke was in action that day too, only four days after being rescued from the North Sea, and managed to shoot down a Fortress without harm to his own aircraft. Two days later, on Sunday, 10 October – the same day that Bob Johnson became the fifth pilot in the Mighty Eighth to become an ace – Knoke was in action yet again. 'The Yanks do not leave us alone,' he scribbled in his diary. 'Today they attack Münster in strength.' Knoke and his *Staffel* were about to dive down on the Fortresses when they were attacked by Thunderbolts, very possibly including those of the 56th Fighter Group. He was soon caught up in a swirling dogfight, but then spotted an Me110 fire four rockets, two of which hit the enemy bombers. As they exploded, several Thunderbolts tore after the Me110. Knoke, along with Barran and Führmann from his *Staffel*, went after the Thunderbolts. Knoke opened fire at close range and saw one of the American fighters blow up, while Führmann shot down a second. Suddenly, an entire pack of P-47s descended on them; in rapid succession, the attacker became the attacked. 'It is all we can do to shake them off,' Knoke recorded later. 'I try every trick I know, and put on quite a display of aerobatics.' Eventually he managed to escape by executing a corkscrew climb, a trick he knew the Thunderbolt could not perform as well.

Knoke might have been safe, but he could see that Barran and Führmann were not, with as many as a dozen Thunderbolts still on their tails. Choosing what he hoped was the best moment, he dived down again, shooting wildly to distract the enemy, but was hit badly across the tail and left wing. Flipping over, the Messerschmitt began diving downwards out of control. On his dashboard, the altimeter circled backwards. Desperately, Knoke tried to bring it under control. Breaking out into a cold sweat, he thought this time he really was done for. At just 3,000 feet off the ground, the stick was still jammed stuck. He now took his feet off the rudder pedals, pushed hard against the stick and at last felt a violent jolt, knocking his head hard, and as if by magic the Gustav was suddenly flying straight and level.

The nearest airfield was Twente in Holland and so, nursing his plane carefully, he swooped in low, only to discover one of his undercarriage wheels had been destroyed. That meant a belly-land. With a grinding and screeching of metal, he hit the deck, sliding and slewing to a halt. Miraculously, he was still in one piece. Clambering out, he saw half his tail plane had been shot away.

Soon after, a crippled Focke-Wulf came in, also with a broken undercarriage, but this time the pilot tried landing on one wheel. It didn't work. The fighter overturned and burst into flames. The pilot, trapped in the cockpit, was burned to death right in front of Knoke. 'I am powerless to help,' he wrote later. 'I have to watch him being slowly cremated alive in the wreck. I am trembling at the knees.' A few minutes later, several heavy bombers flew over and pasted the airfield with bombs.

Taking cover, Knoke felt he had had more than enough for one day.

No matter how desperate the situation may have seemed to Heinz Knoke, and regardless of how short they were of fuel, well-trained new pilots and other vital resources, the Luftwaffe remained a highly dangerous and potent force and a major thorn in the Allies' side. The issue for the Allies in late 1943 was no longer the outcome of the war against Nazi Germany but, rather, the time it would take to achieve total victory over an enemy whose leadership still had complete control over its people and seemed determined to keep fighting for as long as humanly possible. A generation earlier, Germany had ended the First World War because it had reached a point where it had run out of money and resources and could no longer win. Those conditions had long been reached by Nazi Germany – even as early as November 1941, when Operation BARBAROSSA, the invasion of the Soviet Union, had unravelled with Germany still a long way from victory – but Hitler had always viewed the future of the Third Reich as being one of two dramatically opposite outcomes: the war would lead either to a thousand-year Reich or to Armageddon. Armageddon had not yet been reached by the second half of 1943; so long as Hitler remained in power, Germany would continue fighting until the bitter end.

From the Allies' perspective, the aim was a swift end with minimum casualties, but how to achieve that was a matter of debate. Central to the Anglo-American strategy was a cross-Channel invasion of the continent. Immediately after the United States had entered the war in December 1941, President Franklin D. Roosevelt and the US Chiefs of Staff had confirmed an earlier agreement with the British that destroying Nazi Germany would be the first priority, above the defeat of Imperial Japan. The re-invasion of Europe had been the cornerstone of that joint strategy, and especially that of the Americans.

What followed had been the start of preparations for that cross-Channel attack, with the build-up in Britain not only of American troops but also of air forces. The Eighth Air Force had been formed in July 1942 and its first daylight bombing raid had taken place in August that year. Some still believed, a year on, that Nazi Germany could be brought to its knees by air power alone – General Carl 'Tooey' Spaatz, the first commander of the Eighth Air Force, for one, and Air Marshal Sir Arthur Harris, commander of RAF Bomber Command, for another. These men, passionate believers in the efficacy of air power, were, however, in a minority, and both the American and British war leaders accepted that the war could be won only by putting boots on the ground. Operation OVERLORD, as the Allied cross-Channel invasion had been code-named, was planned for May 1944 – that is, in seven months' time. By then, they had to be ready. Any longer, and the war could easily drag on and on, with the deaths of yet more of their countries' young men. On the other hand, to launch OVERLORD and for it to fail was unthinkable.

The Allied leadership might doubt that air power alone could win the war, but all accepted it held the key to a successful re-invasion of the continent. Control over the skies – not just of the immediate invasion area but of much of France and northern Europe – was an absolute prerequisite. To achieve that, the Luftwaffe had to be defeated first, or, at the very least, considerably reduced and driven deep into Germany, away from the skies over western Europe. The problem was, for all the growth of the Allied air forces by the autumn of 1943, and for all the many troubles facing Germany, the defeat of the Luftwaffe was still a long way off.

CHAPTER 3

Black Thursday

THURSDAY, 14 OCTOBER 1943. Another cold, damp and hazy morning at Thorpe Abbotts, a village lying a few miles east of the quiet country town of Diss in Norfolk and home to the 100th Bomb Group. The airfield had been laid down the previous year on requisitioned farmland and brought up to heavy bomber standard with the construction of three concrete runways laid out like a giant 'A', with the long main runway running west–east. The mass of fighter and bomber airfields in England needed to be as close to the continent as possible. What a huge advantage it was that, by a quirk of geography, the flattest part of this otherwise largely hilly and mountainous island should be in the east of the country.

Although the control tower at Thorpe Abbotts stood two-thirds of the way along on the northern side, the main base was to the south. Anyone entering the control tower could easily have been deceived about this, however, because although the airfield and runways were big enough, in terms of acreage they accounted for only about half the space of the entire base. To the south, hidden by Billingford and Thorpe Woods, a large village had emerged – one made up of rows of Nissen huts, looking like long cylindrical tubes of corrugated iron sliced down the middle. There were also hastily constructed brick buildings – two messes, one for officers and one for other ranks, as well as headquarters buildings, sick quarters and ammunition dumps. Newly metalled roads had been built, sometimes on old farm lanes and others completely new. The hamlet of Upper Street had been transformed and dwarfed. The speed of the development had been extraordinary: just over a year earlier, this had been a quiet, peaceful rural community, but now it was a large American heavy bomber base of thousands. Like all these hastily built airfields – thirty-nine were currently occupied by the Eighth Air Force, with more to follow – it had no perimeter fence of razor wire. For local schoolboys from the nearby villages of Thorpe Abbotts, Dickleburgh and Thelveton, their proximity to the base could hardly be more thrilling. Watching these giants fly off or land back down again was exciting, but the place was also full of friendly Americans, who, more often than not, were only too willing to share their supplies of chocolate, chewing gum and other luxuries rare to the average British schoolchild during the war.

A palpable sense of gloom had settled over Thorpe Abbotts this October week, however. Around the perimeter of the airfield itself, most of the standing B-17 Flying Fortresses showed battle damage. Some had a row of bullet holes, others had huge tears and gaping rents. One Fortress had an entire wing shredded, while two others had whole engines ripped off. These B-17s had witnessed and somehow survived an intense battle in the skies.

In fact, the Hundredth had been in three consecutive

days of battle, the last of which, the mission to Münster on the 10th, had been the worst. Already badly depleted after operations on the 8th and 9th, the Hundredth had been able to put up only thirteen Forts. Just one had returned, and that against the odds with two engines missing. In these three operations, the group had lost almost one hundred men. Four months earlier, it had reached England with 140 officers; now only three of those were still fit to fly. In the past fortnight, two squadron commanders had gone, four lead crews and three operations officers. The Hundredth had been decimated.

Now, in the early dawn of this Thursday in the middle of October, the Hundredth was preparing for yet another mission, the fourth in a week and a particularly difficult one: Schweinfurt, far into central Germany. The city had been identified as important by the American Committee of Operation Analysts (COA), which had been set up by General Henry 'Hap' Arnold, the commander-in-chief of the United States Army Air Forces, late the previous year. The COA had made their first report back in March and had recommended enemy fighter aircraft production as their number-one target priority, and ball bearings as the second. These latter were crucial anti-friction bearings used not just in aircraft – although German aircraft factories alone needed more than two million a month – but also in tanks, vehicles, guns and other equipment. Ball bearings were therefore a vital resource and, as the COA pointed out, their manufacture was particularly suited to a knock-out blow because production was largely limited to six cities and because almost half of all German production was based at one single factory in Schweinfurt. There was no doubt that if the ball-bearing plant there could be destroyed completely, the German war effort would take a massive blow.

The Eighth had first hit Schweinfurt on 17 August with 315 heavy bombers in a joint attack that also targeted the Messerschmitt plant at Regensburg. This was one of the first big tests of the Eighth Air Force and the American pre-war belief that a B-17's robust construction and heavy armament of thirteen .50-calibre machine guns would be enough, when they flew in close formation, to see off any attacks by enemy fighters. Operations thus far had shown that it was far better to have fighters escort the bomber force, but Schweinfurt was well beyond the range of fighter cover and so it was accepted that on this occasion the heavies would have to fend for themselves. But those pre-war beliefs had been badly tested that day, as a slaughter had unfurled. A staggering sixty bombers – 19 per cent of the attacking force – had been shot down, thirty-six of them from the force targeting Schweinfurt. The attack on Regensburg had been accurate and had caused considerable damage, but nothing like as much as Major-General Fred Anderson, the commander of the Eighth's VIII Bomber Command, had claimed that day. In his diary he had noted that his bombers had destroyed the capacity of the Regensburg factories to build 2,400 Me109s a year. This, he wrote, meant there would be no need to repeat the attack. In fact, nearly 300 tons of bombs of varying weight and size had hit the plant, destroying a number of newly built aircraft, killing 400 and causing widespread damage. However, the large assembly shop, the most important building of all, had not been hit, and the majority of the all-important machine tools were undamaged. The reality was that aircraft production was barely affected at all.

The bombing of the Kugel-Fischer ball-bearing plant at Schweinfurt had been even less successful. Luftwaffe fighters had badly mauled the attacking force before they even reached the city, but the navigators of those that did had struggled to spot the target because it had been hidden by fog generators. Just 424 tons were dropped, of which only 35 tons of high explosives and 6 tons of incendiaries actually struck the ball-bearing works; the rest mostly landed on residential areas. Production was reduced by 34 per cent for a short while, but there was enough spare capacity and the damage was quickly righted.

Aircrews had also made claims that amounted to 228 enemy fighter planes shot down on the raid, which would have been a notable aerial victory. In the confusion and the melee of swirling fighters, over-claiming was both inevitable and understandable, but in truth Luftwaffe pilot casualties had been just seventeen dead and fourteen wounded, around a tenth of what had been claimed.

In other words, the results had not matched the effort and cost, especially since the aim had been to stop production altogether for between three and six months. Not only had the Eighth lost 60 bombers and 600 aircrew, but a further 11 bombers had later been scrapped and 164 were damaged, some badly so. In all, a third of the total attacking force had had to be written off. It had been a crushing blow, to put it mildly, and called into question whether daylight precision bombing, as strenuously advocated by America's air chiefs, could be either precise enough or even sustainable without finding some better way to protect the bombers all the way to the target.

Both Lieutenant-General Ira Eaker, who in December 1942 had taken over from Spaatz as commander of the

Eighth, and Major-General Anderson had gradually learned from a combination of photo-reconnaissance and other intelligence sources – not least decrypts of German Enigma code traffic – that the Schweinfurt–Regensburg raid had fallen some way short of their initial aims. Both had accepted that before very long they would have to send their boys back into the heart of Germany. The trouble was, the horrific losses had set them back. The Eighth Air Force was still growing, but first of all had to make good the losses of Schweinfurt–Regensburg, then build up strength even further. Nor had the weather helped; it had not been good in the late summer of 1943. Together, these concerns meant that not until early October had the Eighth felt ready to have another crack at enemy targets beyond fighter range.

Once again, the aircraft industry was the prime target: the Arado works at Anklam on the Baltic coast, the Focke-Wulf plant at Marienburg, as well as Münster and Bremen. Finally, this Thursday, 14 October 1943, it was the turn of Schweinfurt once again. Mission Number 115. Brigadier-General Curtis LeMay, commander of VIII Bomber Command's 3rd Division, had rung Colonel Neil 'Chick' Harding, commander of the 100th BG, and suggested they could sit this one out after the mauling they had suffered in the past week, but Harding had replied, 'The Hundredth go off ops? Never!' So the Hundredth would be flying again.

Among those from the group due to be flying that day were the crew of *Nine Little Yanks and a Jerk*, captained by Lieutenant Bob Hughes, a 25-year-old from Bryant in Washington State. Mission 115 that day was to be Hughes's tenth, but the briefing early that morning was unlike anything he and his navigator, Lieutenant Len Wickens, had yet experienced. Normally, the briefing room would be crammed before a mission, but as the curtain went back to reveal the map and a route to Schweinfurt, there were officers from just eight crews. As was then revealed, a number of those crews were to have key positions filled by the loan of personnel from other units. Nor would they be flying all together as a bomb group. Rather, the eight were to be split into two flights, one of which would fly the mission attached to the 390th BG, and a second, led by Hughes, which would accompany the 95th.

From the briefing, they went the short distance over to the mess hall for breakfast: dried eggs, Spam, coffee, toast, English marmalade and what Hughes called 'wonderful English dark bread'. It had been an eventful few months for Hughes. He had joined up the previous year, been selected for pilot training and had finally passed out with his wings from Class 43-B at La Junta in Colorado. From there he had been posted to Walla Walla back in his home state of Washington, where he had joined the 'Saunders Provisional Group', which was made up from twenty-five rookie crews. A key part of daylight bombing was formation flying, because it was believed that only by sticking together in close formation would crews be able to bring the full weight of fire to bear. With thirteen heavy .50-calibre machine guns per aircraft, twenty Fortresses, for example, multiplied to an impressive 260 machine guns. Yet flying and fighting together required practice and coordination, so, along with a number of other rookie crews, they had carried out Secondary Phase Training together from Walla Walla, which had involved plenty of navigational practice, formation work and also gunnery.

Final Phase Training had taken place across the state border at Redmond, Oregon, and then they had all flown on to Grand Island, Nebraska, for staging to England.

At this point it had not been clear to Hughes and his fellows whether the Saunders Provisional Group would remain together as a new bomb group or whether they would arrive in the UK and then be posted to other groups already there. It says much, though, about the exponential growth of the US Armed Forces that entire regiments in the army, as well as bomber and fighter groups, were being formed and were training together from scratch. The United States Army Air Corps – as it had been when Germany had invaded Poland in September 1939 – had had just seventy-four fighter planes and even fewer modern bombers. Now, America was producing barely comprehensible numbers of aircraft: in 1942, just under forty-eight thousand had emerged from new American factories. That figure had already been surpassed in the first nine months of 1943.

As a first lieutenant who was slightly older than many of his fellows, Hughes had earlier been appointed personnel officer to the Saunders Provisional Group. On 23 June, Colonel Saunders had mustered his charges together. The colonel would not be making the trip across the Atlantic; rather, his task was to train up yet more new crews. However, someone needed to be nominally in charge of the group as they headed to England, and Saunders had appointed Hughes. He and the crew of the already christened *Nine Little Yanks and a Jerk* would be leading the way.

The next day, they had flown to Bangor, Maine, and carried out some further training to study long-range cruise control – vital before flying across the Atlantic. There, a further nine B-24 Liberators had been added to the Provisional Group and then it was finally time to make the epic trip across the Atlantic, staging at various airfields along the way, from Nova Scotia to Iceland, before finally touching down at Prestwick in Scotland. All thirty-four had arrived safely, although as Hughes had made his approach, Joe Boyle, his radio operator, forgot to pull in the trailing radio antenna, which then caused a bit of damage as it whipped over the trees and hedgerows at the end of the airfield. 'Now we thought we knew who was the "jerk" on the crew,' noted Hughes in his diary. He had handed over command, and then the crews promptly had their new bombers taken from them and were all packed off to Combat Training School. Two weeks later, Hughes and his crew were assigned to the 351st Bomb Squadron of the 100th Bomb Group.

Although crews would be kept together through a tour of twenty-five missions, each member was first given a taste of a combat mission as part of a more experienced crew. Hughes, for example, had flown his first official mission on 25 July as the co-pilot to Lieutenant Tom Murphy and the crew of *Piccadilly Lily*. It had been to hit the U-boat pens in Kiel in northern Germany and had certainly been no easy milk run. By the time they landed again, *Piccadilly Lily* had twenty-seven holes in it. Two more trips with Murphy's crew had followed in quick succession. During a mission to Hanover, they had had the right elevator shot off and an incredible 168 holes drilled through the plane in an attack by an Me210, and next they had been attacked by German fighters during a mission to Oschersleben. Finally, the crew of *Nine Little Yanks and a*

Jerk had all flown together for the first time on 15 August, and this time it had been a milk run to Merville in northern France.

Since then, Hughes had notched up another five trips, including the Regensburg mission, which he had again carried out as co-pilot on Murphy's crew. That had been his last trip with *Piccadilly Lily*. Murphy and all his crew had been lost on 8 October, along with five other crews from the Hundredth that day. A further crew had managed to bail out and were now prisoners of war.

On this Thursday, 14 October, Hughes was about to fly his tenth official mission, although only his fifth with his crew on *Nine Little Yanks and a Jerk*. And as was all too evident from the rows of empty beds and the ghostly atmosphere in the mess hall and briefing room, and from the sight of far too many battle-scarred Fortresses, Hughes had done pretty well to survive as long as he had. Now, he and his crew were to fly to Schweinfurt, scene of a slaughter just two months earlier.

General Fred Anderson had sent the order to bomb Schweinfurt just after 11 p.m. the previous evening. 'This air operation today is the most important air operation yet conducted in this war,' he wrote on his orders. 'The target must be destroyed. It is of vital importance to the enemy. Your friends and comrades that have been lost and that will be lost today are depending on you. Their sacrifice must not be in vain. Good luck. Good shooting and good bombing.'

Around 90 miles further west of Thorpe Abbotts, at Podington, near Wellingborough, the crews of the 92nd Bomb Group were also learning what the day's target was with a mixture of incredulity and dread. The 92nd had been among the first to join the Eighth Air Force. They had reached England the previous summer and had taken part in several early missions that September. From then until May, the 92nd had built up strength, absorbing and training up new crews and getting ready to go back into combat.

Among those originals who had flown to England the previous year was Lieutenant J. Kemp McLaughlin. Now twenty-four years old and from Braxton County in West Virginia, McLaughlin and his crew had not been sent to North Africa, but instead they and the rest of the 407th Bomb Squadron had been instructed to help set up the 1/11th Combat Crew Replacement Center. This had been established by General Ira Eaker to help newly arrived air-crew orientate themselves around the UK, as well as learn about escape and air-sea rescue, and escape and evasion procedures, flying near barrage balloons and in poor weather. It was a good idea, but while McLaughlin had been singled out to become an instructor pilot, he was also asked to fly a number of VIP flights to Gibraltar, then on to North Africa and back again. Not until May 1943 did he finally rejoin his original bomb group.

Then, in early July, McLaughlin had been transferred from the 407th Bomb Squadron to the 326th, where he had been given an entirely new crew, a new Fortress – swiftly named *Fame's Favored Few* – and been made a flight leader. He and his crew had been one of the leading bombers for the first attack on Schweinfurt and had had a comparatively easy time of it, but now, on the morning of 14 October, McLaughlin was in no doubt about what lay in store. 'We all knew that we'd be going back to this target,' he noted, 'and each of us hoped he'd not be selected for that raid. No such luck.'

In fact, McLaughlin and his fellow officers on *Fame's Favored Few* had been put on alert the previous day. What the target would be was never revealed until the morning of the mission, but there was a clue to be had from a visit to the base weather office. There, they learned another low front lying over much of England and stretching across the Channel and over the continent was forecast for the following day. Better weather was predicted for central Germany, where the skies would be clear – ideal for bombing. At dinner that night in the officers' mess, many of them had been trying to guess what the target might be, but when they woke early the following morning not just to thick cloud but also to drizzle and fog, McLaughlin, for one, was convinced there was little chance they would be sent up in such poor conditions, no matter how clear the skies over Germany.

Still, they had been taught to prepare for a mission, even if it was likely to be scrubbed, and, after an early breakfast, trucks pulled up at the mess to take them to the briefing. At the far end of the room was a curtain and a middle-aged intelligence officer.

'Gentlemen, may I have your attention?' he said once all the pilots, navigators, bombardiers and 92nd staff officers had settled. 'This morning we have quite a show.' He then drew back the curtain to reveal the large map on the wall. The men leaned forward, craning to see the lines of the route and the target. Then the intelligence officer added, 'It's Schweinfurt again.'

For a moment there was a profound silence, then came the groans and whistles. 'Son of a bitch!' said one man loudly. 'This is my twenty-fifth mission.' The last of his tour before returning to the States.

'What the hell are you crying about?' responded one youthful-looking pilot. 'This is my first!'

McLaughlin, meanwhile, was more interested in what was to follow. He accepted it was a vital target, but just how tough it was likely to be depended on which route they took, the number of fighters, or 'Little Friends', that would be escorting them and the likely number of enemy fighters. The intelligence officer now explained that only light flak was expected along the route and P-47s would escort them all the way to the Ruhr. From then on, they would be on their own until the return leg, when more Thunderbolts would pick them up north-east of Paris. That was more than 400 miles and over two hours' flying. It was quite a long stretch without any protection. And over the Reich. Over the target itself, they could expect some 380 anti-aircraft guns firing twelve rounds per minute. That equated to well over fifty thousand shells fired at the main formations from the moment they reached the initial point (IP) through to the end of the target run.

Even worse, they would most likely be met by some seven hundred enemy single-engine fighters and four hundred twin-engine, attacking them with cannons, machine guns and the advantage of far greater speed and manoeuvrability.

Most of the men assembled sat aghast as the briefing continued with details of flight formations, the runway take-off line-up and the composition of the bomber force. That day the 92nd would be leading not only their wing, but also the 1st Division and the entire Eighth Air Force. And McLaughlin and the crew of *Fame's Favored Few* would be the lead ship. Finally, Colonel Budd Peaslee was introduced. Formerly commanding officer of the 384th BG, he had, two weeks earlier, taken over as Chief of Staff of the 40th Wing. He was going to fly with McLaughlin and his crew as Eighth Air Force commander.

McLaughlin was tall and lean, with short, dark hair and pale eyes, and although his height lent him an obvious natural authority, he still looked incredibly young, as did most of the boys about to take off that day. There was no getting around it: this was likely to be a horror show. McLaughlin's only cause for optimism was the weather here in England, which was still terrible. He reckoned there was still a very good chance the mission would be scrubbed.

Even so, they had to assume otherwise and so he arrived at his aircraft half an hour before take-off in order to make his own personal checks and, after walking around and satisfying himself all was in order, he climbed up through the rear hatch with his parachute and flying kit, conscious that the weather remained as dreadful as it had been. Captain Harry Hughes, his navigator, and Lieutenant Ed O'Grady, the bombardier, arrived from their additional briefing and clambered up directly behind him. Once on board, they discovered the rest of the aircrew and ground crew inside the ship already, keeping out of the rain. 'One quick glance,' noted McLaughlin, 'told me they were worried, scared, and that morale was down.' McLaughlin did his best to reassure them, while still silently praying that the mission would be cancelled. If anything, the weather appeared to be worsening and there was still no sign of their passenger, Colonel Peaslee, which augured well. They were not to be saved, however. As McLaughlin was starting the engines for the warm-up and carrying out his preparatory drills, Peaslee arrived and clambered into the cockpit. The mission was on.

As the lead Fortress, *Fame's Favored Few* was the first to taxi out, slowly inching around the perimeter and then lining up at the end of the runway. Behind him, other Forts followed. There were still a few minutes before take-off and, peering out into the worsening fog and rain, McLaughlin struggled to see how they could possibly go ahead. He now broke radio silence to ask the control tower if there was any message, hoping against hope they would be ordered to stand down. 'I did not relish the idea of a zero-zero take off,' he wrote soon after, 'with a full bomb load, extra gasoline, and maybe bad icing conditions.'

Before any reply arrived, however, the clock reached take-off time and so, reluctantly, at 10.12 a.m., McLaughlin began revving his engines, released the brakes and the Fortress sped down the runway, 50 miles an hour, 60, 70. Asking Peaslee to keep a close eye on the runway in case of any swerving, he watched the speedometer reach 100 m.p.h., then, pulling back on the control column, felt the big bomber ease into the air. He was flying purely on instruments, a nerve-wracking experience with so many other laden bombers right behind him. Climbing up through the cloud, they finally broke out at around 7,000 feet and kept climbing, circling to wait for the rest to form up behind them. Over the Channel, he spotted Thunderbolts flying on over them, ready to intercept any enemy fighters.

There had been no such crowding for take-off at Thorpe Abbotts. Bob Hughes watched the first bomber squadron go and then it was their turn, with his ship in the lead. It was 10.15 a.m. Thirteen minutes later, they managed to clear the cloud base and successfully rendezvous with the 95th Bomb Group, although their hosts for the day were four ships short. That meant a bit of realigning so that they were in a tight defensive square as they flew. Without fighter escort, they were still extremely vulnerable. But without a flying formation, they were dead in the air.

They now rendezvoused with the 390th Bomb Group and that made their 13th Combat Wing complete. As they neared the continental coast, they spotted their escorts. It was now around 12.30 p.m. They were a little south of course and around four minutes behind schedule. Over his headset, Hughes heard chatter on the radio from the lead units and escorts ahead of them. It seemed the enemy were already swirling.

Hughes and the rest of the boys from the Hundredth might have successfully formed up and joined their wing, but in the lead ship it was clear to Kemp McLaughlin and Colonel Peaslee that not all units had joined up in their proper sequences; it was hardly surprising in the terrible weather, but as a result the mission had begun with some confusion – and that was unlikely to help their cause.

On they flew. As they entered German air space, the fighter escorts, at the limit of their range, turned and left them. The bombers were on their own. 'A large formation approaching at 5 o'clock,' called out Lieutenant Augustus Ahrenholz, who was usually McLaughlin's co-pilot, but who had taken the tail of the plane to make room for Peaslee. At first they thought this must be the 40th Combat Wing behind them, but it rapidly became clear that it was instead a large gaggle of twin-engine Messerschmitts. Rather than attack from behind, the enemy fighters passed them on their starboard side, ready to circle in for a head-on strike; sure enough, the moment the fighter escort had departed, the enemy began their attacks. As McLaughlin flew on, he could hear his own crew calling out attacks from all around them.

Flak now appeared – puffs of angry black smoke and the clatter of shrapnel. The Fortress lurched. This was coming from the southern tip of the Ruhr – the great industrial heartland of Nazi Germany; they were too far north. A swift adjustment to avoid anything more, but then they were under attack again from yet more fighters – over a hundred this time. At this point, McLaughlin noticed that the low group ahead and below them had already lost five out of sixteen ships.

'Oh, hell!' called out Sergeant Ford, one of the waist gunners. McLaughlin asked him what was wrong. There were, the sergeant reported, a mass of twin-engine enemy fighters gathering for attack. Never before had they come under such a heavy and concentrated onslaught. Two Me110s attacked from the starboard flank, while an Me109 suddenly sped down out of the sun and opened fire on the Fortress of the deputy leader on McLaughlin's right, Major George Ott. One engine was knocked out immediately, possibly even two. The stricken B-17 could not keep up and fell back. Nine parachutes blossomed, but Ott was still flying. Then the bomber disappeared from view.

Two Ju88 twin-engine bombers now attacked from ten o'clock. Sergeant Edison in the top turret called it out.

'My God, Mac, take some evasive action!' shouted Harry Hughes, the navigator. McLaughlin did so at the

moment two rockets exploded just off their nose. Everywhere they looked were enemy fighters. The low group
had now lost more than half their ships, most exploding
from rockets or burning mid-air. Sergeant Van Horn now
called out that Lieutenant Clough's Fortress had been hit
and was on fire; one of the wings had been blown off. And
two parachutes had appeared. Now came yet another
attack by Me110s in groups of four, each firing two rockets
from around 600 yards. Twin streaks of black smoke were
left behind as the rockets passed, but single-engine fighters were following. Those already hit and straggling had
no chance at all.

Yet the formation was not even close to the target.

'Captain,' said Peaslee over the intercom, 'I think we've
had it.'

McLaughlin barely had time to think about what their
chances were; he had his hands full trying to keep the formation together and maintain some sort of slight
protective position behind the low wing up ahead. Even
so, he had never been more scared in his life. The Fortresses to his right and behind had been shot down and
only four now remained of the sixteen up ahead. Peaslee
was surely right.

Repeatedly ordering the survivors to close up and keep
a tight formation, they flew on and, by what seemed like a
miracle, they were still in one piece as they finally drew near
to the target. Lieutenant Ed O'Grady, the bombardier, now
reminded him to turn on the Automatic Flight Control
Equipment (AFCE). This allowed the bombardier to control the aircraft using the Norden bombsight as they flew
the bomb run over the target. It also meant flying straight
and level, with O'Grady peering straight down through

the bombsight's lens. The aim was to make only minor adjustments until they were right over the bull's-eye. Even now, though, McLaughlin had to un-clutch the AFCE and regain control in order to take further evasive action. They had been flying for three hours. Glancing around, McLaughlin realized his group looked more like a squadron. Only twelve planes remained of the twenty-one with which they had taken off.

They now finally began nearing the target. Flak began bursting around them, but fortunately it was not accurate, so McLaughlin switched the AFCE back on. 'Okay, O'Grady,' he told his bombardier. 'It's all yours.'

On the plane flew. The sky was clear, the ground easily identifiable. Enemy fighters continued to swirl and peck at the formation, and twice Ed O'Grady saw them fly through his optics. On board no one spoke, but the gunners continued to fire, their heavy .50-calibre guns drumming away. The flak became denser, but then, suddenly, there was the target: the Kugel-Fischer ball-bearing plant. Pressing down on the bomb release, O'Grady called out, 'Bombs away.'

Immediately, McLaughlin took back control and pulled the Fort into a right turn. 'We've flown this far for Uncle Sam,' he told Peaslee and the rest of the crew. 'From here we fly for the U.S. – us.'

Not far behind, the 95th Bomb Group, including Bob Hughes's squadron from the Hundredth, were approaching the IP for the final turn towards the target. It was now 2.47 p.m. and suddenly the leader of the 95th was hit and began rapidly descending. By this time the flak had intensified and a loud burst knocked their neighbouring ship, lifting it and rolling it directly towards *Nine Little Yanks and a Jerk.*

'Move, Bob!' yelled the co-pilot, Lieutenant Don Davis. With enormous skill and quick thinking, Hughes kicked hard on his left rudder, pushed the control column forward with a bit of left aileron, then pulled back again, swiftly peeling off and out of the way of the neighbouring Fortress, which was still completely out of control from the flak burst. A mid-air collision had been avoided by a whisker, but it meant that *Nine Little Yanks and a Jerk* was now ahead of the rest of the formation, on her own and, in effect, the lead ship. They had been due to drop their bombs following the lead bombardier's release, but both Hughes and Dick Elliott, his bombardier, had earlier attended the Intense Target Study and so were already familiar with the primary target. Elliott also realized the target was dead ahead and reported this to Hughes. They would now be first over it in their group and bombing out of formation, something they had never done before. With increasingly intense flak up ahead and the prospect of emerging alone into the waiting clutches of swirling enemy fighters, Hughes worried about proceeding with such an action.

'Dick,' he said over the intercom, 'I do not have the right to commit a man to this course of action against his will. It would have to be 100 per cent volunteer.'

Elliott now carried out a quick vote. All agreed they should go for it; they had to hope the flak would not open up on one lone bomber around the target for fear of revealing the ball-bearing plant. Also, by not opening the bomb bays until the very last moment, Hughes and Elliott hoped to dupe the enemy flak gunners below into thinking they were a lone and stricken bomber that had lost its way.

They were now almost upon the target and still in one piece, so the bomb bays were finally opened and at 2.54 p.m. Elliott called out, 'Pickle barrel!' The bombs were away and all in the mean point of impact (MPI). That was a good job done, but it was still a long way back home. Key to survival would be helping the struggling Fortresses of the 95th get back into close formation, and to get into that formation themselves as soon as they possibly could.

Meanwhile, McLaughlin's crew on *Fame's Favored Few* had been attacked the moment they turned for home, but then, miraculously, had been left alone for more than ten minutes. Clearly the enemy aircraft had been forced to return to base to refuel and rearm. They all knew it was only a matter of time, however, before more fighters appeared. McLaughlin reckoned about half their bomber force had now gone, which made those that remained more vulnerable than ever. Sure enough, enemy fighters soon returned, making yet more frontal attacks from above, and diving down and past them at enormous speed. Sergeant Foley asked how long it would be before the Little Friends rejoined them.

'An hour and thirty-eight minutes,' replied Harry Hughes. McLaughlin could sense the inward groans, although no one made a sound. On they went, the gunners firing relentlessly as the fighters continued to pounce and fire on them, but despite being clattered by bullets, no one was hit and the sturdy Fortress continued flying. Eventually, over France, the enemy fighters broke off. Of the Little Friends, there was no sign. This was because a fog blanketing England had grounded them. In truth, it made little difference, because the enemy fighter force had attacked the bombers out of their range in any case, and it certainly hadn't prevented even more bombers from being shot down on the return leg than on the way out. Three more had gone from the 92nd BG. But not *Fame's Favored Few*. 'From there on,' noted McLaughlin, 'we had a sort of awed peace as we momentarily looked back, the view broken only by a few negligible bursts of flak against the white clouds below. The evening sun was bright in a clear blue sky, but we were not quite up to enjoying it.'

Eventually, they reached the Channel, but they were certainly not out of the danger zone, because now they faced the same thick, ten-tenths cloud they had left all those hours earlier. It was bad enough flying up out of this at the start of an operation, but worse at the end of a long, terrifying and stressful mission, by which time everyone was utterly spent. They had been airborne for seven hours and on oxygen for six. Now, 12,000 feet of cloud seemed to mock the thought of landing.

After McLaughlin had ordered his crew to unload their guns and come out of the turrets, they then moved forward up towards the cockpit and opened a can of pineapple, which they passed around. The sweet, succulent taste was like nectar at that moment.

Then, a miracle: a hole in the cloud large enough to guide the formation through. As they descended, a weather report came in: they could expect a cloud ceiling of 1,000–2,000 feet and visibility of 2 miles. That was something, and certainly enough in which to land, although as they flew lower and lower conditions worsened again. Rain pelted them and not until they were dangerously low, at just 500 feet, could they see the dark patchwork of fields and patterns of villages and towns. Using radio fixes, they managed to find Podington. Their wingman, pilot

Lieutenant 'Smoke' McKennon, had a badly damaged ship, so, after leading them in, McLaughlin pulled up again and allowed the stricken Fort to land first. Finally, after leading two more Fortresses in, McLaughlin brought his own aircraft down. 'A long, tough, soul-searching day,' he noted, 'I'll not soon forget.'

A little while after, Bob Hughes and the crew of *Nine Little Yanks and a Jerk* also touched down safely. A few days earlier, just one Fortress had made it back from Münster, but this time, miraculously, all eight from the Hundredth had safely reached home at Thorpe Abbotts. It was a lottery, but that day a number of other bomb groups had been decimated. The 305th had lost thirteen crews out of sixteen; the 306th ten out of eighteen; the 92nd, 379th and 384th Bomb Groups all lost six crews. In all, sixty Fortresses were lost and 594 men killed or captured, with a further forty wounded. Seven more aircraft had to be written off and 138 were damaged to varying degrees.

The question, though, was whether this huge sacrifice had been worth it, because the harsh reality was that, in seven days of bombing operations, the US Eighth Air Force had lost 148 heavy bombers. That was not sustainable.

'Black Thursday', as it would soon be called, had brought the Combined Bomber Offensive to crisis point.

CHAPTER 4

America's Bomber Men

GENERAL IRA EAKER, THE commander of the US Eighth Air Force, had followed the progress of Mission 115 with General Fred Anderson at VIII Bomber Command Headquarters at High Wycombe, code-named PINETREE, some 40 miles west of London. A large, sprawling Gothic mansion in 250 acres of grounds, Wycombe Abbey had been rebuilt 150 years earlier and, since 1896, had been a boarding school for girls. However, with the girls and school evacuated away from perceived danger, it had been requisitioned and handed over to the Americans. Not only did it have the space to house a large headquarters, it was also only down the road from RAF High Wycombe, the headquarters of RAF Bomber Command. Collaboration and cooperation had always been seen as a key part of the Combined Bomber Offensive. Old panelled schoolrooms had been converted into a war room, with maps covering the walls from floor to ceiling, and an operations room, complete with yet more maps, telephones and the means to plot and follow the progress of any mission.

Following the Schweinfurt raid must have been a chilling experience, yet both Eaker and Anderson had known it would be costly. The key issue was whether the gains would outweigh the sacrifice, so both men had remained there waiting for intelligence reports and after-action reports, plus the all-important photographic evidence, to start pouring in. Bob Hughes's strike photos, for example, had proved their bombs had, indeed, hit their mark.

Nor were Hughes's photos the only ones to indicate serious damage to the plant. Subsequent intelligence reports confirmed this, and the following day, Friday, 15 October 1943, Eaker was able to cable his chief, General Hap Arnold in Washington, to report that all three Kugel-Fischer factories had been destroyed. There was no hiding the bomber losses, however, although Eaker was quick to add that the horrific mauling did not 'represent disaster'. He asked Arnold to rush through more crews and aircraft, and more fighters too – a minimum of 250 bombers and crews a month. Eighth Air Force, he wrote, had to become bigger, not smaller. 'We must show the enemy we can replace our losses,' he wrote to Arnold. 'He knows he cannot replace his. We must continue the battle with unrelenting fury. This we shall do. There is no discouragement here. We are convinced that when the totals are struck yesterday's losses will be far outweighed by the value of the enemy material destroyed.'

Arnold responded to this news by announcing to the world that Schweinfurt had been completely destroyed. This, however, was not the case; despite the accuracy of the bombing, only 482 tons of bombs had been dropped and inevitably a large part of that had failed to hit the Kugel-Fischer plant. Output fell by 67 per cent, which was no small amount, but already dispersal of factories had begun and, in any case, the Luftwaffe was moving away from bombers to fighters, and fighters required far fewer ball bearings. In other words, the damage caused had been significant but was still a way off from proving decisive. Eaker had said there was no discouragement, but that was palpably not the case.

Arnold then followed up his comments on Schweinfurt II by telling the press that losses as high as 25 per cent on some missions might be expected and could be accepted. Even Eaker, always so loyal to Arnold, had to protest at these comments. In the context of the wider war such losses were not especially high, but in the context of the structure and base organization of the Eighth Air Force they were absolutely not sustainable. Certainly there was no question of going back into Germany any time soon – the week's efforts had been far too damaging and the losses too great for that, and yet only by sustained bombing could more decisive results be achieved.

At Podington, for example, Kemp McLaughlin and a number of others in his squadron were sent for a week of rest and recuperation at Stanbridge Earls, a large manor house near Southampton. At Thorpe Abbotts, meanwhile, the bomber base had seemed like a ghost town for a while. It was the same across the board in VIII Bomber Command. Captain James Good Brown had the unenviable task of being chaplain to the 381st Bomb Group based at Ridgewell, to the east of Cambridge. Like other bases, Ridgewell sprawled well beyond the limits of the airfield itself. Brown's office lay at one end of a hastily constructed brick and metal-frame-roofed hall, the main part of which was used as the base cinema. It was Brown's job to offer solace, moral support and spiritual guidance, but it could be hard to convince 18- and 20-year-olds of God's wisdom and mercy when they had just seen friends atomized in mid-air, or returned to confront rows of empty beds. Youthful confidence went only so far; bomber crews were increasingly coming to understand their chances of making it through a twenty-five-mission tour unscathed were very slight. The 381st had got off comparatively lightly at Schweinfurt, but had suffered over Bremen and Anklam earlier that week, when ten planes had been lost. The shock had been enormous, because many of those crews had been the original members of the 381st. 'Therefore it took all the hope out of any man left,' noted Brown, 'the hope of finishing twenty-five missions. The possibility of reaching twenty-five missions seemed gone . . . when they saw that the men who had eighteen to twenty raids did not return, all said, "What hope is there for us of ever coming through?" The truth is, there was little hope.'

A few days after the Schweinfurt mission, Brown sat next to the chaplain of the 305th BG at a division chaplains' meeting.

'How did you fare on the Schweinfurt II raid?' he asked.

'Let's not talk about it,' came the reply.

But Eaker had to talk about it. He was the one sending these young men to their deaths and, at that moment, he was following a doctrine and a strategy that were clearly failing.

Eaker was a good and decent man, but suddenly trapped in a situation where immediate solutions seemed to be in short supply. In October 1943 he was forty-seven years old, balding but with a handsome face. Square-jawed, he had piercing dark eyes and an air of resolve that was entirely in keeping with his character. The son of poor farmers from Texas, he had managed to break free of rural poverty by proving an excellent student. This had helped him win a commission as an officer soon after joining the army. In November 1917, while he was on the parade ground of the 64th Infantry at El Paso, an aeroplane had got into trouble and landed nearby. At the time, Eaker had never seen a plane before, and as the nearest officer on the scene he had hurried over. The pilot's problem, Eaker spotted almost immediately, was a loose spark plug. Putting it back in and reconnecting the lead did the trick and the engine whirred back into life.

'You ought to come into the Aviation Section of the Signal Corps,' the pilot told him.

'How do I do it?' Eaker asked.

The pilot reached into his pocket and produced a form. 'Fill this out,' he said, 'and send it in and you'll probably get a call to fly.' Eaker did exactly that and five months later he was transferred, learning to fly and becoming a skilled pilot. His rise up the ranks was slow, as it was for most in the small US armed forces of the interwar years. However, he also proved a talented writer, in 1933 gaining a degree in journalism from the University of Southern California and becoming the unofficial public relations man for the Air Corps. He also attended the Air Corps Tactical School as well as the Army Command and General Staff School at Fort Leavenworth, a sure sign that he was being marked out for higher command. In between, he still found time to fly and in 1936, along with his friend Major Bill Kepner, became the first pilot to fly across the United States 'blind' – on instruments only and with a black-out hood over his cockpit.

By the outbreak of war in 1939, Eaker was in Washington as executive officer to Major-General Hap Arnold, the Chief of the Air Corps, and with Brigadier-General Carl 'Tooey' Spaatz as Air Corps Chief of Staff. This made Eaker effectively Number 3 behind Arnold and Spaatz. He even collaborated with Arnold to write three books on air power, of which the last, *Winged Warfare*, became something of a standard text. In the summer of 1941, Eaker was in Britain as an observer and met many of the leading commanders of the RAF, not least Charles Portal, soon to become Chief of the Air Staff. He even got to fly a Spitfire and learn about RAF fighter tactics from Bob Stanford-Tuck, one of the RAF's leading aces.

After the US entered the war in December 1941, Eaker was promoted to brigadier-general and sent back to Britain along with Spaatz. Their task was to prepare for and then establish the Eighth Air Force, with Spaatz as commanding officer and Eaker as CO of VIII Bomber Command. When Spaatz was sent to North Africa to become USAAF theatre commander, Eaker was the obvious choice to take over the Mighty Eighth. Operationally, the challenge had been to build up a big enough force quickly enough to make an impact. Even more airfields had to be constructed by British and American engineers; aircraft had to be sent from the States – no small matter when coming all the way from factories in the Midwest and beyond; ever more crews had to be trained and shipped over; and vast numbers of staff and ground crew needed to be sent, along with equipment and, of course, bombs. Roughly fifty men were needed on the ground to keep ten aircrew in the air. On top of that, many of the Eighth's original bomb groups had then been transferred to North Africa.

There had been strategic challenges too. American troops had first arrived on British soil in January 1942, part of Operation BOLERO, the build-up of US forces in Britain for the planned cross-Channel invasion of Nazi-occupied Europe. Yet American – and British – strategy had never been just about getting troops back on to French soil, but also about gradually tightening the noose around Germany's ability to wage war. This was to happen largely through air power and specifically strategic bombing, part of the policy to use 'steel not flesh' wherever possible. The idea was a simple one: in order to avoid the wholesale slaughter of a generation of young men, as had been experienced by Britain in the last war, they would use technology, modern science and machinery to do much of the work. The number of men thrust on to the coalface of war would thus be kept to a minimum. Air power was central to this strategy, so much so that even in the autumn of 1943, it was not the British Navy or Army or RAF that had priority in manpower, but rather the British Ministry of Aircraft Production.

In the years leading up to the outbreak of war, much thought had been given to air power, not just in Britain but all around the world. One of the most influential prophets had been the Italian Giulio Douhet, a former artillery officer, who in 1921 wrote *Command of the Air*. Douhet's book, which was revised and reissued six years later, was widely read and argued that in future warfare would be dominated by air power. Large numbers of bombers were key, he claimed; they would operate independently, striking at the heart of an enemy power's industrial base, centres of communication and even cities. Winning control of the skies was obviously central to this vision and, although Douhet predicted some air defence, he argued that the side with the biggest, most powerful air force would prevail. In Douhet's vision, the bomber, not the fighter plane, would be king.

The idea that the bomber would dominate also held sway in Britain, where Marshal of the Air Force Sir Hugh 'Boom' Trenchard, the first commander of the RAF, was an ardent and messianic bomber man who continued to wield enormous influence even though he had formally retired. That Britain had established a fully coordinated air defence system – the world's first – and its own independent Fighter Command was, in many ways, thanks to the dogged stubbornness and enlightened thinking of a handful of individuals, including the former Chancellor of the Exchequer and Prime Minister Neville Chamberlain, Air Chief Marshal Sir Wilfrid Freeman, and Air Chief Marshal Sir Hugh Dowding, Fighter Command's first commander-in-chief and a man who had repeatedly clashed with Trenchard and his lackeys. There were others, but these men, especially, had fought to buck the prevailing thought that it was bombers that would dominate the skies in any future conflict.

In the United States, the supremacy of the bomber had also taken root. Arguably the most influential of the pre-war theorists was William 'Billy' Mitchell, who had finished the First World War as commander of US Army air operations in France and then, post-war, had become assistant chief of the Air Service. So outspoken was he about the need to build up a strong air force and the importance of the bomber, he was even court-martialled in 1925 for accusing the War and Navy Departments of treason for their neglect. Resigning from the air service, and now unshackled from military rules and decorum, he spent the next decade writing and continuing to push his theories. The key, he argued, was to build up an air force that was superior to that of any potential enemy and then unleash it aggressively and swiftly, so ensuring an end to any further hostilities before land or naval forces even came into the fight. This way, future wars would be over quickly without the wholesale slaughter of America's young men.

The trouble was, the United States in the 1920s and 1930s was not only isolationist, but its leaders believed that maintaining large armed forces inevitably led to them being used in conflict, while a small army and navy would ensure America kept out of future wars. In any case, the United States was distancing itself from Europe – and the Atlantic was in the way. Mitchell drove himself to an early death, in 1936, in his efforts to change people's minds, frustrated that the powers that be refused to listen to his warnings and his ardent belief in the primacy of air power.

However, Mitchell's preachings had not fallen on entirely deaf ears. It was true that in September 1939, when Germany invaded Poland, the US Army Air Corps had just seventy-odd fighter planes and even fewer bombers; none the less, not only did the Army Air Corps exist, but air doctrine had also been developing alongside some very important technological advances. The Air Service Tactical School, founded at Langley Field in Virginia in 1920, was the spiritual centre of the Air Corps. Renamed the Air Corps Tactical School six years later, as well as effectively being the US air college, its staff were also given the task of developing air doctrine. And at the heart of this doctrine was bombing, although not, it must be said, without considerable debate.

In the first half of the 1930s, a doctrinal air battle had raged at the Tactical School. Captain Claire Chennault was an ardent believer in the power of the fighter plane, or pursuit aircraft as they were known at that time in the Air Corps. Pursuit aircraft, he argued, were more flexible and could both stop bombers and give support to ground forces. While at the Tactical School, he argued two key tenets: first, that pursuit aircraft would always be able to intercept bombers if given enough warning of an attack, and second, that bombers, flying deep into enemy territory, needed a friendly fighter escort to prevent heavy losses if not complete failure.

Others, however, such as Harold George and Kenneth Walker, argued that the long-range bomber was the preeminent weapon of air power, and that pursuit aircraft could not achieve any strategic influence on any future war in the way that a bomber could. In truth, both were needed, but Chennault left the Tactical School in 1937 and headed to China, where he became a mercenary and led a group of American fighter pilots flying for Chiang Kai-shek's Nationalists against the Japanese.

With Chennault gone, it was the influence of the bomber men that was felt most keenly, and what they promoted was high-level, precision and, crucially, daylight bombing. Central to this focus was technological advancement: dreaming of long-range heavy bombing was useless without the kind of aircraft that could deliver such a vision. However, in the United States new, modern civilian commercial aircraft were being developed with far stronger cantilevered wings made of metal spars and covered with stressed lightweight aluminium sheeting. This meant that suddenly the age of fabric-covered biplanes was drawing to a close and, in its place, modern, all-metal and much larger aircraft were emerging.

Among the early civilian airliners was the Boeing 247, which first flew in 1933, the year Hitler came to power and Roosevelt was sworn in as president of the United States for his initial term. The Boeing had a retractable undercarriage, something quite different, and could fly at around 200 m.p.h. It looked shiny and modern and new – and it was. That it could take a maximum of only ten passengers was, frankly, neither here nor there. Anyone looking at the Boeing 247 was looking at the future and seeing enormous possibilities. The same was true of the Douglas DC-3, which appeared three years later and, similarly, was all stressed metal and had cantilevered wings. This mighty machine could carry up to thirty-two passengers. In the United States, private commercial business in an economy slowly but surely emerging from catastrophic economic depression was leading the way to rearmament and future military strength.

In terms of a vision of future air power, it was the Boeing company that set the bar. A year after the Boeing 247 had dazzled the aviation world with its modernity and shininess, the War Department, at the urging of the men of the Tactical School, issued a procurement brief for a new multi-engine heavy bomber, which was to be able to fly at upwards of 200 m.p.h. for ten hours and carry a bigger payload than any American plane up to that point. Three firms, Douglas, Martin and Boeing competed for the prize – and all at their own expense, as America's strict amortization laws would not be repealed until the autumn of 1940.

The outcome was a planned 'fly-off' at Wright Field,

Dayton, Ohio, between the three manufacturers' proto-
types. The Boeing 299 first flew on 28 July 1936 from their
Seattle base. Sleek, powerful, and unlike anything that
had come before, it had an internal bomb bay, a largely
retractable undercarriage and even air brakes, and – a
first in aviation – an automatic pilot that could keep the
aircraft flying straight and level during a bomb run. It also
had five machine guns, protruding with obvious venom,
which prompted one Seattle reporter to say, 'Why, it's a
flying fortress!' Boeing were delighted with the line and
swiftly trademarked the name. They were even more
delighted when it effortlessly flew from Seattle to Dayton
in just under ten hours at an average speed of 252 m.p.h. –
far in excess of the requirement. In truth, the prize was a
foregone conclusion: the Boeing had four engines, while
Martin's and Douglas's bombers each had just two. It was
also faster and could carry more. The plane was redesignated the B-17 'Flying Fortress' and Boeing was given an
order for sixty-five.

The quantity was hardly huge and certainly did not
reflect the kind of overwhelming air supremacy the har-
bingers of air power were predicting, but it was the weapon
that the bomber advocates within the Air Corps had been
dreaming of: fast, powerful, with range, fire-power and a
bomb load of more than 2 tons. Even better, around the
same time, the US Army took possession of the Norden
bombsight, originally designed for the navy in the late
1920s by the Dutch émigré Carl Norden, and a marvel of
modern technology and science. This ingenious piece of
equipment enabled a bomb-aimer to look at the target
through the eyepiece and accurately compute the aircraft's ground speed and direction, then, after taking into

account the weight and size of the bombs, calculate when to release them to best achieve accuracy. Gyroscopic stability, which was also added into this remarkable instrument of scientific wizardry, ensured the telescopic sight was kept on the target despite the roll or sudden jolt of the aircraft from flak bursts. It was a truly extraordinary invention and unrivalled anywhere else in the world. It also meant that the Air Corps not only had a long-range, heavily armed four-engine bomber, they now had the technology to land drops on the enemy from height more accurately than any other air force in the world.

By the time war broke out in Europe in September 1939, the US Army Air Corps was still tiny at just 17,000 personnel, but it was led by men firmly rooted in the bomber philosophy, not least Major-General Henry 'Hap' Arnold, its commander-in-chief. The vision of Arnold, and of men like both Spaatz and Eaker, was not only to use massed bombing to spearhead any future military operations, but to carry out such bombing by daylight when visual siting was possible and the precision of the Norden bombsight could come to the fore. If the bombs struck their target accurately, then less ordnance would be required to do the job and, as a result, fewer aircraft. And the more efficiently and accurately the Air Corps could carry out their tasks, the smaller the number of Americans who would be needed to risk their necks in any future war. That, in essence, was the theory.

There was, however, always likely to be a gap between theory and practice. Imagining rafts of American bombers pulverizing key industrial and military targets while watching B-17s flying across the clear, azure-blue skies of the southern United States was easy, but on the other side of the Atlantic the weather was altogether more fickle, even in summer, and the Norden bombsight was less effective in cloudy conditions when the bombardier could not actually see the target.

Such considerations had little effect on those now leading America's burgeoning air capability, however, even though several senior air commanders – Spaatz and Eaker among them – had visited Britain well before the US entry into the war.

A highly regarded and hugely competent air commander, Spaatz – pronounced 'Spots' – had been at the very heart of the development of US air forces and strategy. Aged fifty-two by October 1943, he was stocky, square-jawed and handsome, with a trim moustache, and he carried an instantly identifiable air of authority, sagacity and charisma, which he backed up with an intuitive intelligence. These were fine attributes for a senior commander. Spaatz also had plenty of experience. He had flown as a fighter pilot in the First World War, shooting down several enemy aircraft and winning a Distinguished Service Cross.

In the years that followed, he took on various commands, first in a pursuit role and then in bombers. In January 1929 he captained a tri-motor Fokker aircraft called the *Question Mark*, which set a world endurance record for remaining airborne for more than 150 hours, thanks to repeated air-to-air refuelling. Ira Eaker had also been part of his *Question Mark* team. In the 1930s, Spaatz had been among those helping Boeing develop the B-17 and later the Consolidated B-24 four-engine bomber. Like Eaker, he had spent a year at the Command and General Staff School. From there he held staff posts at what was then called GHQ Air Force and in January 1939 took command of the Plans Section in the office of the Chief of the Air Corps, with a secret brief to draw up an expansion plan that would raise the Air Corps to ten thousand aircraft within two years. This had placed him at the core of the Air Corps' preparations for war, a position that was further augmented by a trip to England in the summer of 1940 in the role of special military observer as the RAF tussled with the Luftwaffe over southern England. Spaatz had regarded himself as a 'high-class spy'.

Under-resourced during the 1920s and 1930s the US Army Air Corps may have been, but from the summer of 1940 onwards, as President Roosevelt began mobilizing the American war industry, air power lay at the heart of that expansion. Like the British, the US was determined to use technology and industrial output to limit the number of their young men who had to put their necks on the line. Back in 1940, Roosevelt had promised 50,000 aircraft a year. That had seemed fantastical at the time, but had been proved a reality since. The Army Air Corps had also become the US Army Air Forces in June 1941 and, although strictly speaking it was still part of the US Army, it had been given its own staff and its commander, the newly promoted Lieutenant-General Hap Arnold, had a seat on the Combined Chiefs of Staff alongside General George Marshall and Admiral Ernest King.

Once America had entered the war, Spaatz, with Eaker as his right-hand man, arrived in Britain on 18 June 1942 to take command of the newly formed US Eighth Air Force. The plan had been to build up a force of sixteen heavy bombardment groups, each with thirty-two heavy bombers, three pursuit – or fighter – groups of 75–80 fighters each, as well as medium and light bomber groups. The first units started arriving that summer.

Spaatz had reached England already a committed supporter not only of strategic air power – that is, air forces operating independently of ground forces – but specifically of daylight precision bombing. Nothing he had witnessed in England in the summer of 1940 had dissuaded him from that firmly entrenched stance, but he did learn a great deal in the few weeks he was there. He had correctly predicted that Germany had nothing like enough aircraft for the task and would lose the Battle of Britain, but he had also accepted the crucial role of fighter aircraft and having a fully coordinated air defence system. A modern, well-dispersed air force protected by an effective early-warning system, he recognized, could not be destroyed on the ground. So it had proved.

Spaatz had left Britain in September 1940, but not before the Luftwaffe had turned on Britain's cities and begun night bombing. 'The Germans can't bomb at night,' he told an American reporter over dinner in London. 'Hell, I don't think they're very good in daylight – but they haven't been trained for night bombing. Nope, the British have got them now. They've forced them to bomb at night. The Krauts must be losing more than we know.'

Night bombing meant sacrificing accuracy. And without accuracy, there seemed little point in bombing, because it wouldn't achieve its aims; what he had seen of the Blitz convinced him that civilian morale would not collapse in the wake of area bombing – and in this he was quite right, as the Luftwaffe's failed Blitz went on to prove and as Bomber Command had learned after long and costly years of bombing Germany up to March 1943.

So it was that in the summer of 1942, when Spaatz had returned to England as commander of the fledgling Eighth Air Force, he had done so as committed to daylight bombing as ever he had been. And in this he had the absolute backing of the C-in-C of the USAAF, General Hap Arnold. Heavy bombers, Spaatz and Arnold had hoped – and particularly the B-17 Flying Fortress, which by 1942 had improved armour and armament – would be able to operate deep inside enemy territory without fighter escort. They would fly in mass formation, so that, rather like the merchant shipping convoy system, there would be safety in numbers. At the time, there had been some grounds for this confidence. Unlike the British Lancasters and Halifaxes, for example, which had a seven-man crew and were equipped with .303 Brownings that had already proved to be little more than pea-shooters, the Flying Fortress had a crew of ten and was equipped with a whopping thirteen .50-calibre machine gun in eight different positions. The .50-calibre was everything that an air-to-air machine gun needed to be and that a .303 was not: it had a good velocity and rate of fire and could pack a hefty punch. The B-17 was, quite simply, designed for daylight, not night operations.

There was also another important reason for pursuing daylight bombing. Spaatz wanted the Eighth to operate independently of the RAF. He did not want them playing second fiddle to the British or to be sharing assets. Moreover, he, Arnold and others in the USAAF were determined not to sing to the RAF's tune before testing their own carefully thought-through doctrine. As coalition partners with their own doctrine, this approach was entirely fair. More to the point, it meant that at some stage in the not-too-distant future, they would be able to deliver round-the-clock bombing, with the RAF bombing by night and the USAAF by day. For the Germans, there would simply be no let-up.

On paper, that all seemed a reasonable, clear and sensible approach to protracting the strategic air campaign against Germany. By the beginning of 1943, however, a rather dramatic divergence of doctrine and aims was emerging between the American air chiefs and the man in charge of British strategic bombing, Air Marshal Sir Arthur Harris. These were fundamentals about precisely what it was that such a campaign was attempting to achieve and how best it should be done. The stakes could hardly have been higher: the success or failure of the planned invasion of Nazi-occupied Europe and, with it, the swift conclusion of the war.

CHAPTER 5

Learning the Hard Way

WHILE THE EIGHTH WAS getting pummelled over Germany, RAF Bomber Command continued to bomb targets well within the Reich almost every night. Kassel, Frankfurt, Stuttgart, Hanover, Bremen and even Leipzig, deep in central Germany, were all targeted in October 1943. All were large cities with their own industrial areas and every one of them was involved in war work of some kind. On the night of Friday, 22 October, the target was Kassel for the second time that month. Kassel lies about 100 miles north of Schweinfurt and was a major base for the Henschel company, which made tanks, not least the fearsome Tiger, as well as railway locomotives. The German railway, the Reichsbahn, was very much the glue that kept the German war effort together; most arms, men, equipment – and, of course, Jews – were transported by railway, so locomotive factories and railway works were a good target. The aircraft manufacturer Fieseler also had a factory in Kassel, and the city was home to the regional military headquarters for Wehrkreis – Military District – IX. In other words, Kassel was a more than justified target for Bomber Command.

Among those flying that night were George and Bill Byers. Identical twins, they were both captains of Halifax heavy bomber crews in 429 'Bison' Squadron in the Royal Canadian Air Force, and part of Bomber Command's 6 Group. Although both now had two missions under their belts as second pilots, the attack on Kassel was to be their first operation with their own crews.

The twins were born in Vancouver in March 1921. Their mother's first husband had been killed in the last war and then she had met their father, who was working in lumber. When the twins were about six, they moved to Burbank in California, but after a few years returned to British Columbia.

Bill and George were inseparable. 'Our thoughts were often identical,' said Bill. 'Whether it was some kind of telepathy I don't know, but if we thought about some problem, we'd be sitting there looking at each other and both get the same idea at the same time.' Both were practically minded and cared little for academic work, so left school when they could and undertook a course in aeronautics. When war broke out, the brothers signed up as ground crew.

Kept together, they were posted to Saskatoon and then to Manitoba. Around that time, it had been decided that ground crew should sometimes fly in the aircraft they were working on. Both the Byers enjoyed this, so Bill suggested to George that they ask to retrain. To get in they had to pass an IQ test, which they did easily and in half the time allowed. Their subsequent medicals revealed they had perfect twenty-twenty eyesight and, after scraping through algebra and geometry tests, they were sent off to begin training as pilots. By December 1942 they had both passed their wings examinations but were told they had been earmarked to become instructors. This was a major disappointment, as they both wanted to go to England. 'We were gung-ho,' Bill admitted. However, two Australians who had trained with them had fallen in love with Canadian girls and were desperate to stay in Canada, so they were allowed to swap places.

George and Bill sailed to England in January 1943 and were finally split up when Bill fell ill with appendicitis. However, when he had recovered, George was still stuck at the holding camp in Bournemouth and so, reunited, they were posted together once more, this time to RAF Pershore for further training. Here they were put in a large room along with navigators, bombardiers, flight engineers and radio operators and everyone was told to sort themselves into crews. Incredibly, this ad hoc method of crewing up worked surprisingly well, and the brothers had soon teamed up, although not without confusion: the twins really were identical and it took a while for their respective crews to work out which was which.

By the end of the summer they and their crews had been posted to Croft-on-Tees, a Heavy Conversion Unit outside Darlington in North Yorkshire, where they were joined by the last members of their seven-men crews and converted to flying the large, lumbering four-engine Handley Page Halifax. It was quite a jump, as a four-engine aircraft was a lot more to handle than one with two engines. Then, on 29 September 1943, they were posted to 429 Squadron, based at Leeming, near Thirsk, also in North Yorkshire.

By this time, they had already formed strong bonds with their crews. Both Bill and George were sergeant pilots rather than commissioned officers and so did not mess separately from the rest of their crew. In fact, the twins ended up sharing a room together, because on arriving at Leeming they were allocated a married quarters house along with Dick Meredith, Bill's wireless operator. 'They were so much alike, you could barely tell them apart,' recalled Meredith. 'And so close. They never said, "Where's my shirt or socks?" but "Where's *our* shirt?"'

Neither the twins nor their new crews knew much about what to expect. Like most young men, their horizons were narrow and they were both ignorant and naïve about what lay in store. They had thought little about wider strategy or whether endless night-time bombing was actually achieving very much. Rather, they had joined Bison Squadron simply eager to get on with the job in hand and to do their bit.

Unlike American bomber crews, the RAF did not have second pilots, but did send up new men in such a role in order to show them the ropes and to ensure that when they flew as a crew for the first time they at least had some idea of what to expect. Bill and George Byers flew their first combat missions on 3 October – coincidentally also to Kassel – and both returned early with mechanical trouble. They were sent out again the following night, to Frankfurt, two bombers of just over four hundred in what was the first major attack on the medieval city. Bill and his adopted crew reached the target unscathed and, with good visibility, dropped their bombs on the red flares of the bomb markers. George's plane, on the other hand, came under repeated attack by a German night-fighter on the way to the city. They only just managed to escape, having flown into the sphere of the enemy anti-aircraft guns with one engine knocked out and two of the fuel tanks holed. There had been fires on board and the electrics on the bomb-bay doors had been damaged, so they had opened them manually, which took time and caused them to delay releasing their bombs. Where the bombs landed was unclear, but the crew managed to avoid further attack on the return leg despite flying with just three engines, which made them both slower and more vulnerable.

Before they reached Leeming, however, it became clear they no longer had enough fuel to get them home. What's more, their landing gear had been shot up and was now inoperable. Once over the English coast, the pilot, Flight Lieutenant Pentony, gave the order for them all to bail out. Six, including George, managed to do so safely, but two of the crew, the bomb-aimer and flight engineer, did not and were killed when the Halifax crashed into the ground. As a first full mission, it had been quite an eye-opening ordeal.

Now, on the night of 22 October, both brothers were piloting their own crews for the first time and were among some 247 Halifaxes and 322 Lancasters targeting Kassel. Bill was airborne by 4.55 p.m. – one advantage of the coming winter was that they could get under way sooner – and George thirty-five minutes later. Bomber Command did not fly in formation like the Americans, but in what was called a 'bomber stream'. Crews would be given a route to follow – one that avoided known flak concentrations and included a number of turns and dog-legs – but were left to follow that route on their own. Both brothers reached the target unscathed and, with the marker flares accurately dropped, Bill and his crew managed to drop their bombs without any hitches. George's crew again had some technical problems with the bomb-bay doors and were forced to jettison their load later, but both then made it back to Leeming safely, Bill touching down twenty minutes after midnight after being airborne for seven and a half hours, and George a short while later.

The German air defence system, however, had correctly tracked the bomber stream and its night-fighters were ready and waiting. Forty-three bombers were shot down that night – not far off the number of American bombers lost over Schweinfurt – but this was only 7.6 per cent of the attacking force rather than nearly 20 per cent, and well over five hundred bombers accurately hit the heart of Kassel, which was gutted by a massive and horrific firestorm. That night of devastation, the city lost 63 per cent of all its living accommodation – either destroyed or damaged – leaving up to 120,000 people homeless. In addition, 155 industrial buildings were destroyed or severely damaged. Three Henschel aircraft factories were badly damaged, the railway was seriously hit and some 5,599 people were killed. As Bill Byers recorded, 'It appeared to be a good raid.'

By October 1943, Bomber Command was not only hitting Germany very hard, it was doing so with the kind of accuracy that had been unachievable just a short time earlier. This was massed bombing on a scale that was also out of all proportion to what had been witnessed by either side early in the war. It had been a long and difficult road for the British, and had been achieved by a considerable degree of trial and error and by learning the hard way.

In fact, such lessons had early on persuaded both the British and the Germans to abandon daytime bombing in favour of night operations. They had quickly accepted that daylight bombing was unsustainable because bombers did not have the speed, agility or defensive power successfully to fend off much faster and more manoeuvrable fighter planes. Claire Chennault had been absolutely right. Nor, in those early years, had bomber fleets brought the kind of Armageddon predicted by Douhet, Trenchard and Mitchell, despite the German destruction of the Basque town of Guernica in 1937, or the devastation wreaked on Warsaw in September 1939 and Rotterdam in May 1940.

Since those heady days, the Luftwaffe's fortunes had suffered. They made an entirely unsuccessful attempt to destroy the British Air Force in the summer of 1940, only ever managing to knock out just one of the RAF's 138 airfields for more than twenty-four hours. Nor had they even remotely brought the country to its knees during the sustained Blitz upon Britain between September 1940 and May 1941. Rather, Britain had continued to build ever more factories at breakneck speed and to produce rapidly increasing numbers of tanks, guns, ships and, most of all, aircraft. In fact, the greatest cost of the Blitz to Britain was in the defensive measures prompted by the Luftwaffe's bombing rather than in actual damage done.

By the time of the Blitz, the Luftwaffe had largely given up daylight attacks, preferring the comparatively increased safety of night-time raids. Of course, bombing by night meant less accuracy, but then again, daylight bombing had not proved particularly accurate either. The Germans had no bombsight comparable to the Norden and this was one of the reasons they had put so much emphasis on dive-bombing earlier in the war. The theory was that dive-bombing ensured bombs were dropped closer to the target, which meant they would be more accurate. This, in turn, ensured less ordnance was required and so fewer aircraft. As the first year of war demonstrated, however, dive-bombers were only really effective against large fixed targets and with air superiority over the battle space. The moment the Luftwaffe did not boss the skies, their Junkers 87 Stukas were shot down in droves. By that time, however, they had already got a twin-engine dive-bomber, the Ju88, lumbering into production and, incredibly, despite the evidence, they were developing a four-engine dive-bomber too, the Heinkel 177.

In all, the Luftwaffe lost some 2,200 aircraft in its attempt to subdue both the RAF and Britain, which amounted to 100 per cent of the force with which it started, and although every one of the 41,000 British civilians killed in the Blitz was a personal tragedy, all those lives, all that effort, and all the diversion of resources into such a sustained aerial assault achieved little more than inconvenience to Britain's war machine. It did not bring about a collapse of British morale, did not stop Britain from continuing dramatically to increase its production of war materiel and, most importantly, did not provide the tactical or strategic victory Nazi Germany so desperately needed. The Germans invaded the Soviet Union in June 1941 with not only Britain still very much in the war, but with fewer aircraft in the Luftwaffe than when they had launched the invasion of France and the Low Countries the previous year. The Luftwaffe's defeat at the hands of the RAF in 1940 had proved catastrophic.

The British had also suffered in those first years of the war in the air. Entire bomber squadrons had been decimated during the Battle of France. Number 18 Squadron, for example, had lasted just ten days in France. During that time they had set off on one bombing mission after another, but by 20 May, when they were posted back to Britain, they had just four crews left out of twenty. A day later, they lost another while operating from England.

Meanwhile, RAF Bomber Command had begun bombing targets within Germany from the middle of May 1940, but had swiftly realized that if they were to have any chance of survival they needed to focus on night-time operations. When they bombed Berlin four times in August and early September 1940, they did so at night. Their accuracy was woeful, although these raids achieved a small psychological victory in that they infuriated and humiliated the Nazi leadership and proved to the German people that the war was still far from over. None the less, whether the benefits outweighed the downsides is questionable.

The RAF did learn from the Luftwaffe, however. The German attack on Coventry in November 1940, in which the heart of the medieval city was destroyed, demonstrated the benefit of attacking in waves, in clear moonlit skies and with a light breeze, and of dropping a mixed ordnance of high explosives and incendiaries. Those conditions, of course, were not something anyone could rely on, but they certainly set the bar. The British also learned that a few hundred twin-engine bombers capable of delivering a ton or so of bombs were simply not enough. For bombers to be decisive, there needed to be hundreds, if not thousands, of aircraft and preferably bigger, four-engine 'heavies' capable of carrying a much greater payload.

One of the men who had watched the Blitz with bitter interest was Air Marshal Arthur Harris, who had been at the Air Ministry in 1940. By February 1942 he had become commander-in-chief of Bomber Command and was, like his boss, Air Chief Marshal Sir Charles Portal, the Chief of the Air Staff, an avowed believer in the power of the bomber and in bringing Nazi Germany to its knees by pulverizing its cities and industrial infrastructure.

Despite Portal's support and despite factories in Britain producing more and more aircraft, faith in his new command was at an all-time low at the point Harris took over. The previous year, in August 1941, the Butt Report had been published, an independent investigation into the accuracy of Bomber Command's bombing effort. The killer statistic was the claim that only one in three bombers had been managing to drop their bombs within 5 miles of their target. This had been a devastating blow to Bomber Command and there were many who had questioned the ongoing bombing strategy, which was, after all, using up a considerable amount of effort and resources, not to mention young men's lives; even at night, bombing remained perilous.

There was to be no change of heart, however. Portal persisted in his conviction that strategic bombing would dramatically shorten the war and save the lives of many British servicemen. More importantly, Winston Churchill, the Prime Minister, was also certain that air power was key to ultimate victory. In any case, British factories were, by 1941, producing more aircraft than any other country in the world. It was simply too late, mid-war, to reverse this strategy.

Furthermore, new, bigger aircraft were on their way. Some of the finest minds in Britain were dedicated to pushing the country's aviation industry to new levels of sophistication and technological advancement – not only aircraft, but also scientific instruments. On its way was the four-engine Avro

Lancaster, capable of carrying a staggering 10 tons of bombs. Also in development were sophisticated new navigational aids.

Thus, despite the fallout of the Butt Report, the British remained committed to both air power and bombing, with more aircraft, more bombs, and even greater research and development. And, until bombs could be dropped with greater accuracy, RAF Bomber Command – and the air chiefs – accepted they would simply continue to strike at Germany with whatever means available.

It was very bad news for German civilians, but collateral damage was not something that weighed on the minds of many of Britain's war chiefs at this time – not with parts of London in ruins, with tens of thousands dead thanks to the Luftwaffe, and with Britain committed to an attritional and brutal war that was not of their making. Towards the end of 1941, Air Marshal Sir Richard Peirse, C-in-C of Bomber Command before Harris took over, told an audience in London's Thirty Club that for a year British bombers had been quite intentionally targeting German civilians. 'I mention this,' he told them, 'because for a long time, the Government, for excellent reasons, has preferred the world to think that we still held some scruples and attacked only what the humanitarians are pleased to call Military Targets . . . I can assure you, gentlemen, that we tolerate no scruples.' No one could claim the Nazis had a monopoly on cold-hearted ruthlessness.

Air Marshal Harris tolerated few scruples either, but recognized that a major period of rebuilding was needed before RAF Bomber Command could deliver the weight of force that was needed to have a strategic impact. His belief in air power – that it could dramatically shorten the war and save the lives of many young British – and American – servicemen had not been shaken in the slightest. What had changed was his realization that strategic bombing had to be on a far larger scale than had earlier been appreciated. He needed more bombers – heavy four-engine varieties and especially the new Lancasters that had started to arrive from early 1942. Up to that point, the highest monthly average for aircraft had been 421 bombers available each day, but only 68 of those had been heavies. Ten months later, at the end of 1942, the total figure had been 419, but the number of heavies had risen to 262. It had been an improvement, but creating the size of heavy bomber force Harris envisioned was taking a painfully long time.

Harris also needed more airfields with proper concreted runways that could take the weight of these heavies in all weather conditions; all-grass airfields were no longer sufficient. And he also needed the promised new and improved navigational aids. These were in development, but they were taking time: time to design, manufacture and implement, and time to train crews to use them.

Some successes had been achieved. At the end of May 1942, Harris had launched the first 'Thousand Bomber Raid'. Bomber Command had only had some four hundred aircraft at the time, but by scouring the Operational Training Units and other commands, and by using a number of largely obsolete aircraft, they had managed to reach the magic number of a thousand bombers. The target had been Cologne and heavy damage had been caused. It had also profoundly shocked Hermann Göring, the C-in-C of the Luftwaffe, and the Nazi leadership. Two more such raids followed and, although it was too risky and stretched resources too tightly to repeat them regularly,

Harris had been able to use these attacks to give his command a huge boost and their success had done much to convince sceptics that large-scale strategic bombing had a vital part to play in the ongoing war.

None the less, not until March 1943, after more than a year in the post and with the war already three and a half years old, was Harris at last ready to launch his all-out strategic air offensive against Germany. Expansion had been slow and hugely frustrating. Precious resources had been diverted to the Far East and to the Middle East. Nor had new Lancasters been rolling out of the factories as fast as he would like, but the line on the graph was heading upwards at long last. What's more, developments in navigational aids were also about to make a significant impact. By the time of the Thousand Bomber Raids, Harris's crews had been able to use a recently developed aid code-named 'GEE'. This was a radar pulse system that enabled a navigator on board an aircraft to fix his position by measuring the distance of pulses from three different ground stations in England. First trialled in 1941, it was being fitted into bombers by early 1942. It was a leap forward, although nothing like as accurate as scientists had hoped; its range was short and it was certainly not effective enough to aid blind flying. However, by the spring of 1943, Harris also had two more new and exciting navigational aids to work alongside GEE.

The first of these was 'Oboe', which relied on a radio signal pulse repeater in an aircraft linked to two ground stations back in Britain. It had limited range and could handle the signals of no more than six aircraft every hour, but it was accurate and appeared to be impervious to enemy jamming. That just a small number of aircraft were equipped with Oboe was fine, because only a handful were needed to find the target and then drop flares that would mark the way for the bombers following behind. Oboe was placed on the new De Havilland Mosquitoes – twin-engine aircraft, largely made of wood rather than stressed metal, which could fly at over 30,000 feet, so out of range of the flak guns below, and at more than 400 m.p.h. These Mosquitoes were part of the Pathfinder Force (PFF), which had come into being in August 1942. Harris had originally been against the move, as he didn't want any of his other squadrons to feel that an elite force was being developed – he believed it would be detrimental to fragile morale. However, the PFF had soon proved its worth and, because the bombers were now finding their targets more easily, morale had not taken the dip he had feared. By the spring of 1943, the Pathfinder Force had become a crucial and highly valued part of Bomber Command.

Another new navigational aid just entering service in the spring of 1943 was H2S, effectively the first-ever ground-mapping radar. H2S produced an 'echo map' created by radar pulse returns. The 'map' was a little crude and required training and skill to use, but, unlike Oboe, it was not limited by range and could be accurate up to around a mile. Nor was it affected by weather.

So, with all-weather runways and navigational instruments that could find targets through cloud, by March 1943 Harris's force could start bombing both remorselessly and with an accuracy that had earlier eluded them. These were massive strides forward.

Furthermore, bomb-aimers were now using a new bombsight, first designed in 1939, which had finally started to be introduced the previous year. The RAF had begun the war using a bombsight brought in as long ago as 1917. Science had moved on since then – as had aircraft, and the height and speed at which bombers dropped their loads – and, quite simply, the existing bombsight had no longer been good enough. Across the Atlantic, the Americans had developed the superb Norden bombsight, but had been unwilling to release it to the British. Although later details of the Norden were willingly shared, by that time the British had developed their own bombsight. This was the Blackett sight, or, more formally, the Mk XIV Computing Bomb Sight. By March 1943, the Blackett was standard in all bombers and was proving quite a success. It was easy to use and as good as the Norden at levels below 20,000 feet, although above that height it did lose accuracy. However, a new Stabilized Automatic Bomb Sight (SABS) was now also coming into service in limited numbers and was another technological bound forward; it could also be used by the Pathfinder Force.

Nor were these the only technological developments. British scientists were introducing new methods of jamming German radar. 'Mandrel' was a device that spread noise to cover the frequencies of the enemy's Freya radar. 'Monica' was a tail-warning radar that could be fitted to bombers; 'Boozer' was a radar-warning receiver. There was also 'Window' – tens of thousands of tiny strips of tinfoil that could be dropped by the Pathfinders in advance of a raid. These strips, or 'chaff', would very effectively jam any radar.

One of the reasons Harris had been forced to wait for enough all-weather airfields was because the Americans needed them too. Expansion of Bomber Command had to go hand in hand with the build-up of American air forces in Britain and, because they too had heavy four-engine bombers that needed airfields with paved runways. Now, however, by the autumn of 1943, the realignment of bases had successfully taken place to accommodate the Americans. Broadly speaking, Bomber Command's groups were in the north-east of England, with the Americans in the Midlands and East Anglia.

Since the launch of his all-out offensive in March, Harris had been pretty pleased with the way his campaign had been going and remained unwavering in his belief that area bombing alone could bring about the collapse of Nazi Germany. He compiled information on Germany's cities and towns in his 'Blue Books', which he kept at High Wycombe and which he constantly updated and refined. Each city had its own rating in terms of industrial importance. Pie charts and diagrams indicated what section of the city was doing what, and also demonstrated the proportion of its population directly involved with war work and how much the city was dependent on that particular industry. Harris would show his Blue Books to anyone who visited High Wycombe. They were his means of justifying his pursuit of area bombing, and they underlined his basic point: that almost everyone in Germany was up to their neck in it and therefore a justifiable target. It was a neat way of convincing himself, and others, that the wholesale slaughter of vast numbers of German civilians was acceptable.

This, too, was underpinned by a simple logic: destroy large numbers of German cities and the factories in and around them, and Germany would no longer be able to manufacture war materiel. Without weapons and munitions, they would be unable to fight. 'We are bombing Germany, city by city,' he had written in a pamphlet dropped on Germany the previous summer, 'in order to make it impossible for you to go on with the war. That is our object. We shall pursue it remorselessly.'

He had been as good as his word, and there was no denying that since March the results had been impressive – or at least, far more so than anything that had come before. By July 1943, Harris could call on nearly eight hundred bombers daily, of which more than 80 per cent were now heavies. The Ruhr industrial heartland had taken a hammering. In May, nineteen specially adapted Lancasters carrying a bouncing high-explosive depth charge had destroyed Germany's two largest dams, the Möhne and Eder, and badly damaged a third, the Sorpe. The levels of devastation had been enormous and the amount of urgent work required to repair and make good the destruction had prompted a vast diversion of men and resources at a time when Germany was losing the battles on the Eastern Front and in the Mediterranean. Repairing the dams had cost the Germans billions of dollars in today's money.

Then, in the last week of July, some 3,500 aircraft had pummelled Germany's second city and biggest port, Hamburg, over three consecutive nights. The result had been truly apocalyptic levels of destruction. Some 42,600 German civilians had been killed by Operation GOMOR-RAH, as the raids on Hamburg had been called – that was more than had died in the entire eight-month Blitz of Britain. A further 37,000 had been wounded and the old Hanseatic city had been all but destroyed as a colossal firestorm had developed – so big, so hellish, that the flames rose to nearly 1,500 feet. Some 6,200 acres out of 8,382 had been erased.

One night during the Blitz, Harris had climbed out on

to the roof of the Air Ministry to watch the fires caused by enemy bombing of London's East End. 'Well,' he had muttered before heading back inside, 'they are sowing the wind.' Coventry had provided the template for night-time bombing of an old city, and wave after wave of British bombers continued to pound Hamburg for three nights with grim ruthlessness, helped by the first-ever deployment of Window. Although it had been developed some time earlier, it had not been used for fear that the Germans would adopt it in turn when attacking Britain. It proved devastatingly effective over Hamburg, however. For the first time in a long while, the Germans had had no warning at all that Hamburg was the target.

Such was the overwhelming destruction of Germany's second city that, combined with the downturn of fortunes in Sicily and at Kursk, it might very well have brought about the end of the war in any generation other than that of the Nazis. The pictures of Hamburg after the firestorm are enough to make anyone gasp, even to this day.

The essential logic of Harris's stance was undeniable. By launching vast bomber fleets in a strategic air campaign, he was unquestionably ensuring fewer young men had to risk their lives on the ground. The casualty rates among his boys were appalling: in early 1943, only 17 per cent of bomber crews could expect to survive the thirty completed missions of their first tour. None the less, the numbers involved were comparatively small. It was reckoned some forty-eight men on the ground were needed to keep one crew of seven in their Lancaster – forty-eight men who were not staring death in the face each night they flew. This meant that Harris needed only around four thousand men to keep the 570 heavy bombers he had by October 1943 in the air. A single infantry division was about 16,000 men, and an army as many as half a million. In other words, the bomber war was fulfilling the pre-war pledge of using steel not flesh as far as possible. In terms of young men putting their necks on the line as a ratio against damage caused, it was certainly more efficient than relying on vast armies on the ground. That was indisputable.

In other words, by the autumn of 1943 Harris was pleased that his command was finally living up to its billing and starting materially to grind down the Germans' ability to wage war. And a bombing raid like that on Kassel proved, as far as he was concerned, that his approach was the right one and the Americans' continued determination to bomb by day and get shot down in droves was a mistake. That, however, was their affair; in the meantime, his command would continue with ever heavier night attacks. And next on his main target list was none other than the capital of the Third Reich itself. With Berlin in ruins, Harris was confident the Germans would soon see sense, in which case there would be no need for a cross-Channel invasion after all.

CHAPTER 6

The Defence of the Reich

CRISIS ALSO GRIPPED MUCH of the senior Luftwaffe command in the summer and autumn of 1943. In many regards, the bombing of Hamburg in July had been the Luftwaffe's Stalingrad – a terrifying glimpse of Armageddon. 'A wave of terror radiated from the suffering city,' noted General der Jagdflieger Adolf Galland, 'and spread through Germany. The glow of fires could be seen for days from a distance of 120 miles.' Streams of refugees trudged down the roads from Hamburg, while the realization that what had befallen the city could happen elsewhere struck a note of panic throughout the urban civilian population. Berlin was largely evacuated and the country gripped by a palpable sense of doom. Stalingrad had been a traumatic blow, but was 1,000 miles away deep in the Soviet Union. Hamburg was Germany's second city in the very heart of the Reich. The world had never before witnessed man-made destruction on such a catastrophic level.

Operation GOMORRAH stunned the leadership of the Luftwaffe. Reichsmarschall Hermann Göring, the commander-in-chief, was at the Wolf's Lair in Rastenburg in East Prussia, Hitler's eastern headquarters, when details began to reach him. Teleprinter messages arrived in quick succession revealing increasingly grisly news: entire suburbs erased; twenty-six thousand bodies and counting; a firestorm still raging; widespread panic. Around noon on the 28th, Göring told Feldmarschall Erhard Milch that from now on the main effort of the Luftwaffe was to be focused on the defence of the Reich.

Officially, Milch was State Secretary for Aviation and Inspector General as well as Director of Air Armament. Effectively, he was Göring's number two, and was also the man responsible for procurement and aircraft production. A brilliant administrator, he was part of the Zentrale Planung, which, as its name suggested, was a central planning committee for all armaments production and which was presided over by Milch, Albert Speer, the Armaments Minister, and Paul Körner, Göring's secretary. In reality, it was run jointly, and with unquestioned authority, by Speer and Milch. Both men had been determined to streamline the bloated and rivalry-riven armaments industry, which, like most areas of the Nazi state, had proved toxic and corrupt.

Broadly speaking, the Zentrale Planung had achieved those aims. By the summer of 1942, Milch had the three largest aircraft manufacturers on a much tighter leash. Willi Messerschmitt had been forced to give up all managerial control, and upfront payments to any aircraft companies had been cancelled. This had pushed Ernst Heinkel into a purely development role, and the Junkers company had also become more tightly controlled. The days of waste and minimal focus were over. Rationalization measures had been introduced, enabling production figures to rise, while aluminium consumption, for example, had remained the same.

Cost was also being driven down. By the early summer of 1943, just as the Mighty Eighth was getting into its stride, German fighter production had risen more than tenfold: from just 200 a month at the end of 1941, Milch had overseen an astonishing rise to 2,200 a month in May 1943. It was an impressive turnaround and, in truth, Milch's increase in aircraft production rather than Speer's improved figures for tank production had been most responsible for the so-called recent 'armaments miracle'.

Yet pilots were being rushed through training, there was a woeful shortage of fuel and, as Milch was all too aware, there were major question marks over the quality of the aircraft now being produced. He had cancelled the Me309, the replacement for the Me109, in the spring because flight tests had shown the new fighter would probably have a rate of climb and manoeuvrability inferior to its predecessor; in fact, in trials an Me109 had easily turned far more tightly than the new fighter. In truth, the Me309, as well as other aircraft emerging, simply needed more development time, but that was a luxury the Germans no longer had. As a consequence, the development process was being hurried, corners were being cut, and the net result was aircraft that were falling some way short of what was urgently needed.

The alternative was to stick with what they had, and by keeping with existing models, jigs and machine tools, and cutting down on overheads Milch had been able to increase production significantly. However, there was no getting away from the fact that the Me109, for example, was a mid-1930s fighter whose zenith had been the 'Emil' variant, which had reigned supreme in 1940 – a lifetime ago in the context of the war and recent technological advancements. Superior Allied fighter aircraft had followed, knocking the Emil from its lofty perch, so it had been necessary, at the very least, to improve the engine performance. The trouble was, the Me109's airframe was not really designed to take on any larger engine. Despite this, the most recent Gustav model had been fitted with the latest Daimler-Benz, the DB605, which was 250kg heavier and which performed poorly at low altitudes. It was also a brute to fly initially, which wasn't good for the mass of young pilots emerging from the training schools with less than an ideal number of hours in their logbooks. Flying straight and level, the Gustav was quick enough, but what it had gained in speed it had lost in manoeuvrability.

Just as concerning, this latest Me109 had suffered one too many engine fires when it had first rolled off the production line. Such a fire had killed one of the Luftwaffe's greatest aces, Hans-Joachim Marseille, in September 1942. The cause was Milch's economizing, as the engine construction had switched from ball bearings to plain bearings. On the face of it, this was a small thing, but roller bearings caused more friction. With half-decent lubricants, this should not have been an issue, but by this stage of the war the Germans were using synthetic lubricants, which were not as good. As a result, the bearings were overheating and occasionally causing the oil to catch fire, which was obviously far from ideal when flying at 20,000 feet and in the middle of a dogfight. This technical glitch was being rectified, but the outcome of all these decisions was a dramatic quantitative increase but at a qualitative cost.

Another Messerschmitt reaching the end of its shelf-life

was the twin-engine Me110. This was well armed and good at shooting down bombers, but was vulnerable when up against an Allied fighter. Nor were there enough of them. The Me210 had been supposed to be an upgraded version, but, again, Professor Messerschmitt had been allowed to get carried away and had designed an almost entirely new aircraft, which tended to go into a spin at the slightest provocation. Numerous modifications were made, but the accidents continued and, although the problems were eventually resolved, by then it had become the Me410 instead. In any case, it wasn't significantly superior to the Me110 – slightly faster and with a higher service ceiling, but certainly not worth all the time, expense and lives it had already cost. The net result of this drain of precious resources was the continued over-dependence on the Me110.

So far in the war, those flying aircraft inferior to their enemy's inevitably tended to fare poorly; as large numbers of Luftwaffe fighter aces had discovered over the Eastern Front, shooting down masses of enemy aircraft was easy enough when those aircraft were palpably of poorer quality and performance. Fortunately for the Luftwaffe fighter arm, the gulf between their aircraft and those of the RAF and USAAF was not yet a wide one, but it was certainly hampering their cause.

There was, however, one exciting new aircraft in development with the potential to put all others in the shade. On 22 May 1943, General 'Dolfo' Galland had flown the experimental Me262 jet for the first time. He had been stunned by the speed and manoeuvrability of this amazing new machine, and on landing back down again had clambered out from the cockpit determined that this wonder-plane should be put into production immediately.

'This model is a tremendous stroke of luck for us,' he told Milch, 'it puts us way out in front, provided the enemy continues to use piston engines.' Flying at over 520 m.p.h., it was faster than any other aircraft and, Galland discovered, handled well. New possibilities for fighter tactics were spinning around in his mind; suddenly, the Luftwaffe had a future once more. Milch, who had learned to trust Galland, accepted his General of Fighters' judgement. The Me262 was to go straight into production and all other interim piston-engine fighter projects were to be scrapped. Göring approved the decision on 5 June.

On paper, this seemed quite possible because by that time the Air Ministry – the Reichsluftfahrtministerium, or RLM – had narrowed down the jet-engine programme to just two models, one made by BMW and the other by Junkers Motoren (Jumo). Helmut Schelp, the head of the Air Ministry's Technical Office, had overseen this programme of jet development, but he had never intended that either the Jumo or BMW engines should go into service, but rather that they be used in further development of both the airframes being designed and to resolve the many inevitable issues of high-speed jet-powered flight. In other words, both engines were somewhat immature and not considered ready for mass production. What's more, the current engines were using materials such as nickel and chrome that were far too precious for large-scale manufacture. Alternative materials would need to be found, further testing carried out, and then machine tools and facilities built and a workforce trained – all of which meant the Me262 was still a long way off going into production, no matter how much Milch and Galland might have wished it to be otherwise.

There had been some other spanners thrown into the works too, not least by the Führer, who still thought of himself as a military genius but whose judgement and decision-making was proving worse and worse the longer the war continued. In March, Milch, during a long conversation with Hitler, had tried to win the Führer's backing for a defensive air strategy. Instead, Hitler told him to go back on to the offensive with high-altitude, high-speed bombers as the main focus of Luftwaffe production.

This was an absurd suggestion on a number of levels. Fighters were easier and cheaper to make than bombers because they were smaller and required fewer resources. The Luftwaffe had no effective bomber that could cause significant offensive damage and nothing in the pipeline that could be hurriedly brought into mass production. The only option was to fall back on obsolescent models such as the pre-war Heinkel 111 and Ju88. They had not made a massive impact back in 1940–41 when there had been lots of them; they would make even less of an impression now, but to the detriment of the defence of the Reich. Kampfgeschwader 2 – Bomber Wing 2 – had been conducting small-scale bombing raids against Britain; average life expectancy for those crews, who were achieving so little, was just twelve missions. Sending bombers to Britain was simply a waste and depletion of effort.

Milch was always operating with one arm tied behind his back and the full force of a Hitlerian tirade cowed even him. 'The Führer sees it as taking too great a risk,' he explained of Hitler's decision not to back the Me262. 'But I have my orders. I am a soldier, and must obey them. We must observe the prudence demanded by the Führer.' Hitler and prudence, however, were words that in no way went together.

Nor did Milch get much help from Göring. Although the Reichsmarschall had been a celebrated fighter ace in the First World War, like Hitler he had never been to staff college and had not commanded at middling ranks. He was a far better politician and businessman than military leader. During the 1930s his power had been second only to Hitler's, and much of the structure and success of the Nazis had been down to him. Since the Luftwaffe's failures had begun to be felt, however, his influence had been significantly on the wane. In his efforts to curry favour he had become increasingly sycophantic and cowed by Hitler's rants and attempts to humiliate him. As a result, Milch had no one at the highest level to back him up.

Soon after, the full weight of the RAF's bombing campaign began to have an impact as the Ruhr was pummelled. Because of the bombing, by the summer of 1943 the Zentrale Planung had faced a shortfall of 400,000 tons of steel and any further increases in Luftwaffe aircraft production had been brought to a halt.

And now Hamburg lay in ruins. Speer questioned whether they could even maintain production of fighter aircraft, let alone more bombers. He warned Hitler that if six more cities suffered like Hamburg the war would be over. On 2 August, on Hitler's instructions, ministers and gauleiters – regional Nazi governors – met in Berlin, where Josef Goebbels, the propaganda chief, planned to put some fire back into their bellies. At one point, Milch, normally so calm and outwardly unemotional, interrupted him. 'We have lost the war!' he exclaimed. 'Finally lost the war!' Goebbels had to appeal to Milch's sense of honour to get him to calm down. The following day, after Hamburg had been hit yet again, Milch cabled Göring. 'It is not the front which is under attack and struggling for survival,' he wrote, 'but the home base, which is fighting a desperate fight.'

Hitler now vacillated repeatedly. On 28 July, in the middle of the Hamburg raids, he approved the decision to make defence of the Reich the Luftwaffe's priority, yet the next day he refused to authorize a higher production of fighters and instead once more insisted on retaliatory strikes against Britain. 'I want bombers, bombers, bombers!' he raged at a meeting of senior Luftwaffe staff. 'Your fighters are useless!' Milch tried to get round this by ordering fighter output to three thousand per month and referring to the V1 flying bomb project, still in development, as a 'bomber replacement'.

Then on 17 August, when the Americans bombed Schweinfurt, a number of jigs set for making Me262 fuselages were destroyed, while later that night the RAF bombed Peenemünde, the research establishment on the Baltic coast where V2 ballistic rockets were being built and tested. Some 596 heavies hit the plant pretty accurately, although they also tragically hit the camp for forced labour. It was estimated this set back the V2 rocket project by at least two months. Hitler was incensed and immediately insisted on giving the project all priority. Britain was to be brought to her knees by these weapons, he said; attack was the only way to deal with Germany's enemies. Prioritizing the rocket programme, however, came at a cost, as skilled workers were taken from the aircraft factories and sent to Peenemünde instead. 'Not one swine is helping us,' said Milch in utter exasperation.

At the beginning of September, Göring called together all his senior commanders to Schloss Rominten, a hunting lodge he had acquired near the Wolf's Lair. Milch was there, as was General der Jagdflieger Adolf Galland. The Luftwaffe, Göring told them, had achieved outstanding successes but now needed to turn entirely to defending Germany's western front. With focus and concentration of force – *Schwerpunkt* – on one aim, he was certain the Allied bomber threat could be halted. The role of the Luftwaffe had never been more important than at this critical hour; it had to protect the lives and property of German people, but also safeguard war industry. He then outlined the measures he intended to take: an end to offensive action for the time being; the vast majority of forces brought back to Germany; and new tactics for maintaining air superiority over the Reich.

Galland, for one, was profoundly moved by this speech. 'Never before and never again,' he noted later, 'did I witness such determination and agreement among the circle of those responsible for the leadership of the Luftwaffe.' Rivalries and rifts had been put to one side. Satisfied that his commanders were all in agreement, Göring then left them to visit Hitler in person at the Wolf's Lair and outline to the Führer the new measures for the defence of the Reich.

Some time later, Göring reappeared, followed by his senior adjutant. The Reichsmarschall did not say a word, but walked past the assembled men and disappeared into an adjoining room. Galland and others looked at each other in amazement, wondering what on earth had happened. Soon after, Galland and Oberst Dietrich Peltz, the Inspector of Combat Flight, were called in to see Göring. 'We were met with a shattering picture,' wrote Galland. 'Göring had completely broken down. His head buried in his arm on the table.' Galland and Peltz stood there in embarrassment until eventually the Reichsmarschall pulled himself together. The Führer, he explained, had rejected all his proposals and had angrily told him he had lost all faith in the Luftwaffe. A change from offensive to defensive was out of the question. The Luftwaffe would be given one last chance to regain some trust, but this could only be done by a resumption of large-scale attacks on England. Attack was to be the only word. Terror had to be met with counter-terror. The Führer, Göring said, was right; he was always right.

'Oberst Peltz,' said Göring, now pulling himself to his feet, 'I herewith appoint you assault leader against England!'

Galland could scarcely believe what he had heard. He thought of resigning there and then, but wondered whether Hitler might not soon change his mind. 'I was mistaken,' he noted later.

Dolfo Galland was one of the most celebrated pilots in Germany and, still aged only thirty-one, also one of the Wehrmacht's youngest generals. Lean, dark and debonair, with a raffish dark moustache and equally dark piercing eyes, he was rarely without a cigar, which rather added to his swashbuckling image, and had even insisted on flying only aircraft that had an electric cigar lighter. The Nazi state was always quick to make celebrities of fighting heroes and Galland was one of the most visual, gracing magazine covers and featuring in newspapers and on newsreels. He had been given a house in Berlin, had been awarded the Knight's Cross with Oak Leaves, Swords and Diamonds – the highest award for gallantry – and made sure he slept with as many women as possible.

The son of well-to-do minor aristocrats from Wester-
holt, in the Ruhr area of western Germany, Galland had
become obsessed with flying at a young age. Learning the
basics through gliding, he had been among the first to join
the Luftwaffe following a stint as a pilot for Lufthansa, the
fledgling civilian airline. As part of the Condor Legion, he
had successfully commanded a squadron in Spain during
the civil war there and was among a group of young officers to start developing tactical doctrine for the fighters.
He later flew during the Polish campaign in 1939, over
France and then in the Battle of Britain, amassing large
numbers of victories. By the end of 1940, he had fifty-seven
confirmed enemy aircraft shot down and was *Gruppe*
commander of III/JG26.

Never afraid to stick his neck out, Galland had quite
openly criticized Göring's tactics and mismanagement of
the German fighter force during the Battle of Britain, but
because of his skill, qualities as a leader, and celebrity, he
got away with it. Through much of 1941, he had led JG26,
based in the west, and had taken on the Spitfires of RAF
Fighter Command. By the middle of November 1941, he
had amassed ninety-six personal victories, second in the
world only to his friend Werner Mölders.

That month the Luftwaffe had been rocked by the suicide of Ernst Udet, its Armaments Minister, swiftly
followed by the death of Mölders, who was killed when an
aircraft he was not piloting crashed en route to Udet's
funeral. Mölders had only recently been appointed General der Jagdflieger. 'A few days later at the interment of
Mölders,' said Galland, 'Göring announced, with exquis-
ite taste at the side of the open grave that I was to be the
next General der Jagdflieger.'

At the time of his appointment, Galland had been just twenty-nine and at the peak of his career as a fighter pilot. Only a few weeks earlier he had been awarded the Swords to his Knight's Cross, the first man in the entire Wehrmacht to have been given such an accolade. Up to that point, he had focused entirely on flying, leading his *Jagdgeschwader* – his fighter wing – and honing tactics. To the reverses in the Soviet Union, the imminent entry of the USA into the war and the increasing power of the RAF he had given little thought.

Promoted to Oberst – colonel – he had handed over JG26 then tried to work out what he needed to do in this new leadership post. None of his predecessors had put in place any long-term programmes or done any kind of planning. Liaison with the Air Ministry was non-existent; nor did Galland himself have any staff training. On the one hand, this made his post a rather daunting one; but on the other, he was confident, outspoken, had the backing of both Göring and Hitler, and had been given the opportunity to shape the position as he wished. 'I functioned,' he said, 'as adviser, consultant, administrator, inspector, formulator of doctrine, and on some occasions as an operational authority.' This meant he oversaw training, advised on procurement, supervised tactical developments, and acted as the direct liaison between the fighter units and Göring, Milch and other senior figures. In fact, his remit was wide-ranging but his overriding concern had been to develop the German day-fighter arm for the defence of the Reich. His offices were in Berlin and he had a train coach at the Wolf's Lair, but much of his time had also been spent touring the Reich and occupied territories, and visiting fighter units.

Galland understood the importance of talking to those serving under him.

His first year in the post had been tough as, on all fronts, the Germans had suffered reverses and the Luftwaffe had become increasingly stretched. Although he had come into contact with Göring frequently over the years, only in his new role did Galland see his chief at close hand. He soon realized that the Reichsmarschall had no technical understanding and very little appreciation of the circumstances in which fighter pilots were living and operating. Opinions were formed on the basis of advice from a small clique of sycophants. 'His court favourites,' said Galland, 'changed frequently since his favour could only be won and held by means of constant flattery, intrigue and expensive gifts.' Since he refused to play such games, Galland discovered that his master's fickle nature was a near-constant bugbear, with repeated changes of mind, contradictory orders and decision-making that frequently defied any kind of logic.

On top of that, Galland's own staff were overly bureaucratic, with little practical knowledge. He swiftly brought in new men – old colleagues and fighter leaders who understood the demands of combat flying and whom he could trust. In the east, the fighter units continued to amass great scores against largely inferior opposition and morale remained high. In the west, however, the situation was gradually worsening, with fighter units horribly understrength and morale taking a hit. New breeds of Spitfire and the fast, high-altitude Mosquito were also cause for technological envy. The Focke-Wulf 190 was still considered by the pilots to be inferior to the latest Spitfires above 20,000 feet and it had taken too long to iron out the flaws in its engine, the BMW 801. Then had come the problems with the DB605 engine that powered the new Me109G. At times the Luftwaffe had appeared to have no good fighter engine at all.

Nor had the air defence system been working well. Germany had begun the war with no air defence system at all. One had started to be developed, but it was inefficient and interception rates had been low. The whole system needed overhauling.

Later that summer of 1942, the first American daylight attacks had begun. German fighter pilots had never before encountered heavy bombers so well armed and able to fly in such close formation. 'The defensive fire-power of the bombers,' Galland admitted, 'was regarded as extremely effective and actually instilled considerable apprehension into the minds of the fighters.' Pilots were clearly avoiding combat with enemy bombers and not until Major Egon Mayer, of JG2, began shooting them down by attacking head-on had new tactics to deal with the Flying Fortresses been developed. Soon after, Galland issued new Tactical Regulations. Fighter units were to fly on a course parallel to and on one side of the bombers until about 3 miles ahead of them, at which point they were to turn in by *Schwärme* – 'swarms', or fours – and then fly on a level with the bombers for the last 1,500 yards before opening fire at around 900 yards. This was quite a distance, but such were the closing speeds they would still be firing at very close range. They were then to fly on flat over the top of the bomber formation. Galland himself flew a number of missions to test these tactics and was satisfied they were the right ones. At any rate, they were beginning to bring down a lot more.

Only at the start of 1943, however, was much thought given to creating a proper, fully coordinated defence system. The German way of war was to attack with overwhelming and concentrated force and to win the battle – and war – in a very short time. This had evolved over the centuries and stemmed from Germany's – and, before it, Prussia's – geographical location in the heart of Europe and its lack of natural resources. Wars needed to be quick out of necessity. This meant front-loading the war effort into all-out attack. Fighting a war defensively had not even been considered, and during the early victories the Luftwaffe had been the spearhead of that offensive mindset. It had simply not occurred to anyone to create an air *defence* system. Nor had the Luftwaffe begun the war with any kind of ground control such as had been developed by the RAF. Individual squadrons – *Staffeln* – could communicate with one another once airborne, but otherwise, when in the air, bombers and fighters were on their own.

By early 1943 the situation was very different, and what air defence system there was had been developed piecemeal and initially in response to the night raids by the RAF. Oberst Josef Kammhuber had established a nightfighter group in 1940. By the following summer, this had become an air corps, XII Fliegerkorps, and Kammhuber had been promoted to general and made Inspector General of Night-fighters. He had then developed a defensive line in which a system of controlled sectors, equipped with radar and searchlights, were each linked to a nightfighter unit. Each sector was known as a *Himmelbett* zone, an area of around 20 miles by 15 that included a Freya and later two Würzburg radars. Both of these were highly sophisticated, 360-degree rotating sets that put early British radar into the pale. Also in each *Himmelbett* zone were a 'master' radar-guided searchlight, a number of manually controlled searchlights and two night-fighters, one primary and one back-up. If an enemy bomber crossed into the range of the radars, one set tracked it while the other followed the movement of the night-fighter patrolling that particular zone. The zone's controller then radioed interception vectors to the night-fighter and, once the attacker was close, his target was lit up by searchlights.

The RAF's Thousand Bomber Raids in the summer of 1942, however, had highlighted how inadequate the fledgling air defence measures were. The *Himmelbett* system and the so-called Kammhuber Line had worked because a night-fighter could be vectored – directed – to a lone enemy bomber in any one zone at a time. However, the British had realized that if bombers crossed over into enemy-held Europe using the same route and in quick succession – in a 'stream' – then the *Himmelbett* system would be overwhelmed. So it had proved, and the bomber stream had become the preferred method of British night-time bombing. Nor had the increase in anti-aircraft guns been enough to stop the British bombers. More was needed: more night-fighters, more day-fighters, more guns, better and more sophisticated radar, plus a fully coordinated system that brought these various cogs of defence together.

This had been gradually implemented throughout 1943, with Milch, Galland, Kammhuber and another pioneer, Generaloberst Hubert Weise, overseeing much of the development and doing so without much support from General Hans Jeschonnek, the Luftwaffe Chief of Staff – who, like Hitler, was obsessed with offensive action – and with little or no input from Göring. Jeschonnek's management of air defence was 'dragging' and suggestions for streamlining and coordinating air defence 'remained a mystery to him.' Ultimately, this attitude cost him his life, even though for much of the time it had chimed with that of the Führer; such were the contradictions of the Nazi regime. It was easy for Göring to blame his Chief of Staff for the catastrophe of Hamburg – after all, it couldn't possibly have been the Reichsmarschall's fault – and the subsequent raids on Schweinfurt, Regensburg and Peenemünde sealed his fate. The day after those latter raids, 18 August 1943, Jeschonnek shot himself.

Kammhuber, too, fell from favour after Hamburg – his night-fighters had failed to stop the enemy. His solution was to demand more night-fighter boxes in his *Himmelbett* system. In fact, he planned on creating a further 102 of them in north-eastern, central and southern Germany, as well as in Italy, Austria and along the Channel coast. That, though, required more radar, more radar stations, more operations rooms and more staff, at a time when manpower was in as short supply as any other asset. Just to keep one night-fighter in the air required 116 support personnel.

However, since Hamburg a new band of night-fighters had come very much to the fore. The *Wilde Sau* – 'Wild Boar' – were three brand-new *Geschwader* of fighter aircraft under the command of 30-year-old Major Hans-Joachim 'Hajo' Herrmann. An extremely bright, single-minded Luftwaffe officer, with stern Aryan good looks and piercing pale blue eyes, Herrmann had been one of the first to join the fledgling Luftwaffe in the 1930s and had become a bomber pilot. Since then, he had served with the Condor Legion in Spain, over Poland, during the campaign in the west against France and the Low Countries, and then throughout the Battle of Britain. By mid-October 1940, when he had won the Knight's Cross, he had already flown nearly a hundred bomber sorties. Later, he had served in the Mediterranean against Malta and Greece, and managed to blow up a British ammunition ship in harbour in Piraeus. In turn, it had destroyed ten other ships, which had taken with them 41,000 tons of supplies and, in so doing, had effectively sealed Britain's fate in Greece. He had flown over the Eastern Front and within the Arctic Circle. Few men had flown as many bomber missions in as many different theatres as Hajo Herrmann.

However, since July 1942 Herrmann had been serving as a staff officer with Gruppe T of the Luftwaffe General Staff, based in Berlin. Gruppe T was the tactical and technical section and Herrmann was placed on the Bomber desk. He had soon realized what Galland and Milch had also understood: that the Luftwaffe was no longer really capable of sustained offensive action and the sheer numbers of aircraft being produced in Britain alone, never mind the USA, were such that the Luftwaffe had no realistic means of competing. And rather than continue to make lots of different types of aircraft, Herrmann had recognized that it made more sense to build just fighters – fighters that could be used day or night and could perform a variety of roles.

The suggestions he had put forward to this effect had got him nowhere, but he was determined that at the very least single-engine fighters could be used both day and night. One of the problems was that day-fighter pilots were not taught night flying – that is, to fly blind using only instruments. However, he reckoned a cadre could be brought in and others trained up – it would be easier, for example, to train bomber pilots to become fighters as they already knew about blind flying. These *Wilde Sau* night-fighters would be given information about the likely course of enemy bombers and the target to which they were headed. They would then take off and, without ground guidance or on-board radar, would use search-lights to light up their target and hit the bombers over it.

Kammhuber had been against Herrmann's plan, but Galland had been all for giving it a try and had supported him by providing the aircraft from his precious day-fighter force. On the night of 3/4 July 1943, Herrmann had led twelve fighters against a large raid on Cologne and Mülheim. Blind flying initially, they then used the fires and flares caused by the bombers and the searchlights from the flak units below, and shot down sixteen of the thirty bombers destroyed that night. It had been a resounding success. It was estimated that it took 2,000 anti-aircraft shells to bring down one bomber, so Herrmann's *Wilde Sau* were certainly an improvement in terms of efficiency.

The following morning, while sleeping off his night's antics, Herrmann had been woken with the words, 'The Reichsmarschall is on the line.' He was to fly to Berchtes-gaden to see Göring and Jeschonnek right away. When he had eventually got to Hitler's favourite Alpine part of the Reich, Jeschonnek had told him to form a new special single-engine night-fighter *Geschwader*, JG300. They were to be known as the 'Wild Boars'. Fired with enthusiasm, Herrmann had got on with training up and creating his new special night-fighter group right away. It was Galland, however, who had helped him lick his *Wilde Sau* into shape, ordering staff officers like Edu Neumann, a legendary ace and fighter leader, to teach them the principles of fighter tactics.

After the first attack on Hamburg, Göring had rung Herrmann personally. 'How near to being operational are you?' he had asked. Mid-September at the earliest, Herrmann had replied. In a calm but insistent voice, Göring told him he would be ready that night with as strong a force as possible. As a result, Herrmann and his fledgling force had found themselves flying over the burning city and had shot down some twenty RAF bombers.

At the time, Herrmann had still been a major. At a conference immediately after the Hamburg raids, however, and at which General Kammhuber was present, the Reichsmarschall had humiliated the Inspector General of Night-fighters by giving Herrmann command of XII Jagdkorps. 'Seldom in the history of the war,' noted Herrmann, 'can a soldier have received an order such as that: a *major* was to give orders to the General in Command.'

Such was the unpredictable nature of Göring's command. However, Herrmann, like Galland, was young, dynamic, full of energy and fire, and had the intelligence and determination to match. He had thrown himself into this new role and his *Wilde Sau* continued to do well. By the end of September, Göring had ordered two more Wild Boar wings, JG301 and JG302; by the time they were all fully operational, they would amount to around a hundred. Because they were using single-engine day-fighters, with greater speed and manoeuvrability than twin-engine night-fighters, if intelligence was able to pick up a likely target early enough, Herrmann's *Wilde Sau* could be swirling over it, no matter where it was in the Reich, by the time the British bombers reached it.

Ironically, the introduction of Window had forced the Luftwaffe to break out of the rather rigid *Himmelbett* system. New formations of more traditional twin-engine night-fighters were now starting to attack retreating bomber streams in packs rather than singly and strictly in their own box as before. These were called *Zahme Sau* – 'Tame Boars'. The day-fighters were also better organized for defence; Galland had brought his fighters into newly created *Jagddivisionen* – fighter divisions – and these had then been formed into two new *Jagdkorps*: I Fighter Corps was created on 15 October, the day after Schweinfurt II, under the command of Generalleutnant Josef 'Beppo' Schmid, absorbing Kammhuber's old XII Fliegerkorps in the process. Meanwhile, II Fighter Corps was also formed in France.

By October, then, and despite the innumerable obstacles thrown in the way, increasing numbers of day- and night-fighters were operating in a highly coordinated manner over a wide area, and now supported by an early-warning system that was the most sophisticated in the world – none of which augured well for the Allies at this moment of crisis in their strategic bombing campaign.

As with the British, several features of the German early-warning system, when brought together, added up to more than the sum of their individual parts. The Horchdienst – the Radar and Radio Listening Service – more often than not picked up radio chatter from bombers forming up and gave the first indication of an impending raid. The Flugmeldedienst – the Aircraft Warning

Service – used radar stations of dramatically increased sophistication. By the autumn of 1943, the Germans were using a 'giant' Würzburg as well as an improved version of Freya, known as 'Mammut'. Both had larger reflectors that enabled substantially increased range. A further new radar, the Wassermann, was the finest early-warning radar yet designed and was fully rotational with a range of 150 miles in any direction. The only area where the Germans lagged was with on-board radars. While the British had developed the cavity magnetron, which enabled them to build radar sets small enough to put on board an aircraft or ship, the best on-board radar the Germans had developed was the Lichtenstein, which had a maximum range of 2 miles and a minimum of 200 yards, but which required huge aerials and reflectors to be added on to the nose of the aircraft, acting like an air brake and badly affected handling.

In addition to the Horchdienst and the radar network, the Flugwache – the Ground Observer Service – covered every inch of the sky and its members reported their visual assessments of numbers and height with an accuracy that could not be matched by any radar reading. On top of these purely Luftwaffe systems were four further watch groups: the Civilian Aircraft Warning Service, the Railway Aircraft Warning Service, the Aircraft Warning Service of the army anti-aircraft artillery, and the Navy Warning Service, which used shipborne and coastal radars.

Their collected information was fed to the control part of the system, which was managed by Aircraft Warning Regiments and Air Communications and Control Regiments, with three battalions each, which were placed throughout the Reich and the occupied territories.

Initially, Kammhuber's XII Fliegerkorps HQ at Deelen in Holland had housed the principal operations and control room, but by October 1943 each fighter division set up by Galland had its own. Each contained large vertical plotting screens, some even on frosted glass and with lights illuminating progress, with details of position, course and number of enemy aircraft. To the right of the glass screen was a board on which were listed the various crews, aircraft numbers and take-off and landing times. There were plotters, meteorologists, people to collate information from the Horchdienst and radar stations, as well as ground controllers and an overall commander. Observers fed reports to First Order Radar Stations, which would then combine their visual and radar data before forwarding it on to the fighter division control centres. All other component information would be sent directly to the control rooms, where this collected information would be synthesized and given to the ground controllers. It would be updated constantly and the movement of aircraft mapped on the plotting screens.

Ground controllers would then speak directly to the fighter units, warning them of the nature of the threat, what weather to expect, and helping them vector towards the enemy. Updates on what was happening during the course of an air battle were also channelled to the pilots. In addition, there was a system for distinguishing friendly and enemy aircraft from one another.

Despite the ad hoc nature with which it had evolved, this newly developed air defence system meant that, for the most part, the Luftwaffe always knew when, where and in what numbers the Allies were likely to attack. What's more, the defenders had the home advantage, just as the RAF had

had over southern England during the Battle of Britain. Allied aircrew who bailed out over Nazi-occupied Europe usually remained prisoners of the Germans for the rest of the war, while every time Heinz Knoke was shot down, for example, assuming he was fit and well, he could take to the skies again almost immediately.

By October 1943, there was no doubt that the Luftwaffe was in serious trouble, but despite the interference of Hitler and the vacillations of Göring, the Reich was being defended by increasing numbers of fighters, both day and night, organized by a highly efficient air defence system. It remained, over home soil, an incredibly tough nut to crack.

CHAPTER 7

The Nub of the Matter

DESPITE THE SUCCESSES OF Hamburg and Kassel, and the continued almost nightly pounding of German cities, crisis was looming for the British as well as for the American strategic bombing campaign against Germany. The difference was that, while the Americans recognized that they were failing in their aims, the man in charge of RAF Bomber Command remained utterly convinced that his strategy was the right one.

Air Marshal Sir Arthur Harris was not known for suffering fools. Although quite jovial and good company out of hours, once he arrived at Bomber Command HQ at High Wycombe he became focused, gruff and altogether more taciturn. Bull-faced, with piercing pale eyes, greying, gingery hair and a trim moustache, he was prepared to be utterly ruthless in his pursuit of strategic bombing: ruthless with other commands or other parts of the RAF that challenged his own command for resources; ruthless with anyone who crossed him; and ruthless most of all with the Germans, whether they be servicemen, civilians, factory workers, women or children. As far as Harris was concerned, any resources being used to further the

German war effort – factories, supplies or manpower – were legitimate targets for attack. That meant all cities in Germany, as every one was involved in war work of some kind, whether it be the major industrial centres such as Essen, home to the Krupp works, which made tanks and many other weapons, or Dresden, known throughout Europe for the production of fine porcelain, but also an urban centre with no fewer than 127 separate factories and businesses conducting war work. All were fair game.

The trouble was, by the autumn of 1943, smashing cities was not enough in itself. Harris was still wedded to the belief that area bombing alone could foreshorten the war, but even with improved accuracy and with increasingly sophisticated navigational aids and other scientific instruments, area bombing was still not accurate enough. The morale of the German people was certainly on the wane; most German citizens wanted the war to end and feared deeply for the future. No one wanted their home to be destroyed. But bombing in itself, even the destruction of Hamburg, had not brought the German population to the point of collapse. Rather, if anything, the grip of the Nazi leadership was even tighter than it had been before. As had been spelled out in February by Josef Goebbels, the Propaganda Minister, Germany was now embroiled in 'total' war; the choice for Germans after the recent reverses was clear: keep fighting or face Armageddon. It was negative propaganda, but very effective propaganda all the same.

Perhaps more crucially, however, night-time area bombing was not, in itself, destroying the Luftwaffe. In other words, it was not enabling the Allies to gain and then maintain air superiority over Nazi-occupied Europe. Both winning and keeping air superiority were absolutely vital before any offensive land operations could be undertaken. The invasion of Sicily in July 1943 had been successful because the Allied air forces had very effectively neutralized the German and Italian air forces over the island and specifically the invasion beaches during the landings. Some 702 German aircraft had been destroyed over the Eastern Front between June and August that year, but the figure had been 3,504 in the Mediterranean. In all, in the three months between 30 June and 30 September 1943, the Luftwaffe had lost 4,100 aircraft destroyed and a further 3,078 damaged. Back in 1940, even someone as militarily obtuse as Hitler had understood there could be no invasion of Britain until the Luftwaffe had cleared the RAF from the skies. They had not come close, and so there had been no invasion. Instead, Germany had turned eastwards to the Soviet Union, and far earlier than had ever originally been planned.

The Allies well understood there could be no cross-Channel invasion until they had control of the skies, not only over the invasion beaches and anticipated immediate bridgehead, but over a large swathe of western Europe as well. It was accepted, quite rightly, that the success or failure of the invasion would depend on the ability of the Germans to launch a massed and concentrated counter-attack within days of the landings and before the Allies had had a chance to successfully reinforce any bridgehead. Therefore, restricting Germany's ability to counter-attack swiftly was of the most vital importance. Deception was a key part of this plan, but so too was the role of air power. In the nine weeks leading up to D-Day, air power was to carry out a heavy interdiction operation. This meant blowing up bridges, roads and especially railways and marshalling yards. Given the Germans' dependence on the Reichsbahn to transport the bulk of the war effort, the more lines that were cut, bridges destroyed, cuttings blown in and marshalling yards hammered, the harder it was going to be for the German mobile units – the elite of the army – to move quickly from one part of Nazi-occupied Europe to another. The successful slowing-up of any potential German counter-attack could not possibly have been more important to Allied chances of success.

Although the strategic heavy bomber forces had a role to play, such an interdiction campaign was largely the preserve of the tactical air forces: two-engine medium bombers and ground-attack fighter aircraft, which would be operating at far lower heights than the heavies and with greater accuracy – the kind of accuracy that was needed to destroy bridges and narrow railway lines rather than sprawling factory complexes. In order to do this successfully, however, the Allies really needed to operate in skies where they held air superiority. That meant ensuring the Luftwaffe was sufficiently contained to offer little interference anywhere over France, the Low Countries or even the western edges of Germany itself. This had to be achieved not by D-Day in May 1944, but nine weeks earlier, by March 1944. That was now just five months away.

Furthermore, there was a limit to how much strategic bombing could achieve while increasingly skilled and well-directed night-fighters stalked British bombers, or hordes of Messerschmitt and Focke-Wulf fighters equally skilfully attacked the daytime fleets of American bombers. In both cases, the German fighters attacking these bombers were faster, more agile and could often pack a bigger punch than their Allied opponents. British heavy bombers, especially, were thin-skinned and under-armed. Once an enemy night-fighter locked on to them the chance of survival was slight.

In January 1943, at the Casablanca Conference – the meeting of President Roosevelt, Winston Churchill and the Joint Chiefs of Staff – the British had questioned the point of America continuing with daylight bombing and voiced their concerns that the losses would soon prove prohibitive. Dropping this policy was unthinkable to General Arnold and all the other senior American air force commanders: their entire pre-war thinking had been built around it, as demonstrated by the B-17 Flying Fortresses and B-24 Liberators with their arsenals of heavy machine guns. Nor did they want to be beholden or play second fiddle to the RAF – after all, the United States and Britain were coalition partners rather than formal allies.

Tooey Spaatz had been brought to Casablanca to fight the American corner, as had Ira Eaker, then the new commander of the still fledgling Eighth Air Force. Unlike most of the senior US commanders, Eaker had come properly prepared, so determined was he to win over Churchill, who had voiced doubts about daylight bombing more vocally than most. Eaker's impassioned plea did the trick. He argued that it would bring about 'round-the-clock' bombing and give the Germans no rest. It would prevent putting excessive strain on British air space and communications. It would be more accurate. And he also pointed out that daylight bombing would force the Luftwaffe back to the Reich, where the enemy day-fighter force would be compelled to take to the skies to defend their empire.

Churchill had accepted that the Americans should persevere with daylight bombing, but Eaker's point about taking on the Luftwaffe day-fighter force was arguably most pertinent, because only by continuing with daylight bombing could there be an effective means of gaining air superiority over mainland Europe. The American bombers could hit targets such as the ball-bearing plant at Schweinfurt, essential for aircraft production; or the Messerschmitt plant at Augsburg and the Heinkel factory at Rostock, for example; and they could bomb other component manufacturers, such as the Bosch factory at Stuttgart, where dynamos, injection pumps and magnetos were manufactured. But at the time of Casablanca, Eaker had also believed his heavily armed bombers, and Flying Fortresses especially, could take on the Luftwaffe in the air, and had argued that they could shoot down two or even three enemy fighters for every bomber that was lost. This had since been tragically disproved.

At Casablanca the British had accepted that the Americans would stick to daylight bombing and a directive had been issued that demanded the 'progressive destruction and dislocation of the German military, industrial and economic system, and the undermining of the morale of the German people to a point where their capacity for armed resistance is fatally weakened.' Effectively, both the Americans and British were now being given carte blanche and official authorization for all-out strategic bombing campaigns, but each on their own terms.

By the Washington Conference in May 1943, however, this original directive was no longer sufficient, not least because a firm commitment to make a cross-Channel invasion the following year, in May 1944, had been made;

for that to happen, the necessity of clearing the skies of the Luftwaffe suddenly became dramatically more pressing.

In April 1943, General Eaker had been the main driving force behind the Combined Bomber Offensive from the United Kingdom Plan (CBO), which had then been worked on and approved by the British Air Staff. It became known unofficially as the 'Eaker Plan'. This acknowledged that German fighter strength appeared to be growing and therefore the success of bombing German industry was dependent on also destroying German fighter strength. In this draft plan, the immediate objective – referred to as the 'intermediate objective' in the Eaker Plan – was to neutralize German fighter strength. 'The German fighter force,' ran the draft, 'is taking a toll of our forces both by day and by night, not only in terms of combat losses, but more especially in terms of reduced tactical effectiveness. If the German fighters are materially increased in number it is quite conceivable that they could make our daylight bombing unprofitable and perhaps our night bombing too.'

While many had pointed out that the cost of daylight bombing might well prove too great, this was the first time the growing threat of enemy night-fighters had been acknowledged as potentially decisive. Specifically, the destruction of the Luftwaffe was to take place by targeting airframe, aero-engine, aircraft component and ball-bearing plants. Aircraft repair depots and storage facilities were also to be hit. Finally, both RAF and VIII Fighter Commands were to seek and destroy as many enemy fighters in the air as possible. 'It is emphasized,' the draft stressed, 'that the reduction of the German fighter force is essential to our progression to the attack of other sources of the enemy war potential and any delay in its prosecution will make the task progressively more difficult.'

Harris was fully aware that German fighter strength was growing, but believed this latest plan was misguided. His night-bombing force could not hope to destroy enemy night-fighters in the air; nor did he believe the American Flying Fortresses could do much better. Since no Allied fighter was then capable of accompanying the bombers deep into Germany, there was little point in even suggesting such a course of action. It frustrated Harris intensely that others thought there was some easy solution out there that could make bombing more precise and efficient; he despised what he termed 'panacea mongers'. Technology had come on leaps and bounds, but it was, he argued, important to do the job with the tools in hand, not try to achieve something with tools that did not exist. To his mind, there was only one way to destroy the Luftwaffe – and with it, Nazi Germany – and that was by relentless heavy bombing of cities.

However, while he certainly had a point, his stubborn refusal to be deviated from his chosen path was somewhat blinkered. It was not impossible to give fighters greater range, for example. Rather, the Air Ministry had simply not yet given it enough time, thought and effort. What's more, navigational aids and bombing techniques were continuing to improve. At the time Harris had taken over Bomber Command, there really was no alternative to night bombing than area bombing. That did not necessarily need to be the case now. The know-how was emerging to allow a different path.

That washed very little with Harris, however, and

consequently, when he was given the chance to tweak the Eaker Plan, he changed the wording so that Bomber Command would not be hidebound to attack the Luftwaffe as the primary target. In effect, he was safeguarding his right to choose whatever targets he liked and leaving the destruction of the Luftwaffe to the Americans. This amended version of the Eaker Plan was then approved by both Portal and Arnold, rubber-stamped by Roosevelt and Churchill, and issued on 10 June 1943 as a new directive code-named Operation POINTBLANK.

On the face of it, as the summer wore on, Bomber Command's successes and the losses suffered by Eighth Air Force twice over Schweinfurt appeared to prove Harris right and the Americans wrong. However, while Bomber Command was certainly causing more damage at proportionally less cost, it was far from achieving its aims: Germany was still in the war and bombers by both day and night were being met by increasing numbers of Focke-Wulfs, Messerschmitts and Junkers.

On 15 August, two days before the first Schweinfurt mission, Air Chief Marshal Portal told the Joint Chiefs of Staff that since January the German fighter force on the Western Front had doubled. 'If we do not now strain every nerve to bring enough force to bear to win this battle during the next two or three months,' he said, 'we may well miss the opportunity to win a decisive victory against the German Air Force which will have incalculable effects on all future operations and on the length of the war.' The 'future operation' he was especially referring to was Operation OVERLORD, the planned cross-Channel invasion. Only Harris still believed bombing alone was enough to defeat Germany; all the other senior Allied commanders accepted that the Combined Bomber Offensive was intended to wear down the Germans and make OVER-LORD possible.

By September, concerns were starting to mount that even night-time bombing might soon be seriously affected by the resurgent German fighter force. Air Marshal Sir Norman Bottomley, the RAF's Deputy Chief of the Air Staff, warned Portal at the end of September that unless something could be done, 'we may find that either we are unable to maintain the night offensive against Germany, or that the Germans can sustain the intensity of attack which we can develop.' Bottomley proposed that Harris be given far less of a free rein to choose his targets and should instead focus directly on the POINTBLANK plan and targeting the German aircraft industry. This would force Harris to abandon plans to attack Berlin, a campaign he was convinced could well prove decisive. Back in 1940, the Luftwaffe had switched from attacking airfields to mounting a sustained offensive against London and other British cities, and this change of tack had achieved little. It certainly hadn't destroyed the RAF and had done nothing to help preparations for an invasion. Admittedly, Harris was now bombing Germany with a considerably larger force and with far more bombs than the Luftwaffe had had three years earlier, but the comparison was not entirely unfair.

The truth was, Harris's conviction that bombing alone could prove decisive was badly misplaced. There was no question it was making the German ability to wage war harder, but that was not the same thing. The nub of the matter was this: winning air superiority was vital both to the chances of success of OVERLORD and to future bombing operations. Air superiority could not be won by bombing alone, but winning air superiority would make bombing considerably more effective. Harris did not accept this, but an equal truth was that night-time bombing was not going to win air superiority either, even if Bomber Command began religiously targeting the German air industry.

Ultimately, destroying the Luftwaffe could only be achieved by day. It was for this reason, rather than more spurious arguments about greater accuracy, that the Americans had been quite right to persist with daylight bombing.

The trouble was – and this was the crux of the deep crisis the Allies were now experiencing – they had no real idea of how to defeat the Luftwaffe's fighter force. Eaker was demanding ever more bombers and bomber crews, but there was no getting round the fact that bombers, even those full to the gunwales with heavy machine guns, were not sufficient to destroy a decisive enough number of German fighter planes in the air. They had neither the speed nor agility to do the fighter's job.

However, nor were they particularly effective bombers; armour plating and all those heavy machine guns came at a price. They added both weight and drag, which meant the aircraft could carry fewer bombs than they might otherwise have done. In fact, the payloads of both the B-17 and the B-24 were not large. The Lancaster, for example, designed without much thought to self-defence but with everything to do with payload, generally carried over 6 tons and as much as 10. The B-17, meanwhile, could carry just over 2 tons. This meant one hundred Lancasters could drop the same number of bombs as nearly five hundred Flying Fortresses. That was a big difference. It was one of the reasons why five hundred British heavies over Kassel could destroy much of the old city in one raid, and why 270 American heavies could not completely destroy one factory complex.

What Black Thursday had proved was that, while B-17s could bomb with a fair degree of 'precision', the numbers getting through were still comparatively small, which in turn meant the number of bombs dropped was also nothing like as high as it might be. The task of neutralizing the Luftwaffe over Europe was going to be considerably more difficult and take far longer than had originally been appreciated, and time was not a luxury the strategic air forces had in October 1943, with OVERLORD scheduled to take place the following May.

What the Allies needed were fighter planes superior to those of the enemy, in greater numbers than those of the enemy, which could escort the bombers deep into Germany and were piloted by men with superior flying skills. Such aircraft would not only defend the bombers but also take on and destroy the enemy fighter force. For the most part, by the autumn of 1943, the Americans had achieved three of those four criteria. Pilots were arriving from the US far better trained than their German equivalents and were then rapidly learning the ropes thanks to an abundance of further practice and training time once in theatre. The P-47 Thunderbolt was robust and could dive faster than any other fighter plane in Europe, and the numbers were increasing all the time.

This meant that, on paper at any rate, the Allies now had the superior aircraft as well as increasing numbers of better-trained pilots. What was lacking was a modern and superior fighter plane with the range to reach far into Germany and back. Finding such a machine seemed to be an unsolvable problem, because the small size of a fighter plane compared with a bomber restricted its ability to carry the large quantities of fuel needed to fly such distances.

However, at the very moment the Allies were confronting the stark reality of this potentially catastrophic crisis, succour was at hand. The answer lay in the truly remarkable P-51 Mustang.

CHAPTER 8

In the Bleak Midwinter

AFTER BLACK THURSDAY, THE rest of October 1943 was quiet for the men of the Eighth Air Force. In part this was because they were licking their wounds, but it was also because the weather was terrible. Lieutenant Bob Johnson called it the 'North Sea Stratus'. 'It was really heavy ground fog,' he said. 'The trees and telephone poles would stick up through it. All of England seemed to be covered.' As a result, the bombers flew a single mission to Düren, on the German–Dutch border, but otherwise a couple of night-time leaflet-dropping operations was all they managed until November.

On 29 October, Bob Johnson and the other 56th FG pilots at Halesworth waved goodbye to their chief, Colonel Hub Zemke, who had been sent to Washington as part of a team led by Brigadier-General Curtis LeMay to make a report on progress to their superiors and to Congress; Zemke had agreed to go on the understanding that he would soon be allowed back to the helm of his fighter group. Colonel Robert B. Landry, an old man of thirty-four, had arrived to take charge in his absence.

Bob Johnson, Gabby Gabreski and the men of the 56th

finally flew again on Wednesday, 3 November, to support a maximum-effort raid on Wilhelmshaven, Germany's major North Sea port. Before taking off, they were joined by the 4th Fighter Group from Debden, who were to use Halesworth as a staging post. After refuelling, the 4th took off again ahead. Johnson was watching from his cockpit on the perimeter near the far end of the main runway when one of the 4th's pilots, Lieutenant Waterman, got airborne only to spin and crash back down again, the plane flipping over in flames. Before the crash wagons – the fire service – could reach him, one of the airfield's military policemen, a large fellow called Delaney, ran over to the burning wreckage and pulled Waterman free.

The pilot was hysterical. 'Go away!' he shouted. 'Let me die! Let me die!' Johnson could see he had suffered bad burns and his clothing was still smoking. Ignoring Waterman's pleas, Delaney pulled him clear then fell on him to protect him just as the Thunderbolt exploded in a ball of flame. Such accidents could happen to anyone, and Johnson, like everyone else, had to put it behind him and get on with the mission.

Major David Schilling led both groups that day – a total of fifty-four P-47s, the largest number ever put up for a mission from Halesworth. After the drama of taking off, the operation itself proved easy. The entire mission flew at high altitude, Johnson looking down at the many streaks of white from the contrails of 539 B-17s and B-24s. They saw nothing all the way to their target, but on the return leg Johnson spotted a lone Me109 away to his left and below, working its way up behind the bombers using the contrails to hide its sneaking approach. But the German pilot failed to spot Johnson's Thunderbolt. As Johnson dived down he saw two rockets slung on to the underside of the German fighter: while deadly for a bomber, they made the Messerschmitt slow and ungainly, easy meat for an attacker. 'Two hundred yards back,' noted Johnson, 'I squeezed the trigger; white flashes all over the airplane. The Kraut snapped over in a roll to the left and started to dive.' It was no contest, not against the fast-diving P-47. Johnson tore down after him and got so close he almost rammed the enemy fighter. A squeeze of the trigger and this time the Messerschmitt – and pilot – blew up, Johnson hurtling through the remains.

Since their attack on Kassel on the night of 22/23 October, RAF Bomber Command had been grounded by the weather too, but that night, 3/4 November, they were to strike at Düsseldorf in Germany's industrial heartland. Harris was continuing to pay scant regard to the POINT-BLANK directive and instead was gearing up to strike Berlin itself.

In attacking the capital of the Reich, Harris did have the backing of the Prime Minister, who, while fully supportive of POINTBLANK, none the less believed that heavy night bombing might well gain the Allies the best results. On that same day, 3 November, Harris had written to Churchill for blessing for his renewed assault on Berlin and reported that forty-seven German cities had so far been targeted by his command. Nineteen, he told Churchill, were now virtually destroyed, another nineteen were seriously damaged and nine merely damaged. As Harris pointed out, nearly all this destruction had happened since the advent of a much larger heavy bomber force, as well as tools such as Oboe, H2S, Window and the

Pathfinders. He urged the Prime Minister to put pressure on the Americans to give up costly, and in his view inefficient, attacks on specific targets and join the RAF instead in striking at Berlin. 'We have not got far to go,' he told Churchill, 'but we must get the USAAF to wade in in greater force. We can wreck Berlin from end to end if the USAAF will come in on it. It will cost us 400–500 aircraft. It will cost Germany the war.'

Harris was again singularly failing to acknowledge or accept that winning air superiority and successful area bombing were not different strategies; rather, they needed to be symbiotic parts of the same overall plan.

In any case, night-time bombing was proving hardly much safer than daylight bombing, not least because numbers of Luftwaffe night-fighters were on the rise. There had been 553 night-fighters defending the Reich in January 1943, but by November that figure had risen to 748. Of those, just under five hundred were ready to fly at any moment. That equated to around the same number of day-fighters with which the RAF had defeated over a thousand Luftwaffe bombers back in 1940. At the start of November 1943, Harris had 879 bombers of all types available, which was also comparable with Luftwaffe bomber numbers of three summers earlier.

One of those flying into the darkness every time the 'Tommies' came over was Leutnant Wilhelm Johnen, of 5/ Nachtjagdgeschwader 5, who had just turned twenty-two but who had already been flying in a front-line squadron for more than two years. From Homberg, south of Kassel in central Germany, he had decided to join what had then been the fledgling night-fighter arm in the autumn of

1940. At the time, he had still been training at fighter school in Munich when Major Wolfgang Falck, one of the first of the Luftwaffe's night-fighters and the first successfully to shoot down an enemy aircraft, had arrived at the school on a recruitment drive. 'Major Falck was a genial and plausible speaker,' wrote Johnen later. 'I trusted him and after due consideration I decided to become a night fighter.'

After completing his training, he had been posted to 3/NJG1 and since then had become a night-fighter ace with eight victories to his name. His first downed bomber had very nearly cost him his life, because on the same sortie he had then spotted a Stirling heavy bomber but had been shot at in turn. His navigator-gunner had been killed, his Me110 had become a flaming torch, and Johnen had only just managed to bail out in time, although not before being hit in the leg and badly burned. That had been in March 1942, and although these injuries had kept him out for several months, he had been back into the fray by June that year and barely out of it since. For the increasingly manpower-starved Wehrmacht, pilots had to fly and fly until they were physically unable to do so. All too often that meant death.

By the autumn of 1943, Johnen and his comrades in NJG5 had accepted this with a mounting sense of fatalism. They understood the Luftwaffe was in decline. On one occasion in the summer, a number of bombers had staged at their airfield of Gilze in Holland. Johnen and his fellows had watched them, discussing how the once mighty bomber formations were a shadow of what they had been. 'In the old days,' said one of his longest-serving comrades, Heini Strüning, 'they set out in armadas of between 400 and 600 aircraft and today there are only about 100 of them left. Moreover, those old crates are out of date and an easy prey for the British night-fighters. If thirty of them set out tonight, probably only twenty would return.' This underlined the futility of Hitler's insistence on continued offensive action.

Johnen was aware of the new jet aircraft in development and he and his fellows all wondered why they were not getting these sooner. Enemy-aircraft envy was rife and they had all been demanding aircraft of greater speed, armament and range on a regular basis. For the night-fighters, the De Havilland Mosquito had caused the biggest stir. They considered the Mosquito 'vastly superior' to their own night-fighters, which, in terms of speed and altitude, it was. The new Heinkel 219, which was just reaching the squadrons, offered some cause for hope, but once again its development had been fraught with setbacks, arguments between Kammhuber and Heinkel, and production difficulties as a result of Allied bombing.

Despite this, Johnen and the other night-fighters were still flying aircraft that were faster and far better armed than any British heavy bomber. Johnen's was the Me110, a G-4 night-fighter variant, albeit slower than the Me110s in which he had first flown. And as with the British and Americans, new technology was never far away. His aircraft was now equipped with the latest on-board radar, the SN2, which was a development of the Lichtenstein. Its advantage lay in using several ultra-short waves so that it could change frequency should one of them get jammed; this enabled it to overcome Window, for example. The flipside was antennae that were even larger and more drag-inducing than the Lichtenstein's; also, highly sensitive fingers and a great deal of practice were required in order to get an enemy bomber clearly on the screen of this new instrument.

New tactical developments included the *Zahme Sau* system. By the beginning of November, both the SN2 and Tame Boar methods were being widely used. This way, as soon as an enemy raid was picked up and the estimated course and target of the bomber stream established, the night-fighter squadrons would be scrambled and directed towards it by ground controllers using another new VHF radio navigation system called 'Ypsilon', or 'Y', and also by providing night-fighter crews with updated radio commentary in plain language on the bombers' position, course and height. The night-fighters would then become part of the bomber stream as soon as possible, usually flying below so that enemy bombers might be silhouetted against the sky and their own aircraft hidden by the dark of the ground.

The new *Zahme Sau* system had prompted Johnen's boss at NJG5, Major Rudi Schönert, to introduce a new method of mounting twin 20mm cannons into the fuselage just behind the pilot's head. With the barrels pointing upwards at an angle of around 70 degrees, the idea was to use the SN2 to latch on to an enemy bomber, then fly underneath it, where both Lancasters and Halifaxes were most vulnerable and least able to see any attacker. Using a reflector gunsight mounted in the top of the cockpit cover, the pilot would then open fire with both barrels, aiming high-explosive cannon shells directly into the fuel tanks. Schönert nicknamed this new system *Schräge Musik* – 'slanting music'.

Johnen had used these new techniques to good effect

when Bomber Command had attacked Berlin at the end of August in what had been a one-off raid by over seven hundred bombers. On this occasion, his SN2 set had packed up, but it hadn't mattered. 'Here over Berlin,' he noted, 'radar was superfluous. We could see the enemy circling over the city with our naked eyes.' Just after 1 a.m., a Halifax had crossed his path and Johnen had fired directly into the bomber's petrol tanks. The bomber exploded and fell in burning fragments. Not five minutes later, he had spotted a Stirling, quickly silenced the rear gunner and seconds later had destroyed the plane. 'At 1.08 this heavy bomber fell like a stone out of the sky,' he wrote, 'and exploded on the ground.' That night, NJG5 had accounted for no fewer than twenty enemy bombers; Bomber Command lost fifty-six in all, almost as many as the Americans had suffered over Schweinfurt.

'We all knew,' noted Johnen, 'that the hour of victory had passed and that Hitler only wanted to gain time. But was there any sense in brooding over this?'

Johnen was not alone in thinking like this, but on the night of 3 November 1943, as the bomber stream headed to Düsseldorf, he and his fellow night-fighter crews – more than five hundred of them – would be there in the skies over the Reich, using their cannons and *Schräge Musik* and on-board radar, and supported by what had become a highly sophisticated early-warning and ground control system. While the glory days of the Luftwaffe were in the past, it was also true that those in Bomber Command had very good reason to fear the night-fighters. In November 1943 they still posed a considerable – and increasingly sophisticated and efficient – threat.

*

RAF Leeming was a bleak place to be that autumn. Lying on a long stretch of flat land sandwiched between the high hills of the Yorkshire Dales to the west and the Yorkshire Moors to the east, with the town of Darlington to the north, and Thirsk and then, further off, York to the south, it was a place where the icy northerly winds from the Arctic swept in and where low cloud seemed to stay rooted. Bob Johnson might have thought the perpetual fog and cloud was bad enough far to the south in Suffolk, but compared with Leeming it was almost tropical.

The Byers twins, laid-back and phlegmatic, took the weather in their stride – after all, they were used to snow and cold in Canada – but Leeming looked particularly spectral that morning of Wednesday, 3 November, the hangars and buildings, not to mention the Halifaxes parked up around the perimeter, little more than dark looming shapes amid the mist and drizzle. Yet shortly after 10 a.m., a cipher clerk received a signal from Bomber Command Headquarters at High Wycombe that there would be an operation that night. A WAAF immediately put a call through to Wing Commander Jack Pattison, the CO of 429 Squadron. 'There's a "war" on tonight, sir,' she told him. A short while after, Pattison was in the operations room.

Pattison was handed the fully decoded message in silence. Düsseldorf, and another maximum effort. The city had been designated by Harris as a 'Primary Industrial Target' – although it had little specifically to do with the Luftwaffe – but it had been attacked only four times so far. Bomber Command were demanding six hundred bombers for the attack. Pattison had fifteen aircraft available to fly, including his own.

A bomber squadron was split into three flights, each with an establishment of six aircraft and each usually commanded by a squadron leader. George Byers had been put in 'A' Flight, his brother Bill in 'B'. They headed to their respective flight rooms at around 10.30 a.m., where they learned, via a notice on the ops board, that they would both be flying operationally that evening. Of the target, there was no mention. Bill then went to see the meteorological officer to find out whether there was likely to be any improvement in the weather – there was not – and then, having assembled his crew, they took a truck, or 'blood wagon' as it was known, over to their Halifax, *Z for Zebra*.

The Halifax was a big bomber – at over 100 feet wide, 20 feet off the ground and nearly 72 feet in length, it sat on the concrete hardstand – parking area – with its all-black underside like a giant menacing beast. In its vast bomb bays it could carry nearly 6 tons of ordnance – not as much as a Lancaster but more than the American heavies – but while its payload more than matched its deadly appearance, it was horribly vulnerable, as all the British bombers were, to enemy attack. In order to carry that load and to cruise at over 220 m.p.h., it was very thin-skinned. Halifaxes were little more than tin cans, more cramped than their outward appearance suggested, with few concessions to the comfort of the crews. As they were unpressurized, at altitude the crews existed on oxygen and thick, electrically warmed sheepskins. To reach the cockpit, the pilot had to clamber over wing spars and, once seated, was aware that little other than a thin wall of aluminium protected him from tearing cannon shells, bullets and fire. On board, their only defence was eight

.303 Browning machine guns, the same as a Spitfire or Hurricane from the Battle of Britain. They were little more than pea-shooters.

George Byers and his crew were doing the same – pre-flight checks and running up the engines – as was everyone else due to be flying later, so that, despite the cold, mist and drizzle, the whole airfield was a hive of activity. Soon the comparative quiet was ripped apart by the sound of sixty Merlin XX engines, while Jeeps, fuel bowsers and ammunition carts also sped around the field. Getting fifteen Halifax IIs ready for ops was no small operation in itself.

Lunch followed the pre-flight tests – a hot meal of stew, then chocolate or biscuits. The food was a small perk of the job; while the rest of the country was on reasonably stringent rationing by 1943, the bomber boys had no shortage of food or even drink; beer and whisky were plentiful in the mess. Between the end of lunch and the final briefing there was little time – perhaps the chance to write a letter or a quick game of cards – but by 3 p.m. they needed to be ready in their flight kit. In the flight rooms the crews would put on silk underwear, thick pullovers underneath the dark blue battledress, then wool-lined leather flying boots, then they would head to the briefing room. The briefing was for 429 Squadron and 427 'Lion' Squadron, also based at Leeming. The pilots, navigators, flight engineers, bomb-aimers, wireless operators and air gunners would all pile into the briefing room, where rows of chairs and desks were already set up and where the aircrew could make notes. Ahead of them, on the far wall, was a large map, covered in cloth until the station commander and briefing staff arrived.

Waiting for the destination could be a tense moment: the further into Germany the target, the tougher the mission was likely to be, with more time over occupied territory, more flak to contend with and, of course, more enemy night-fighters. So, it was to be Düsseldorf, on Germany's western extreme. Plenty of flak, but there were worse targets. The navigation officer explained the forming-up procedure and the route of the bomber stream, which was marked on the map with tape. Next up was the met officer. Despite the persistent low cloud over England, the target area was expected to be clear. The Byers twins listened carefully, each jotting down a few notes on a scrap of paper.

With the briefing over, the crews collected the rest of their kit – flight suits, Irvin jackets, flak jackets and Mae West life vests – while Bill Byers squirrelled away some apple juice and chocolate. Then it was into the blood wagons once more to be taken around to their aircraft. It was nearly 4 p.m. by the time they reached their Halifaxes, and the light was already fading. Once aboard, they waited for nearly half an hour. In the cockpit, there were final checks with the flight engineers – Sergeant Jim Moore in Bill's crew and Sergeant Ted Bates in George's. It was cold without the engines running and smelled of metal and oil and rubber. The crews were quiet. No jokes, no laughter. Nicknames and Christian names were put to one side; proper titles only were used – Navigator, Mid-upper Gunner, Skipper – and communication was through the intercom and headphones. Time seemed to slow. Already, Bill Byers had learned this was the worst part of the whole trip. Too much time to think. He felt scared, as well he might. Anyone who said they didn't feel the same was a liar as far as he was concerned.

At 4.20 p.m., the flare was fired and they all began to move off, slowly creeping around the perimeter. At 4.25 p.m., Squadron Leader Alban Chipling and his crew began their take-off. Twenty minutes later, it was George Byers' turn, two ahead of his brother. Along the edge of the airfield and away by the hangars and control tower were the usual collection of ground crew, WAAFs and staff come to see the station's two squadrons go. At 4.48 p.m., *Z for Zebra* was at the head of the runway. Opening the throttles, Bill felt the engines roar and the Halifax surge down the runway. Then, with both hands, he pulled back on the control column and felt the Halifax lift from the ground, the perimeter hedge disappearing beneath them, and then they were climbing up, through cloud, into the dark mass of the sky beyond.

Taking off, fully laden, in such weather was one of the more dangerous parts of the mission, but flying in a stream rather than in any kind of formation made life easier. None the less, collisions did happen. The twins managed to clear the cloud and by around 5.30 both were crossing over the Channel and joining the bomber stream of 589 aircraft: 344 Lancasters and 233 Halifaxes led by 12 Pathfinder Force Mosquitoes.

Already Luftwaffe radar and the radio listening service of the Horchdienst had begun to pick them up. They managed to avoid heavy flak concentrations, but it was easy to drift even slightly off course and find guns peppering the sky as they crossed the coast of Europe. And from then on the night-fighters might begin stalking them, directed to the stream by the Tame Boar system. On board the bombers, gunners strained into the darkness.

The coastline came and went. Now they were flying

over occupied territory. In *Z for Zebra*, Bill Byers glanced out of his side window and saw that some of their aircraft were under attack from night-fighters; he saw one Halifax plummet in flames. He pushed on until he was well into Germany. As he neared the target, flak began peppering the sky, shells exploding all around them, the Halifax rattling and shaking. Now they were on the bomb run, flying straight and level until at last Dick Fawcett, the bomb-aimer, called out, 'Bombs away!' Immediately, the bomber rose, lightened now the bombs had gone, up and out of the fray. Most of the bombs dropped that night were reasonably accurate, hitting the centre and south of Düsseldorf and destroying a number of industrial buildings as well as homes in the area.

Nearly four hours after they had taken off they were approaching Leeming once more. Three from 429 Squadron had already returned home early with technical problems, but of those who had made it to Düsseldorf, the first landed back just before 10 p.m. Wing Commander Pattison and his crew touched down at 10.04 p.m. Bill called up Leeming flight control and told them they would shortly be joining the circuit, flying around the airfield waiting their turn to land.

Most had landed by 10.30, but Bill Byers continued circling, waiting to hear George's voice crackle through his headset. But there was no sound from his brother. 'Skipper, I think you'd better land,' said Jim Moore, the flight engineer, eventually, 'we're getting low on fuel.' Reluctantly, Byers did so, the 16-ton bomber touching down with a lurch and a screech of rubber. They were the fourteenth aircraft from 429 Squadron to make it safely back. Byers hung around for as long as he could, then made his report to the intelligence officer. Tots of rum and cups of tea were handed out to the exhausted crews, but as soon as Bill had changed out of his flying kit he made his way over to the control tower, and waited. The minutes passed slowly. Eleven o'clock came and went, then midnight; but there was nothing. No distant beat of engines, just a dark, empty sky.

He waited up all night for George, but in his heart of hearts Bill had known earlier that night that his brother wasn't coming back. No one had seen them hit or crash near the target, so the chances were it had been a night-fighter that had got them. The following morning, Wing Commander Pattison offered Bill some compassionate leave – everyone knew how close the twins had been – but he turned the offer down. The CO accepted his decision, but insisted on accompanying him on a twenty-minute flight to see how he was holding up. All right, it seemed – but even so, he and his crew would not be sent out again for a fortnight.

The crew did their best to help him, but it was difficult. Dick Meredith moved into George's old bed to keep Bill company, but otherwise no one ever mentioned it. Bill hoped that word would come through that his brother was in a POW camp – that was not uncommon – but days passed and then a couple of weeks and there was nothing. And by that time, Harris was launching his offensive against the capital of the Third Reich: Berlin.

CHAPTER 9

Mustang

THICK FOG HAD STOPPED the *Athlone Castle* from docking at Liverpool on 1 November 1943, so not until the 4th did the ship finally pull in alongside the quay. On board were some seven thousand servicemen, including over a thousand pilots, ground crew and staff of the 354th Fighter Group, a further three squadrons that had been formed and trained together in the States before being shipped across the Atlantic. Among them was 23-year-old Lieutenant Dick Turner, who, like most of his fellow pilots, had always been quite happy with his own two feet on the ground, even happier in the air, but was not so keen to be out at sea, especially not on an ocean as large as the Atlantic and with the possibility of a lurking U-boat striking at any moment.

The Battle of the Atlantic might have been won by then, but U-boats were still operating and ships were still being sunk, as Turner had witnessed all too vividly. One night, he and his pals had been about to turn in for the night when suddenly the 'Abandon ship' alarm rang out. Breathlessly hurrying to his lifeboat station and strapping on his life jacket as he did so, he had been stopped in his tracks by the sight of a sheet of flame mushrooming into the sky away off their port beam as one of their convoy was hit. Fortunately, the *Athlone Castle* had sailed on safely and they had all remained on board, but it had been an unsettling experience and a reminder that they were heading ever closer to the war.

After a warm welcome speech from an RAF group captain, they finally began to disembark. As they did so, Turner was carefully watching cargo nets hoisting their foot lockers on to the quayside, conscious that one of them contained their squadron mascot, a white bull terrier. They had smuggled him aboard in New York, but the ship's captain had discovered the dog's presence and insisted the mutt be destroyed before landing. The pilots had responded with a wall of silence and protested ignorance, but now Turner prayed the winch operator wouldn't be too rough and the terrier be injured in the process. Then something else caught his eye: the sight of aircraft being off-loaded. Presumably these were their fighters, and what was particularly exciting was that these planes were not the P-39 Airacobra with which they had trained, but brand-new P-51 Mustangs. Soon after, Turner was reliably informed that they would indeed be assigned to the 354th. 'Rumor or not,' noted Turner, 'it served as an excellent omen on the arrival of our fighter group in the European Theater of Operations.'

Rumour became a reality when the pilots were posted south to Greenham Common near Newbury in Berkshire, while the ground crews, support staff – and the crates of P-51s – were sent direct to Boxted in Essex. Greenham Common, meanwhile, was home to the 67th Tactical Reconnaissance Group, already flying P-51As. For over a week, the boys of the 354th were to share these Mustangs while their new base was set up at Boxted. Turner was thrilled. Before reaching England he had never even seen a P-51, but they all knew about this exciting new fighter plane and the first few flights did not disappoint. It was fast, forgiving, highly manoeuvrable and vastly superior to the old P-39s they'd been flying in the US. The only drawback was that the P-39s had a tricycle undercarriage, giving them excellent forward vision when taxiing, whereas the Mustang was a tail-dragger so that when on the ground all the pilot could see ahead of him was the fighter's nose. However, it didn't take them long to learn to taxi in an 'S' movement, from side to side, to see better.

On Saturday, 13 November, Turner and the rest of the pilots headed to Boxted, near Colchester, where they discovered everything already in place and three squadrons of brand-new P-51Bs – the latest high-altitude, high-speed and, crucially, long-range version. The 354th Fighter Group was to be the first to use this new wonder-plane operationally. Turner and his fellow pilots could not have been more delighted.

That they had them at all had been the result of much high-level wrangling, about which the new pilots were completely unaware. It had also been the subject of a number of missed opportunities by those who, frankly, ought to have known better, and not least Hap Arnold and Ira Eaker. In fact, that new P-51Bs were now in England at all was, in a large part, down to a civilian, rather than to any military commanders; Robert A. Lovett, the US Assistant Secretary of State for War, had identified its long-range potential to Arnold back in June, before the slaughters of the Eighth's bombers over Germany. There was, he had

The cockpit of the Boeing
B-17 Flying Fortress.

Above: The waist gunner's station in the B-17, with the ball turret beyond. It was little more than a tin can.

Below: The prototype B-17, gleaming and silvery. It was the most modern heavy bomber in the world when it first flew in July 1935.

Above: Don Blakeslee briefs pilots of the 4th Fighter Group. James Goodson, with moustache, sits to his left. Drawn from the American volunteers who made up the original RAF Eagle Squadrons, the 4th FG were tough, highly experienced pilots. And of those, Blakeslee was the toughest.

Below: The identical twins from Canada, George (*left*) and Bill Byers, who arrived in England to fly Halifax bombers in RAF Bomber Command's 6 Group.

America's air leaders, committed not only to daylight strategic bombing but also to gaining air superiority and defeating the Luftwaffe.

Fred Anderson

Hap Arnold

Jimmy Dolittle

Ira Eaker

Bill Kepner (*far left*) and Carl 'Tooey' Spaatz (*2nd left*)

Bud Anderson

Some of the Eighth Air Force's most celebrated aces. Increasingly, American fighter pilots had greater flying hours, skill and combat tactics than their German adversaries.

Duane Beeson

Don Blakeslee

Gabby Gabreski

Don Gentile

Jim Howard

Bob Johnson

SHORT-FUSE SALLEE

Dick Turner

Hub Zemke

The prototype P-51 Mustang (*left*) showed immense promise from the outset, but not until the P-51B model (*right*), harnessed with a Rolls-Royce Merlin engine, did it become one of the most important aircraft ever designed.

Above: The 4th FG were thrilled to be among the first units to get Mustangs.

Right: The Thunderbolt P-47 and its firing scheme.

Below: Newly arrived P-47 Thunderbolts transported through Liverpool.

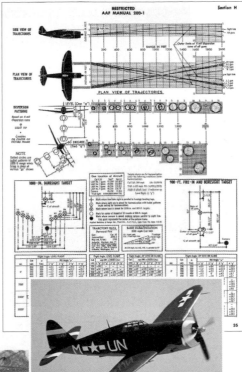

Above: B-17s lined up ready to taxi for another mission.

Below: Some of the crew of *Worry Wart*.

Ace Conklin
(co-pilot)

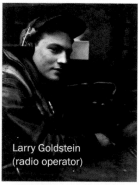

Larry Goldstein
(radio operator)

Kent Keith
(bombardier)

Right: Jimmy Stewart, from Hollywood
star to outstanding air leader.

urged Arnold at the time, 'an immediate need for long-range fighters', and he had identified both the twin-engine P-38 and the new P-51B. Despite this, and despite a number of tests proving the Mustang's ideal suitability, the 354th Fighter Group had arrived in England originally destined to join the fledgling Ninth Air Force, currently forming as a tactical rather than a strategic force. The Mustangs were to have a ground-attack and reconnaissance role.

The story of the Mustang was certainly a remarkable one. In 1940, both Britain and France had been trying to increase their war production dramatically, and Britain was already committed to a strategy in which air power was to play a central role. More factories were springing up and increasing numbers of aircraft were being built, but the worry was that even this was not enough. The USA, at the time neither at war nor under threat, and with huge industrial potential, had been an obvious place to turn to the moment the war had begun, and by January that year the Anglo-French Purchasing Board had been established in New York. Although the United States still had its Neutrality Acts in place preventing the sales of arms to overseas customers, a loophole had been introduced the previous November that allowed for purchases on a cash-and-carry basis. This worked for the British – and French – rather than Germany, because only Britain and France had both the ready cash and the shipping available successfully to conclude any arms deal in the US.

Among the first orders made by the British had been for three hundred Curtiss P-40 Warhawks, but although the Curtiss–Wright Corporation had already sold a number of the earlier model P-36 Hawks to the French, they told the British they no longer had the capacity to build such numbers of their latest fighter for the RAF as well as for the now expanding US Army Air Corps. In desperation, the British had then turned to North American Aviation, a far smaller company based in California, which specialized in building training aircraft. Initially, they asked North American to produce Warhawks under licence. James Howard 'Dutch' Kindelberger, the North American Aviation president, asked to be given some time to consider the matter, to which the British conceded.

Kindelberger recognized his company had been presented with a wonderful opportunity. The Warhawk was, even by 1940, a relatively old design and, although rugged and reasonably well armed, it was slower than other leading fighters, not so manoeuvrable at higher altitudes and would most likely soon become obsolescent. On the other hand, if they could produce an entirely new and better fighter aircraft, they would have an incredible chance to advance and expand their company significantly. Edgar Schmued, a German-born engineer who had moved to South America after the First World War and to the US in 1931, had drawn up the first designs of a new fighter for North American in February 1940. The British officials had been impressed and two months later, they were presented with a further design, which looked sleek and smooth and included a revolutionary laminar-flow airfoil wing, which meant a much narrower leading edge and, theoretically, less drag; in a nutshell, the pressure that produced lift was more spread out than on a traditional wing. The fuselage, too, was narrower than on other fighters. Another design first placed the radiator and oil-cooler intake centrally on the underside of the plane, just behind the cockpit, which not only reduced drag further but also produced a far more efficient cooling system. Furthermore – and quite by accident – the radiator design provided around 300 lb of jet thrust as the heat energy left the exit scoop.

Schmued's design was approved on 4 May 1940 with an order for 320 planes at $50,000 each – roughly £14,500 – but with the caveat that the prototype be completed within 120 days. It was an enormous – and potentially costly – gamble by the British, but an even greater one by North American Aviation; even by the standards of the day this was an exceptionally short period within which to design, construct and fly a brand-new fighter aircraft. The development rule of thumb was four years, not four months. Cutting development corners had repeatedly come back to haunt the Germans over the course of the war so far, but such had been the urgency back during the desperate days of 1940 that both the British and the team at North American had accepted the risk.

Incredibly, however, after some 78,000 man-hours and a mere week over schedule, the prototype, NA-73X, was rolled out. With very few problems during testing, production began equally seamlessly and, although a bit behind schedule, the first Mustangs reached England and the hands of the RAF in October 1941. By the time of Pearl Harbor in December that year, the British had orders for some 620 and North American's gamble appeared to have paid off.

However, the Mustang, as the British had named it, was not proving to be quite the aircraft that had been hoped. It was undoubtedly fast, with a top speed of 388 m.p.h., and highly manoeuvrable too at heights of up to 5,000 feet; but performance tailed off dramatically with altitude, and at

15,000 feet and above it was nothing like as effective. Consequently, the RAF used it purely for low-level operations, while the USAAF showed absolutely no interest in the fighter.

The issue, however, was not Schmued's design but the plane's engine. The Allison V-1710 simply did not have the power. The Mustang might well have been relegated for ever had it not been for Ron Harker, a test pilot at Rolls-Royce. Harker, who had joined the company before the war, had flown a large number of aircraft and liked a lot about the P-51. It reminded him of the Me109F, a captured model of which he had also flown. 'The point which strikes me,' he wrote in his subsequent report, 'is that with a powerful and a good engine, like the Merlin 61, its performance could be outstanding, as it is 35mph faster than the Spitfire V at roughly the same power.'

The new Merlin 61 had a horsepower of 1,565 compared with the Allison's 1,150. Furthermore, it had a two-speed, two-stage supercharger, which, crucially, gave it greatly increased performance at medium and high altitudes, as well as improved boost. These were the kind of refinements that had been giving the latest marks of Spitfire such improved performances. The Merlin 61, for example, was now being fitted out in the Spitfire Mk IX, an aircraft that could out-perform both the latest Me109 and FW190. The problem with the Spitfire, now that the air battle was moving ever further from England, was its lack of range.

On paper, this should not have been an insuperable problem. In early 1942, for example, Spitfires had successfully flown off aircraft carriers and then travelled over sea more than 800 miles to the island of Malta. Auxiliary drop tanks had been fitted and had worked well. Photo reconnaissance Spitfires also regularly flew deep into German air space. At the very top of the RAF command, however, there was a fundamental unwillingness to engage in the notion of long-range fighters. Early in the war daylight bombing had been judged too dangerous and so both it and the need for escorting fighters had been brushed aside along with any further notions of daylight bombing.

The other issue was the lack of will on the part of Harris's opposite number at RAF Fighter Command, Air Marshal Sir Trafford Leigh-Mallory. It is baffling how Leigh-Mallory rose so high, because as a commander he was conservative, unimaginative and, worst of all, complacent. Nor did he make a great effort to learn much about fighter tactics, despite having been first commander of Fighter Command's 12 Group and then 11 Group before taking the top job. As Johnnie Johnson, Fighter Command's leading ace, admitted, Leigh-Mallory 'did not pretend to know about fighter tactics and relied on us to keep him up to date.' He guarded his precious Spitfires – and their use – religiously and gave short shrift to anyone trying to encroach on his patch. Any number of reasons had been given as to why Spitfires could not be sent overseas, all of which had proved fallacious the moment the RAF's best fighter began operating from Malta. By then it was the spring of 1942 and, although it was a case of better late than never, sending them to the Mediterranean and North Africa far earlier might well have proved decisive. It is extraordinary to think the RAF could have fought with significantly superior aircraft in this theatre earlier and yet did not because of internecine small-mindedness.

As a result of this asset-hogging – an attitude Leigh-Mallory had also inherited from his predecessor, Air Chief Marshal Sir Sholto Douglas – Fighter Command's swollen squadrons had spent the two years following the end of the Battle of Britain flying mostly ineffective and costly cross-Channel raids to northern France. More recently they had been coerced into providing escorts for the Eighth's bombers, but only within their normal – and limited – range.

Instead, the seeds of a future long-range fighter had been transferred to the Mustang. After Harker's report, Rolls-Royce converted five models, the first of which, with Harker at the controls, flew in October 1942 and with a four- rather than a three-blade propeller. The results were stunning. Meanwhile, Major Tommy Hitchcock, the Assistant Air Attaché at the US Embassy in London (and the inspiration for the character Tom Buchanan in F. Scott Fitzgerald's *The Great Gatsby*), who was a friend of Harker's, had already been urging his bosses back home to do the same, as the Packard automobile company had an agreement to build Merlin engines under licence. Both the Merlin 61-equipped Mustang III and the newly designated P-51B Packard Merlin* had a performance that did not decline at altitude but, rather, rapidly improved. With the Packard-Merlin V-1650-3, for example, it could fly at 375 m.p.h. at 5,000 feet, 400 m.p.h. at 10,000 feet, 430 m.p.h. at 20,000 and a stunning 455 m.p.h. at 35,000 feet, some

---

* The Merlin III was the British name for the Rolls-Royce Merlin 61-powered P-51. The P-51B was equipped with the Packard-built version of the Merlin 61, the V-1650-3. In effect, they were the same aircraft.

6½ miles up. This made the P-51B faster than both the FW190 and Me109G – some 70 m.p.h. faster than the Focke-Wulf above 28,000 feet and 50 m.p.h. faster at 20,000. It could also dive faster than either – which had earlier in the war been one of the great strengths of the Me109 – and had a tighter turning circle than the 109 and much the same as the 190.

The P-51B also had a quicker roll rate than either of these German aircraft or than any other Allied fighter. In addition, its internal layout and essential construction were both more logical and more straightforward than many other contemporary fighters, and it was smaller overall than most others too, all of which made it well placed for mass production and, crucially, some $30,000 cheaper to build than the P-47 Thunderbolt. With its small laminar wings and high wing-loading, the P-51B Mustang now combined power with phenomenal manoeuvrability. In short, it was an absolutely stunning new fighter.

But that was not all the Mustang had in its favour. The aerodynamics of Schmued's design, originally drawn up in early 1940 and using very smooth surfaces with sunken and filled-in rivets and thick, glassy paintwork, combined with the Packard-Merlin and a much lighter take-off weight than other fighters, meant it was more fuel-efficient too. What really made the difference in fuel efficiency, however, was less the sleekness of its design and more the amount of extra thrust derived from the placement of the radiator and the way air passed through it in such a way that its net coolant drag was only one sixth of that of a Spitfire. Although the standard Mustang's fuel tanks allowed a range of only around 415 miles, which was not exceptional, it had a fuel economy that was more than 30 per cent better than that of the P-47 and more than 60 per cent better than that of the twin-engine P-38, the only other fighter that was being considered to fill the long-range escort hole. The implications of this far superior fuel efficiency were obvious: add drop tanks and that extra fuel would go far further than on the other Allied fighter aircraft – even a Spitfire equipped with extra fuel-carrying capabilities.

The USAAF had ordered 1,350 Packard-Merlin Mustangs on 8 October 1942, even before Rolls-Royce had tested their Merlin 61 versions. The re-tooling and subsequent production took time but, by the summer of 1943, they were ready. Interestingly, though, during this time the Mustang's potential as a long-range fighter had not registered higher up the chain.

'Attached are Mr. Lovett's comments,' Arnold told his deputy, Lieutenant-General Barney Giles. 'This brings to my mind very clearly the absolute necessity for building a fighter airplane that can go in and come out with the bombers. Moreover, this fighter has got to go into Germany.' Arnold, who had been the leading champion of US bombers defending themselves, had now, following the Schweinfurt and Regensburg raids, accepted that fighter escorts were needed throughout any mission. 'Within this next six months,' he continued, 'you have got to get a fighter to protect our bombers. Whether you use an existing type or have to start from scratch is your problem. Get to work on this right away, because by January '44, I want fighter escort for all of our bombers from UK into Germany.' Crucially, he was not giving Giles six months to find a solution, but half a year to find a solution *and* have enough aircraft built and shipped to England and enough pilots trained and ready to fly them.

Even in this instruction, Arnold did not specify, as Lovett had, that Giles should look into the range potential of the P-51. Giles, however, correctly recognized that the answer to the long-range fighter was already right under their noses and immediately flew to California to see Dutch Kindelberger and Edgar Schmued at North American Aviation. There, Giles suggested replacing the radio set behind the pilot's head with a 100-gallon fuel tank and putting new bulletproof fuel tanks along much of the length of the two wings. Kindelberger initially doubted the wings were strong enough, but Giles insisted and was swiftly proved right: the sturdy Mustang could handle an extra 300 gallons on board without difficulty. That gave it a range of up to 750 miles. When two 75-gallon drop tanks were added, tests showed it could manage a stunning 1,474 miles. That was a round-trip from England that went beyond Berlin. And that was a game-changer.

Incredibly, however, most of the P-51Bs now rolling off the production line had continued to be sent to reconnaissance units or to the new Ninth Air Force. Only at the end of September did Arnold appear to realize what an asset they had wasted, and fired off a cable to Portal asking him for any P-51s operating in England to be sent either directly to, or for service in support of, the Eighth. The RAF's Mustangs, however, were nearly all P-51As – that is, with the Allison engine and therefore not entirely suitable as long-range escorts. Consequently, Portal didn't send over very many.

Then on 14 October, the same day as the second Schweinfurt Raid, Arnold sent another tense letter to Portal.

Both men had incredibly difficult jobs; no matter the material superiority they had over the enemy, their air forces were needed globally and in a multitude of different roles. The pressures on them were immense and the lives of many young men were held in their hands. Much has been made of the tensions between British and American commanders, but it is remarkable how comparatively few spats and strained relations there were considering the gargantuan levels of responsibility on their shoulders. For their part, Arnold and Portal got on well and there was undoubted mutual respect, but Portal was in England, where so much of the USAAF was now based, whereas Arnold, for much of the time, was on the other side of the Atlantic in Washington. Portal had eyes on the ground; Arnold did not.

Arnold's letter to Portal on 14 October revealed both his mounting frustration and anxiety and his distance from the epicentre of the Combined Bomber Offensive. 'Overlord hangs directly on the success of our combined aerial offensive,' he wrote, 'and I am sure that our failure to decisively cripple both sources of German air power and the GAF itself is causing you and me real concern.' His concern was that not enough was being done to take on the Luftwaffe directly. He was, he said, pressing Eaker as much as he could to get as large a force off the ground as possible in order to strike hard against the targets outlined in POINT-BLANK. But why, he wanted to know, was RAF Fighter Command not doing more? As he understood it, the RAF had 'thousands' of fighters. Surely they could help with escorting bombers? Couldn't more drop tanks be put on to Spitfires? 'Is it not true,' he asked, 'that we have a staggering air superiority over the German and we are not using it?

Should we not make it possible to put all fighters in an effective offensive action against the German Air Force at this critical time?'

Arnold had a point. Undoubtedly, the Mustang was the best bet for a long-range fighter, but the Spitfire, equipped with extra internal and auxiliary drop tanks, could easily have been capable of flying a round-trip deep into Germany. In fact, the previous year, in the summer of 1942, Fighter Command had been asked to provide long-range escorts for RAF Coastal Command's attacks on Germany's vital iron trade down the coast of Norway and into the Baltic. Calculations had been made, somewhat disingenuous conclusions drawn, and the notion summarily dismissed. Despite hard evidence to the contrary, it was decided there was not enough margin for error; nor did they want their pilots flying alone over water for the length of time it would involve. That US Navy fighter pilots, meanwhile, were carrying out lengthy flights over the Pacific and accepting the demands of such flying does not appear to have been considered.

Arnold's frustration was entirely justified, but he was coming up against a culture in which long-range Spitfires – except in special circumstances, such as flying to resupply Malta – had already been dismissed as not practicable. And he was also coming up against Leigh-Mallory, because, before he replied, Portal passed Arnold's note to the commander-in-chief of Fighter Command. Nor was it just Spitfires Leigh-Mallory was zealously guarding. He had not permitted a single Hawker Typhoon, nor the new Hawker Tempests, to be sent to other theatres either. The Typhoon and Tempest were fast, powerful, bristling with weaponry, and quite superb ground-attack aircraft, so, although there was sound logic to keeping them in the UK, the decision didn't help overcome Leigh-Mallory's – and Fighter Command's – reputation for hoarding or for being parsimonious with their assets.

In his reply to Portal, Leigh-Mallory pointed out that he didn't have 'thousands' but rather some 750 Spitfires and 270 Typhoons. There was also a difference between what was available on paper and what was ready to fly on any given day. The latter figures were more like 580 Spits and 216 'Tiffies', as they were known, and some of these, he claimed, were needed for defence purposes. However, despite Hitler's orders, the numbers of enemy bombers and fighter bombers coming over were low. Leigh-Mallory could have spared plenty more fighters if he had been inclined to do so.

He had also weighed in on the issue of drop tanks. 'Acceleration of production of the 45 gallon drop tank has been urged by Fighter Command for some months,' wrote Leigh-Mallory, 'but the Fleet Air Arm, for whose use these tanks were originally designed, have prior claim.' It was an admission of the failure of Leigh-Mallory's command to plan for them earlier and betrayed either a total lack of understanding or even greater levels of disingenuousness. In fact, Spitfires were capable of carrying up to 216 gallons internally plus two 62-gallon drop tanks, giving them a theoretical range of 1,904 miles.* What's more,

---

* In fact, later models of Spitfire were capable of carrying as much as 500 gallons: 85- + 75- + 20- + 106-gallon internal fuel tanks and a 90-gallon slipper tank and 2 × 62-gallon drop tanks. This gave it a theoretical range of 2,700 miles, compared with the 434-mile range of an ordinary Spitfire.

if Leigh-Mallory had demanded them earlier and more emphatically, the Ministry for Aircraft Production would have produced them. Suggesting Fighter Command did not have drop tanks because of the Fleet Air Arm's superior claims was nonsense. It was a lack of will at the top that was the issue.

'It is becoming increasingly difficult,' Leigh-Mallory added, having dismissed the drop-tank option, 'to bring the German Fighter Force into action, for Germany's policy is to conserve her fighters and to use them only against large bomber formations, while avoiding engagement with escorting fighters.'

Portal gave his response to Arnold a leisurely ten days later. Fighter Command, he told him, was currently devoting 73 per cent of its total effort to offensive operations, of which 76 per cent was devoted to escorting American bombers. 'We intend to continue the offensive effort,' he wrote, 'and to continue the tactics designed to cover offensive operations or to provoke air battles.' But only within the limits of the Spitfire's standard range. He was emphatically drawing a line. The RAF was simply not prepared to engage in this discussion. They did not believe in long-range fighters, so it was left to Arnold, who had belatedly woken up to the urgent realization of what was required, somehow to find the solution before it was too late.

Even Eaker was only slowly realizing what was needed. Immediately after Schweinfurt, he had sent a long cable to Arnold, which included a list of three urgent requirements. The first was to rush through replacement aircraft and crews. Currently, Eaker told him, he was getting 143 planes and crews a month, but he needed at least 250. Second, 'send every possible fighter here as soon as possible. Especially emphasize earliest arrival of P-38s and Mustangs.' Finally, he wanted eight thousand drop tanks each month.

However, not until the end of October, more than two weeks after the second raid on Schweinfurt and a week after Portal's response, did Arnold order that all Mustangs, as well as P-38 Lightnings, should be sent exclusively to the Eighth Air Force. This was why Dick Turner and the rest of the 354th Fighter Group were now part of the Eighth Air Force after all, although they remained under administrative control of the Ninth. The trouble was, it would take time to bring enough of these superb fighters to England to make a decisive difference – one fighter group was not enough – and almost certainly longer than the January deadline Arnold had given Barney Giles back in June.

It was a case of missed opportunities: first, the RAF had failed to pursue long-range fighters with more drive earlier; and second, the length of time required since the revelation of the P-51B to realize its full potential. Had its long-range capability been thought about the previous autumn, the crisis now facing Allied air commanders might very well have been avoided altogether.

Meanwhile, in Germany, those in charge of defending the Reich were largely ignorant of the emergency facing their enemy. As far as they were concerned, the crisis seemed largely with them and the ongoing problem of how to find more and better fighters and, more importantly, more and better pilots. On 6 and 7 November, the commander of the newly formed I Jagdkorps, Generalmajor Beppo Schmid, called a meeting in Berlin with his senior commanders, including Dolfo Galland, General Hubert Weise and those in charge of the fighter divisions. Schmid had just received an order from Göring to destroy all enemy four-engine bombers while avoiding combat with Allied fighters. It was, of course, easier said than done, particularly with one hand tied behind their backs by the demands and restrictions imposed by the senior leadership.

Galland had already been trying to increase the size of the day-fighter force by poaching units from the Eastern Front and increasing the size of each *Geschwader* by adding an extra *Schwarm* of four aircraft to each *Staffel*, so bringing it up to sixteen aircraft, and an extra *Staffel* to every *Gruppe*, and a fourth *Gruppe* to each *Geschwader*. So far, he'd managed to enlarge both JG2 and JG26 in such a way. In all, this had bolstered the size of the fighter defence by nearly a thousand aircraft, which was no small number.

It was still not enough as far as Galland, Schmid and their divisional commanders were concerned. They were conscious only of a hydra's head developing in England with more and more bombers and fighters inevitably heading their way, and with their own numbers bleeding away badly. Göring's new order meant a switch in tactics was now necessary and at the Berlin Conference Schmid persuaded his commanders to move all fighter units back into the eastern part of Holland and to the Rhine area in order to avoid short-range fighter escorts and any attack by tactical bombers. He also accepted Weise's suggestion that, regardless of Göring's order, a small number of single-engine fighters should try to draw off the escort force, and in turn got agreement that the day-fighter force should concentrate efforts against one part of the bomber stream at a time. This played into time-honoured German principles of concentration of fire, but was a different approach to the successful tactics of Air Vice-Marshal Keith Park during the Battle of Britain; he had deliberately used his squadrons in pairs to peck away at and continually disrupt the flow of the Luftwaffe's bomber formations.

Another problem that was harder to square was the vast number of aircraft and pilots lost in flying accidents and to friendly fire. In the last four months of 1943, 967 Luftwaffe pilots would be shot down over Germany by the Allies, but a staggering 1,052 more without any help from the enemy. In part this was due to trigger-happy and inexperienced anti-aircraft gunners, and in part due to inexperienced pilots with sub-standard training. Galland had been trying to improve training by insisting each *Geschwader* sent its own instructors to the training schools from which it recruited its new pilots; this, he hoped, was improving the quality of the instructors. Since the Americans were still coming over in poor winter weather, there was now an urgent need for blind-flying training – flying using instruments only, rather than relying on being able to see out of the plane – but this was a corner that had been completely cut from the training schools. Galland had insisted on reintroducing blind-flying training, but the lack of fuel was hindering this. The truth was, Germany had long been fighting a war it could no longer afford.

At least good, competent and dynamic men were in charge. Schmid himself had begun the war as an intelligence officer on Göring's personal staff. A veteran of the Nazi's Beer Hall Putsch of 1923, he was a personal friend of his boss with very few qualifications for the role. His intelligence briefing on the RAF back in July 1940, before the Luftwaffe had launched its all-out attack, had been risible, but he had matured considerably since then and was still only forty-two. Göring had given him command of his ground panzer-grenadier division in Tunisia, and it was certainly true that many still regarded him as little more than one of Göring's lackeys. 'Some malicious tongues,' noted Hajo Herrmann, 'had said that we should have let the Americans have him, because he would have told a big pack of lies as he had previously told his own leaders.' However, Schmid's long years of observing the Luftwaffe high command and working alongside men like Galland, Falck and Weise had taught him much, so that by the autumn of 1943 he had a far wiser and more astute head on his shoulders. He also understood the importance of diplomacy – a vital characteristic when working through the myriad dynamics of Nazi command structures and politics. Herrmann, for one, thought Schmid was up to the task. 'I found him to be interested, ready to learn and of a practical turn of mind,' he noted.

The Berlin meeting resolved some tactical issues, but Schmid was already thinking of ways to wrest greater control of the flak units to his fighter units – and with it, he hoped, to cut the amount of home losses dramatically. Furthermore, the night-time defence of the Reich was in far better shape than it had been in July when Hamburg had been hit. That attack had caught the Luftwaffe out; they had not been prepared, but the combination of the intensity of the attack and the use of Window had forced dramatic changes. Kammhuber's *Himmelbett* system, quite sensible when first suggested, had long ago begun to creak and at Hamburg its limitations had been horribly exposed. Since then, not only had *Himmelbett* been super-seded, but Kammhuber himself had, in October, been posted away to take command of the Luftwaffe in Nor-way. How long Herrmann's *Wilde Sau* would prove effective was questionable, but there was no doubting the efficacy of the *Zahme Sau* tactics. Since Hamburg, the defence system had been further refined, the number of aircraft had been increased, as had the number of anti-aircraft guns: now more than twelve thousand were defending the Reich. Whatever Germany's long-term chances, this did mean the Luftwaffe was now a much tougher proposition than it had been back in July.

On Wednesday, 17 November, at Achmer to the north of Münster, Leutnant Heinz Knoke was awarded the German Cross of Gold for his sterling efforts. The presentation was made by the Reichsmarschall himself and beforehand a number of men from JG11 and other fighter units had been ordered to line up for an inspection. Göring eventually appeared in a motorcade of some thirty vehicles, then stepped out to speak to a number of the men, Knoke included; he was currently the leading ace in 2 Jagddivi-sion, with some fifteen heavy bombers to his name. Such a score hardly compared with the massive tallies gained by some on the Eastern Front, but few others had as many American heavies to their name. This impressed Göring, who paused to talk to him for around ten minutes. The Reichsmarschall was particularly interested that the previ-ous year Knoke had also managed to destroy a Mosquito – an aircraft with which Göring had become increasingly obsessed. The Mosquito, he told Knoke quite emphatically, was 'an infernal nuisance and pain in the neck.'

'Göring makes a most peculiar impression,' Knoke scribbled in his diary later, with his fancy grey uniform, plentiful gold braid and bulging legs sticking out of scarlet doeskin boots. 'The bloated puffy face makes him look to me like a sick man,' Knoke added. 'Close up, I am forced to the conclusion that he uses cosmetics.' On the other hand, he was cordial and seemed genuinely interested in what Knoke and his fellows had to say.

After the presentation of the medals, Göring then made a speech, talking openly about the difficulties that now faced them. They should, he told them, use the RAF's defence of Britain back in 1940 as an example of courage and determination. Knoke did not disagree, but he was left with a clear feeling that the commander-in-chief of the Luftwaffe had very little idea or understanding of what they now faced when engaging American bombers and fighters. 'The inescapable fact,' noted Knoke, echoing Wim Johnen's views, 'is that on the technical side our perform-ance is inferior in every respect.' As far as Knoke was concerned, the early victories of the war had led to the Luftwaffe leadership becoming complacent and resting on their laurels, and he blamed them for the chronic short-ages of decent planes and pilots. What successes they continued to have were, Knoke thought, purely down to the excellent morale and fighting spirit of the aircrews. 'We need more aircraft, better engines,' he noted in his final lines for that day, 'and fewer Headquarters.'

In England, Ira Eaker's demands for more men and more machines were being answered, but he was competing with a new strategic air force being established in Italy. Following the successful invasion of Sicily, the British had urged their American coalition partners to press on and invade Italy too. The Fascist dictator, Benito Mussolini, had been deposed and his replacement, Marshal Pietro Badoglio, had agreed an armistice, which had come into effect on 8 September 1943. The American chiefs were initially against invading Italy, which they saw as a further distraction and drain of resources from the main goal, the cross-Channel invasion in May 1944. However, both General Dwight D. Eisenhower, the Supreme Allied Commander in the Mediterranean, and General Tooey Spaatz, now US Twelfth Air Force commander in North Africa, were big advocates of the initiative, as it would put other vital POINTBLANK targets within easier range. So too was Portal, and soon enough both General George Marshall, the US Chief of Staff, and Hap Arnold were persuaded by these arguments. Further boosting the strategy was the revelation, from decoded German signals, that Hitler intended to abandon Italy up to the Pisa–Rimini Line, some 150 miles north of Rome. What's more, it was agreed that the build-up of strategic air forces would be given priority over ground forces.

British Eighth Army had invaded the southern tip of Sicily on 1 September, but the day after the armistice, 9 September, US General Mark Clark's Anglo-American Fifth Army had landed at Salerno, to the south of Naples. Although the landing had been successful, the German commander, the Luftwaffe Feldmarschall Albert Kesselring, had defended so voraciously that Hitler had been persuaded to fight for every yard of that mountain- and river-covered peninsula. Then the weather swiftly turned, with persistent and heavy rain. Suddenly, instead of an easy victory and Rome captured by Christmas, the Allied forces faced a resource-sapping and soul-destroying slog up one of the most brutal places imaginable in which to fight. Nor were the ground forces helped by the priority being given to the build-up of air forces.

That, however, went largely according to plan, with the capture of the all-important Foggia airfields on 27 September. Roughly a third of the way up the leg of Italy, Foggia was one of the few flat areas in the country and its capture meant that, at the beginning of October, Arnold had been able to draw up plans and get approval for the creation of the Fifteenth Air Force, with the existing Twelfth Air Force becoming the tactical force to support the ground operations. Transferred to the new strategic air force would be the Twelfth's six heavy-bomber groups, plus fifteen more from the United States. Unsurprisingly, Eaker had protested against such a move. From 15 October, he had become commander-in-chief of all US Army Air Forces in Britain – the equivalent of an army group commander – and was in charge of both the Eighth and Ninth Air Forces. The demands on him were enormous, the expectations incredibly high, and yet he was simply not getting the tools he needed. In a long memo to Arnold he pointed out that of the 113 key targets outlined by POINTBLANK, only 10 per cent were closer to Italy than England. He also argued that, while the weather was probably better in Italy – actually, it wasn't – the weather over the target was what really mattered and aiming and navigation devices like H2X and Oboe were available only to crews operating from England. What's more, facilities were better and more established in England and it was an easier place to maintain operationally. The defenders of the Reich, he pointed out, faced west, not south, and in order to beat them he needed the largest force possible. 'It is axiomatic,' he argued, 'that our loss rate goes down as the force builds up. The movement of several groups out of the UK leaves a diminished force which must face the concentration of defenses in Western Europe. It can be expected, therefore that our losses will be heavier.'

These arguments fell on deaf ears and, valid though they were, there was no doubting that having strategic air forces operating from Italy put huge extra strain on the German defence of the Reich. The oilfields of Ploesti in Romania, for example, Germany's one real source of that liquid gold, were in range only from the bombers in Italy. There was also a psychological benefit in attacking not only from the west but also from the south – a theatre about which Hitler had always been hugely paranoid and to which he attached enormous strategic significance. In any case, while weight of numbers was unquestionably important to the success of the Eighth's bombing efforts, the rapid build-up of long-range P-51s was even more vital and none of those precious fighters was heading to the Fifteenth Air Force. Not in 1943 at any rate.

The Fifteenth had been formally activated on 1 November, but although heavies were now operating from the Foggia area and the build-up of supplies was continuing apace, the 2nd Bombardment Group was still based at Tunis in North Africa. Despite its number, the 2nd BG was actually the first US bomb group and had been formed in September 1918 in France as the 1st Day Bombardment Group. It had survived the cuts at the end of the First World War and been redesignated the 2nd in 1923. Although it had not been the first group to be sent across the Atlantic, it had been in action – first on anti-submarine watch – since America's entry into the war. Stationed in North Africa since April, it had more than played its part in the final stages of the Tunisian campaign and subsequent invasion of Sicily and mainland Italy.

Only recently arrived, however, was Lieutenant T. Michael Sullivan, a replacement bombardier from Elgin, Illinois. Sullivan had joined the Army Air Force in April 1942, and, having completed his training, had finally been shipped overseas on 23 September 1943 in a large, 65-ship convoy to Casablanca, arriving after what had seemed like an interminably long voyage on 11 October. Just under a week later, he flew the final leg in a C-47 Dakota along with fourteen others plus baggage. A storm, however, brought them an early landing in Algiers. 'Went to town, ate, I drank wine,' he scribbled in his diary. 'Just like the movies . . . Harbor littered with sunken ships. Town torn up a bit.' The following day, he finally reached his allotted squadron, the 429th of the 2nd BG at Tunis. For a young man who had barely left the Midwest before joining up, it was quite an eye-opener: burned planes and tanks all over the place, tented accommodation and almost no facilities, and only two crews on base, as the rest were busy bombing Araxos aerodrome in Greece. This involved a three-day trip, staging at Foggia, bombing the target, remaining another night and then flying back to Tunis.

On 22 October, Sullivan had flown a practice mission over the islands of Pantelleria and Sicily, then the next day, Saturday, 23 October, he had joined Lieutenant John C. Goodfellow's crew in Flying Fortress *Wolf Pack* and flown to a B-25 base at Grottaglie, near Taranto in the heel of southern Italy, each man equipped with his flying kit, mess kit and a bed roll. 'Ate a rotten supper,' noted

Sullivan. 'Slept on marble floor in operations.' At 5.30 a.m. they were woken and by 8 a.m. were airborne. The target was Wiener Neustadt, the site of seven Messer-schmitt facilities in Austria, which, according to Allied intelligence, were now producing 20 per cent of all Ger-man single-engine fighters and 40 per cent of Me109s.

There were some two hundred bombers and fifty P-38 escorts for the mission, of which the 2nd BG was provid-ing forty-two Fortresses. Unfortunately, a petrol-dump fire at Ponte Olivo airfield on Sicily prevented the thirteen B-17s staging there to take part, but despite this and des-pite thick ten-tenths cloud, the entire force managed to form up over Foggia and then head north towards Aus-tria, although the four bomb groups involved struggled to keep in formation and soon became strung out. The bad weather, however, played into the Americans' hands, as the Luftwaffe remained firmly on the ground; on the other hand, visibility over the target was almost non-existent and only a mere five bombers managed to drop their loads in the vicinity of the target. 'Impossible to see target,' noted Sullivan. 'Washout mission.' All that effort had been for nothing, but at least Sullivan had chalked up his first mission. Tours were of different lengths in the Mediterranean theatre – fifty missions rather than twenty-five. So only another forty-nine to go.

A few days later, on the 29th, Sullivan flew with a dif-ferent crew to bomb a ball-bearing factory at Turin, but the Fortress developed engine trouble and so they were forced to turn back early. Then weather once again inter-vened. 'Raid called off. Bad weather,' he noted on 5 November. 'Raid again called off, bad weather,' he scrib-bled two days later. That same day he learned that his friend, Frank McGinley, had been killed on the group's second attempt on Wiener Neustadt five days earlier. They had been in the same training crew together back in the States. 'It cut me deeply,' wrote Sullivan. 'He was an old friend and a swell kid. I'll pray for him.' Two days after that, he and his crew suffered a flat tyre on their Fortress and so could not take off. Three days later, engine trouble kept him grounded again. Then, on Saturday, 13 November, he hitched a ride into Tunis in a 'Limey truck' which then crashed and rolled four times. Sullivan was lucky to get away with a bruised arm and sprained leg, but his pal 'Mac' McKew cut his head, which bled profusely. Next day, Sunday, was Sullivan's twentieth birthday. 'I'm out of my teens,' he scribbled in his diary. 'I feel as if someone beat me with a baseball bat. Can scarcely walk.'

Not until Monday, 22 November did he finally fly another mission – this time to bomb the naval base at Toulon – but once more bad weather intervened. Neither Sullivan nor the Fifteenth was having much luck. On paper, establishing the new strategic air force had seemed a sound idea. After all, Italy was a place of sunshine, azure skies and citrus groves, where the dense fog of England could never be found.

Except in the winter of 1943, when the cloud, rain and cold seemed to have descended over much of war-torn Europe. Nor was it about to change.

CHAPTER 10

New Arrivals

AIR MARSHAL SIR ARTHUR Harris had wanted to hit Berlin in August, immediately after Hamburg, but at that time he had been hamstrung: the capital of the Reich had been beyond the range of Oboe; he still did not have enough Lancasters for the job; and he had to contend with the vagaries of the weather. As if to prove the point, the three times he had sent his bombers there at the end of August and the beginning of September the raids had been marred by the limitations of H2S radar. By the middle of November, however, Harris had more aircraft – over eight hundred heavies most days – and a number of Pathfinder aircraft were now equipped with H2S Mk IIIs, as well as with a new Ground Position Indicator, making it possible to carry out accurate timed runs to the target even when flying through heavy flak. The time had come, Harris believed, for a sustained assault on Berlin. Other cities would continue to be hit, but the German capital was to be the focus and nearly all operations were now to take place deep inside the Reich. This would place an extra strain on the crews, but Harris believed that if these attacks were properly driven home, the sacrifices made by his bomber crews would save the lives of many, many more. Berlin, though, was further away than Hamburg, better defended, and its attack would not be catching the Luftwaffe off guard again. Nor were Hitler and the Nazi leadership conducting the war in a rational and logical way.

What Harris would call the Battle of Berlin began on the night of 18/19 November, although only 444 aircraft were sent to the city, while 395, mostly Halifaxes and Stirlings, were sent to Mannheim and Ludwigshafen. Among those leading the way were twenty-one Halifaxes from the Pathfinders of 35 Squadron. The Pathfinder Force, of necessity, had among the best and most experienced navigators, as its task was to direct the rest of the bomber stream on to the target as accurately as possible. Flight Lieutenant Gordon Carter had been posted to 35 Squadron straight from training the previous October, when still only nineteen, but with consistently high marks at every step. His night vision had been 'exceptional'; his navigational skills 'Well above average'. He had also been praised for his maturity and singled out for a commission. 'Calm and confident. Very mature for age. Intelligent. Deep thinker.' He had also proved a brilliant navigator. 'This man,' wrote the examiner in his final navigation report, 'knows his navigation and exploits it to the Nth degree.'

Carter had never really intended to join the RAF. The son of a New Zealander father and English mother, he had had a peripatetic upbringing, living in Paris until he was thirteen and then in New York. In the summer of 1939, with war looming, the family made trip to see Europe and England, after which Carter began his freshman year at Dartmouth College in New Hampshire. He spoke French fluently, though by this time he had become thoroughly Americanized; none the less, he felt fiercely British and patriotic, despite never having lived there, and as he completed his first year at Dartmouth he became increasingly concerned about Britain's plight and certain that he needed to do something to help. To begin with, he thought about joining the navy, but then decided it would be better to get involved directly without actually having to kill people – a 'mild sort of conscientious objection'. Getting passage to England proved next to impossible, but as his eighteenth birthday approached in the summer of 1941, he took himself to Montreal in Canada to try to join some non-combatant relief outfit.

He was turned down by a Canadian Scots field ambulance unit preparing to ship to the Far East for being too young – or so he was told – although extreme disappointment became relief some months later when Singapore was overrun by the Japanese. Instead, he turned to the RCAF, which he formally joined on 8 July 1942. Although quickly side-lined away from becoming a pilot, he swotted up his maths and made sure he applied himself to the considerable challenges of becoming a navigator. Immediately earmarked for the Pathfinder Force, in 1943 he was commissioned and a few weeks later finally headed back across the Atlantic and, eventually, to 35 Squadron at Graveley, near Huntingdon in Cambridgeshire.

The PFF had been formed only a couple of months earlier, and Carter swiftly realized that, for all his high marks in training, navigation was both difficult and challenging, especially in a Pathfinder and supposedly leading the way. GEE, Oboe and the advent of H2S all helped, but navigating still involved a fair amount of dead-reckoning – or

DR – which meant manually calculating courses and times on the strength of predicted winds. Weather forecasting was notoriously difficult and far too often the weather briefings proved inaccurate. Carter always had to make his own estimations of wind speed by repeatedly calculating drift and then making the appropriate adjustments. This was not necessarily easy, particularly once deep in Germany and beyond the range of GEE, which would otherwise help determine position by providing a 'fix', as it was known. Astro-navigation was used too, but relied on the pilot flying straight and level until stars could be lined up – which was fine over the North Sea, for example, but not such a good idea over Germany. Multiple challenges remained, even by the autumn of 1943. 'We were blinded by darkness and thick clouds,' Carter noted, 'which often used to shake us up quite badly and which were the cause, every so often, of very near misses, another aircraft suddenly flashing past or "sitting" on us, or just squeezing past beneath us.' Carter's was a job of constant calculations and anxiety, of checking and double-checking his Dalton computer – a kind of slide-rule – as well as maintaining an event-by-event log throughout any trip. He kept his eye glued to his watch and desperately tried to keep his jottings and course markings neat and clear, despite operating in temperatures as low as –50°C at 20,000 feet and with flak bursting all around. The demands on pilots, bomb-aimers and navigators like Carter are barely comprehensible.

Carter joined Flying Officer Tommy Thomas's crew at Graveley and soon began to rack up missions. On 13 February 1943, the target was the U-boat pens at Lorient in France. Carter found the Blavet river and led them directly to the target. No sooner had they released their target indicators, however, than they were hit by flak. In moments, fire was pouring from the port inner engine. Thomas dived to try to put it out, but to no avail, and soon after gave the order for them to bail out. Carter had snapped back his folding table and seat, clipped his parachute to his harness, pulled up the floor hatch and lowered himself so that his feet were dangling out. Immediately, one of his boots was whipped off in the slipstream. 'Navigator bailing out!' he called, then remembered in the nick of time to pull off his flying helmet with its intercom and oxygen leads. Clutching the ripcord, his guts cramping with fear, he jumped into the void. After the worst anguish he had ever known, the parachute opened and he was jerked upwards before drifting gently down to the ground.

So began two months of escape and evasion. All but one of the crew had successfully made it out of the aircraft. Carter had landed in Brittany, south-west of Carhaix, and was immediately picked up by the Resistance. Passed from one safe house to another, he and another of his crew, 'Nap' Barry, who had also bailed out but landed elsewhere, were due to be picked up from the coast by a British submarine, but the rendezvous failed and instead they were sent to Paris, where they were due to meet with Tommy Thomas. That failed too, so they returned to Brittany, where Carter fell in love with and became engaged to Janine Jouanjean, the sister of a local Resistance leader. Eventually, in early April, he managed to get away on a forty-foot Breton sardine boat and, despite a storm and heavy swell much of the way, safely reached Newlyn in Cornwall. Tommy Thomas, meanwhile, had reached Switzerland, where he was interned, while three others, including Nap Barry, got to Spain and eventually back to England. Only one of the crew had been caught. After a formal debriefing by MI9, by 27 April Carter was back at RAF Graveley.

Since then he had flown a further twenty-five operations with a new crew, including over Hamburg in July, had been awarded the Distinguished Flying Cross and now, still aged only twenty, was one of the most experienced navigators in the squadron. It didn't make the trip to Mannheim on the night of 18/19 November any easier, though – not with 40-knot winds, intense flak and plenty of night-fighters about.

Carter and his crew, skippered by Squadron Leader Julian Sale, were designated 'visual markers', rather than 'supporters' or 'back-up' who followed behind the initial markers. Their task was to drop flares on top of the target, which was primarily the Daimler-Benz factory. For once the sky was clear, with no cloud at all over the city. Having got them there, Carter handed over to the bomb-aimer for the bomb run – although they were not bombs but flares. This was always the worst moment: flying straight and level, flak bursting all around, and a terrible feeling of helpless vulnerability. The crew were silent, almost breathless.

'Bomb doors open,' came the voice of the bomb-aimer, who then called out for minor adjustments of course. Then, at 8.40 p.m., 'Bombs gone,' and they dropped their load from the comparatively low height of 10,000 feet: four lots of white flares and three batches of marker candles, which floated down in parachuted canisters then burst, spewing a cascade of a thousand marker candles each, falling pools of glowing light that caused a photographic flash as they triggered the camera. Then the pilot flung the plane into heavy evasive action, pushed the stick forward to gain speed and got away from the inferno as quickly as possible.

Also flying that mission were Bill Byers and his crew, on what was their first trip since the loss of George. The strong winds pushed them far off course and instead they hit Frankfurt, but made it back safely. It was unusual to fly two nights in a row, but they were back in the air again the following night – this time to Leverkusen, near Cologne. 'I think if I had stopped,' said Bill, 'I might have broke down.'

Berlin was hit again on the night of 22/23 November, this time by 764 aircraft, causing several firestorms due to the recent stretch of dry weather. The next day, the smoke cloud over the city reached 19,000 feet and could be seen for miles. Some 3,000 houses and 23 industrial plants were completely destroyed and many thousands more properties damaged. More than 175,000 people were left homeless and over 50,000 troops were brought in to help clear up the damage. It was on this night that the famous Kaiser Wilhelm Memorial Church was destroyed. So too were more than 2,000 people. Another 383 bombers returned the following night and 443 on the night of 26/27 November, both raids killing a further 2,000 and more. Harris was certainly hitting Berlin hard, but at a cost: between 18 and 27 November, Bomber Command lost 131 aircraft – and over 900 aircrew.

In his new offices near the Olympic Park in the west of Berlin, Hajo Herrmann was now not only Inspector of

Night-fighters but also commander of the *Wilde Sau* 30 Jagddivision. Göring, like Hitler, favoured a divide-and-rule approach to leadership and, with it, lots of parallel command structures, which meant that although the *Wilde Sau* came under the jurisdiction of Beppo Schmid as CO of the Jagdkorps, Herrmann was subordinate not to him but rather to General Hans-Jürgen Stumpff, commander of the Central Area. In practical terms, this meant Herrmann had free rein and, if answerable to anyone, it was to Göring.

Suddenly, he was a colonel with his own staff and far-reaching responsibilities, with influence in areas of training, tactics and even procurement. To discuss matters of procurement and supply he had driven through Berlin to the giant Zoo Flakturm – flak tower – complex for a meeting with the Armaments Minister, Albert Speer, on the evening of 22 November. Three of these monster edifices had been built in the capital, each enormous and utterly dominating the part of the city in which it stood. The main Zoo Flakturm – the 'G-tower' – was 135 feet high and over 200 feet wide, contained seven levels including a hospital, ammunition stores and offices, and had walls 8 feet thick. It could hold up to eight thousand civilians and the array of anti-aircraft guns on the roof were connected by underground cables to a smaller 'L-tower', which contained the radio and radar systems. It stood over the old zoological gardens like a massive concrete Norman keep.

Herrmann met Speer in the L-tower, which was the command and control post. During the meeting, the air-raid sirens sounded and, once he had finished his meeting with the Reichsminister, Herrmann hurried up to the roof of the tower where the Würzburg and Mannheim radars were situated along with the rangefinder. Young Luftwaffe soldiers were busy manning this sophisticated technology. Not far away, fallen incendiaries were stuck in the trees and burning on the pavements. 'There was a shrill organ concert of thousands of flak splinters whistling down and striking sparks from the concrete as they landed,' Herrmann noted, 'punctuated by the cracking of bombs and the pressure waves of aerial mines. All around me was a light-grey to white luminous sea of fog. In the centre of this chaos the young men on their exposed tower carried out their duty. I was appalled. This was what the terror looked like to the eyes of a defenceless victim.'

Herrmann left and drove back to his headquarters at Staaken through burning streets. He felt utterly overwhelmed, his mind stunned and conflicted; he wasn't sure whether there was any hope left. Should they now admit defeat? This was exactly what Harris had been bargaining on, but by the time he arrived Herrmann felt resolved to do more to take the fight to the enemy; the weather might be awful, but his *Wilde Sau* would have to brave it. They could not sit back and let this carnage happen in the city.

Bomber Command were back the next night, but the weather was terrible once more: the cloud base was at just 100 feet and it was treacherously cold. Herrmann agonized over whether to send his men up in such conditions, so instead asked for volunteers. Only those who felt confident enough should put themselves forward, he told them. Of the thirty pilots at Staaken, seven raised their hands. Herrmann followed them out; he was forbidden to fly – on Göring's direct orders – so watched them from the control tower. The visibility had not improved. 'It was cold and damp,' he wrote, 'and I found myself shivering again. But it wasn't only because of the weather. I was asking myself where the war was taking us, and wondering whether we were asking too much of our airmen and of our civilian population.'

He waited up, cursing himself for having sent any of them out, but after several long, cold and dispiriting hours they all returned and landed safely. 'I gave thanks to God,' wrote Herrmann.

New crews were arriving during the autumn of 1943 to bolster the Eighth's bomber force, some flying over the Atlantic, others taking the long voyage by sea. Factories in the USA were building more and more bombers and fighter aircraft; American industry was operating at full speed, reaping the rewards of the conversion from civilian to war economy. At Willow Run, for example, what two years earlier had been a rather featureless creek east of Detroit was now the world's largest single factory, more than a mile long. The brainchild of Charles Sorensen, one of the Ford automobile company's senior executives, it was an assembly-line building under licence Consolidated B-24 bombers. With no threat from any enemy bombers, it could afford to be the world's largest room, and could operate round the clock and with maximum efficiency. Factories like this were helping the US build a staggering 8,574 heavy bombers in 1943 alone. Even so, Eaker was still receiving fewer than the 250 per month he had demanded.

Among the newcomers were Lieutenant Belford J. 'BJ' Keirsted and his B-17 crew, who arrived at Knettishall in Suffolk in October to join the 563rd Bomb Squadron of the 388th Bomb Group. The radio operator was 21-year-old Larry Goldstein, a New Yorker from Brooklyn. From a large Jewish family, Goldstein was the fourth child of six. Soon after Pearl Harbor, his older brother joined the Marines and Goldstein tried to follow suit, but was turned away. Instead, he joined the Air Corps and, to his delight, was sent straight to Miami Beach for basic training. Having always had an interest in aviation, from reading about aircraft to making models as a kid, he had dreamed of one day becoming a pilot, but instead was earmarked to become a radio operator and posted to a school in Chicago. Passing out in March 1943, he then went back to Florida to attend radar school in Boca Raton, and from there to a replacement depot at Salt Lake City, which was where he volunteered for flying status. 'I was impressed with the glamour of flying,' he said, 'and all that went with it – the silver wings of the gunner, the promotions, and the flight pay.' Hustled off on to a gunnery course, he had no idea that plans were already afoot to create the largest air force in the world.

After gunnery school he was sent to a brand-new airfield at Moses Lake, Washington State, where he saw his first B-17 and was allocated a crew, with Keirsted as pilot and Clifford 'Ace' Conklin as co-pilot. 'I must admit,' Goldstein recalled, 'that when I sat in my radio position of the B-17, I was overwhelmed in not knowing where I was, what I was supposed to do.' He had sat in mock-ups during training, but the reality seemed very different. This was hardly surprising. The B-17 looked solid and rugged from the outside, but on board it was a slightly different matter. The prime objective of wartime heavies was to drop bombs. On board, the Fortress, like other bombers, was little more than a tin can: cramped, difficult to move about in and a largely alien environment for new aircrew experiencing the plane for the first time. The entry hatch was about two-thirds of the way down the fuselage on the starboard – right-hand – side. Only the tail gunner turned left to his isolated position at the rear of the plane. The two waist gunners had the easiest route to their stations along a narrow wooden walkway, but the machine guns were open to the elements, with wooden ammunition boxes either side hooked to the aircraft's sides. No part of the aircraft was pressurized and so at bombing heights the crew all had to operate with oxygen and at sub-zero temperatures. This meant they had to wear electric sheepskin flying suits that could all too often short-circuit with all the movement the crew had to carry out. Goldstein's station as a radio man was better than some – he did at least have a small table and chair – but he could see little and it was incredibly noisy, and it took a bit of adjusting to be able to use his hands freely while wearing gloves in a heavily vibrating aircraft.

Then there was the ball-turret gunner, who had to squat into a hydraulically controlled ball that was fixed to the underside of the plane and had an entry and exit hatch that was, again, in no way generously proportioned. Wearing a parachute while in the ball turret was inconceivable and the position was a lonely and isolated one. Most tended to sit up in the fuselage until over enemy territory, but that could still mean spending several hours squashed into the turret.

Up front were the navigator, pilot, co-pilot and bombardier, who accessed the aircraft from a hatch on the lower port side of the cockpit. This stood quite high off the ground with no ladder, so the technique was to grip the sides, swing the legs upwards and then hoist oneself in. The four up front had reasonably comfortable seats, but the noise was incredible; communication without headsets and a fully functioning intercom was inconceivable. All around were a multitude of wires and electrics, any one of which might get damaged and cause problems. The truth was, young men were not really designed to fly in tight formation on oxygen in temperatures of up to minus 50° for hours on end and in rattling, noisy, cramped, largely comfortless conditions – and that was without being shot at or flying through dense flak. It was a feature of the war that, while technology and mechanization were taking a giant leap forward, much less thought had been given to those expected to operate these machines.

None the less, Goldstein soon got to grips with the demands of the job, helped by the immediate gelling of the crew, who nicknamed him 'Goldie'. Like so many other aircrews, they were a mixed bunch and unlikely ever to have worn a military uniform had it not been for the war. BJ Keirsted, the pilot, had been a professional ballroom dancer with his sister, with the stage name 'Jan and Janis'. Ace Conklin had been a business student and had initially been a bit sceptical about playing second fiddle to a dancer, but Keirsted soon proved a natural leader. 'I'm not interested in your personal life,' he told his new crew. 'I'm only interested in what you can do for the crew. And I want every man to learn his position. Maybe in combat, one of us may save the lives of the other nine.' Only the rear gunner, Bob Miller, seemed to be the odd one out. 'Strange guy,' wrote Goldstein in his diary. 'A loner, never seemed to hang out with us as a crew.' Miller aside, by the time they had finished working up together and were finally posted overseas in early October, they were not only firm buddies but also trusted one another implicitly.

Goldstein hated the five-day crossing aboard the *Queen Mary* – the constant zig-zagging to avoid U-boats, the cramped conditions and the terrible English food. He soon stopped eating the issued fare and lived off Hershey bars instead. They docked in Greenock and there followed a train ride, then a truck ride, until finally they were at Knettishall, just down the road from Thorpe Abbotts. It was another vast airfield, seemingly sprung up, as if by magic, over the past year: 50-yard-wide concrete runways, a 2,000-yard main runway, two T2-type hangars and a new airfield village hastily completed, with brick operations rooms, airfield headquarters, mess quarters and accommodation blocks. American war production was impressive, but so too were the speed and efficiency with which British construction firms were laying down huge numbers of new airfields. The 388th BG had been there since June, but for new crews like Keirsted's it seemed as though the bomb group had been there for ever.

A stark reminder of what faced them now they were in England and on the bomber front line occurred the night they arrived. Larry Goldstein, along with the five other enlisted men in the crew, were shown their barracks – a Nissen hut, with six others already there and a number of empty beds. 'Where are these guys?' one of them asked.

'Oh, they all went down in the last few days.' That was when Goldstein realized he had volunteered for this. He wondered why he hadn't taken the trouble to find out a little bit more about it beforehand.

When they first met their new ground crew, BJ asked

the crew chief how many crews he had had. 'You're my third,' came the reply. 'The other two went down.' That was since June – just four months.

'We will make it,' Keirsted assured him. 'You can mark that down.'

Mission No. 1 for the crew of *Worry Wart* – as they had named their ship – finally took place on Friday, 26 November. The target was Bremen, and it was the first time the Eighth had ventured into Germany for almost a fortnight. Goldie Goldstein and the rest of the crew were woken at 3.30 a.m., the world outside still pitch black. Trucks came to collect them and take them to breakfast, which included fresh eggs rather than the powdered version. Then it was to the crew rooms to get their flying kit before heading to the briefing. 'It was all very strange to me,' Goldstein scrawled in his diary, 'but will probably be into the swing of things soon.' From the briefing, they were taken by trucks to their waiting Fortress. Take-off was 8 a.m. They climbed through the cloud and began the forming-up process. There were three bomb divisions in the Eighth, much like the groups of Bomber Command. Each flew in its own formation, and each bomb squadron flew in a formation with its bomb group. In all, 440 heavies were flying that morning on the Bremen trip, with five bomb groups contributing to the 3rd Division's effort, of which the 388th from Knettishall was one. They sent up forty-one B-17s.

As bomber raids over Germany went, it was a comparatively quiet one. The crew of *Worry Wart* didn't see any enemy fighters, although Goldstein found the flak uncomfortable. 'The two most welcome expressions heard over the interphone are, "Bombs away,"' he noted, 'and "England just ahead."' Twenty-five bombers were lost that day, including one from the 388th that collided with another Fortress and one that was hit by incendiaries dropped from a bomber above them.

Goldstein was absolutely exhausted by the time they landed safely back down again. It shocked him how tired he was. Five hours on oxygen hadn't helped, he supposed. 'I will have to work out a system of preparing for the missions,' he wrote in his final entry that day. 'Only 24 more to go.'

Three days later, it was the turn of Hugh 'Mac' McGinty to notch up his first mission with 524th Bomb Squadron in the 379th Bomb Group, part of the 1st Division, at Kimbolton, not far from Gordon Carter and the Pathfinders at RAF Graveley. McGinty had turned twenty-one on the 27th and, like Goldie Goldstein, had been rapidly discovering the reality of what he had let himself in for. From Philadelphia, he had put himself down for the Air Corps because he had always loved aviation, but because he hadn't completed high school he had been denied his choice and was instead sent to the Field Artillery along with one of his brothers, Lucky. A reprieve came soon after, however, when he was told he could apply to join the Army Air Forces as an air gunner. It had been the chance he'd been waiting for. His brother, however, had not been impressed. 'Lucky couldn't believe I could be so stupid,' he noted, 'but in his usual way said, "If you go, I'll go too."' Both were packed off to gunnery school, but were also taught armoury and then were put into the air to further hone their skills. The brothers had loved it. By June 1943 they were at Salt Lake City and sent to join their respective crews. Hugh became tail gunner and 1st armourer under Lieutenant Ernal Bridwell. 'The ten-man crew,' noted McGinty, 'made you feel like you were part of a team. We soon became a family.'

Just before they departed for England, they heard about the Schweinfurt raid and the huge losses, but despite this they headed across the Atlantic with morale high, full of youthful eagerness to get on with the job. Kimbolton, however, dampened McGinty's spirits. The relentless grey weather and the rain got to him; he felt the chill all the way to his bones; the mess hall was half an hour's walk away; the mattress on his bed was thin and filled with horsehair. The showers were invariably cold and he was usually even colder by the time he got back to their hut. Although still every bit as keen to get on with the job, now it was so that he could get his twenty-five missions done and get back home – yet for the first two weeks, all they were allowed to fly were practice missions.

Then he heard there was a shortage of tail gunners, so he volunteered to fly as a spare gunner with one of the veteran crews. 'I figured it would give me valuable experience,' he wrote, 'and get my missions completed quicker.' Training on the job like this happened fairly often for all crew positions. The tail gunner had an unenviable location in the B-17. To get to his position, McGinty had to clamber to the left of the entry hatch in the fuselage, then over the elevator spar, by which time he was on his hands and knees. The fuselage now began to narrow dramatically. At the very far end of the bomber was his station: a narrow padded seat on which he perched on his knees with his legs back. Sitting like this for any period of time – especially in the bulky flight suit – was uncomfortable to say the very least. The entire position was cramped, claustrophobic and isolated from the rest of the crew. It was next to impossible to sit there with a parachute attached, so that tended to be left just behind. He had an escape hatch, but it was about 8 feet back and to one side and not big – not big enough to readily slip out of in full flying gear, at any rate. And while his immediate visibility was reasonable, he still had a twin .50-calibre machine gun in front of him and could see absolutely nothing behind. How so many put up with operating in such appalling conditions is hard to fathom.

McGinty, however, seemed to take it in his stride and, two days after his birthday, flew his first mission with Lieutenant George E. Hemphill's crew. They had already flown fifteen operations, but had recently brought back two wounded and one dead. McGinty's normal crew's bombardier, Matty Nathan, also flew with him that day. The target, once again, was Bremen.

All went well on the journey out, although McGinty was not impressed by the idle chat over the intercom – in Keirsted's crew, they had trained to keep radio silence unless speaking was essential. There were only 154 bombers for this mission, but some 314 Thunderbolts escorted them, including Bob Johnson and Gabby Gabreski from the 56th Fighter Group, and while these Little Friends were with them, the German fighters, as ordered by Göring, kept away.

All too soon, however, the Thunderbolts turned for home and suddenly Me109s, Me110s and FW190s were hurtling into them. From his position in the tail, McGinty could see much of this and watched as bombers started to smoke and burn. Tracer criss-crossed the sky and as the wounded bombers fell out of formation, so the enemy fighters tore into them like jackals. He tried to count the parachutes, but not everyone was getting out.

Then came the flak, which grew progressively thicker as the fighters became more aggressive. Now all their guns were clattering, while the men were calling out over the intercom, warning of fighters. Then they were gone and the Fortress was jolting and rattling with the flak burst, which battered against the airframe like hail. They were supposed to be flying straight and level on the bomb run, but it didn't feel like either, they were being jolted so much. At last it was 'Bombs away' and they climbed with a surge, but as they turned the enemy fighters reappeared and McGinty found himself firing almost without respite. He wasn't sure whether he hit any, but it seemed to keep them from getting too close.

And then, at long last, the P-47s returned and they were back over the North Sea, heading for home. McGinty had never seen a more welcome coastline, but what was clear one moment was then lost as the fog rolled in once more. Suddenly, they were on their own, the formation completely scattered, and flying through dense cloud. Only by calling a fix did they eventually find Kimbolton again, the pilot touching down through the fog with their fuel dangerously low. Nine hours they had been airborne, and the Fortress had three bullet holes to prove it, but unlike two others from the group and thirteen in all on the mission, they had made it. McGinty had chalked up mission number one, but the reality was that only 26 per cent – that is, one in four crews – could expect to make it through the next twenty-four.

*

The Flying Fortress might have been the mainstay of the Eighth's 1st and 3rd Divisions, but the 2nd was equipped with the Consolidated B-24 Liberator. This rather ungainly-looking four-engine bomber had begun life in 1939 after Consolidated Aircraft had been asked by the Air Corps to build B-17s under licence. Instead, and rather like North American Aviation with the P-51, they had reckoned they could produce something even better. On 1 February 1939 the Air Corps had issued a Type Specification C-212, which demanded a new heavy bomber with greater range, speed and a higher ceiling than the B-17, and had been prompted by Consolidated's early design ideas. They had duly been given a contract on the understanding that the prototype be ready for flight by December that year.

Not only had Consolidated made the deadline – just – they had also created a heavy bomber with a revolutionary high-efficiency airfoil wing system, designed by David R. Davis. The wings were larger than those of the B-17 and, with the airfoil design, thicker at the centre too, which allowed for greater fuel capacity. In terms of range, there was nothing to touch it. The high wings also allowed for a chunky fuselage, which could accommodate up to 4 tons of bombs – more than the B-17 – and made the plane more comfortable for those crewing it. Furthermore, it had a tricycle undercarriage, which gave it far greater visibility on the ground and made it easier to operate while taxiing. It was also slightly faster than the Fortress, with a top speed of 290 m.p.h. but a significantly higher cruise speed of around 215–20 m.p.h., compared with around 180–85 m.p.h. for the Fortress.

The British and French had immediately ordered

heavily, but when France fell in June 1940 the French orders were transferred to the British. Because of its range, the B-24 was used primarily by the RAF for anti-submarine patrols, but also in the Middle East, and its range ensured it was the first heavy bomber to fly regularly across the Atlantic. Furthermore, the first USAAF bomber unit sent to join the war against Nazi Germany was a group of twenty-three B-24s, known as the Halverson Provisional Detachment, posted to fly side by side with RAF Middle East in Egypt in June 1942. The B-24 became the most produced bomber in the world.

None the less, its payload was nothing like as large as that of a Lancaster, nor was the plane as robust as the B-17; those highly efficient airfoil wings, especially, were vulnerable. It was one of the main reasons why there were more B-17s in the Eighth than B-24s. Opinion about and loyalty to the two US bombers was divided.

One of those who favoured the B-24 was Hollywood film star Jimmy Stewart, now a captain in the USAAF. On Thursday, 25 November, he arrived in the UK to take command of the 703rd Bomb Squadron in the 445th Bomb Group, part of 2nd Division's Liberator units. There were few more effective gauges of the totality of the war than the number of sports and movie stars now in uniform. Stewart could undoubtedly have avoided front-line action, not least because at the time of being drafted he had been thirty-three and was now thirty-five – some eight years older than the maximum age for USAAF flying training.

Stewart had been a keen aviator for years, however; he had gained his private pilot's licence in 1935 and even a commercial licence three years later, and he privately owned a Stinson 105 two-seater, which he often used to fly back to see his parents on the East Coast. He had even taken part in a cross-country air race in 1938 and by the time of Pearl Harbor had logged almost four hundred hours. 'You're like a bird up there,' he said of his love of flying. 'It's almost as if you're not part of society anymore.'

Despite being one of the best-loved male actors in Hollywood – he had won his first Oscar in 1941 for *The Philadelphia Story* – Stewart came from a long tradition of military service. Both his grandfathers had fought in the Civil War in the 1860s and his father had served in both the Spanish–American War of 1898 and on the Western Front in the First World War. Stewart always claimed his father was his greatest inspiration. Then there was a fundamental sense of duty. 'It may sound corny,' he told a reporter, 'but what's wrong with wanting to fight for your country? Why are people so reluctant to use the word patriotism?'

Stewart had become the first major Hollywood star to enter the military, although he had initially been turned down by the Air Corps for being underweight. He soon put that right and was in, but his age, status and considerable flying experience made him an obvious choice to remain at home, training recruits and helping with both recruitment and the raising of war bonds. Reluctant to become a PR agent for the Army Air Forces, he did none the less make a recruitment film called *Winning Your Wings* in early 1942; it was reckoned he helped drive some 150,000 volunteers into the service on the back of this.

By the summer of 1942, Stewart's worst fears had been realized: he was posted to Kirtland Airfield in New

Mexico as an instructor and then to the Operational Training Unit, 29th Bombardment Group, at Gowen Field in Idaho. Rumours reached him that he was soon to be taken off flying duties altogether, but his CO at the 29th BG, Lieutenant-Colonel Walter 'Pop' Arnold, had heard that a new group was being formed – the 445th – and in need of personnel, and so rang the commander, Lieutenant-Colonel Bob Terrill, to recommend Stewart, assuring him the film star wasn't starry in the least, but instead was a high-class pilot and a natural-born leader. On 3 August 1943, Stewart was told he had been posted as operations officer to one of the four squadrons, the 703rd.

Although he had been flying B-17s, he had earlier tried out on a Liberator and favoured the big 'Flying Boxcar', as they were known. Intense training followed at Sioux City in Iowa and, within three weeks, Stewart had taken over command of the 703rd, having quickly proved himself to be every bit the man recommended by Pop Arnold and with the novelty of his celebrity soon worn off.

Before they left Sioux City, Stewart invited his parents up from Pennsylvania for a farewell dinner. As they left the next day, his father, the old warrior Alex Stewart, handed him a letter. 'I feel sure that God will lead you through this mad experience,' he had written. 'I can say no more. I continue only to pray. Goodbye, my dear. God bless you and keep you. I love you more than I can tell you. Dad.' It was dated 11 November – the anniversary of the end of the First World War in which he had played his own part.

Two weeks later, Stewart was in England, at Tibenham in Norfolk, just a few miles north of Thorpe Abbotts, and among the fifteen hundred new aircrew to reach England that month.

But for all this influx of manpower, and for all the hundreds of thousands of tons of bombs dropped already that year, it was clear that the Luftwaffe was still far from beaten, and Germany's leadership was still a long way from putting up the white flag.

PART II

The Turning Point

CHAPTER 11

Fighter Boys

WHILE GENERAL IRA EAKER was concerned that not enough new crews were reaching him quickly enough, the continued poor weather was allowing him to replenish his bomb groups and even add entirely new ones, such as the 445th BG. Many of the new crews arrived as replacements, though, and that included pilot Lieutenant William R. Lawley and his crew, who had flown a brand-new B-17 from the US air base at Presque Isle, Maine, coast-hopping north to Canada, Greenland and Iceland, then on to England.

Lawley was twenty-three, tall and of slender build, and from Leeds, Alabama. The youngest of ten children, he was none the less the only child of his mother, and his nine half-siblings from his father's first marriage were all a lot older. He had enlisted a little over a year earlier, in August 1942, and had applied for the Air Forces because, ever since Charles Lindbergh's solo flight across the Atlantic in 1927, he had wanted to learn to fly. He had never had the money to do much about it, but the war had presented him with a great opportunity finally to take the plunge and become a pilot.

Unusually, he chose bombers rather than fighters. 'I liked the idea of the heavy equipment,' he said. 'I felt a little on the large size for WWII cockpits and I didn't like the idea of that single engine out in front of me.' By the beginning of October 1943, Lawley had formed his crew and been placed in a provisional group at Scott Field, Illinois. On 3 October, they were told to fly to Maine and get ready to head overseas. That day saw the opening of the World Series and so, along with the other five pilots scheduled to depart, Lawley asked permission to buzz Yankee Stadium in New York on the way. 'Just don't get too low,' they were told.

Unfortunately for Lawley and his crew, they soon developed engine trouble and had to abandon hopes of overflying the baseball. Instead, they landed at Bridgeport, Connecticut, where by chance the legendary aviator Charles Lindbergh happened to be passing through. An engine change at Bridgeport did the trick and they made it without mishap to England, where the B-17 was promptly taken from them and they were posted to Chelveston, about 15 miles from Bedford, home to the 305th Bomb Group. Once there, they joined the 364th Bomb Squadron and were given a new ship, which they christened *Cabin in the Sky*.

Meanwhile, at Tibenham, the newly arrived members of the 445th Bomb Group were settling into their new environment and working up to go into action. The crews had all flown over in their longer-range B-24s, using a route from Florida south to Puerto Rico, British Guiana and Brazil – now an ally – then across the Atlantic to Dakar in West Africa, on to Morocco and then north to England. It took two weeks, and Captain Jimmy Stewart had flown much of the way himself, riding with Lieutenant Lloyd Sharrard's crew. They had lost one crew, the *Sunflower Sue*, which had also been carrying a further four passengers, including Stewart's master sergeant. Out over the Atlantic, they had given a mayday then disappeared. One of Stewart's first tasks on reaching Tibenham was to write letters to the families of the fourteen men who had been lost, possibly the most unenviable task of an air commander.

Cold and wet, Tibenham, like all other air bases, covered a vast area that included accommodation for some six thousand men as well as all the offices, ammunition dumps, fuel stores, firing butts, hangars and workshops. In many ways, airfields such as Tibenham were like small new towns. Hastily built concrete roads linked the various parts of the complex, but plenty of rough tracks, puddles and mud remained. Their last staging post had been Marrakesh; the contrast could not have been starker. Stewart was sharing quarters with Captain Howard Kreidler, CO of the 701st Bomb Squadron, in a flat-roofed concrete-and-brick barracks block. It was basic, with a single Franklin stove for heat, which they soon got working, but better than the Nissen and Quonset huts that housed the majority of crews.

Among those also settling in were the men of *Bullet Serenade*, piloted by Lieutenant George Wright. While Wright and his fellow officers had been put into a Quonset hut, the enlisted men had been allocated a Nissen hut. These cheap and easy-to-erect buildings looked like giant cylinders sliced in half and put on a concrete base, with roofs and walls made from semicircular sheets of corrugated iron. The waist gunner and 3rd engineer was

Sergeant John 'Robbie' Robinson, from Memphis, Tennessee, who had turned twenty-two only that month. 'So this is going to be home,' he thought as he walked into their allotted hut: six beds either side, brick walls at each end, two dangling light bulbs hanging on cords and a pot-bellied stove in the middle. Outside was an unfinished block that contained latrines, showers and washstands, though no evidence of any hot water. That evening they were issued only C Rations – a rather tasteless hash. It was Thanksgiving Day 1943.

Later that evening, Robinson sat on his cot writing to his young wife, Elizabeth, who was back home in Memphis working a night shift in an aircraft factory. They had been married just over a year when his draft had arrived in the post. He was madly in love with her, thought of her almost constantly and missed her desperately.

That same day, Friday, 26 November, Feldmarschall Erhard Milch was overseeing a display of new aircraft and weaponry at Insterburg airfield in East Prussia for the Führer. It had been Göring's idea, organized at very short notice and with the aim of currying favour for the Reichsmarschall. Consequently, when Hitler arrived with his entourage, including Heinrich Himmler, the head of the SS, Göring snubbed Milch entirely and not only personally introduced each of the machines to the Führer but made it clear their existence was largely his doing, not Milch's.

Using Milch's list, however, Göring did not realize that one fighter prototype that had not been expected had made the trip from the experimental base at Rechlin after all, so there was an extra plane in the line and the rest had all moved forward one place. Completely unaware of this change, Göring now started introducing medium bombers as single-engine fighters, and fighters as bombers. Hitler, unimpressed, swiftly put him right. Soon after, they reached the new Me262 jet, at which point Hitler asked whether it could carry bombs. Before Milch could intervene, Professor Messerschmitt stepped forward and told him yes, it could carry either one 1,000kg bomb or two 500kg. 'This at last is the aircraft I have been demanding for years!' the Führer replied. 'Here it is – but nobody recognized it!' Although Göring had earlier argued vociferously that an aircraft such as the Me262 was a fighter and not a bomber, neither he nor Milch offered a single objection to this pronouncement. Once again, it looked as though Hitler's absurd insistence on aggression and further bombing would trump sound military logic.

The display at Insterburg had also included new bombers, rockets and flying bombs. Hitler called these last 'vengeance weapons', but Allied attacks had taken their toll – the raid on Peenemünde had lost them three weeks' development, while the raid on Kassel had forced the complete evacuation of the Fieseler works. Both rocket and flying-bomb projects were sucking up increasing resources, which could then not be used on aircraft production. Mass production of flying bombs still required the creation of a further seven hundred machine tools, one of the most time-consuming and resource-heavy parts of the production process.

Meanwhile, Adolf Galland was deeply frustrated that his current fighter aircraft were increasingly lagging behind those of the Allies. This had led to a spectacular clash with Göring at Burg Veldenstein, near Nuremberg, another of the Reichsmarschall's properties. Pacing up and down in the courtyard of this imposing castle, Göring once again berated Galland for the perceived failures of the fighter arm. Although used to this, Galland rarely took these reproaches lying down. What was needed, he told Göring, was better aircraft and better training – then they might get somewhere. Göring brushed this aside and told him Hitler wanted the twin-engine fighters equipped for a 50mm cannon. The Führer had reasoned that it would pack a much bigger punch and could be fired from greater distances. Large-calibre, long-distance cannons would be a very effective way of improving the performance of the fighter arm. And in this, Göring told Galland, he was in agreement with the Führer.

Galland, however, pointed out that the proposed KWK 5 cannon was incredibly heavy, causing drag and reducing the speed of the aircraft, which was already inferior. Also, it could hold only fifteen shells, was prone to jamming and was most certainly not effective at 500 yards, let alone the 3,000 Hitler had been claiming. The discussion grew increasingly heated until Göring was shouting at Galland. Eventually, the General der Flieger offered his resignation, which Göring accepted.

Meanwhile, Galland's fighter pilots continued to take off and meet whatever incoming American missions were launched into the bleak winter weather. II/JG11, which included Heinz Knoke's 5 Staffel, was now based at Plantlünne, south-west of Bremen. On 18 November, he led his *Staffel* against another American raid, but they failed to make an interception and, when it was time to turn for home, the weather had closed in and the light began to fade. Worrying they wouldn't make it back to base, Knoke radioed to the airfield of St-Trond in Belgium instead. Below, Holland and Belgium lay covered in snow after some heavy blizzards, and Knoke was concerned about icing: it could badly affect the weight of the aircraft as well as the controls. He could feel his breath freezing on the inside of his oxygen mask.

They headed north in close formation, but Unteroffizier Erich Führmann, who had been posted to his squadron several months earlier, was struggling and lagging behind. He was, he told Knoke over his radio, having engine trouble. They were all aware that in these murky conditions it was better to bail out than risk complete engine failure, but Führmann soldiered on. Knoke managed to bring the rest of the Staffel down to St-Trond through a welcome gap in the cloud, but Führmann was some way behind and by the time he finally touched down, it had begun snowing. The engine trouble was quickly resolved and an hour later he joined Knoke and the rest of the pilots as they huddled in a crew hut drinking hot rum punch and playing cards. Although he was invited to join the game, Führmann declined. As always, he was short of cash. One of the others lent him some and then something unprecedented happened: he began winning, over and over. Everyone was stunned. Hours passed and the room became heavy with cigarette smoke, the floor littered with empty bottles. Finally, they called it a night and Führmann coolly placed six 100-mark notes in his battered old wallet.

At midday the following day, they set off for home, the weather still overcast and cold. All made it back safely, except Führmann, who had once again been suffering with engine trouble. This time, however, he did not show up. Knoke reported him missing, increasingly worried. Darkness fell and then a call came through: an Me109 had crashed near Lütjenholm; a peat farmer had found the wreckage of wings and the tail, but the fuselage and cockpit, with the pilot still inside, had sunk into the marsh. The salvage crew recovered bits of uniform and a wallet filled with six 100-mark notes. 'The comrades stare at me, frozen,' noted Knoke. 'I have a feeling that in future something will always be missing.'

A few days later, on 23 November, Knoke learned that Hauptmann Werner Dolenga had been killed in a crash too. On the wall in the crew room, they hung his picture alongside those of the others who had gone. Beneath each was their name, rank and date of death. Some had humorous dedications scribbled on them. Wolny, Steiger, Kolbe, Gerrard, Kramer, Dölling, Killian, Führmann, Dolenga . . . All from one *Staffel*, which usually amounted to just nine men.

Knoke wondered who would be next, while another of the pilots, Methuselah Barran, just sat in a chair staring at the picture of Führmann; the two had been inseparable friends. 'He cannot get over his death,' jotted Knoke in his diary. 'He does not make a fuss or complain; but seems to find an outlet for his grief in quiet, bitter cursing that of all people it would have to be Führmann who went down in the northern moors.'

Knoke himself was struggling to make sense of what was happening to them. He was passionately addicted to the life of the fighter pilot – the thrill of flying his 109 and the adrenalin-fuelled excitement of combat flying, and the pride. He remained fiercely patriotic and loved the ethos of the fighter arm: there was, he believed, a code of chivalry that still existed in the battles that took place high above the clouds, while the prospect of death added to the intensity of life. 'We regard life as a jug of delicious Rhine wine,' he wrote, 'intoxicated by the sense of compelling urgency to savour every last drop while we can, draining it to the dregs in an atmosphere of companionship.' He tried not to think of his lost comrades as dead but, rather, just gone away.

In the crew room, Jonny Fest spoke up. 'Fellows, do you not think they would die laughing at the sight of our gloomy faces down here? You can bet that old scoundrel Führmann is just waiting for the next one to join him to start another card game.'

Barran was not convinced. 'It makes me sick,' he said. He had written 'Swearing is the laxative which purges the soul' under his own portrait. 'In case it, too,' added Knoke, 'has to join the others on the wall.'

One pilot who would have agreed wholeheartedly with Barran was Lieutenant-Colonel Don Blakeslee, who was well known for his liberal use of profanities. On 1 December 1943, he landed in his P-47 at Boxted in Essex, there to teach the greenhorns of the 354th Fighter Group – newly arrived with their shiny P-51Bs – a thing or two about combat flying and to lead them on their first-ever combat sortie. Blakeslee had turned twenty-six just a couple of months earlier and, while delighted to be given the opportunity to fly the new P-51B, he was equally frustrated that this bunch of Johnny-come-lately greenhorns had been given this stunning new aircraft rather than his veterans at the 4th Fighter Group.

Certainly, Dick Turner and his fellows were impressed to see Blakeslee that first December morning, which, for a change, was bright and sunny. Wasting no time, as was his way, Blakeslee got them all airborne for a training flight in which initially he merely observed them. That afternoon, before they were due to take off for their first combat mission, he had them all in the briefing room. Turner was struck by his presence and his steely, penetrating pale eyes. 'He was all business,' wrote Turner, 'and the business was killing. In the briefing, he let us know that he was a master of his craft, and that he would brook nothing less than perfection from those who flew with him.' He underlined the vital importance of radio and air discipline and left Turner wondering whether it was scarier to meet the Germans or displease Colonel Don Blakeslee. He also talked about tactics: the importance of speed and height, which gave the attacker such an advantage, and one it was vital to maintain. One piece of advice that particularly struck Turner was to never, ever turn away from a head-on attack. There was a short silence after this proclamation, until one of the young pilots tentatively asked what would happen if a German pilot proved every bit as bull-headed? Blakeslee smiled, then fixed his eyes on the pilot. 'In that case, son,' he said, 'you'll have earned your extra flight and pay.'

Briefing over, they headed to their waiting Mustangs. Turner clambered in, parachute pack strapped on, then clipped his harness and attached his radio and oxygen leads. Cockpit checks followed: trimming tabs 5 degrees back, rudder 5 degrees right and aileron neutral. Propeller: speed control fully forward. Fuel: check content of tanks. Flaps: up. Supercharger: auto. Radiator shutter: automatic. Oil cooler shutter: automatic. RI compass: on. Then it was time to fire up the Merlin, which ticked over then fired, brief flames spurting from the exhaust tabs before the propeller whirred into life. Airframe shaking, engine roaring, he taxied forward towards the assembly area at the end of the runway. Turner was leading his flight of four, with Bob Klopotek on his wing. The weather had turned – blue skies gone, with a new front sweeping in, so that Turner couldn't see the end of the runway through the mist. That meant they would be on instruments the moment they were airborne. 'Every pilot who took off,' noted Turner, 'would feel the cold play of fear, for no one took off blind in a fighter without fear unless he was too stupid and unimaginative to recognize the possible dangers involved.'

Suddenly it was Turner's and Klopotek's turn. A thousand feet down the runway, they were airborne, Turner trimming up, then gingerly raising the nose and beginning a gentle turn, praying they would not crash into someone else. As he concentrated hard on the instrument panel in front of him, they continued to climb for what seemed like an eternity. He was feeling increasingly tense, but just at the point where he felt he could stand the suspense no longer, suddenly they broke into the clear at some 12,000 feet to find others already circling and waiting to form up. In what seemed like a miracle to Turner, everyone made it safely up through the soup and then, in brilliant sunshine and with deep blue skies above them, they headed across the Channel towards Holland, each squadron at a different height and in staggered line abreast. Each squadron split into four flights of four: red, blue, white and green. Red was the squadron leader, and green was the flexible group designed to ward off any potential enemy attack before rendezvous with the bombers, although all pilots were expected to keep a sharp look out at all times.

Turner made sure he kept his eyes peeled, swivelling his head constantly, but there was no sign of the enemy out there and gradually he began to feel the earlier tension ease away. A few bursts of flak as they crossed the Dutch coast reminded him they were now over enemy territory for the first time, as did the constant undulating whine in his headset – this was the effect of German radar on their radios and another warning that, down below in German operations rooms, their path was being watched and plotted every step of the way.

But although they found the bombers they saw no enemy fighters and after around forty minutes started heading for home. The mission had been a milk run – but it was a start. The demystifying of combat flying had begun and an hour and twenty minutes after take-off they were all back down again, safely through the cloud, their first mission complete.

Captain James Stewart had been ordered to London to face the press on Thursday, 2 December. He had been promised this would happen only once. The questions were ridiculous and he found the exercise painful and embarrassing, but then he returned to Tibenham to get on with being a squadron commander.

On Sunday, 5 December, a sergeant came to Robbie Robinson's hut and told him and his crew-mates to prepare – briefing at 9 a.m. and ready to fly. It was to be a 'shakedown' flight – a training flight to see whether they were ready for combat operations. Out by *Bullet Serenade*, they were just getting ready to move off when a Jeep pulled up and Captain Jimmy Stewart stepped out. 'Fellas,' he told them, 'I'll be riding with you.'

On board, Stewart went to the flight deck, but once they were airborne he came back down, speaking to each of the crew, then went back to the cockpit. Over the intercom, Robinson listened to him asking questions of every man. 'What are you doing now, Sergeant Robinson?' he asked. 'What do you see out of the waist window?' Robinson told him. More questions followed. 'Can you see the supercharger gate position? Are the exhausts smoking? What colour is the engine exhaust? How much fuel do we have on board? Are you checking it? Are the fuel gauges off and drained?' He then called them up in turn to the cockpit. Robinson, like the rest of the crew, had gone through incredibly thorough training. Although a waist gunner, he was a fully qualified flight engineer and even had sixty hours' piloting in his logbook. The idea was to ensure there was always back-up if anything happened to the main operating crew members. 'Robinson,' Stewart asked once he had reached the flight deck, 'can you fly as first engineer?' He also wanted to know whether he could man all gun turrets and arm the bombs. It was quite a grilling, but Robinson was impressed. 'Stewart really knew this airplane,' he noted. 'He wanted us to know it too.'

They were due to form up on the lead ship, which was painted orange with black checks, but it never showed up. Despite this, they flew on, Stewart checking everything, including how well their electric flight suits were working; outside, it was −30°C. Wright made a smooth landing after four hours and fifteen minutes.

'Well,' said Stewart after they had drawn to a halt back on their hardstand, 'I suppose you fellas are going to make it okay together. I just don't know where the, uh, forming airplane went today.' They had passed the test. Soon enough they and the rest of the 445th would be heading out on their first mission.

The weather remained wretched. Up at Leeming, Bill Byers got so down because of the endless grey and fog and rain that he took his crew out on a test flight just so that they could get up above the clouds and see some sunshine. Operations continued, however: a short hop across the Channel to hit U-boat and E-boat pens on 5 December, which gave Dick Turner and the rest of the 354th FG their second official mission. Then early morning on the 11th the target was Emden, a port on the north-west German coast. Bob Johnson, Gabby Gabreski and forty-six other men of the 56th were among nearly four hundred fighters escorting the biggest effort the Eighth had mounted since Schweinfurt – some 583 bombers dispatched that day. These were the kind of numbers to deflate the stoutest German hearts, and because the target was north-west Germany, it meant the bombers could be escorted all the way. Also joining the American fighters for the first time over German skies were forty-four P-51s of the 354th Fighter Group, although Dick Turner was not among them; it was his turn to sit one out. Even so, this was a shallow-penetration raid, not the heart of the Reich or indeed the German aircraft industry.

As they headed out over the North Sea, the bomber formation presented an awesome sight. Bob Johnson, looking down, could only wonder at how all those squad-rons, bomb groups, wings and divisions managed to get themselves into formation, majestically droning over the sea in their staggered boxes. From 30,000 feet, he saw the bombers as little more than dots, streaming long contrails of vapour across the bright, deep blue sky high above the cloud.

The 56th had been ordered to support the first two boxes of the 3rd Bomb Division, which would take them to the limit of their endurance. The three squadrons of the 56th were only over the Frisian Islands off the Dutch coast when they spotted a formation of around a dozen enemy fighters above and away from them, and it looked as though they were in the mood for fighting. As far as Johnson was concerned, it was a sign they might be running into some of the more experienced and aggressive Luftwaffe pilots.

The men of the 56th kept flying and then, when the Germans were abreast and with the sun behind them, down they came. Orders now arrived through their headsets for the 62nd Fighter Squadron to take the enemy on, but for the 61st – Johnson's and Gabreski's squadron – and the 63rd to stay out of the fight and rendezvous with the bombers as planned. 'Which is exactly what the Krauts were trying to prevent,' wrote Johnson. 'They hoped we would be stupid enough to commit all forty-eight fighters to a brawl with the dozen airplanes, eliminating the escort our Big Friends needed so desperately.' The sixteen Thunderbolts of the 62nd turned in towards the enemy, with four soon disengaging and joining the other two squadrons. This left thirty-six Thunderbolts in the group now swinging north at 35,000 feet towards Bremen in a wide turn. It was bright up there, with the sun reflecting off the puffs of high cloud and making it hard to see. Turning is a difficult manoeuvre in a finger-four formation, because the outer aircraft has to increase speed and the inner one drop off the pace, and then the two swap places. Halfway through this procedure two of the aircraft in the flight directly in front of Johnson drew together and, before he could shout out a warning, one had sheared the wing off the other, fuel tanks had exploded and the two planes were torn apart in a blinding explosion. He watched two parachutes billow out, but his relief quickly turned to horror as he realized only pieces of the two pilots remained to swing gently downwards. 'Just like that, two good men lost,' noted Johnson. 'We couldn't help either Larry Strand or Ed Kruer by watching the wreckage fall. There was nothing to do but to hold our course and continue towards our rendezvous with the bombers.'

Gabreski, leading the squadron, had not seen the incident and initially thought they had been bounced, but up ahead he now spotted a large number of enemy fighters – perhaps forty twin-engine 110s – manoeuvring to attack from the rear of the bombers and more than sixty single-engine fighters already tearing into the Big Friends, one of whom was Heinz Knoke, about to shoot down his twentieth bomber.

Gabreski ordered the squadron to attack and the P-47s dived down. Johnson immediately spotted an Me110 below him and at ten o'clock to his position. He dived, but the Messerschmitt's rear-gunner clearly spotted him and so the pilot flipped over his aircraft and dived himself. Following, Johnson was almost at ground level by the time he caught up, having hurtled down almost 6 miles in no time at all. He thought the 110 was going to plough straight on into the ground, but at the last moment the pilot rolled the plane over and began to pull her up, then dived down again, Johnson following each time. Eventually, Johnson saw the Messerschmitt fill his sights. 'Perfect!' he noted later. 'One short burst knocked the bottom out of his bucket! The airplane tore itself apart in mid-air.'

Meanwhile, Gabreski suddenly found himself all alone and, aware how dangerous that could be in the middle of the fray, he looked around for some P-47s to tag on to. Instead, he spotted three more Me110s about 5,000 feet below him. It was just too good an opportunity, so, against his better judgement, he dived down and opened fire on the last of the three, keeping his finger on the firing button until he was close enough to see the crew bailing out.

Unlike Bob Johnson, Gabreski recovered at 23,000 feet and soon spotted a formation of P-47s, only to find as he drew closer that they were, in fact, Focke-Wulf 190s. Fortunately, they had not seen him and he was able to turn and get away. By this time, his fuel was getting low. Flying high at comfortable cruising speed, it was quite possible to eke out the miles, but the moment a fighter was in a dogfight, fuel consumption rose dramatically and Gabreski told himself to head home. Turning westwards, he had begun flying away from the melee when he spotted an Me109 passing below at nine o'clock. Gabreski held his breath, hoping he hadn't been spotted, because he knew he didn't have the fuel to get embroiled in another tussle. But the German pilot had seen him and was soon turning his machine up to meet him.

Another glance at his fuel gauge told Gabreski that he simply didn't have enough to try to outrun his pursuer. Instead, he decided he would fly at about 80 per cent throttle and hopefully present the German with as tough a shot as possible. Diving a little to build up speed, he throttled back, watching his back for all he was worth. Sure enough, the Messerschmitt was soon on him but, at the moment the German opened fire, Gabreski pulled up then kicked the plane over, throwing off his pursuer's aim and giving him nothing better than a 90-degree deflection shot, which was incredibly difficult to pull off.

This ploy worked the first time, and the second, but on the third attempt the enemy pilot got his bead spot on and fired into Gabreski's cockpit with a loud explosion. A cannon shell tore off one of his rudder pedals and also smashed the heel of his flying boot. Suddenly, his engine was losing power too and, with his foot throbbing, Gabreski accepted it was all over and time to bail out in quick order.

He was now at around 20,000 feet. Pushing the stick forward and using the ailerons, he picked up air speed and began rolling the plane so that he could drop out, but with the canopy already half-open he realized he still had some manifold pressure and r.p.m.s of around 1,000. The engine was not dead quite yet. This persuaded him not to give up.

Hastily closing the canopy, he dived towards a bank of cloud and reached it just as the Messerschmitt was closing in for the kill. It did the trick, but the German was not to be easily put off and each time Gabreski pulled back up and looked around, he saw his pursuer skirting the clouds, looking for him. Eventually, Gabreski decided it was better to stick in the cloud and rely on his instruments. Pulling further back on the throttle and calling mayday just in case, he prayed hard and spent an anxious half hour hoping he would find landfall before his engine cut out.

Luck was with him. Eventually, the cloud thinned and he saw England and the long finger of Kent up ahead. Spotting Manston air base at the south-east tip, he called up and was able to land. No sooner had he begun taxiing, however, than his engine cut out, and only then did he summon the nerve to look at his foot. Fortunately, there was no blood at all – the cannon shell had merely skimmed his boot, which had a gash across it, but he was miraculously uninjured.

Stuck on the runway, Gabreski was soon rescued and towed clear. A call was put through to Halesworth and someone sent to collect him, leaving him a little time to ponder his lucky escape. There were holes all over his cockpit, an oil tank that was almost dry and a completely bust turbocharger unit. It said much about the ruggedness of the P-47 that it had got him home, but equally it was testimony to Gabreski's own experience and skill.

CHAPTER 12

Change at the Top

AIR CHIEF MARSHAL SIR Arthur Harris's battle for Berlin continued. Some 450 aircraft flew over the capital on 26 November, the same day that Goldie Goldstein and others in the Eighth attacked Bremen, and a similar number attacked the capital of the Reich a few days later on 2 December. Far heavier winds than had been forecast affected the latter raid, with a number of aircraft blown way off course. German intelligence had correctly identified the capital as the target nearly twenty minutes before the first bombers attacked, so that by the time the Lancasters reached the city there was a mass of night-fighters waiting for them. Forty bombers were lost on the raid, including five of twenty-five from 460 Squadron, made up mostly of Australian crews. One of those that went down was carrying two reporters, Captain Nordhal Grieg, a Norwegian working for the British *Daily Mail*, and Norman Stockton of the *Sydney Sun*. Both were killed.

Then the following night, 3/4 December, the target was Leipzig. Margarete Dos was an 18-year-old Berliner studying medicine in nearby Jena. An athletic girl, she had once hoped to compete at the Olympics, but such ambition had been dashed by the war. On the other hand, she had done well in her school exams, had completed her compulsory Arbeitsdienst – the Reich labour service – and, as there was an urgent need for doctors, medics and nurses, in September she had begun her first term at the ancient university where Goethe had once lived and worked.

Jena had avoided the bombs so far and, although she worried for her mother, who was still in Berlin, Margarete was relishing the medical training she had begun; as her mother had urged her, she had been concentrating hard on her studies and trying to put the shifting fortunes in the war behind her. Even so, the sirens rang out all too frequently in the picturesque town, as it lay on the path from England to Berlin. Loudspeakers around the town and university would announce, 'The enemy has been sighted and is advancing from a northerly direction,' although so far the planes had passed on over them.

On the night of 3 December, however, Margarete was working late in the laboratory, dissecting a dog, when suddenly the sirens rang out again and the loudspeakers blared. Soon after, she heard the sound of bombs dropping. Putting down her instruments, she hurried out of the lab and ran to the bomb shelter just outside the main entrance to the medical school. A number of students and professors were already there. They looked bewildered. More bombs were falling, closer this time. Margarete put her arms over her head and prayed hard to God.

When the all-clear sounded, no one dared move. Instead they remained where they were in silence until a commotion outside the hatch roused them. 'Open up, open up!' someone shouted. 'We have a wounded man!'

The hatch was opened and two men came in carrying a third, who was grimacing in agony. Blood was spattered over his front, and below the knees his trousers and his legs had been shredded. Strips of skin hung off them. His feet had gone entirely.

'There are medical students here, aren't there?' cried one of the men. Margarete called out that she was. 'Bring him down into the bunker,' she told them. 'At least we can lay him down somewhere and keep him warm.' Only when she had him lain down and others were tying tourniquets around his legs did Margarete realize the wounded man was Professor Schmitt, one of her lecturers.

When she eventually emerged from the shelter, she was shocked by the level of damage. Wandering over the rubble, she headed into the town, walking dazed and exhausted towards the tavern where she and her friends would meet. A few students had had the same idea and together they stood by the statue of Hanfried in the market square. 'No one spoke, but we wept,' wrote Margarete. 'We wept for the friends we knew we would never see again. We wept for the professor whose booted feet were missing. But mostly we wept because our dreams were dead. We would no longer be able to study and we wept deeply for that.'

Margarete Dos and her friends regularly used the phrase 'Until better times.' It might well also have been adopted by General Hap Arnold, who, by December, was committed to providing new impetus for the Combined Bomber Offensive, and particularly the aims laid out in POINT-BLANK. Ever since August, he had been considering an overhaul of the air command structure in the European

Theatre of Operations – a belief that had become only more entrenched with the creation of the Fifteenth Air Force in Italy and with his belated acceptance that his heavy bomber force could not, after all, successfully defend itself without fighter escorts. By December, the hard reality was that POINTBLANK was at least three months behind schedule. Looming ever closer was the planned cross-Channel invasion, yet there was no sign of any reduction in German fighter production, which Allied intelligence sources put at 645 per month. In fact, the figure was over two hundred more than that. Injecting as many long-range Mustangs as possible, as quickly as possible, into the Eighth Air Force was one clear way to improve matters, but there was a growing feeling that fresh eyes, a new look at tactics and a burst of energy might also be needed.

One increasing concern was the need for better coordination. RAF Bomber Command and the Eighth and Fifteenth Air Forces were three strategic bombing forces now operating collaboratively in many ways but hardly as one. Arnold wanted a single Allied Strategic Air Force Commander in overall charge of all three, with a headquarters in London and status equal to other theatre commanders. Such a move would make all Allied strategic air forces in the west independent of any ground forces commander and allow them to pursue the Combined Bomber Offensive entirely independently. On top of that, it would further Arnold's agenda to create a US air force unshackled from the army.

He also wanted a US Strategic Air Force Commander in Europe, also based in London, who would have operational control of Fifteenth Air Force in Italy and Eighth and Ninth

Air Forces in England. Again, this was the better to oversee and coordinate efforts in Britain and Italy. In late August and early September, when Arnold had visited Britain, he had started to talk to various people about these ideas, not least Air Marshal Harris. After a dinner on 4 September at Harris's house, where Arnold was staying as a guest, the conversations had continued the following morning in Harris's garden, underneath plum trees dripping with fruit and with geese and chickens wandering about. Harris, unsurprisingly, was against a joint Allied air commander because it threatened his autonomy.

When he returned to the US, Arnold managed to persuade Harry Hopkins, President Roosevelt's senior advisor, and also got the conditional support of General Marshall, although the US Chief of Staff warned him not to press the matter just yet – at least, not until the new Supreme Allied Commander had been appointed and other issues of command in the Mediterranean had been resolved.

Thus not until the Joint Chiefs of Staff conference in Tehran in November was Arnold able to raise the matter more formally. On the trip out, aboard the USS *Iowa*, he won the backing of President Roosevelt and then the support of the American Chiefs for the creation of the US Strategic Air Forces in Europe (USSTAF) – a decision that could be made independently of the British. They also agreed with Arnold's suggestion that the new commander should be Tooey Spaatz, who, since November, had been C-in-C Fifteenth Air Force in the Mediterranean Theatre. He was liked, respected, had the seniority and experience, and shared Arnold's views on strategic bombing.

At the Tehran Conference, however, the British made

clear their considerable objections to Arnold's plans. Portal had been given the task of coordinating the Combined Bomber Offensive, which enabled him to ensure Bomber Command maintained its independence. Soon the number of American heavy bombers in Britain would exceed those of the RAF, so looking ahead it was even more important for the British to maintain that independence, and especially so since British and American attitudes and approaches to strategic bombing were different. Portal also objected to creating a new and what he believed to be unnecessary headquarters, plus all the staff that would go with it. Why add another level of command, which threatened to hamper rather than help future operations?

The matter was left up in the air at Tehran, but resolved in early December at the Cairo Conference, which was attended by just the Western Allies. Arnold's plan for an overall Allied air commander was rejected, but the British did not object to the creation of a new overall American air commander for Europe. It was also agreed that POINTBLANK must remain the absolute priority.

Clearly, with the new command, General Ira Eaker's position as US commander of both the Eighth and Ninth Air Forces in England had effectively been made redundant, which meant he had either to be given the leg-up instead of Spaatz or moved somewhere else entirely. What became apparent in Cairo was that Arnold had no intention of further promoting Eaker. Rather, he had lost confidence in his old friend, who, he told his fellow Joint Chiefs, had shown inflexibility during recent months. The frustrations Arnold had been feeling for some time emerged in a blistering critique of Eighth Air

Force's performance. He had, he told them, sent a number of inspectors, who had reported that the Eighth was using only 50 per cent of the available aircraft instead of the 60–70 per cent used in other theatres where operating conditions were more primitive. Arnold felt that the lack of key targets destroyed had been because of a failure to employ bombers in sufficient numbers. Not enough focus had been given to the priority targets of POINTBLANK. Training, technique, tactics and operational efficiency all needed improving.

Only some of this was fair. The weather had been atrocious and it was also hard, when looking at numbers on a piece of paper, properly to appreciate the devastating effect on morale and operational capability that the huge rates of attrition had caused individual bomb groups and their bases. Arnold might have been head of the US Army Air Forces, but he had never commanded even a group in combat and perhaps lacked the sympathy held by those with operational experience. And from Eaker's perspective, the insufficient numbers combined with the terrible weather had caused the setbacks, not a lack of either ruthlessness or operational efficiency. He was convinced, for example, that attacking Schweinfurt with 600 heavies rather than 300 would still have resulted in the loss of 60 bombers, but the percentage of the overall force would have been halved, while the weight of bombs dropped would have been double, and very probably decisive.

Arnold was, to a certain extent, finding in Eaker a scapegoat for his own mistakes. He had overestimated the destructive power of his bombers and their defensive strength; and he had not foreseen the need for a long-range fighter when one was already there in front of his eyes. Yet it was true that Eaker did lack vision and tactical acumen. Whenever Arnold had shown his frustration and criticized the efforts of the Eighth or suggested to Eaker that he change some of his senior commanders, the response had always been the same: more aircraft and crews needed urgently. Eaker never fired anyone.

Perhaps Eaker's biggest failing, however, was his misunderstanding of the role of the fighter. Even though transforming the Mustang with a new engine had been initiated in the UK, Eaker had never once mentioned this remarkable machine before Arnold was suddenly alerted to its potential in the summer of 1943. The tactics used were also unimaginative. Insisting on close escorts was a mistake and a tactic that had proved woefully bad for the Luftwaffe back in 1940. This was because fighters flew much faster than bombers, so the only way to stick with them was by weaving back and forth, which used far more fuel and meant the fighters' range was badly affected. To Arnold, it was absurd that the Americans were still sending fighters over in such a way. As he had learned, but Eaker had not, fighters were the key to defeating the Luftwaffe. That Eaker still believed sheer weight of bombers was enough betrayed a fundamental misunderstanding of the battle in which his forces were now engaged.

Over the ensuing days in Cairo, a large change of senior Allied command was discussed, agreed and put into motion. General Dwight D. Eisenhower was appointed Supreme Allied Commander for OVERLORD, which meant him moving from the same post in the Mediterranean. His deputy would be Air Chief Marshal Sir Arthur Tedder, who was currently C-in-C Mediterranean Allied Air Forces. This meant the two most senior air commanders in the Mediterranean would be leaving the theatre, which, Spaatz warned Arnold, might upset the balance between the RAF and US Army Air Forces there. A solution was to put Eaker into the position vacated by Tedder; it would mean a promotion of sorts for Eaker and would allow the Americans to maintain influence in a theatre dominated by the British. A final shift of command came at Spaatz's suggestion: that Major-General Jimmy Doolittle take over leadership of the Eighth Air Force.

General Jimmy Doolittle was one of the most famous men in the United States Armed Forces and certainly one of the best regarded within the air force. Diminutive, balding, but with fiery dark eyes and a ready smile, he turned forty-seven on 14 December, having already had a long and highly distinguished career in aviation. Born in California, he had gone to university in Berkeley before enlisting in the Signal Corps Reserve as a flying cadet and was commissioned the following year. Kept in the States as an instructor rather than being sent to France, he later undertook a number of aeronautical engineering courses and became a famous aviation pioneer, carrying out a number of first-ever flights, including the first transcontinental flight in September 1922, for which he was awarded the Distinguished Flying Cross. But Doolittle was also increasingly interested in the technical side of aviation and completed a master's thesis, drawing on his own practical experiments with aeronautical acceleration, and then went on to gain a doctorate, the first ever awarded for aeronautical engineering. Using his knowledge and skill to good effect, he then became a test pilot and a high-speed pioneer, winning the world-renowned Schneider Cup air speed race for the United States in 1925.

However, possibly Doolittle's most important contribution to aviation during the 1920s and 1930s was his development of instrument-only flying. Up until that point, little thought had been given to flying in anything other than daylight and fair weather, but Doolittle recognized that true operational freedom in the air could only be achieved by blind flying using just instruments. In 1929, he became the first man to take off, fly and then land without any view at all outside the cockpit, and over the next few years he helped develop and test instruments still universally used to this day, such as the artificial horizon and directional gyroscope. He collected numerous awards and further air speed records before finally retiring from air racing, not least because of his beloved wife, Jo, and his children, but also because, for him, racing was all about the development of aviation; as far as he had been concerned, air racing had, by the mid-1930s, outlived its usefulness. By this time he was as famous as a Hollywood film star: in a progressive nation emerging from the Great Depression, aviation was an impossibly glamorous and exciting pursuit, and Doolittle was one of its greatest and most heroic advocates.

A major in the Air Reserve Corps, he had also worked as manager of Shell Oil Company's aviation department and in that role had travelled the world, including to Germany a number of times; he even became good friends with Ernst Udet, the former fighter ace and head of the Luftwaffe's procurement. Doolittle was brought back into the US Army Air Corps in July 1940 in the role of aircraft procurement and a year later was sent to England as part of a special observation mission.

By the time of Pearl Harbor in December 1941, Doolittle was not only one of America's most celebrated aviators and a highly successful aeronautical engineer, but he was still young, dynamic and a man of proven flair and vision. Not surprisingly, he was singled out and promoted to lieutenant-colonel and given the job of planning the US Army Air Forces' first retaliatory raid on Japan. He had also volunteered to lead the mission he had devised: flying sixteen B-25 twin-engine bombers off the USS *Hornet* to bomb a number of targets, including Tokyo.

The Doolittle Raid, as it became known, launched on 18 April 1942. All the planned targets were hit, and Doolittle was among those who, with his crew, subsequently bailed out over China, coming down in a rice paddy. Helped by Chinese Nationalists to get through Japanese lines, he made it to safety along with all but seven crew. For planning, leading and executing the raid, Doolittle was awarded the Medal of Honor, America's highest award for gallantry.

Since then, he had been given key appointments for America's first major contribution to an active campaign: Twelfth Air Force commander in Northwest Africa, then C-in-C of the new Northwest African Strategic Air Force. He oversaw the Allied strategic bombing of Sicily and Italy, and at every promotion and step up the chain of command proved more than capable of rising to the challenge. In terms of practical knowledge, experience and leadership by example, Jimmy Doolittle ticked all the right boxes, and he commanded the utmost respect from those who served under him. It was a shrewd move on the part of Spaatz to suggest Doolittle take charge of the struggling Eighth.

Arnold conducted his lengthy discussions with Spaatz, Doolittle and the other senior air commanders in the

Mediterranean during a trip to Italy following the Cairo Conference. The weather was just as dreadful in Italy as in England, and made worse by the war damage already wrought on the country and by the far more primitive conditions. Arnold was shocked by what he found there. 'Foggia hard hit by bombs,' he jotted in his diary on 9 December. 'Debris all over the streets. Station and railroad yards a mess.' Two days later, he was staying in the old palace at Caserta, headquarters of General Alexander's Allied Armies in Italy. 'Modern battle,' he wrote. 'Jeeps and mud, trucks and tanks, more mud, trucks and road jams, bridges and culverts blown out by bombs and demolitions of the Germans. Bomb holes, mine holes . . . Villages and towns demolished, partly demolished. Destruction and devastation everywhere, mud and more mud.' Compared with Italy, England was like the Garden of Eden. And compared with England, America was the land of luxury. Four days later, he was back in Washington, his mission complete and most of the changes he had wanted in place. He hoped they would give POINTBLANK the renewed impetus that was so desperately needed. Now all he had to do was tell Eaker.

This Arnold did on 18 December. It came as a complete bolt from the blue, which was surprising, since Eaker had fielded no small amount of criticism from Arnold over the past few months. What's more, on the 14th, Portal, back from Cairo, had visited Eaker and relayed Arnold's sharp criticisms. He had also briefed him about Spaatz's new command. Eaker had chosen not to see the writing on the wall, but instead had accepted what Portal said and agreed wholeheartedly with the need to pursue the POINT-BLANK targets more vigorously. But now, on 18 December, he was staring at the cable from Arnold, his old friend, collaborator and close colleague, telling him he was to become Commander Mediterranean Allied Air Forces. 'As a result of your long period of successful operations,' Arnold wrote to him, 'and the exceptional results of your endeavors as Commander of the Air Force in England, you have been recommended for this position.'

Taken at face value, this was a decent promotion, but for Eaker it was the darkest moment in his career. He felt as though he had been 'kicked upstairs'. No matter that he was moving to a more senior post; as far as he was concerned, he had been sacked and no amount of sugar-coating could disguise it. 'I feel like a pitcher,' he wrote to a friend, 'who has been sent to the showers during a world series game.'

Immediately, he cabled Arnold urging him to reconsider. 'Believe war interest best served by my retention command Eighth Air Force; otherwise experience this theater for nearly two years wasted.' Then he added a personal plea: 'It would be heart-breaking to leave it just before climax.' It was also, however, heart-breaking to be shot down in flames in a B-17 over Germany, so a degree of perspective was needed. Portal weighed in on Eaker's behalf – the latter was popular with the British and had even been given an honorary knighthood – but popularity with coalition partners was not enough, and Arnold was not to be swayed.

In any case, he had made the right decision. Spaatz would be a tougher and altogether more influential senior air commander in England, Doolittle had far better vision, tactical intuition and general chutzpah, and someone of Eaker's standing and experience was absolutely needed in

Italy. No matter how hurt and upset Eaker might feel, the new team was a better one for the all-important next phase in the strategic air war.

Change affected the Luftwaffe too. In the second week of December, General Beppo Schmid ordered the nine surviving defence districts to hand over operational control of all anti-aircraft units to the fighter divisions in order to ensure better cooperation between fight and flak forces. His fighter divisions were also given control of the air-raid warning system. This was a sensible streamlining of the air defence, which, for all its sophistication, had become somewhat unwieldy and, like so many organizations in Nazi Germany, was operating with too many parallel command structures. From now on, Schmid's fighter divisions would be responsible for bringing together the different strands of information available on each enemy raid and then managing the coordinated defences for each enemy air attack. Air Command Centre was renamed Luftflotte Reich – Air Fleet Reich – and by Christmas Schmid had further disbanded the old original fighter command centres – or *Jafü* – and handed over all tactical control of fighters to the divisional operations rooms. Fighter tactics were also changing. Small groups of thirty-plus fighters were not enough to make a significant impact on daylight bomber formations. From now, Schmid wanted fighters to attack with two or even three groups, that is, between sixty and ninety aircraft.

They were still, however, flying the same Focke-Wulfs and Messerschmitts. After Galland's falling-out with Göring, no further appointment was made and so the General of Fighters had continued in his role. Two weeks passed, then a further two, and then Göring apologized and Galland was formally reinstated. His task was no easier, however. Rockets and flying bombs were still absorbing much of the Luftwaffe's potential resources and a new upgraded version of the FW190 had still not reached the squadrons. Nor had training improved much.

By this time, a mounting sense of fatalism had unquestionably crept into the Luftwaffe's fighter units. It was hardly surprising, but earlier wartime enthusiasm had been replaced by the growing belief that they were now involved in a numbers game in which the odds were stacked against them. Most still felt a sense of pride, loyalty and even patriotism, but they were like a once-great sporting team that had suffered a string of defeats and was now in a slump from which there appeared to be no means of emerging. There were still some very good pilots – Heinz Knoke, Wim Johnen and Hajo Herrmann to name but three – but the best were suffering too. The Wehrmacht had always celebrated individual success. U-boat aces were feted and given Knight's Crosses and then had Oak Leaves, Swords and even Diamonds added to the original award. Panzer aces were similarly treated as heroes and decorated in much the same way. So it was with fighter aces too. These warriors were the idols of Nazi Germany: brilliant men whom other young Germans could aspire to emulate. A fighter ace with more than twenty-five 'kills', or 'victories', was known as an *Experte* and once an *Experte* had proved himself to be a cut above the others, the job of the lesser mortals in the *Staffel* was to support him and protect him so that he could get on with the job of shooting down enemy aircraft and ensuring his score and his celebrity continued to rise.

There were, however, three big drawbacks to this approach. It completely ignored the fact that the U-boat commander had a crew and officers under him who more than played a part in any success they might achieve. The same was true in a tank. A panzer commander was supported by the gunner, or loader, and driver – the men who were actually getting into position and taking the shot. Being in a U-boat or in a tank was a team effort. It was a team effort being in a fighter squadron too. The second problem was that putting a chosen few on a pedestal often stifled the development and skills of those following behind. After all, if so much focus was on supporting the ace, how were the new aces to come through? Finally, it did little for either performance or morale if these heroes were then killed in action – something that was increasingly becoming an occupational hazard. The attrition on German manpower had been grinding down their war effort for a couple of years; ever since the autumn of 1941, Germany had been struggling to fill the hole caused by the huge casualties already suffered in the war. This meant there was little chance for rest and recuperation. *Experten* were expected to keep flying. And keep flying. And then fly some more.

During 1943, just twelve Luftwaffe aces claimed 1,160 Allied aircraft. The over-dependence on these men was, of course, completely unsustainable. On 4 December, Hauptmann Wilhelm Lemke, one of the Luftwaffe's leading aces with 131 victories to his name, was killed by American pilots far superior in skill and in machines than their Soviet counterparts. In mid-December, Heinz Knoke was due to go on leave and see his beloved wife, Lilo, but was unable to get away. The *Gruppe* had moved once more, albeit not very far – this time to Wunstorf, to the south-east of Bremen. On 17 December, he was sitting in the car and about to go to catch a train to Berlin when the alert sounded and he was forced to run to his Gustav instead. 'My driver shook his head,' he wrote in his diary, 'and even Arndt said that I really needed a few days' rest.'

There was a palpable sense of fatalism among many of the American bomb groups too. At Ridgewell, home to the 381st Bomb Group, which had suffered so in August and again during the Blitz Week of October, Chaplain Captain James Good Brown noticed a huge change. One evening, a new pilot accosted him in the chow line and asked him whether Brown knew Millheim, Pennsylvania. The chaplain did – he had been brought up there. The relief in the pilot was obvious – at last, a connection to home! New crews arriving into established bomb groups often felt distant and isolated, like unwanted strangers. Often they were given bunks only recently vacated by those just killed or now POWs. The old hands were often wary of becoming too friendly, because that just made things harder when a new comrade was subsequently lost. When Chaplain Brown had arrived at Ridgewell with the original 381st BG, the confidence had been exceptional. 'Not a single man expected to be shot down,' he wrote. 'We were innocent. We did not know war.' When their numbers started to be decimated, the trauma was immense. To begin with, the survivors had clung together ever more tightly, unable to process what was happening. Then, in October, even more had been taken. 'It nearly killed us,' he wrote. 'As for comradeship, this was no more, for our comrades were gone.'

In the 100th Bomb Group at Thorpe Abbotts, the vast majority of those crews who had been in the group when Lieutenant Bob Hughes had arrived back in July had gone. Some had finished their twenty-five missions, but most had become casualties. His crew had stuck together, but Sergeant Joe Boyle, his radio man, had been killed on a mission to bomb the synthetic fuel plant at Gelsenkirchen on 5 November. It wasn't easy flying home with a dead comrade bleeding all over the ship. Nor was it easy writing the condolence letter to Joe's mother.

In sharp contrast to the bombers, morale could not have been higher among the American fighter units now in England. In the early years of the war, the Luftwaffe's fighter pilots had strutted around with the brazen cockiness of young men who knew they were good, flying the world's best fighter in the Me109E, and winning. A very similar attitude now pervaded most of the American fighter units.

For every mission, each squadron was expected to provide four flights of four, with an extra flight of four on standby in case operational gaps had to be filled. This still left a lot over. In Dick Turner's 356th Fighter Squadron, for example, there were forty-three pilots, which meant a ratio of more than two to one in terms of operational requirement. Turner quickly found that choosing who should fly was one of the more challenging tasks facing a flight commander on the ground. 'By now,' he wrote, 'my pilots were all clamouring to fly every mission.' He and the other flight commanders were forced to set up a strictly impartial rotation system 'in the interest of fair play.' As a flight commander, he was expected to fly two out of every three missions, which enabled another pilot to gain valuable leadership experience and which, as far as he was concerned, brought the added privilege of allowing him to fly more missions than most.

Fighter squadrons tended to be competitive towards one another too – another sign of high confidence. 'Anything you did in an airplane,' said Bob Johnson, 'you were watched and criticized by other squadrons and, of course, you broke that competitiveness down within the squadron itself between flights. C Flight of the 61st was always the best! That was my flight!' Johnson believed the 56th was the finest fighter unit around. They had a new nickname: 'Zemke's Wolfpack'. Hub Zemke had even given his pilots the target of reaching a hundred confirmed victories by 6 November, a total they achieved the day before. 'The 56th was by now an experienced, effective fighter group,' wrote the slightly more restrained Gabby Gabreski. 'But we never stopped experimenting and looking for better ways of doing things.' With the 4th Fighter Group at Boxted Don Blakeslee regarded the air war as adrenalin-fuelled sport, an approach that inevitably rubbed off on others. He made a point of telling his pilots to be aggressive and imbued his men with a cast-iron belief that the 4th was the best in the entire United States Army Air Forces.

A survey carried out by Eighth Air Force showed that fighter pilots were usually younger than bomber pilots, were much more likely to sign up for another combat tour and nearly all admitted that if they were asked to join the air force again, they would choose to become a fighter pilot again. 'Fighter pilots,' the report noted, 'are more likely than bomber pilots to report that they are in good physical condition.'

This all augured well for General Doolittle as he prepared to take over command of the Eighth. In the weeks to come, his fighter boys would be given the task of knocking their counterparts out of the sky. High levels of confidence and skill were vital. But so too were new tactics.

CHAPTER 13

Berlin

THE OLD YEAR FINALLY drew to a slow close. There had been only a handful of missions in the second half of December, and two of those had been back to Bremen yet again. Hitting Bremen three times in a month was only partially fulfilling the aims of the POINTBLANK directive, however. It was an important industrial centre and a major location for the manufacture and assembly of U-boats, but it was not quite the key German aircraft industry target it had been earlier in the war when a major plant for Focke-Wulf had been located there. 'The Focke-Wulf Company are believed to have transferred about two thirds of their Bremen plants to Eastern Germany, East Prussia and Poland,' wrote the latest update in the Air Ministry's *Bomber's Baedeker*. 'It is believed that the Hast-edt and Hemelingen works are now engaged on the production and modification of components for the air-port works.' On the other hand, it was a major industrial city, and of targets in Germany was closer than most to England. And the Luftwaffe seemed keen to defend it, which – every bit as important – brought their fighters into the skies.

The poor weather and comparative lack of missions had, however, allowed Eaker both to build up strength and to give new crews time to acclimatize and carry out practice flights in conditions very different to those back home. This period of comparative recuperation for the Eighth may have frustrated General Arnold, but as a result the raid on Bremen on 13 December had involved over 700 bombers and nearly 400 fighters, while the next trip to the city, on 16 December, had been carried out by 631 bombers and 201 fighters, and similar numbers struck again on 20 December. Then had come Osnabrück and Münster again on the 22nd, a milk run to Calais on Christmas Eve and another big effort of over 700 bombers and nearly 600 fighters to Ludwigshafen on 30 December.

New boys like Captain Jimmy Stewart and Sergeant Robbie Robinson had chalked up their first missions, along with the rest of the 445th. 'We were all terrified,' Stewart later admitted. But they managed to get through them. So too did Larry Goldstein and his crew on *Worry Wart*, while Hugh McGinty had his fifth mission under his belt by the end of the year and Bob Hughes, up at the 100th BG at Thorpe Abbotts, had managed to complete his seventeenth, eighteenth and nineteenth missions.

Meanwhile, RAF Bomber Command had continued to pummel Berlin – four times in December alone. The capital wasn't the only target, however; on the night of 20 December, Harris sent 650 bombers to Frankfurt, including the Pathfinders of 35 Squadron. Excellent visibility had been predicted, but when they reached Frankfurt there was thick cloud and they had decided against releasing their target indicators after making four unsuccessful runs at the dangerously low height of 5,000 feet. After dropping their three 1,000lb bombs on what looked like a factory, they had turned for home.

This was Gordon Carter's forty-sixth mission, one more than the normal tour of duty in the Pathfinder Force, but he was conscious 'keen types' tended to press on to sixty and he wanted to reach that magic number. In any case, he had become very good friends with his skipper, Julian Sale, and liked the rest of the crew; he wanted to stick with them. What's more, a few weeks earlier he had been to Buckingham Palace to receive a Distinguished Flying Cross from the King himself and on 7 December had been given temporary promotion to squadron leader.

The return leg was uneventful until Sale brought the Halifax down to 1,200 feet and then suddenly all hell let loose as flares started lighting from the bomb bay. Somehow, the safety cover for a TI fuse had detached itself and now that they were below the flares' normal detonating height they had gone off. All too rapidly, the bomber began to fill with smoke and flames. Sale gave the order to bail out, which Carter, not for the first time, did right away. One moment he was upside down, then he righted himself, his parachute opened and he hit the ground heavily – and just beyond the perimeter track at Graveley.

Meanwhile, Sale had also been about to jump when he became aware of Roger 'Sheep' Lamb, the mid-upper gunner, beside him. Lamb's parachute was burned and, realizing that meant certain death for one of his crew, Sale opened the side window and, with his head half out so he could see, succeeded in bringing the Halifax around and landing it. As soon as they had taxied off the runway and on to the grass, he and Lamb jumped down and ran for their lives. They managed to cover just enough distance before the entire Halifax blew up. For his actions, Sale was awarded a Bar to his Distinguished Service Order. An article in *The Times* ran the headline, 'Landed Blazing Bomber to Save Comrade'.

The next trip after Frankfurt had been, once again, Berlin. Among those being sent to the capital of the Reich was pilot Flight Sergeant Russell 'Rusty' Waughman and his crew, who had joined 101 Squadron in Bomber Command's 5 Group only in November. It had been their misfortune to be thrown straight into one of the furthest and best-defended targets in Germany; there had been no milk run to help ease them into operational flying. Nor had their first two trips gone at all well.

Waughman was only twenty years old and from Consett in County Durham. From a working-class background, he had been a sickly child, suffering from typhoid among other illnesses, and had missed a lot of his schooling. Somehow he had survived and when he was seventeen decided to volunteer for the navy as his father had done. However, when he realized the local naval recruiting officer was his own doctor, he went next door to the RAF recruitment office instead. Incredibly, he was accepted, even though during his medical he was told he had a heart murmur. Then he was packed off to the Air Crew Receiving Centre at Lord's Cricket Ground in London; it was the furthest he had ever been from home by quite some margin.

That he might be earmarked for pilot training had never occurred to Waughman, but, despite his childhood hindrances, he passed all attestation, progressive and aptitude tests and to his utter amazement was soon after sent to

Canada to learn to fly. Like most others, he requested to be a fighter pilot, but instead he was trained as a bomber pilot. Almost thrown out at one point, he survived his washout test and got his wings, and by the beginning of 1943 was heading back across the Atlantic to Britain. He passed through his Operational Training Unit, the Heavy Conversion Unit where he learned to fly four-engine Halifaxes instead of twin-engine Wellingtons, and then finally Lancaster Finishing School.

He found it a little tricky to fly the Lancaster to start with. 'My little short legs came into it,' he said. 'When you're on take-off and you've got four engines with 1280 horsepower and 3000 revs, and all the props going, you've got tremendous torque, and with my little short legs I couldn't keep this bloody thing going straight down the runway.' His great friend throughout training, Paul Zankey, was much taller and had no problem, so finished his training a bit sooner and was sent to join 101 Squadron. When Waughman had finally got the measure of the Lancaster and had finished his training, he asked to join 101 Squadron too. At first he was told only the best pilots were sent there, but in the end that was where he went. 'So I asked him, "Why the change of heart?" and he told me it was the squadron with the highest attrition rate in the service and they had first call on the availability of crew.'

As if to prove the point, when he and his crew reached 101 Squadron at the end of November, Waughman learned that his great pal Zankey had been killed the night before on his first mission.

The squadron's home was Ludford Magna, just north of Lincoln. A number of 5 Group bomber stations were scattered around the city, including Scampton, from where

the Dams' Raid had been launched back in May, as well as
Waddington and Coningsby. Ludford Magna was a little
rough around the edges, built in ninety days from scratch
and only ever meant to be a temporary base. There was
only one main tarmacked road on to the base. The men
had renamed the place 'Mudford'. The days were dark, the
rain, cloud and mist seemingly never-ending, but at least
those running the base had a fairly relaxed attitude about
what the aircrew got up to when not flying. There was
plenty of beer in the mess, trips into Lincoln, and a laissez-
faire approach to the men finding 'relaxation' with women.
This was all quite an eye-opener for Waughman, who had
lived a decidedly sheltered life and was hardly worldly-
wise. He learned that around one in five of his comrades
had some form of sexually transmitted disease. 'It wasn't
treated as pornography,' he said, 'it was just a sense of
relaxation.' One friend later said to him, 'Thank God for
sex. It's kept me sane.'

Waughman and his crew had been put in C Flight and,
unlike Paul Zankey, were given over three weeks in which
to train further through cross-country navigational flights,
fighter affiliation flights and practice bomb-drop runs over
the training site at Wainfleet on The Wash. Not until 23
December were they put on the roster for their first mission. As with the Americans, the British system was to
send a new pilot up as second pilot with an experienced
crew for his first mission, but Berlin was a maximum
effort, so Waughman had to forgo that opportunity to gain
much-needed experience. They would just have to trust
their training, trust each other, and hope for the best.

Up to that point, Waughman had been really pleased
with his crew. They were all NCOs, so were able to keep

together when not flying, rather than heading off to separate digs and messes. Crewing up at the Operational
Training Unit was always a haphazard affair, but they
were all young, reasonably like-minded and most instinctively understood that by cooperating and getting on they
were more likely to succeed and get through their tour.
Wartime camaraderie was intense and helped forge firm
friendships. Waughman warmed to them quickly, even
though they were all quite different in background and
character. Norman Westby, his bomb-aimer, had been
born in a gypsy caravan. His navigator, Alec Cowan, had
lied about his age to get in and was only seventeen, not
that Waughman knew this at the time. His wireless operator was a Welshman inevitably nicknamed 'Taffy'. He
liked his beer, but Waughman never doubted his skill or
reliability. 'He was a rogue,' said Waughman, 'an amazing
character. But very conscientious.'

The only member of the crew he had concerns over was
his engineer, Les Reeves, and on that first trip, having successfully taken off and climbed up above the cloud, they
were crossing the Channel when Reeves told Waughman
their instruments were defective and that the GEE was not
working. They should turn back, Reeves told him. Waughman felt he had to listen to his flight engineer; flying all the
way to Berlin was a big task at any time, but on a first operation, and with defective navigational gear and faulty
instruments, the odds seemed insurmountable. And so
Waughman turned for home. And an aborted mission did
not count on their tally of thirty for a first tour.

Christmas Day was spent on standby for an operation
that was then scrubbed, so it wasn't until Wednesday,
29 December, that they flew off again for Berlin. Again,

Reeves claimed that some of the Lancaster's instruments were defective, but this time they flew on. 'Target pretty hot,' noted Waughman in his diary. They encountered both fighters and flak over Berlin, shells bursting all around them during the bomb run and then were twice attacked over the target by Hajo Herrmann's *Wilde Sau* and once again on the return leg. Each time, Waughman managed to take evasive action and the fighters disengaged to attack another aircraft instead, and somehow, after seven and a quarter hours in the air, they managed to make it back in one piece.

By this time, Waughman was starting to have doubts about his engineer, who seemed a little jumpy, but inexperience got the better of him and so he did nothing about it. On the evening of Saturday, 1 January 1944, the target was once again Berlin, and they were one of 421 Lancasters sent off on this first day of the new year. As they crossed the Dutch coast, however, they were hit by flak and the starboard out engine caught fire. At this Reeves panicked. 'He just sat on the floor,' said Waughman, 'and shivered and sweated and cried.' By a combination of diving and using the inbuilt extinguisher, they managed to get the fire out, but Reeves reckoned there was an oil leak. Lancasters were perfectly capable of flying on three engines and, as Waughman admitted, with a bit more experience he might have continued to the target even with one engine down. However, with Reeves in such a state he felt he had no option but to turn back. They then got hopelessly lost.

Eventually, they made it back, but Waughman was hauled in before the CO. Two aborted missions out of three was not a good record, and his crew had got badly lost. 'You know, we can't have this sort of thing going on,' the squadron commander told him. 'Any more of this sort of thing and we'll make you LMF and you'll be posted off.' 'LMF' stood for 'lack of moral fibre'. Waughman was being threatened with being sacked for cowardice. However, it was not Waughman who was kicked out of the squadron for LMF, but Reeves. 'He disappeared off the station,' said Waughman. 'He just left.' Waughman discovered that their plane really had been defective; their G4 compass, so vital for navigation, had been going awry because steel links had been put into the control column. They had been flying on the right compass headings but in all the wrong directions. Fortunately, their ground crew explained this to the wing commander and Waughman was given both a new engineer and an exoneration.

That same evening, New Year's Day 1944, Hajo Herrmann had seen the intelligence reports that the RAF was once more heading to Berlin. Although Göring had expressly grounded him, no one in the *Wilde Sau* had greater experience than him at flying at night in such appalling conditions. After watching his pilots take off into the icy cloud too many times for comfort, he decided that, along with his adjutant and Friedrich-Karl 'Tutti' Müller, a fighter ace just about to take over command of JG3, they would head out of Berlin to Staaken on the western edge of the city. There they picked up their FW190s and scrambled into the darkness. The cloud base was at 1,500 feet, better than it might have been, but it was freezing and there was a high risk of icing until they broke free of the cloud base, which would be at around 12,000 feet. Icing was dangerous, as it caught on the wings and the propeller, slowing the aircraft as it climbed and dramatically reducing the performance and bite of the prop, which could cause an aircraft to stall and simply drop out of the sky.

Herrmann and his fellows decided they should stay under the cloud until they had reached full throttle, then climb steeply and through the ice-zone as quickly as possible. The plan worked, and they broke out of the cloud without mishap. Herrmann then flew up to 21,000 feet, circling at low throttle until the enemy appeared.

Suddenly in his headphones he heard, 'Leading bombers, Brandenburg.' They were now close. Markers began dropping from the sky – red and green – followed by the back-up markers. The British Pathfinders were marking their target. Flak began to erupt, followed by their own illuminating flares, which was just what Herrmann needed. Now he saw a Lancaster heading towards him from the south. Opening the throttle, Herrmann dived down towards it, firing at the wings and cockpit. His aim was good and a large chunk of debris hurtled past him. It was 2.57 a.m. and he radioed that he had scored a probable, then turned back into the bright arena now over the city as flares and searchlights created a light glow that lit up the bombers amply. Below and about half a mile away he spotted another bomber silhouetted against the 'shroud' – the cloud illuminated by searchlights – and although momentarily dazzled by flares, he quickly regained his bead and opened fire again in two quick successive bursts. Flames erupted from the bomber, rapidly taking hold, and the Lancaster fell away. It was 3.05 a.m.

A loud crack resounded in Herrmann's cockpit and he felt pain in his leg. Tracer shot past him: he had been hit by a British night-fighter. 'I had become a victim of my own shroud,' he noted, 'the blazing bomber had made it even brighter.' Herrmann flew on and out of the glare. He had now lost all feeling in his leg, so was relieved to find it still there. When he called Staaken there was no response and he realized his radio had been shot up in the attack. Freezing air hurtled into the cockpit on to his face and neck. He could not land at night in these conditions without radio contact; he had a wound in his leg that was bleeding badly; and the temperature around him was 50° below. Herrmann was starting to feel faint. He knew he had to get out – and soon, before he passed out – but he was too high. A burst of oxygen made little difference. Pushing the stick forward, he dived down, desperately trying to keep himself going, then pulled out at around 800 feet, hoping he might see the lights of an airfield and so take his chances at landing, but there was nothing – just inky darkness and falling snow.

The time had come to bail out. Right leg up against his body, unbuckle the harness, oxygen leads pulled clear, jettison the canopy, push the stick forward, and suddenly he was free, falling through the sky. He pulled the ripcord and, with a lurch, the parachute blossomed and he was drifting down through the sleet. He landed with a painful thump and pulled the parachute towards him, thinking he would wrap himself up in it until dawn, but then he felt the blood in his boot and realized that might be too late. Crawling with his arms and one good leg, he soon spotted a house and made for it, calling out. A woman opened the door. Herrmann was flooded with relief. Within an hour he was recovering in the hospital at nearby Hagen. From his bed he had a message sent to his command post and a short while later he was wheeled into the doctor's office to take a call from Führer Headquarters. It was Hitler's Luftwaffe adjutant on the phone. The Führer was sending his personal congratulations and asking him to report to him as soon as he was fit enough.

Within a couple of days, Herrmann's old *Wilde Sau* friends had him transferred to a sanatorium near their base at Bonn–Endenich. 'It was a great joy to my stressed, worn-out soul to have dear, friendly people coming to visit me,' he noted. 'There, there was no war. In my mind's eye, I saw far-off, peaceful times, small things, fine things, brotherly love.'

Those German civilians still stuck in Berlin, however, enjoyed no respite. Margarete Dos had returned home to find the city in ruins. The colour seemed to have disappeared. Trees were shredded, skeletal shapes. Familiar buildings had collapsed. There was no birdsong, no children laughing. Rubble filled many of the streets. Half-collapsed buildings still held the remnants of the homes they had once been: a bathtub perched precariously, or a wall still papered but open to the elements. Giant potholes filled with water were a feature of almost every street.

Her student days over, Margarete had decided to do something useful and joined the Red Cross at their office on the Berlinerstrasse, near where she was now living with her mother in Charlottenburg. Her own father had died when she was ten and her stepfather, an officer in the navy, was away at war, as was her younger brother, Dieter, now in the army and serving on the Eastern Front. Her mother was also helping out as a railway station nurse, so the two of them had taken to cycling through the ruins to their work.

The days took on a regular pattern. Up early after little sleep. Quickly dress. Feel hungry – rationing in Berlin was severe – and eat some *Muckefuck*, as it was known – rough, almost ersatz bread – with 'IG Farben' jam. As they cycled to work they would see what had been destroyed the previous night. At the main railway station she, her mother and other Red Cross nurses would meet the trains and do what they could to help the wounded, the frightened and the displaced. Often, the best they could offer was comfort and a hot drink. Berlin had become a miserable place – a city where everyone was living on the front line.

Certainly, the accumulative carnage in Berlin was on an incredible scale and already far out of all proportion to anything that had befallen London. The raid on 16/17 December alone caused considerable damage to the Reichsbahn, the German railway system, and to rolling stock. Large numbers of Berliners were deserting the city, so the strain on the railway was proving increasingly debilitating, as Margarete and her mother were witnessing first hand. Because of the shortage of oil and because Germany had never had the motor transport to rival Britain or the USA, they were heavily over-reliant on their railway. This attack alone caused a hold-up of six days to a thousand wagons headed for the Eastern Front. Successful military operations depended on knowing what supplies were arriving and when. The troops at the front were increasingly finding themselves hampered by shortage of vital supplies.

On the other hand, Berlin accounted for only 8 per cent

of Germany's total industrial output. While some 40 per cent of the country's electronic industry was based in the capital, it was well dispersed. And unlike an older city such as Hamburg, Berlin generally had wider streets and far fewer wooden buildings. There had been no firestorm in Berlin.

Harris was doggedly staying on the course he had set for his force, but it was becoming ever more apparent that the Battle of Berlin, as Harris called it, was falling some way short of his initial aims. Germany was not about to collapse and, despite the streets of Berlin steadily filling with rubble, the returns on this huge bombing offensive against the German capital were diminishing, while more and more crews were being lost in the effort. The defences all across the Reich, but especially over Berlin, were stiffening. The number of anti-aircraft guns had doubled since the start of 1943. By December, 3,463 flak batteries were operating in the defence of the Reich, most of them around the key centres. Since the start of the year, heavy gun batteries – 88mm, 105mm and 128mm guns – had risen from 1,578 to 2,236, and medium and light batteries from 1,253 to 1,586. There were also a number of Gerät 50s – 149.1mm guns. The number of guns per battery was also rising: from four to six in a heavy battery, then increased to eight and sometimes more. As many as 15,000 heavy flak guns now defended Germany, with as many as 1,000 in and around Berlin. On top of the flak towers were twin 128mm guns that could fire a 26kg shell 34,000 feet vertically into the air at a velocity of just under 3,000 feet per second and at a rate of up to 14 rounds per minute. German night-fighters circled about as well: Hajo Herrmann's *Wilde Sau* and those of the *Zahme Sau*, the ordinary units like those of Wim Johnen. It was no wonder Bomber Command's casualties were mounting. In ten raids on Berlin from November up to the night of 2/3 January, Bomber Command had lost 239 aircraft. That amounted to more than 25 per cent of the daily availability.

By the end of the first week of January 1944, Harris's earlier claim that the cross-Channel invasion would not be needed was starting to look hollow, which was all the more reason why POINTBLANK, aimed at defeating the Luftwaffe, was so increasingly, pressingly, important. Time, that most precious commodity, was running short.

CHAPTER 14

Spaatz and Doolittle
Take Charge

On 27 December, General Hap Arnold had sent a
missive from Washington DC to the commanding
generals of the Eighth and Fifteenth Air Forces. It was
brief and to the point and made five key points:

a) Aircraft factories in this country are turning out
large quantities of airplanes, engines and
accessories.

b) Our training establishments are operating
twenty-four hours per day, seven days per week,
training crews.

c) We are now furnishing fully all the aircraft and
crews to take care of your attrition.

d) It is a conceded fact that OVERLORD and
ANVIL [the planned invasion of southern
France] will not be possible unless the German
Air Force is destroyed.

e) Therefore, my personal message to you – this is a *MUST* – is to, "*Destroy the Enemy Air Force wherever you find them, in the air, on the ground and in the factories.*"

As a message, it was unequivocal: he had given them the tools and now they should attack with ruthless determination, no matter the cost, because there were more crews and aircraft on their way and the stakes couldn't possibly be higher.

On Wednesday, 29 December, General Tooey Spaatz arrived in London, a place with which he was now very familiar, to take up his new command at a pivotal moment in the fortunes of the US Army Air Forces. From the date of the Eighth's first mission on 17 August 1942 to the end of 1943, they had lost 1,013 aircraft and around 10,000 aircrew. A further 174 aircraft had been so badly shot to pieces they had been scrapped and 1,008 on top of that had been sufficiently damaged to be withdrawn from the battle for repair. Another 5,932 had suffered damage of varying lesser severity. On the other hand, the flow of aircraft was now reaching England uninterrupted. The U-boat menace had been largely eradicated, ensuring the smooth passage of shipping across the Atlantic. American factories, only just starting to get into gear in 1942, were now operating at full steam, while the once tiny Army Air Corps had now grown into the vast Army Air Forces, with huge numbers of training schools and airfields across the USA. At the end of November, Eaker had been able to dispatch 633 bombers; by 13 December – when Jimmy Stewart and Robbie Robinson had flown their first missions – 710 bombers had been taking off. There were now 26 bomb groups and 12 fighter groups operating from England alone. That amounted to 4,242 combat aircraft, a vast total and more than the Luftwaffe had ever been able to concentrate into one theatre. Within another six weeks, Spaatz would have a further 12 heavy bomber and 4 fighter groups in Italy as well.

One of Portal's and General Marshall's concerns over the establishment of USSTAF was that it would absorb extra layers of staff and become too unwieldy, but Spaatz simply moved into Eighth Air Force's HQ at Bushy Park in south-west London, the same headquarters he had first established in 1942, promptly abolished it, then absorbed most of the personnel into his new headquarters and sent what was left to VIII Bomber Command HQ at Wycombe Abbey. This then became Doolittle's new HQ for Eighth Air Force. VIII Bomber Command simply stayed where it was, working under and alongside Doolittle's staff. A major new headquarters had thus been neatly and cannily established without any extra buildings or staff whatso-ever. At the same time, Spaatz and Walter Bedell Smith, Eisenhower's Chief of Staff, agreed to locate the new Supreme Headquarters at Bushy Park too, which would not only ensure close collaboration between air and land operations, but give Spaatz unbridled access to the new Supreme Allied Commander.

There was a palpable feeling of the new year heralding a new dawn and a fresh sense of purpose, one that Spaatz was determined to put into practice. Eaker might have had fewer aircraft to play with, and for much of the time no H2X – which was a development of the British H2S, but used a different band frequency – or many long-range fighters, but Spaatz wanted to inject a far more aggressive approach into the strategic air campaign. Prescribed doc-trine dictated that in the Eighth the main role of fighters was to escort the bombers. Spaatz wanted that defensive mindset thrown out. 'It is my belief that we do not get suf-ficient attrition by hitting fighter factories,' he told staff at the Eighth's War Room, 'therefore we must place emphasis on airdromes and knocking them down in the air. Our mission is destroying the German Air Force.'

On Wednesday, 5 January, General Jimmy Doolittle flew from North Africa to England and two days later took command of the Eighth, moving himself into Wycombe Abbey. Among his first duties was to pay his respects to some of the senior British figures alongside whom he would be working. An appointment was made to see King George VI at Buckingham Palace. At the allo-cated hour, Doolittle arrived and was given a protocol briefing. Never, he was told, speak to the King first – he was to wait to be spoken to. On entering, the King silently motioned to him to sit, but then stony silence followed. Eventually, thinking he had to say something, Doolittle cleared his throat and mentioned how glad he was to be in England and how he intended to ensure that the excellent relationship between both nations would continue under his command. The King eyed him and then said, 'We're certainly sorry to lose Eaker.'

He didn't get much further with Air Marshal Harris. After presenting himself at Bomber Command HQ, he was ushered into Harris's office, where he saluted smartly. Harris motioned to him to sit down, then, without look-ing up, continued shuffling some papers. Eventually, they exchanged some brief pleasantries and Doolittle left. 'The British,' he noted, 'probably since the Middle Ages, have been suspicious of outsiders until they prove themselves loyal to the Crown.' He soon discovered British intelligence had planted an officer at his headquarters who was to report anything that might be worthy of putting into a dossier, so Doolittle started making generally positive and encouraging remarks in a voluble way. He also sent one of his own intelligence men to try to get a copy of the dossier and then report back, which he duly did. Fortunately, it contained nothing to worry him.

As Doolittle wrote in a letter to his old friend General George Patton, he was keenly aware that 'miracles are confidently expected.' His first task was to learn the mood and thoughts of those carrying the war to Germany and so he made a point of visiting every wing and group in his command, and of holding meetings with his commanders in which he asked them for their thoughts and suggestions. These he then brought back for discussion with his own staff. It was clear to him, just as Spaatz had intimated, that new tactics were needed. He was also aware, as was Spaatz, that the fighters, rather than the bombers, held the key to destroying the Luftwaffe. In many ways, he was fortunate. He was taking over at a time when a lot of the shortcomings facing Eaker had been resolved. Still only one group of Mustangs was available, but there was another of twin-engine P-38s and more and bigger drop tanks. Thunderbolts now had a theoretical range of over 400 miles; P-38s could manage 850; Mustangs, with fuselage tanks and 150-gallon 'torpedo' drop tanks, could, theoretically fly up to 1,400 miles. As Spaatz made crystal clear in his operational directive to Doolittle, the key was to destroy German fighter aircraft in the air and on the ground.

Doolittle thought the best strategy was not to hug protectively close to the bombers but to go after the enemy aggressively. 'Fighter aircraft are designed to go after enemy fighters,' he noted. 'Fighter pilots are usually pugnacious individuals by nature and trained to be aggressive in the air. Their machines are specifically designed for offensive action.' He believed his fighters should be told to hunt out and attack the enemy before they reached the bombers.

In this he was unquestionably right. Hugging the bombers had been catastrophic to the Luftwaffe during the Battle of Britain because it had deprived them of the twin advantages of speed and choice of angle of attack. By actively hunting for the enemy, American fighters would be able to climb high, spot them, then, after manoeuvring so that the sun was behind them, dive down at full speed and with the chance of surprise.

When Doolittle visited Major-General Bill Kepner, the commander of VIII Fighter Command, he spotted a sign on the wall of his office that said, 'The first duty of the Eighth Air Force fighter is to bring the bombers back alive.'

'Bill, who dreamed that up?' Doolittle asked him.

'The sign was here when we arrived,' he replied.

'That statement is no longer in effect,' Doolittle told him. 'Take that sign down. Put up another one that says: THE FIRST DUTY OF THE EIGHTH AIR FORCE FIGHTERS IS TO DESTROY GERMAN FIGHTERS.'

'You mean you're authorizing me to take the offensive?' Kepner asked him.

'I'm directing you to.'

Kepner could not have been more delighted. For over two months he had been urging Eaker to allow his boys to go after the enemy, but had been repeatedly turned down. Together, he and Doolittle eagerly discussed how this might work. Some fighters would still be assigned to escort work, but the bulk would go directly after the enemy. 'Flush them out in the air,' Doolittle told him, 'and beat them up on the ground on the way home. Your first priority is to take the offensive.'

Kepner soon reported that his fighter boys were delighted at this new instruction. The same was not so true of the bomber crews, whose commanders swiftly wrote and visited in person to tell him he was, in effect, a murderer. Their bomber formations would now be slaughtered. 'There was no compromise as far as I was concerned,' wrote Doolittle, 'and many bomber crew remained unhappy.' Genial he might have been, but Doolittle was also tough. He was also absolutely right.

At the same time that Doolittle was tearing up the rules of fighter escorts, he was inheriting a bomber force that was not only starting to grow dramatically in size, but also in capability. Few of the pre-war planners had envisaged quite so much miserable weather as had been experienced that winter, which had made something of a mockery of plans for precision bombing. However, bombing techniques were improving further, with the Americans now convinced about the benefits of using H2X, or what they termed 'radar bombing', which meant, in theory, that they would be no longer quite so dependent on having clear skies over the target.

There were currently only twenty sets, enough for a dozen special training aircraft and a few other sets for spares. The first mission had come on 3 November, when just eleven H2X-equipped B-17s and trained crews had led

539 bombers on Wilhelmshaven. Some 1,400 tons of bombs had been dropped through thick ten-tenths cloud, and although the attack lacked the accuracy of a normal raid with clear vision over the target, it had been an encouraging first effort. With considerably more H2X-equipped Pathfinders evenly spread among the bomb groups, accuracy levels looked likely to rise dramatically.

The problem was that, rather like the Merlin-powered Mustang, H2X was arriving just a bit late; only on 10 December had Eaker urgently asked for more and suggested each bomb group be equipped with six H2X-carrying Pathfinders. 'The most critical need of the Strategic Air Forces,' Spaatz cabled Arnold in the second week of January, 'is for more Pathfinder aircraft. A few H2X planes now will profit our cause more than several hundred in six months.' The first production models of H2X would not be reaching Spaatz's forces until February, however. Until then, it was left to the same overworked crews.

Thus in January 1944 little that was especially 'precision' marked the way the Eighth was attacking targets, and nor had the targets chosen since Schweinfurt II been particularly high priority on the POINTBLANK list – something that needed to change. Hovering in the minds of both Spaatz and Doolittle, however, was Operation ARGUMENT, which was in effect a sub-plan of POINT-BLANK and which was meant to be a week-long, concentrated assault on the industrial backbone of the Luftwaffe. It had been drawn up by the Combined Operational Planning Committee (COPC), which in turn had been set up in June 1943 when the POINTBLANK directive had been issued. The COPC consisted of representatives of both RAF Bomber and Fighter Commands, as well as Eighth Air Force, including Headquarters and VIII Bomber and Fighter Commands. The idea was for this new body to come up with coordinated tactical plans for new, specific operations. ARGUMENT was one of these plans, and envisaged using primarily the Eighth and Fifteenth Air Forces to pound key industrial targets while at the same time drawing up enemy fighters. The aim was nothing less than a decisive hammer blow on the Luftwaffe – a blow from which the German Air Force would never recover.

ARGUMENT had been drafted at the beginning of November and approved on the 29th. Key to any possible success, however, was a week of half-decent weather, and so far that had simply not come about. In many ways, that had proved a blessing in disguise, because with every passing week both US air forces were getting stronger and better equipped. None the less, with the clock now ticking inexorably towards D-Day, Spaatz, especially, was chomping at the bit to get on with it. That made Doolittle equally determined to get ARGUMENT under way as soon as he could.

On Tuesday, 4 January a small force of just sixty-eight B-17s from two bomb groups was sent to Münster, while nearly five hundred hit Kiel. Although the diversionary raid on Münster was much smaller, the bombers heading there were escorted by a swarm of fighters – some 430 in all, including three squadrons of the 56th.

Among those heading to Münster was Larry Goldstein and the crew of *Worry Wart*. Goldstein and his mates had been woken at 2 a.m. – the earliest start ever, which made them all worry that the target might be Berlin, so it was something of a relief to learn they would be penetrating only western Germany after all. By 7 a.m. they were airborne and heading up through the early-morning gloom on their ninth mission.

The fighter escort saved them from the worst of the enemy fighters, but the flak was heavy. Over the target and with the bomb bays open, their bombardier, Lieutenant Kent Keith, was looking down through the Plexiglas waiting to signal 'Bombs away' when the nose was hit by flak and the Perspex shattered. A splinter hit him just above the left eye; while it bled a bit he was otherwise all right, but it underlined just how thin the line could be between getting a small nick and being killed. 'No other damage,' noted Goldstein in his diary, 'and I consider ourselves very lucky. It was not exactly a "milk run." '

However, the large number of fighter escorts had been one of the main reasons why not a single bomber was shot down on the mission – in fact, the only casualties were two that collided near the Initial Point. Certainly, the pilots of the 56th FG had been quick to pounce on any enemy they saw. Bob Johnson and Gabby Gabreski were both flying that day and using brand-new paddle-blades on the propellers. This gave the P-47s massive extra bite as well as both climbing and diving speed, as Bob Johnson discovered first-hand. Spotting some Me109s directly beneath him, Johnson rolled over and dived down. 'And wow! What a dive!' he wrote. 'I hauled back on the stick, afraid that the engine would tear right out of the mounts.' Unfortunately, he dived so fast he completely overshot them. Cursing to himself, he vowed to get back and put in some practice time to get used to this new power.

Not everyone made the same mistake, however, as Heinz Knoke discovered to his cost. He was closing in to attack the bombers when his Messerschmitt was hit by German flak. Immediately the tail felt sluggish and he realized his prop and the front part of his engine had been completely shot away. It was all he could do to keep the stricken fighter under control, but a moment later a Thunderbolt dived down on him and shot up his wing, which burst into flames. Knoke was now in serious trouble and only by using all his strength could he keep the control column vertical between his legs. Flames were already licking the cockpit; it was time to bail out. Off flew the canopy and, with his leads and harness undone, he was suddenly jerked out of the cockpit before he was ready, but left dangling, his parachute snagged on something and billowing open. With his right leg outside the cockpit and his left still in, and with the flames growing, the aircraft plunged towards the ground. The force of the slipstream was so great he simply couldn't move.

In intense pain, Knoke could barely breathe and now flames were licking across his body. The pressure was immense and he had plummeted some 12,000 feet when, with one last effort and with blood streaming from his nose, he managed to get his right leg back inside, push over the stick so that the aircraft half-rolled, stood on its tail and then dropped, but in the process Knoke was thrown clear at last. For a fraction of a moment he was falling alongside the fuselage, then something hit his back with a mighty blow and struck his head, knocking him out cold.

He came to surrounded by clouds and dangling from his parachute. Glancing down at the ripcord, he saw it was still in its socket; miraculously, the chute had opened fully by itself. Now the ground was rushing towards him and his parachute was swinging wildly from side to side. Almost horizontal, he managed somehow to avoid the roof of a house and landed heavily on solid frozen ground in the garden. Knoke gasped, then lost consciousness again.

When he awoke, he was in a hospital bed with a fractured skull, fractured lumbar vertebrae, severe bruising of the right pelvis, bruising of the hip, severe concussion and temporary paralysis of the right side due to his back injury. Vomiting continually and in great pain, he wished he could sleep, but that eluded him. He shouldn't have even been flying that day – it was only because of casualties in the group that he had done so. 'And today,' he wrote later in his diary, 'was to have been the last day of my leave with Lilo and little Ingrid . . .'

That same day, Tuesday, 4 January, tragedy struck the 381st BG at Ridgewell. 'Today,' noted Chaplain James Good Brown, 'war came close to us. It hit us in the face like a ton of bricks.' That morning, two of the first pilots to have arrived with the 381st in the summer were completing their twenty-fifth and final missions and would then be shipped back home, their combat service finished. One of them was Lieutenant Cecil M. Clore and the target was Kiel – not the worst trip, because they would have the Little Friends with them the whole way. At the briefing, everyone was patting Clore on the back and wishing him good luck.

Clore took off as normal, but then something went wrong – what, exactly, remained unclear – but suddenly his Fortress was on fire. Quickly, the bombs were jettisoned in a field, about five of them exploding and causing the ground to pulsate for miles around. Desperately, Lieutenant Clore tried to land the plane and so headed towards another field, but it was still not fully light and instead the plane hit the edge of a wood next to the field and was torn to pieces.

Chaplain Brown was immediately called to the hospital, unsure at this stage whether any of the men were alive. On arrival, he saw five bodies – the men who had been hurled from the wreck of the aircraft as it had crashed. The tail gunner, Sergeant Richard E. Ingmire, had been smashed against a tree. 'To stand there and see the bodies of five men whom we loved, men who gave their blood and life for what they were told was a good cause, and who did so willingly, causes us to wonder whether these dead shall not have died in vain,' wrote Brown. 'Let us hope that we shall be nearer a goal than we were before. This is my hope.'

Brown left the hospital along with an ambulance crew to try to find the remaining five members of the crew in the wreckage. The fires had died out by the time they reached it, so they could easily pick out the main structure of the wrecked Fortress. They spotted a head among a pile of twisted metal. They got hold of a leg and tried to pull the man out but he wouldn't budge; more wreckage needed moving first. 'The body emerged,' wrote the chaplain. 'But the head and arms were caught under heavy material. Some wires had to be cut. With our hands, we had to pull aside the burned material.' One by one, they pulled them all free, grappling with bits of shattered aircraft and prising off charred flying suits to collect dogtags and any unburned papers, lockets and mementoes. Brown was horrified and sickened. 'One must see a burned body to know what it looks like,' he wrote. 'Yet we had to face this awfulness in order to identify the bodies. We had no choice. The grim aspect of war was forced upon us whether we liked it or not.' The chaplain tried to convince himself that they had died because of the war as surely as if they had been shot down over Germany, but the stark and vivid sight of ten young lives cut short in such a violent and cruel manner affected him deeply. Nor could he get rid of the smell of the burned bodies. It was as though it had pervaded his very soul.

On Friday, 7 January 1944 the target for the Eighth was Ludwigshafen. All three bomb divisions were being used and Captain Jimmy Stewart, now on his fourth mission, was bomb group leader for the 445th, following the 389th BG and with the 93rd BG off to their starboard. That put Stewart in charge of sixteen ships and sitting in the co-pilot's seat of *Lady Shamrock*, skippered by Lieutenant Bill Conley. In all, the sixteen B-24s of the 445th were part of a 420-bomber force all heading towards the IG Farben plant outside the city on the Rhine. Escorting them were even more fighters: 571 in all.

The boys of the 56th FG were once more among the fighter escorts. By this time, Bob Johnson had thoroughly mastered the new paddle-blades on his Thunderbolt, as he had demonstrated the previous day over Koblenz. Diving successfully down on to fifteen Focke-Wulfs, he had seen Gabby Gabreski lock on to one of the enemy planes, then watched the German's wingman go hard after his squadron commander in turn. Johnson spotted him swing towards Gabreski, so turned hard himself and made a head-on pass. The Focke-Wulf pulled up steeply and turned to starboard, while Johnson, throwing his Jug into a roll, went after him. Pulling his Thunderbolt into a tight turn, Johnson kept rolling and firing, sticking to his opponent's tail like glue as the German tried every trick he knew to shake off his pursuer. Still Johnson kept on him, wounding his enemy like a matador toying with a bull. Bits of airframe were falling off, bullets tearing holes in the metal. Eventually, the German flicked over and dived, yawing the plane from side to side to throw off Johnson's aim. 'He was terrific,' noted Johnson, 'one of the very best.' The German's mistake, however, had been to dive. There had been a time when the FW190 and Me109 could out-dive any plane, so it had been a reliable way to get out of trouble. But not any more. Johnson dived too, quickly gained on him, drew in close and opened fire. 'The bullets tore into his cockpit and left wing root, flaming a fuel tank,' he wrote. 'The Focke-Wulf tumbled crazily, end over end, and tore apart.' It was victory number eleven for Johnson.

Meanwhile, on the 7th, no enemy fighters had so far got near Jimmy Stewart and the B-24s of the 445th, although there was plenty of flak along the 30-mile run-in from the Initial Point to the target and in *Lady Shamrock* the crew were being bounced and jolted about all the way as shells burst around them. None the less, everything was going well: they dropped their bombs, then climbed and began making the turn for home.

Ahead, the 389th BG were already turning, so Stewart intended to tack on behind and simply follow them home, but he and his crew soon realized they were headed on the wrong bearing, some 30 degrees off course.

'What are they doing?' Conley asked, giving his compass a tap. Stewart had been part of the briefing earlier, so knew the course should have been 283 degrees, but the leader of the 389th was steering them on a bearing of 245 degrees instead.

Stewart called up the leader of the 389th and pointed out their navigation error, but to no avail. 'We know what we're doing,' he was told. 'Get off the air.' This presented Stewart with a difficult conundrum. Not far away, another group of bombers was leaving on course and he could have directed his group, and with it the 93rd, to tack on behind and follow it home. That, however, would have meant abandoning the 389th up ahead. A single group, groping its way homeward, would be vulnerable to say the least, and it would also mean splitting the fighter protection that was on offer. On the other hand, if he continued in the interests of keeping the formation close and tight and giving the wayward 389th a better chance, then he would be exposing his own group to possible fighter attacks and flak damage; routes were carefully chosen to avoid flak and enemy fighters. Wandering off even by a few degrees could mean the difference between getting home unscathed and having several bombers knocked out of the sky. To make matters worse for Stewart and his crew, at that moment the de-icer on his starboard No. 3 engine packed up and as a result the supercharger froze, which meant they were now reduced to three good engines.

Ultimately, it came down to which course was likely to cause fewer overall casualties and so, with a heavy heart, Stewart decided to follow the 389th. Pushing the broadcast button on his radio, he said, 'F Lead to Group. All right, listen up. I want this formation as tight as it's ever been. Look sharp. We're covering our wing lead.'

'But they're heading for Paris!' said his navigator.

'Yeah,' replied Stewart, 'that means we all are.' A few moments later, he added to the entire group, 'Radio silence, everybody.' From now on, the only sound would be Stewart urging his group to fly ever tighter together.

Already they had said enough to rouse the Luftwaffe, whose listening services and observers and radar would have picked up on the confusion. Sure enough, enemy fighters soon appeared, tearing into the formations. One of the first B-24s to go down was the lead ship of the 389th. They continued on until they could see Paris, and even the Eiffel Tower, down below. Only then did the 389th realize their mistake and dog-leg westwards. So far, not a single aircraft from the 445th had been shot down, but they were incurring some battle damage, including *Lady Shamrock*, when the de-icer on the No. 1 engine was hit.

Eventually, both the flak and the fighters melted away and soon after they could see the French coast. At this point *Lady Shamrock*'s No. 1 engine packed up; the B-24 could still fly on just two engines, but with less power, which meant dropping out of formation. Fortunately, however, their work was largely done. Stewart radioed to the deputy lead bomber to take over, then told his crew to throw out anything they could to lighten the load.

Lady Shamrock touched down again safely at Tibenham some seven and a quarter hours after taking off. Incredibly, the 445th had not lost a single ship. A few days later, a note of thanks came through from Colonel Milton Arnold, commander of the 389th. 'The good judgement of Captain Stewart, your Group leader,' he wrote, 'in maintaining an excellent group formation yet making every attempt to hold his position in the Combat Wing formation is to be commended.'

CHAPTER 15

Thirty Against One

Tuesday, 11 January 1944. To the meteorologists, it had looked the previous day as though there might be a break in the weather, so Doolittle and Anderson had decided to make the most of this and send a heavy force into Germany to hit targets at Brunswick, Halberstadt and Oschersleben, all quite close to one another to the west and south-west of Berlin, and all with aircraft assembly plants.

At Kimbolton, the crews of the 379th BG were woken earlier than usual. As they dragged themselves out of bed, Hugh McGinty and his pals in their Quonset hut had got into a routine of turning on the radio to listen to the Irish-American traitor and Nazi broadcaster Lord Haw-Haw on one of the German stations. In particular they wanted to hear the 'Guests of the Reich' section in which captured airmen were listed. Today, Lord Haw-Haw specifically mentioned the 379th: 'The Luftwaffe is waiting to welcome you this morning,' he said. None of them was too bothered by this. Then, as they were about to leave for the mess hall, the broadcast ended with a song from *Snow White and the Seven Dwarfs*: 'Heigh ho, heigh ho, it's off to work we go'. 'That put us in a better mood,' noted McGinty, 'and we sang all the way to chow.'

Despite this lightening of the mood, McGinty felt the briefing room was noticeably tense that morning. Everyone could sense it. As the commander entered, they all stood and came to attention, then, as the curtain was drawn back and they saw the long line heading east in the direction of Berlin, a loud spontaneous groan was let out by the crews. But it wasn't Berlin; for 1st Division, including the 379th, the target was Oschersleben, some 50 miles south-west of the capital. That was still a long way to go.

The plan was explained. The 2nd Division was going to Brunswick and the 3rd to Halberstadt. They were shown where they could expect the worst of the flak and warned that they might attract considerable enemy-fighter attention, which was, of course, a major reason for mounting the raid. The fighters would be protecting in the relay system recently implemented: Thunderbolts and P-38 Lightnings to the target in relays; then, over the target area, the new long-range P-51 Mustangs of the 354th Fighter Group would provide protection. As they turned for home, they would be met by yet more P-47s, which would escort them back to England. This made the crews feel a little better – it was the first time the Mustangs had ever been briefed to accompany them on a deep-penetration raid. Just to make sure the bomber crews didn't start taking pot-shots at these new Little Friends, they were shown plenty of identification pictures so that they wouldn't mistake them for enemy planes. 'The chaplain,' noted McGinty, 'was a very popular guy that morning.'

Eighty miles away at Boxted, Dick Turner had been woken as normal and made his way to the headquarters buildings for the 354th Fighter Group's briefing. It was a significant moment in the history of the Eighth Air Force: the first time bombers had ever been sent to the heart of the Reich with escorts all the way there and back.

At Kimbolton, Hugh McGinty and his crew loaded up their kit and headed out to their plane. They were getting a new ship, but it was still undergoing modifications and wasn't ready, so they were flying one of the spares. Whatever the weathermen had thought, at Kimbolton the cloud was low and the atmosphere damp. Take-off was delayed twice, which only added to the tension they all felt. They didn't want to head into the jaws of the lion, but nor did they want to have the mission scrubbed; it was draining to get oneself keyed up only to be stood down, and, of course, a scrubbed mission meant they were no closer to finishing their tour.

Finally, a green flare was fired over the airfield and they began running up their engines. When the second flare went up, they started taxiing. Misty low cloud and drizzle covered the wide-open expanse of the airfield, but at last Lieutenant Ernal Bridwell's crew were at the end of the runway. As the bomber ahead of them disappeared into the mist, Bridwell opened the throttles to 2,500 revs, with superchargers set at 52 inches of manifold pressure, released the brakes and off they sped, hurtling down the runway and lifting off with 1,800 lb of incendiaries in their bomb bays.

McGinty was tired from the early start and the tension he had felt all morning, so instead of getting into his tail turret, he opted to lie himself down on the catwalk in front of his position and try to get some sleep. He soon nodded off and woke only when he heard the navigator,

Bill Rau, calling on someone to check that their tail gunner was all right: McGinty hadn't answered the oxygen check. He now clambered into his gun station and checked in.

Looking around him, he saw the groups all starting to form up on their leaders. It was always an extraordinary sight: hundreds of heavy bombers emerging from the cloud base, circling and climbing and slotting into their part of the formation. The clouds below them were bright, with the group forming up below silhouetted against them. A rainbow seemed to circle their shadows on the clouds. Flying in close formation with bombers either side and ahead and behind was easier said than done, but as Jimmy Stewart and the 445th had shown, good, tight formation flying really did save lives. The trouble was, keeping that tight formation with enemy fighters swooping from all angles, guns blazing, or with flak bursting all around, was difficult and required cool heads, nerves of steel and very steady hands on the controls.

At Boxted, the pilots of the 354th FG were being dropped off at their squadron areas, and with parachute packs swinging behind them and leather flying helmets loose on their heads, they clambered up into their P-51Bs. Dick Turner was feeling keyed up, the adrenalin surging already, certain they would soon be tussling with the enemy as they flew directly over the heart of the hornet's nest. Cockpit drills, the familiar smell of oil, metal and aviation fuel, preceded the engine start: the slow turn of the big four-blade metal prop and then a puff of flame and smoke from the exhaust stubs as the Merlin suddenly roared into life, the prop now a whirr and the Mustang shaking rhythmically. Brakes off, throttle forward, rudder, and they were rolling. Moments later, the throttle now wide, they were hurtling across the airfield, Turner pulling back on the stick as they became airborne. Undercarriage up and almost immediately Essex turned into a thin, spectral landscape and disappeared altogether.

As the bombers crossed the Channel, McGinty worried about the lack of Little Friends – but close escorts had been scrubbed since Doolittle had taken charge, something that had not filtered down to the tail gunner. In fact, nearly six hundred American fighters would be taking part in the day's mission, along with six squadrons of Spitfires to provide cover during the last phase of the return leg. Even so, McGinty was right to be worried, because although the escort plan had been thought out in meticulous detail, the rapidly worsening weather – a situation that had not been forecast the previous day – had ensured all manner of delays in both take-off and then forming up. It underlined just how complicated the organization of a large mission of this kind was, and equally how fraught with potential difficulties it could prove.

As McGinty and his crew crossed the Dutch coast, flak started to pepper the sky and the bomber began to jolt and rattle from the blast. McGinty could also see enemy fighters climbing up through the clouds and, with still no sign of their own fighters, he knew they were in trouble. The first attack came head-on, but soon the bombers were being attacked from all angles. McGinty felt their Fortress vibrate from the recoil of the .50-calibre guns, then saw one Me109 collide with a B-17 and the two go down together in a bundle of burning wreckage.

Suddenly the fighters were gone, presumably, McGinty thought, to refuel. He wondered again where their own fighters were. Was the bomber formation off course? Or were they early or late? From his lonely position at the tail of the plane, there were a lot of unanswered questions and a lot to worry about.

Soon after, another mass of enemy fighters attacked. This time, as single-engine Me109s and FW190s closed for the kill, twin-engine Me110s, 210s and Ju88s fired rockets from a range that was too far for the bombers' .50-calibres. Rockets began exploding in the middle of the formation, showering the bombers with blast and bits of shrapnel; so dense were the formations, inevitably some found their mark. McGinty saw several bombers hit and explode mid-air, a truly shocking spectacle for any aircrew watching.

In England, the worsening weather was causing mayhem. Intelligence suggested the weather had also deteriorated over the targets and the decision was made to recall the bombers of the second and third formations. However, no signal was sent to the B-17s of the 1st Division, which included McGinty's crew and the rest of the 379th BG, because, by the time the decision was made at High Wycombe, they were within 50 miles of Oschersleben. What's more, the lead combat wing of the second formation was far enough into German air space for the bomb leader to decide to press on to the primary target. The remaining three combat wings of the second formation, however, did turn around.

Continuing on its way deep into Germany, the more than 250 bombers of the 1st Division came under further attack as the full weight of the Luftwaffe's fighter force was thrown against them. On McGinty's Fortress, Bill Weigel, their top-turret gunner, called out that friendly P-38s

were now coming in at four o'clock high. While the bombardier in the nose had the clearest visibility, the reality
was that no one position provided a clear 360-degree view.
Even the waist gunners could see only a portion of the sky,
and enemy fighter planes would scream past and be gone
in a flash. This meant crews really did have to work
together and talk to one another once an attack on them
began. At Weigel's warning, McGinty now looked up and
saw the top-turret gunner was wrong, however: the aircraft bearing down on them were Me110s – an easy
mistake to make. In moments, a further three bombers
were falling.

McGinty saw two FW190s close in on the tail of another
B-17. There appeared to be no reply from the tail gunner,
so McGinty guessed he must be dead. Raising his own
twin guns, McGinty realized the Focke-Wulfs were within
his own arc of fire, so he opened up and saw strikes hit the
cowling of the first 190, which promptly broke off and
made for the clouds. McGinty switched to the second and,
again, hit him hard; this time, the Focke-Wulf rolled over
trailing smoke. Adrenalin-fuelled tension got the better of
McGinty and he began shouting excitedly until the co-
pilot, Lieutenant John Talbot, told him to get off the
intercom. Chastened, McGinty realized he had just broken
his own rule never to shoot at any enemy aircraft unless it
was directly attacking their own ship. This was because
the Luftwaffe used the finger-four – or *Schwarm* – as their
basic formation, as did RAF and American fighters, and
by concentrating on two enemy planes it was easy to take
your eye off the other two. McGinty's job, he reminded
himself, was to concentrate on protecting his own crew.
In fact, he had developed a successful technique. If any

enemy fighters looked to be locking on to their tail, he would fire at them until they lined up directly behind, give them an extra second, then call out to Talbot to 'jump'. Talbot would push the throttles forward, pull back on the control column and the B-17 would climb sharply. With luck – and so far it had held – the fighters' bullets and cannon shells would pass underneath and the fighters dive away.

As they finally reached the target, thick cloud covered Oschersleben, so they headed for their secondary target, Halberstadt, and the Junkers factory there. As they approached, they received word that the weather had closed in over the town, so the decision was made to head for Oschersleben after all. The entire mission was turning into something of a fiasco. And still the enemy fighters kept coming.

Listening to the mission unfolding from the operations rooms were not only Doolittle and Anderson but also Spaatz and Lieutenant-General Barney Giles, who were with General Bill Kepner at VIII Fighter Command Headquarters. Giles, Hap Arnold's deputy, was over from the US to see the birth of the USSTAF and both senior commanders were given a crystal-clear vision of the enormous complications of organizing such a raid in rapidly worsening weather conditions. Fighter groups had not arrived where and when they should, and even the forty-four P-51s had reached the target area a little early, which meant they were wasting precious fuel circling before any bombers or enemy fighters showed up.

None the less, eventually they spotted the bombers below them. The three squadrons of the 354th Fighter Group had just begun deploying themselves when a voice

crackled over the RT, 'My God! There are Germans coming up in droves beneath the bombers!' That was precisely
what had been hoped. Glancing down, Dick Turner saw
both Me110s and 109s climbing together like a swarm of
insects, albeit still some 10,000 feet beneath the bombers.
That was good, because it meant the P-51s could dive down
on them with the crucial advantage of height and speed; all
that was missing was having the sun behind them.

'Go down and get the bastards!' Turner heard in his headset. It sounded like Major Jim Howard, so Turner did as
ordered and flipped over, pushed the stick forward and
dived. Down they hurtled, all twelve of Howard's 356th
Fighter Squadron, each pilot lining up a target. Turner sped
towards a gaggle of Me110s, diving down with Frank
O'Connor on his wing. As they neared, the lumbering
Zerstörer – 'Destroyers' – split their flight in half, one element heading north-east and the other to the north-west. With
O'Connor turning towards the latter group, Turner tore
towards those moving north-east, latching on to one, pulling up underneath so that his six .50-calibre machine guns
were aiming at its underside. In a climbing attack at eight
o'clock, slightly to the port side of the twin-engine Messerschmitt he opened fire and felt the Mustang judder with the
recoil. Turner clearly saw sparks flare across the enemy aircraft as his bullets struck, then flames rapidly engulfed the
Messerschmitt. Still climbing, Turner sped past at an angle,
drawing up underneath a second Messerschmitt and seeing
another row of strikes tear across the port wing all the way
to the fuselage.

Then, out of the corner of his eye, another aircraft bore
down – an Me109, its guns flashing. Turner turned his
P-51 away from the 110 directly towards the attacking 109,

firing his machine guns as he passed. As the tracer from his guns flew by his attacker, he saw the Messerschmitt turn, roll over and dive towards the deck, although not before a number of bullets from Turner's guns tore into him. Turner was going back to finish off the Me110 when over the intercom he heard his wingman, who now had two Me109s on his tail trying to 'shoot his ass off.'

'Where are you?' Turner asked, but O'Connor couldn't tell him. All he knew was he was going round and round in ever tighter circles, trying to dodge the Me109s. Turner sped around the sky looking for him. Minutes passed, Turner agonizing for his troubled buddy, then finally he heard him through his headset.

'Never mind, Dick,' said O'Connor. 'I finally caught up with the SOBs and shot one of them down. The other two cowardly bastards ran away.'

Turner cursed to himself. 'Here I was,' he wrote later, 'practically blowing up my engine over Germany hunting for him, and it turns out he's casually having a turkey shoot.' By now, as was so often the case in aerial combat, the sky around them had largely emptied – of both enemy fighters and their own bombers – so Turner called over the intercom that they might as well head home; when to cut and turn back to base was generally up to the individual pilot and usually self-evident: when fuel was getting low or ammunition was almost out. He still couldn't see O'Connor, but found another Mustang for company and together they turned and headed west. As he flew, Turner began thinking of all the potential targets he had passed over in his search for his wingman and decided he would demand a drink per missed enemy aircraft in the mess that night. Then he suddenly spotted an Me410 twin-engine fighter heading in the opposite direction. Clearly the German pilot was as surprised as he, but as Turner began to turn to attack he glanced at his fuel gauge, saw it was already quite low, so thought better of it and continued back towards England.

At the same time as the P-51s descended on the German fighters, the bombers had been on their bomb runs over Oschersleben. McGinty had seen these new long-range Little Friends appear like knights in shining armour. 'The startled Nazis didn't know what hit them,' he noted. 'They thought they had us all to themselves and weren't looking for any American fighters.'

The P-51s had taken quite a toll on the enemy fighters, but the melee had drawn many of them, Turner included, away from the bombers and only one lone Mustang was battling to keep the bombers safe. This was Major Jim Howard, Turner's squadron commander, who had climbed back up to look after the bombers. Although a squadron commander rather than group CO, Howard had been combat lead that day, so in overall charge of the 354th FG for that particular mission. He had already done well in their initial dive with the rest of the group. He had seen an Me110 move up right in front of him, heading straight for the lead B-17s. Waiting until the Messerschmitt's wingspan had filled his sights, he had then opened fire with a four-second burst. The 110 had begun smoking, dived out of the fray and then its wings had torn off. A moment later Howard raked a 109, then sped after a Focke-Wulf 190, opened fire again and watched the pilot bail out. In less than a minute he had shot down three enemy fighters.

Howard had then found himself alone and was about to withdraw when he realized there was no sign of the P-47s due to take over the escorting of the bombers, so he climbed back up, throttling back and turning to attack any enemy fighter that tried to get near the bombers. More enemy aircraft appeared; Howard attacked another Me110 and saw it peel off and plummet with smoke trailing. He next spotted an Me109 lining up behind the formation of Fortresses, but as he turned towards it, the German pilot dived out of the way. Howard chased it, firing and eventually pulling out of a climb some 3,000 feet above the bomber stream as the 109 also started belching smoke and diving away. Then another Me109 attacked, but again Howard dived down on it and drove it away.

For more than half an hour, the American stayed with the Fortresses, diving and aggressively attacking any German fighter that tried to get too close. Eventually, a Junkers 88 twin-engine bomber started trying to move towards the Forts, but Howard again forced it to turn away, driving it off as a lion would a hyena. Three times he forced it away, till eventually it turned and headed off. Only when the enemy fighters appeared to have gone for good did he finally waggle his wings to the B-17s and make for home. Much of his heroics had been witnessed by Lieutenant William Lawley and the crew of *Cabin in the Sky*, who, along with others from the 305th BG, had continued on their way after the recall had been issued. Hugh McGinty had also seen this lone Mustang twisting and turning across the sky. 'The last I saw of him,' wrote McGinty, 'he was diving through the clouds with three FW 190s after him.'

Incredibly, not a single Fortress of the 305th or 401st

Bomb Groups had been shot down while Howard had protected them, yet in the course of that one mission he had downed four confirmed and very probably two more, and also seen off as many as thirty enemy fighters.

The long mission to Oschersleben was not over yet, however. While Howard had seen off one concerted attack, the bombers met still more enemy fighters on the return leg. McGinty saw the plane of one of his best friends hit and disappear into the cloud, but at long last they were approaching the Channel and the enemy finally melted away. Exhausted crews now faced the challenge of flying the last leg of the journey back down through thick cloud to their mass of bases. In their Fortress, McGinty's crew tried to keep in formation, but as they entered the cloud they soon lost sight of one another. Now there was a very real danger of collision, especially with pilots and co-pilots physically and mentally drained after their ordeal; they had been airborne nearly seven and a half hours already. Many of the crews had dead or wounded on board, or had to battle with aircraft that were low on fuel, and many were badly damaged. McGinty could only wait and hope. They had little fuel and Kimbolton was a lot further inland than many of the Eighth's airfields. This meant they had to find another – and unfamiliar – base at which to land. But they managed it, touching down at a B-24 base closer to the East Anglian coast. Miraculously, apart from a bit of shrapnel damage, the aircraft and all ten crew were unscathed.

On the face of it, the mission had been a great disappointment for the Eighth. Of the 633 bombers dispatched, only 139 had attacked Oschersleben, just 52 had hit Halberstadt and a mere 47 had bombed just one of the Brunswick targets – the MIAG plant 5 miles outside the city. That meant they were not attacking with anything like the weight of force they should have done. What's more, another 42 bombers had been lost, 13 per cent of the attacking force. On the other hand, despite the cloud, the bombing had been pretty accurate and subsequent reconnaissance showed the Oschersleben plant had suffered considerable damage.

Despite the problems of getting the fighter escorts into the right place at the right time, 39 enemy fighters had been shot down for not one loss of their own. Perhaps more significantly, the 44 P-51s had shot down considerably more than the 177 P-47s and P-38s. That was truly remarkable and showed that by January 1944 the Allied fighter arm was beginning to reveal its potential. The P-51s, still comparatively few in number, had proved beyond doubt that they had the potential to radically change the air war.

At Boxted, all the group landed back down that day, with claims of some fifteen destroyed and a further sixteen damaged. Major Jim Howard made his claims, but otherwise said little about his exploits. Only a day later did the truth about his victories start to emerge, when Eighth Air Force Headquarters asked that the group examine its claims and find the name of the pilot who had attacked and driven off no fewer than thirty enemy fighters, destroying six in the process, as witnessed by the incredulous bomber crews he had been single-handedly defending. Someone reported that the code letters of the Mustang were AJ-A. That was Jim Howard.

The bomber boys were astounded. 'For sheer determination and guts,' reported the 401st's leader, 'it was the greatest exhibition I'd ever seen.' Others were equally effusive in their post-mission debriefings, so Lieutenant-Colonel Harold W. Bowman, the 401st BG's commander, sent them to Doolittle, who knew a piece of public relations gold when he saw it. A week later, Howard was ordered to attend a press briefing in London, much to his embarrassment. 'I seen my duty,' he told one reporter, his tongue firmly in his cheek, 'and I done it.' It was a joke on Howard's part, but no one cared. That was the headline. In a long, dark and bruising winter, this was a good news story for a change. Little did Howard know it at the time, but his truly incredible air fighting over Oschersleben had won VIII Fighter Command its first and only Congressional Medal of Honor.

CHAPTER 16

Dicing with Death

MAJOR JIM HOWARD'S FEATS high above Oschersle-ben had been something to cheer, but about the raid as a whole General Hap Arnold was not at all happy. His bad mood began when Spaatz, Doolittle and Giles deliberately held back their report on the raid. Normally, Arnold was sent a report the same day but, aware that the 11 January mission had not gone to plan, they decided to wait until they had the pictures in from subsequent recon-naissance flights over the targets.

However, in the meantime, the German press had boasted about the shooting down of a staggering 123 US aircraft, which was then picked up by the American media. By trying to be clever, Spaatz and Giles had only made the situation worse. What really riled Arnold was not the claim of so many downed US planes, but the small number of bombers hitting the target, and in penny packets too. 'I cannot understand why with the great number of airplanes available in the Eighth,' he steamed, 'we con-tinually have to send a boy to do a man's job. In my opinion this is an uneconomical waste of lives and equipment.' What he wanted to see was a really large force absolutely pulverizing one target at a time rather than lots of pecking at many. He told Spaatz he wanted to hear his thoughts and some new lines of approach.

Spaatz had been in his new job barely a fortnight. The poor weather was once again hampering operations. This would improve: the days would grow longer, more HX2 sets were on their way and one day, eventually, winter would be over. Time, though, was of the essence. 'The weather here is the most discouraging of all factors,' wrote Spaatz. 'Nothing is more exasperating than trying to run an Air Force continuously hampered or grounded by weather.'

At least the Americans and British could have their pilots and crew practise flying in such conditions thanks to the plentiful amounts of fuel and resources at their disposal. The same could not be said for the Luftwaffe. The lack of bad-weather flying training was one of General Dolfo Galland's biggest concerns but, despite his insistence on improving it at flying schools, necessity had made such plans impossible to implement properly. With the dawn of the new year, he felt increasingly pessimistic. The Allies were clearly getting ever stronger. To Galland, it seemed utterly futile to send up fighters in bad weather, because whatever victories they gained were invariably more than offset by the losses caused from icing, accidents on take-off and subsequent crash-landings. Heinz Knoke would probably have agreed. So too would Wim Johnen. The statistics were bearing them out: on 4 January, for example, I Jagdkorps had lost twelve fighters to snow and bad weather.

On Thursday, 27 January, at Parchim airfield, the pilots of 5/NJG5 were given a bleak forecast by the meteorologists: a cloud ceiling of just 150 feet, then dense cloud up to 13,000 feet. Temperatures were bitterly cold and from 3,000 feet there was a danger of icing. Snow was falling, covering the machines with a coat of ice before they even started their engines. By evening, it was worse. 'Absolute pea-soup outside,' said Hauptmann Bär, their new CO. 'You can't see your hand before your nose.' Wim Johnen prayed they would not be flying.

In the crew room, they played skat and waited for the hourly weather reports. Outside, the sleet continued. 'Take it easy,' one of the reserve officers said, noting the anxious glances. 'Tommy couldn't come in this muck. He's not quite tired of life yet. In this pea-soup fog, even his radar would not help him.' Everyone murmured agreement, but Johnen suspected otherwise. He was well aware that the British were using more sophisticated ground-mapping radar – that is, H2S, which the Germans now knew about as it had been discovered on a wrecked British bomber – and it seemed to make no odds to them when they flew. As the clock ticked inexorably, the CO began pacing about. Eventually, Johnen suggested to his crew that they head out to their Me110 to carry out cockpit drills and get used to the dark.

Once on board, they went through their checks, then Unteroffizier Fabius, Johnen's radio operator, switched on the Calais radio station. Soon after they heard an interruption in the sugary-sweet music. 'Berlin, you were once the most beautiful city in the world,' came a voice. 'Berlin, look out for eleven o'clock tonight!' So a raid was being planned. At around 8 p.m., the aircrews were put on alert and the others hurried out to their machines. Once all were on board, a green flare was fired into the air from the control tower. Hauptmann Bär was in his machine next to Johnen. Then through his headphones he heard the duty officer ask everyone to check in. Once they had all done so, the officer said, 'Well, happy landings all,' and then Bär rumbled forward, Johnen following close behind. Visibility was terrible, with sleety rain lashing the canopy. Johnen could barely even see the green lights of the flare-path.

The CO took off, sparks swirling in the slipstream, then Johnen opened the throttle, released the brakes and began thundering down the runway, his nerves focused entirely on just getting safely into the air. Flying on instruments alone, he had told himself not to look out any more than he had to. Suddenly, he was airborne, but just as he retracted the undercarriage and was about to retract the wing flaps a loud explosion shook his machine in a flash of angry flame. It jolted him and for a split second he was frozen by fright and the thought that it was his aircraft. But then the truth hit him: it had been Hauptmann Bär and he must surely be dead. Johnen stared grimly at his instrument panel and tried to put what had happened out of his mind. And in truth, just gaining altitude required all his concentration.

At 3,000 feet, however, the propellers and leading edges of the wings began to ice up, something that was blindingly obvious just from the struggling grinding of his twin engines. His gunner, Mahle, shone his torch along the wings and reported a thick coating of ice. The sleet was freezing as it hit the aircraft. Johnen now told Mahle and Fabius to check their parachutes and be ready to bail out the moment he gave the order. The struggling Messerschmitt was growing heavier, the controls sluggish. Johnen debated whether to drop into slightly warmer air or to keep climbing and pray they could push on through the danger zone. He decided to keep going.

His engines were at full throttle and bits of ice were breaking off and hitting the airframe, but the ice was also increasing. 'Herr Oberleutnant,' called out Mahle, 'it's pointless. The tail unit's beginning to ice up. The temperature outside is now four degrees below.' Johnen's control column was no longer responding much either and he reckoned he could keep his engines at full revs like this for five minutes longer but no more. On the other hand, bailing out from that height into the icy unknown hardly appealed, so he decided to press on and hope for the best. Slowly but surely, they were gaining altitude, although the aircraft was groaning and moments away from stalling. Johnen could not help but look at the wings and the struggling engines. The tension was hard to stomach.

Then suddenly the ice layer started to break off, the engines began to sound better and the machine was responding once more to the controls, although not until they reached 12,000 feet did they finally emerge from the thick cloud bank that had shrouded them since take-off. Johnen thanked God – they had made it through into the clear and unfettered skies beyond. 'I almost felt like patting my Me 110,' he wrote, 'as though she had been a human being.'

Now he began thinking about Hauptmann Bär and what could have happened. One of the captain's crew, Kamprath, had been married with children. Johnen was still lost in his thoughts, heading towards the Baltic coast as instructed, when the ground controller's voice suddenly crackled in his headphones.

'White Argus from Meteor – attention, attention! Strong bomber formation at 15,000 feet over the Baltic flying on a south-westerly course.'

The still comparatively new Tame Boar tactics were working. They were flying over Wismar when Fabius first caught one of the RAF's bombers in his SN2 radar. Johnen drew to close range and opened fire. The Lancaster went down after his first burst, spinning away and disappearing into the clouds. Soon after, they latched on to a second and again Johnen drew near, opened fire and saw the Lancaster plummet, crashing just on the edge of Berlin.

Johnen was now approaching the capital in a southerly direction and saw that, above the bomber stream, a number of parachute flares had been dropped, creating a square of light through which the Tommy bombers were flying. Flak was bursting all around, but above he spotted four more Lancasters and tore after them, opening fire on the nearest. It exploded and fell in burning debris, but, with more targets to hit, Johnen now went after a fourth British bomber. Spotting him, the pilot banked steeply to starboard, desperately trying to get away. The gunners on board the Lancaster also opened fire – bright phosphorescent stabs pouring towards him and framing his machine. Undeterred, Johnen pressed on, drawing in behind and then, once the big Lancaster filled his sights, opening fire with his combination of cannons and machine guns. Armour-piercing cannon shells raked the bomber's fuselage then ruptured the fuel tanks in the wings. Tracers set the fuel on fire, while his high-explosive cannon shells tore holes in the wings. Really, the Lancaster, with its thin skin, stood no chance. Nor did the crew. The Lancaster went down, burning as it spiralled, like a slain dragon.

By Johnen's reckoning he had shot down four that night in just forty-five minutes. He felt all in and had to circle for a further ten minutes just to calm down, but then reality was restored and he knew he faced the ordeal of trying to get back down to the ground. There were some forty other night-fighters in the vicinity and all faced the same problem. Weather reports continued to be fed into his headset, but none of them was good. Every airfield within easy flying distance was reporting the same thing: a cloud ceiling of 150 feet, terrible visibility, snowstorms and temperatures several degrees below freezing.

'Go through that again, Herr Oberleutnant?' Mahle asked him. 'No, it's better to get above Parchim and fall out of the sky like Father Christmas.'

Johnen, though, did not want to abandon ship and bail out; his trusty Me110 had got him up and it would get him down. Another airfield, Leipzig–Brandis, was reporting a cloud base of 240 feet, but Johnen thought that would make everyone try for there. Far better, he reasoned to himself, to aim for Parchim where he knew every hill, every contour, and therefore had the best chance of flying in blind and in a snowstorm.

No one spoke as he flew for half an hour at 15,000 feet until he was circling over Parchim. Calling up the ground-control officer, he made contact. Ceiling was 150 feet, but the snow had stopped. 'Am putting out the shroud and firing radishes,' he told Johnen. 'Reception good.' The shroud meant pointing the airfield searchlights directly up to light up the clouds, which, in such conditions, could reach about 450 feet or so. Johnen now had to descend in a spiral through the dense cloud and ice to find the beacon of light. On paper it was all very straightforward, but at around 4,500 feet the plane began to ice up again, so Johnen throttled back and dived down to 1,500 feet, which seemed to do the trick. Now they were almost there, but he could still see nothing. Outside it was pitch black, and then the flashing lights of the radishes appeared and, a moment later, the shroud. That meant they were directly over the airfield.

Johnen now prepared to land, sweeping in a wide circle so that he could line up on the runway. To help him was the ultra-short-wave Barque approach: if he veered to port of the correct flying-in course, dots could be heard in his headset, while to starboard were dashes. When on track, both sounds merged into a sustained single note. A mile and a half from the airfield, he lowered his undercarriage, which, despite the ice, clicked into position. Wing flaps were lowered to 70 degrees, approach speed was 100 m.p.h. Suddenly he saw blurred lights ahead and moments later he touched down, somewhat fast. He put on the brakes but the aircraft kept going until finally coming to a halt on the edge of the airfield. Johnen said a little prayer and Mahle opened the cockpit so that they were breathing the cold night air.

Back inside, emotions were mixed. There was delight at seeing Johnen and his crew safe – and with four victories! – and Leutnant Kamprath had successfully bailed out of Bär's machine. But Bär was dead and so too were Leutnant Sorko and Oberfeldwebel Kammerer, who had been shot down. Leutnant Spoden and crew had bailed out after bad icing. 'On the one side joy,' noted Johnen, 'and on the other side grief. But we had grown hard in this pitiless war.'

*

On 1 January, Lieutenant-Colonel Don Blakeslee had taken over command of the 4th Fighter Group when his predecessor left to join the Ninth Air Force as combat operations officer. Blakeslee had been waiting for this moment for quite a while and told all his pilots that he wanted them to be aggressive and to become the top fighter group in the Eighth. Anyone who didn't embrace this approach would be transferred to another unit.

Doolittle and Kepner were equally keen for their fighters to become more offensive-minded. The 4th had had a quiet few months and the ramrods they had been carrying out had not allowed for much combat. Most were chomping at the bit and only too willing to follow Blakeslee's instructions to the letter. As if to prove the point, their new commander had led the group into action on 7 January. When a dozen Focke-Wulfs had dived on some straggling bombers, Blakeslee had brought his pilots down on the enemy fighters in a classic bounce. He shot down one with his usual tactic of getting as close as possible, but then had been hammered himself until Jim Goodson shot down the two Focke-Wulfs on Blakeslee's tail. Blakeslee had made it back to Manston; he might not have liked the Jug, but Thunderbolts could certainly take some punishment.

The group was flying a freelance operation on Friday, 14 January. At around 3 p.m. they were at some 26,000 feet near Paris when Don Gentile spotted a gaggle of fifteen Focke-Wulfs around 4,000 feet below them and heading east. Leading his flight, Gentile immediately flipped a wing and dived down, yelling at his wingman, Lieutenant Richards, to stick with him.

'Keep going,' Richards replied over the radio, 'I'm with you.'

As the Thunderbolts were diving down behind them, the Focke-Wulfs spotted them and broke into two groups, each fanning out in a wide arc so that they were turning in towards their attackers. Suddenly, some eight enemy planes were closing towards them. Gentile, out in front, adjusted his gunsight and flicked off the safety switch on his guns. The closing speed was now over 700 m.p.h. 'You can think of a thousand things,' he noted, 'at such moments, and nothing seems to be happening in your life except that the plane is coming slowly toward you and you're living a lifetime – as if it was a speed-up movie reel – and ageing fast and growing old and older and looking suddenly at the end of your life in just about the time it takes to say it.' This was a game of high-speed chicken. Either Gentile or the lead German pilot had to break first or they would collide. Gentile felt calm and, at that moment, unafraid, and then the Germans broke and he knew he had the psychological edge. The Focke-Wulfs dived down towards the deck and Gentile followed, so intent on catching them that he couldn't think what to say over the radio to his wingman, but assumed Richards was still following. Closing in on the first, he opened fire and saw a mushroom of thick smoke as the 190 rolled over into a vertical spin and crashed.

In fact, as they had dived after the lead two Focke-Wulfs, Gentile had been bounced in turn. Richards, seeing a Focke-Wulf open fire at Gentile at some 800 yards, then attacked, and moments later both aircraft were spiralling, each trying to get on to the tail of the other. An FW190 was supposed to be able to out-turn a Thunderbolt, and Richards knew this. It was his first-ever combat, but eventually he managed to get on to the German's tail and, opening fire, saw smoke appear. Moments later, the Focke-Wulf flipped on to its back and dived down straight into a wood and exploded. By this time, though, Richards had lost Gentile and was now out of ammo, so, after wondering what he should do, he set his course west and headed for home.

Meanwhile, the rest of the group had been caught in a melee higher up from where they had first engaged after their dive. Leading his flight in 334 Squadron, Bee Beeson had dived after the Focke-Wulfs, finally closing in at about 6,000 feet. Hurtling in close to the rear four, Beeson opened fire at 250 yards and kept firing until he was almost upon one. He could see strikes and large flashes along the wing roots and in the canopy as he broke over the enemy. The Focke-Wulf plunged downwards, exploding as it hit the ground. That was his sixth confirmed kill.

Gentile was now all alone, miles from the others and about to become embroiled in a titanic death struggle with one of the best enemy pilots he had ever come up against. Having chased after three Focke-Wulfs, he had caught up with one, closing to 150 yards, and opened fire, seeing strikes all around the cockpit. Down and down they went until they were flying only just above the treetops of the Forest of Compiègne, where Hitler had made the French sign the armistice in June 1940. He could feel the turbulence from the slipstream of the German ahead of him and then the Focke-Wulf crashed into the trees in a ball of fire, the force of which Gentile felt as he sped past.

He now climbed back up, but as he did so he came under attack. Tracers sped towards him. Gentile flung the Thunderbolt this way and that, yawing and side-slipping as he tried to shake off the lead Focke-Wulf now on his tail. He was taking hits and two jagged holes appeared in his fuselage and right wing. Horrified, Gentile realized the lead attacker was now so close he could actually hear the chugging of his machine guns and the *poom-poom* of the cannons. Frantically, Gentile looked around and actually saw a 20mm cannon shell hit his wing and a metal flower open up like a torn mouth. He also now realized that Richards, his wingman, was nowhere to be seen.

Gentile had to think quickly and clearly. Pushing the stick over, he turned directly into his attacker, thinking that if he had to die he might as well ram his enemy and take him with him, but instead the lead German pilot pulled up and over him. Gentile stayed in a tight port turn because the lead pilot's wingman was now coming in towards him. But he seemed not to have the stomach for it, because he broke and turned away from the fray. 'Right quick,' noted Gentile, 'I threw my Thunderbolt into a starboard swing and let loose a burst at the guy, but didn't hit him. My nerves at the time were not conducive to accurate gunnery.' Closing in on him, he had a clear shot and pressed down on the firing button, but nothing happened – he had run out of ammunition. The lead Focke-Wulf had now swung around and was positioning himself for a 30-degree deflection shot. That he was even attempting it told Gentile that he was up against a highly experienced and proficient hunter – but with no bullets himself. The tracers were fizzing past some 40 feet in front, then 30 and getting closer. Gentile kept going, turning towards them as his enemy gradually corrected his aim. Gentile had always had a habit of talking to himself in the cockpit. Now he muttered, 'Don, hold on to yourself. Keep yourself steady and you'll get out of this all right. Don't panic, Don!'

The tracers were almost tickling the edge of his cockpit and only then did Gentile throw the Thunderbolt hard to port, with his left foot hard down on the rudder pedal and the stick far to the side. It was a dangerous manoeuvre and he felt his battered aircraft straining, but just as he was on the edge of falling into a spin he pulled out. But his enemy was still there, sending bursts of tracer towards him. Gentile let the process happen all over again: the tight turn, the deflection shooting from the German, watching the tracers getting ever closer and then the flick hard to port.

Then suddenly, in a turn, his Thunderbolt flicked over and he was upside down looking down at the Forest of Compiègne, almost brushing the tops of the trees. Hurtling along at over 300 m.p.h., he flicked the Thunderbolt back the right way, so close to the forest it seemed as though the foliage was in his cockpit with him, but his trick worked, because he was flying alongside the German and, at last, clear of the angle of fire of his guns.

'Help!' Gentile now screamed into his radio. 'Help! I'm being clobbered!'

'Would the individual with the screaming voice please give us his call letters and tell us his exact position as to altitude, longitude, and latitude,' came a muffled reply. But Gentile couldn't tell him because he had his eyes glued on the German pilot in the Focke-Wulf. For a moment they continued flying alongside each other, then the German turned in towards him and Gentile turned in towards him too, which gave his enemy little time to shoot. Still the German wouldn't give up and turned back again as Gentile passed him so that once more they were flying alongside each other. And again, he turned towards him and Gentile followed suit, praying that a lucky shot wouldn't finish him. This went on for quarter of an hour, as both reversed turns from head-on attacks. All Gentile had to do was keep going until his enemy ran out of ammunition. 'And that's what happened,' he wrote later. 'He used up his last bullets and then went home, and I climbed with a great surge into the sky.'

When Gentile touched back down again at Debden, he was weak from fatigue and for a few minutes sat there in the cockpit. Exhausted, he was also euphoric. That day, he had become an ace, an ambition that had driven him from the moment he had arrived in England. He also knew that on that flight he had passed a vital test. 'It showed me what I had learned and it taught me what I was,' he said. 'After it, I felt there was no German alive anywhere who could keep me from killing him when I had an even break in the fight; or if the breaks went against me and he got them all, I felt I could keep him from killing me.'

Now his crew chief was up on the wing beside him. 'Boy, are we glad to see you, Captain,' he said. 'We heard you were a goner.' His Thunderbolt, he added sadly, was going to take a little while to patch up. Gentile nodded silently, then gingerly took off his helmet, pushed himself up out of the cockpit and on unsteady legs, clambered down.

CHAPTER 17

Little Friends

IN CONTRAST WITH THE fighter units desperately defending the Reich, those of VIII Fighter Command were finding life considerably less perilous. On 20 January, the 56th FG lost their only pilot all month when Allen Dimmick was shot down and killed on his first combat sortie. Dimmick had been wingman to Les Smith, who had been chasing after two Focke-Wulfs at the time. Bob Johnson had seen it all: Smith hammering away and then two more 190s bursting out of a cloud. Johnson shouted at them to break, but they didn't hear, or didn't respond quickly enough. Johnson opened fire, hoping to put the enemy pilots off their stride, but he was too far away and he knew it, and so, it seemed, did the Germans. Helplessly, Johnson watched one of the Focke-Wulfs close in to almost point-blank range, open fire with his cannons and knock Dimmick out of the sky. By this time, however, Johnson had caught up and opened fire in turn. His blood was up and he watched with grim satisfaction as his bullets tore into the Focke-Wulf. 'I wanted that German, I wanted to kill him,' he wrote. 'I've never before been so badly afflicted with the urge to kill as I was at that moment.' The German pilot dived, twisting and turning as he did so, but Johnson hung on his tail, firing off short bursts, and eventually the Focke-Wulf flipped over and plunged down into the ground.

On the 30th, the targets were Brunswick and Hanover. Kepner had refined his fighter tactics further after Doolittle had formally introduced his more aggressive approach nine days earlier. From then on, each fighter group would provide two squadrons on close escort duty while the third would be the 'bouncing' squadron, flying higher and given licence to dive down after enemy planes and to remain low in order to roam and hunt any trying to form up for future attacks.

On the way to Brunswick, the 56th's bouncing squadron was able to surprise a large formation of enemy fighters, diving down on them with the twin advantages of height and sun. Bob Johnson went after an Me410 twin-engine fighter. 'It was so easy it was ridiculous,' noted Johnson. Closing in to 150 yards, he opened fire and tore the Messerschmitt to pieces. At one point, Johnson saw at least six German fighters plummeting to the ground trailing smoke and flames. In all, they claimed sixteen that day, which meant the tally for the month stood at thirty-nine for the loss of Dimmick alone. In all, on the two raids on 29 and 30 January, the Luftwaffe lost 109 fighters, most of which were to their American fighter adversaries.

For the Mustang fighter group, the scores at the end of January were fifty-three confirmed enemy aircraft shot down, but with losses of eleven. This was quite high, but the 354th were still new to combat and were flying further than any other fighter group. And they were still massively in credit. Dick Turner had managed to shoot down four and, across the board, the American fighter groups were demonstrating the huge advantage of having superior pilots. A second fighter group, the 357th, had been equipped with Mustangs and was now working up to go operational.

Among the recently arrived pilots of the 357th was Lieutenant Clarence 'Bud' Anderson, just turned twenty-two in January but already with more than 850 hours in his logbook, some eight times as many as a Luftwaffe pilot could expect before going operational. Raised on a farm near Newcastle, to the north-west of Sacramento in California, he had become besotted with flying as a young boy when a tri-motor Boeing Model 80 had crash-landed one December evening just before Christmas 1929 on a nearby farm. Anderson had gone to see it with his best pal, Jack Stacker. 'After that,' he wrote later, 'all we talked about and dreamed of were airplanes and airplanes and airplanes.' Much of his childhood had involved tearing around with Jack in his dad's old Ford V8 truck, going to watch aircraft whenever they could and earning as much as possible on the farm. In the autumn of 1939, he had enrolled at Sacramento Junior College Technical Institute for Aeronautics, which, he knew, would give him the academic qualifications to join the Air Corps. As matters stood, a young man had to be twenty years old to join, which was still more than two years away, so in the meantime he set his sights on enrolling in the Civilian Pilot Training Program, which he finally did in early 1941. By June he had his licence. His first passenger was Jack Stacker, who was a year behind him at college.

On 13 January 1942, his twentieth birthday, Anderson

had signed up for the air force and was not only accepted, but within a week was called up and on 29 September that same year was awarded his wings, commissioned a second lieutenant. He had always wanted to be a fighter pilot. 'I thought that if I was in a single-engine fighter,' he said, 'I would be in control of my environment.' He got his wish and was first assigned to the 328th Fighter Group flying P-39 Airacobras. Not long after, Anderson and four others were singled out to become flight leaders for a new fighter group that was being formed, the 357th. For three months it was based at Tonopah, in the desert in Nevada, where they worked hard, played hard and steadily added hours to their logbooks. Anderson discovered the fighter-pilot mentality beginning to take root. 'Living close to the edge,' he wrote, 'sort of went with the job. Daring, audacity, creativity, flair – those things were as much a part of a good fighter pilot's makeup as skill and sound judgment, and were encouraged.'

In the early summer of 1943, the group split into their squadrons and headed to different bases. Anderson was assigned to the 363rd Fighter Squadron and posted to Santa Rosa, not far from his home in northern California, but was almost immediately sent on a two-week gunnery course in Texas, then back to Santa Rosa and yet more training in clear skies. Finally, on 23 November, they set sail from New York aboard the *Queen Elizabeth* and docked at Greenock on the 30th. By that time, Anderson's friend Jack Stacker was already dead, although Anderson didn't know it at the time. Stacker had joined up slightly behind him, but had been shipped overseas to join a P-38 fighter group ahead of his friend. On his fourth mission, on 13 November, he was shot down and reported missing.

He had, in fact, survived his bail-out, but, badly wounded, had later died in hospital.

Anderson had earlier recognized that flying fighter planes – and in a war – was a dangerous business and that losing friends went with the territory. Pals had already been killed during training and early on in his career Anderson had resolved to control his emotions, no matter how hard this might be. It was a stressful occupation and he realized that men either coped or did not. Death was something he knew he had to get used to, so by the time he arrived in England he already had a tough protective shell around himself.

As with the 354th, Anderson and his fellows in the 357th were initially assigned to the Ninth Air Force but were then transferred to the Eighth, neatly swapping with a new Thunderbolt group. This was a direct result of a conference Spaatz had held on 24 January to regularize and prioritize which newly arriving aircraft and units would be going into which air force. Eaker, before him, had never corrected the earlier decision that all Mustangs should go to the Ninth, which was why the 354th was still officially only on loan to the Eighth and why the 357th had been initially posted to the Ninth. From 24 January 1944, however, all P-51s would be sent to the Eighth and, as they arrived, P-47 units would transfer to the Ninth, where, with their shorter ranges and rugged construction, they were better suited to the demands of supporting the lower-level medium bombers, as well as both ground attack and escort work closer to base.

As a result, the 357th, the Eighth's second new Mustang group, moved to Leiston on the Suffolk coast. That evening they tuned in to German radio, on which they heard the presenter welcoming the 357th as the 'Yoxford Boys' to their new base. Yoxford was a small town some 5 miles from the base and it was slightly unsettling to hear this on enemy radio before they had even unpacked. On the other hand, they had been inadvertently given a nickname. The Yoxford Boys they would remain.

They were all chomping at the bit to get going, but, quite apart from the dismal weather, one of their biggest challenges was their lack of any combat experience. Clearly, it was essential the group, squadron and flight leaders all got some operational hours under their belts, so they were sent to Boxford to carry out some missions with the 354th. The first to go was Captain Joe Giltner, of Anderson's 363rd FS, who had just become their fifth squadron commander in six months. The first had had sinus problems and left; the second had died in a mid-air collision; the third had pretended to be married when he wasn't in order to get his girlfriend on base and had been caught out and fired; and the fourth had been just a stop-gap. The 363rd boys were beginning to wonder whether they were cursed, which wasn't great for morale. Unhappily, on 24 January, his first mission, Giltner was shot down and made a POW. 'The 357th,' noted Anderson, 'was off to a very poor start.'

By 5 February, the 357th had some seventy-four P-51Bs and two days later Anderson headed to Boxted with half a dozen other pilots from the group. They had all assumed that after what had happened to Giltner they would be given a ramrod or some milk run to France, but instead the target on 8 February was Frankfurt.

Anderson's heart was hammering in his chest as he strode out to his plane that morning. In the cockpit, he strapped himself in, attached his radio leads and tightened the harness, then sat there, alone, waiting for the signal to start. He now had a staggering 893 flying hours, of which nearly thirty-one were in Mustangs, but he was well aware that, no matter how good he was, combat flying was a new experience for him. Sitting there, it was neither dying nor getting hurt that worried him, but screwing up. It was, he was aware, difficult following another pilot as he twisted and turned across the sky. The Mustang could travel at over 7 miles per minute at full pelt, and Anderson knew that, travelling at those speeds and swooping all over the place, it could be very difficult to keep glued to the pilot he was supposed to stick to and very easy to find himself miles away, and then lost, with the odds of survival sliding.

They took off and climbed in fours through the cloud, then suddenly they were out in the sunlight and circling slowly while the others joined them. Mustangs would appear every half minute or so, in their fours, then join the sixteen-plane squadron. Once the three-squadron group had formed up, they headed out over the North Sea towards Germany.

Within an hour they found the bombers and climbed to 30,000 feet above them, then throttled back to around 230 m.p.h. and zig-zagged over them. Far down below, occupied Europe was white and grey, but, although it looked peaceful enough, Anderson was keenly aware that it was dangerous out there and full of people who wanted to hurt him. It was unsettling. He had a small knot of fear in his stomach.

Suddenly, he heard someone call out, 'Bogeys!' and he was immediately alert, the adrenalin kicking in.

Anderson was determined to keep close to his leader, whose wing was already up and his Mustang sliding away. He was yelling something over the radio and Anderson realized he was after an enemy fighter. 'I do what he does,' he noted, 'all the time looking around, looking down . . . and then there's a Focke–Wulf 190, right there, a half mile off, maybe less.' Anderson was now almost upside down and looking straight down on the German fighter with its blue-grey camouflage and big black crosses. Glancing around him and behind, Anderson was aware there were now hundreds of planes swirling around, but his leader was pulling out of his dive and closing in on his target.

'Mustang, Mustang! There's one on your tail!' Anderson now heard in his headphones.

Anderson wondered whether this meant him. Looking around frantically, he saw nothing, but again came the warning. 'Mustang! Mustang! He's still on your tail!'

Again Anderson looked around but could see nothing, while his leader opened fire at too far a range. Had he known better, Anderson would have told him not to worry – that the warning was not for them – but he was green and new and so didn't. Instead, the warning came yet again, so he flung his plane around, desperately looking about him, then heard a loud clunk. *I'm hit!* he thought. He pulled back on the stick, put his Mustang into a tight turn, felt himself start to black out from the forces of negative g, but could still see no one. Then his brain engaged and he remembered the clunk would have been caused by the supercharger cutting out after diving through 16,000 feet and more. He cursed, feeling like an idiot and, even worse, realized now he was alone.

Anderson, like Bob Johnson, was fortunate to be blessed with exceptional eyesight and he spotted an aircraft in the distance. As he drew close, he realized it was his leader. Joining him, they then headed back to England. At Boxted, they reckoned someone must have thought Anderson was an Me109, but no one else was admitting to having given the warning. 'Man, was my flight leader pissed!' recalled Anderson. 'He could have gotten that Focke-Wulf and he wanted the victory. It was one more German pilot who would live to fly and fight another day.' Anderson felt bad, but he had gained some much-needed experience and at least he hadn't got the shakes or panicked. And he had made it home, which was more than could be said for his pal, Lloyd Hubbard, with whom he had joined the 357th. The next day, Hubbard flew with the 354th and on the way home they strafed an enemy airfield as per Doolittle's orders. Hubbard was the last of four in the strafing run. 'That morning,' wrote Anderson, 'some German gunner blew him out of the air.'

Next in line to receive Mustangs was the 4th Fighter Group. Don Blakeslee had never much liked the Thunderbolt, but he absolutely loved the Mustang from the outset and, having been lent one with which to lead the 354th FG on their first few missions in December, was determined the 4th should get them too. Blakeslee had even gone to General Bill Kepner in person and pleaded. Kepner was sympathetic, but pointed out that it would take too long for the 4th to make the switch because almost certainly they would be needed in the air rather than out of action while both pilots and ground crew learned how to use their new planes.

'No, sir,' Blakeslee told him. 'Most of these boys flew liquid-cooled types in the RAF. It won't take them long.' He also pointed out that the mechanics were used to Spitfires and also to Merlin engines. 'General, give me those Mustangs,' he pleaded, 'and I give you my word – I'll have 'em in combat in twenty-four hours. I promise – 24 hours.' It was a deal. By the end of February, the Blakesleewaffe, as the 4th was starting to be known, would be the third fighter group to get Mustangs.

By mid-February, the Eighth was in a position to mount the best part of a hundred long-range P-51s on every bombing mission and nearly seven hundred fighters of all kinds, most of which were superior to those of the enemy. Technical advantage counted for nothing, however, if the pilots were not up to the challenge, yet by February 1944 every man had a lot of hours in his logbook, while good combat experience was spread through the entire VIII Fighter Command. Great efforts were made to share this knowledge and expertise. Group, squadron and flight leaders were issued with tactical notes 'which every pilot should know'. The finger-four was the flying formation to be used. Number 1 would be ahead of the others with his wingman, Number 2, on his left and slightly behind. Numbers 3 and 4 would be on the leader's right and also behind, rather as in the ends of the fingers of an outstretched hand. 'No. 1 is free to look all around,' stated one of the tactical memos. 'Nos. 2, 3, and 4 <u>must</u> guard the rear of the Section by looking across and behind. Cross over turns should be practised.' The advantages were that formations could fly straight and level without much fear of being bounced and it helped conserve fuel. The big disadvantage was that a pilot had to rely on another to guard his tail – but that was where training, trust and confidence all played a vital part.

The tactical notes offered lots of other sound advice. 'When flying over enemy territory, always fly as fast as you can. This makes it easier for you to bounce Huns and harder for the Huns to bounce you.' Pilots were to practise air gunnery as much as possible, another skill that was largely denied German pilots. 'Another small but useful point,' the advice added, 'is to cover the sun occasionally when turning or weaving and have a good look around towards it.'

Dick Turner had been hugely grateful for the words of wisdom Don Blakeslee had given them, and, recognizing the value of getting tips from the best in the Eighth, General Kepner began a programme whereby leading pilots jotted down their dollar's worth of top tips, which were then put into a bound publication. David Schilling was one of the top pilots in the 4th FG and, now that Blakeslee was commanding, had become the group's executive officer, or second-in-command. 'Never break upwards [if attacked],' he warned, 'but on the same level, because breaking upwards causes a loss of speed and affords an easier target.' Schilling admitted he wasn't the best marksman. 'I find that my estimation of angle off is usually always in error on the underside,' he added. 'Therefore I am very careful to get a good line of sight and purposely over allow from three-fourths to one-half a ring more deflection [on my gunsight] than I think is necessary. I then decrease my lead to the point when the sight is in the same position as it was just prior to the time I saw strikes.'

Most urged aggression, which was precisely Doolittle's mantra. 'A fighter pilot must possess an inner urge to do combat,' wrote Hub Zemke, the already legendary commander of the 56th FG. 'The will at all times to be offensive will develop into his own tactics.' Bob Johnson warned pilots never to get over-confident and never to stop looking around, even with a wingman. 'Never let a Jerry get his sights on you,' he wrote. 'No matter whether he is at 100 yards or at 1000 yards away.' He also urged practice with those who knew best. So too did Major Walker Mahurin, also of the 56th. 'I think that my group probably does more training than any other in the ETO,' he wrote. 'At least, it seems that way to me. I've been doing training ever since I got to the group and I imagine I'll continue to do so 'til the war is over. It really pays. Every worthwhile hour in the air is the most valuable thing that I know of.'

How it would have pained General Dolfo Galland to have seen a booklet like this. Such words of wisdom flowed easily enough when the pilots had the ability to absorb such advice and the fuel and capacity with which to hone their skills further. All the Luftwaffe had in February 1944 was a rapidly diminishing number of experienced fighter pilots and a reasonable number of fighter aircraft, most of them not as good as those of the enemy. Increasingly, though, and rapidly, the standard of pilots was falling. It says much of the desperate need for half-decent pilots that, just twenty-six days after the horrific injuries he sustained earlier in January, Heinz Knoke was back flying once more.

CHAPTER 18

Waiting for a Gap in the Weather

THE LUFTWAFFE'S BOMBER OFFENSIVE, ordered in a fury by Hitler the previous summer, finally began on the night of 21/22 January. Oberst Dietrich Peltz, the *Angriffsführer England* – Assault Leader Against England – planned to attack in two waves of over 200 aircraft, some five hours apart, dropping around 475 tons, of which 60 per cent were incendiaries. The aim was not to target war industry, but to terrorize Londoners and cause a firestorm. Compared with the raids mounted during the Blitz of 1940–41, these were pretty decent numbers; compared with what the RAF and USAAF were sending over, it was less impressive, and it represented a maximum effort. Throughout the Battle of Britain, for example, the Luftwaffe had had between 800 and 1,000 bombers available on any given day. By 20 January 1944, Peltz could call on 462 operational bombers and fighter-bombers, of which only a fifth were modern types. More worrying was the lack of training. Bombers required even more of that most precious resource, fuel, than fighters did, and training was, by this stage of the war, poor.

Since Göring's failure to deter Hitler from offensive bombing in the wake of Hamburg, the Reichsmarschall had decided to fall in line wholeheartedly with the Führer's strategy, much to the frustration of Milch and just about anyone else with even the remotest grasp on reality. At the end of September, Hitler had told a planning meeting that, come what may, the *Angriffsführer England* was to have six hundred new bombers every month. A few days later, on 5 October, Peltz had issued a memo, 'Bomber Planning', in which he pointed out that most bombers were essentially slightly upgraded versions of earlier models now obsolescent, and that performance was no longer up to the task. There was still no effective long-range bomber, for example. The He177 was now in production, but it was a dog of a machine and everyone knew that; no other wartime aircraft has been responsible for the deaths of more test pilots than this doomed heavy bomber. Demanding it have dive-bombing capabilities was an early – and insane – requirement that set back development significantly. Coupling two engines to one propeller wasn't a great idea either. Collapsing wings, engine fires and a host of other difficulties, including instability and endless tweaking and reworking, caused the He177 to evolve painfully into no less than thirty-four different variants. It also ensured that in January 1944 Peltz had only thirty-five He177 heavy bombers for new attacks against England. It could carry up to 6 tons of bombs, which was impressive, but that was still 4 tons less than a Lancaster. The rest of the German bomber fleet could carry only paltry amounts by 1944 standards. In fact, the original Blitz had demonstrated all too clearly that the Luftwaffe's bomber force had been attacking with nothing like enough aircraft or bombs. Now they were expected to achieve greater results with much less.

A few days after Peltz's memorandum, at another planning meeting Göring stressed the importance of taking the fight to the enemy. 'The German people don't give a damn whether we lose half our fighters, or attack airfields in England. What they want to hear, when a hospital or an orphanage is destroyed here, is that the same has been done in England,' he told those assembled. 'I am anyway, determined . . . to now make use of my Luftwaffe, ruthlessly and totally, so it wins back the faith that has been lost in it.'

Actually, most German citizens wanted to feel they were being protected rather than having precious resources thrown away on bombing operations that had absolutely no chance of making a decisive impact. Göring's ultimatum reflected his desire to get back into the good books of the Führer, not of the German people. In any case, Hitler often vacillated. A week later, Milch learned from Speer that Hitler had said defence of the Reich should take precedence over all other demands. So mixed were the messages that Milch was left trying to build as many fighters as possible while at the same time building bombers – albeit at a ratio of 2:1 – in case Hitler ordered an offensive. Meanwhile, a large amount of resources that would otherwise have gone to Luftwaffe aircraft production were now being directed towards the V1 and V2 programmes, while the Me262 project was being earmarked as a bomber rather than a fighter.

For men like Milch, trying to manage conflicting demands

with resources that were continually being stretched further and further, it was frustrating to say the least. The challenge facing fighter pilots like Heinz Knoke, Wim Johnen and Hajo Herrmann was bad enough without having to compete with an inconsistent strategy and pointless insistence on taking the attack to the enemy.

The first raid of Peltz's bombing offensive was spectacular for its failure, as only half the bombs carried actually hit British soil and of the 475-ton payload a mere 30 tons were dropped on London. A week later, London was hit again, once more in bad weather. Again it was a failure. Not only did most of the bombs land nowhere near their targets, but fifty-seven precious bombers were lost in the two attacks and 101 crews aborted and turned back early. Twelve of the still troubled He177s were destroyed during operations and a further four were lost due to engine fires. The Führer was furious: about the failure to strike a significant blow on the enemy, about British reports that only thirty bombers had reached London and about the failure of the Heinkel 177. This aircraft, Hitler railed, was 'a crap machine – the worst rubbish that was probably ever produced.'

The causes of the failure of the 'Baby Blitz', as the British ridiculed it, were numerous: the low standard of training, especially in poor weather; the weather itself; the lack of reconnaissance aircraft; the shortage of pathfinders. Hitler could not understand why the Luftwaffe didn't have better information from the networks of agents operating in Britain. In fact, not one agent was then active in the UK; the only agents working for Nazi Germany in Britain were those who had been turned or had always been operating on behalf of the Allies.

*

On Monday, 24 January, General Doolittle again recalled his bombers as the weather looked sure to close in completely over England; the last thing he wanted was to lose half his forces because they ran out of fuel or crashed in thick fog. American crews trained hard and long, but few pilots were taught blind flying, so when they could no longer see anything, the chances of crashing were high.

Lieutenant Bob Hughes was leading the 100th BG that day on what was his twenty-first mission, to Brunswick. The recall came as they were passing over from Belgium into Germany, but they had progressed far enough for the mission to count, so that was something. However, on the return leg they encountered a strong headwind and ended up slightly off course, flying directly over an airfield at Ostend. Travelling at little more than 100 m.p.h. because of the wind, they were almost sitting ducks and suddenly came under fire. One of the Fortresses had the end of its tail blown off by flak, the tail gunner disappearing from view, although, incredibly, he survived and was able to pull the cord on his parachute. The B-17 managed to make it home, despite having had its elevators shot off.

That same day, Göring was visiting Luftflotte Reich Headquarters in Berlin and, having seen early reports of the American raid, assumed they had been heading to Berlin rather than to Brunswick. With this in mind, he ordered into the sky every available aircraft, including all day- and night-fighters from I Jagdkorps, from 7 Jagddivision in Austria and from the training schools. Some 821 fighter aircraft of varying types rose into the bleak January skies to meet a raid that had already returned home. The following day, Göring wrote to Generals Schmid and Stumpff at Luftflotte Reich: 'Yesterday's little manoeuvre may be considered a success except for the fact that April Fool's Day is still two months away.'

Also on Tuesday, 25 January, Schmid called a meeting with Galland and his division commanders at which it was agreed that from then on German fighters should engage with American fighters in an effort to make them jettison their drop tanks. It was also agreed that *Gruppe* commanders should give up trying to be everywhere and instead attempt to keep together and fight with local superiority. They all accepted the Americans were growing in number, but none thought the Allies would ever be able to reach Berlin successfully by day; Göring had been fussing about nothing.

What's more, the Reichsmarschall was still insisting that his fighter force avoid combat with the Americans, even though Schmid, Galland and senior commanders had all agreed they should now engage. The difficulties they faced were made worse by the shortage of pilots. Milch's handling of production was ensuring enough aircraft were reaching the fighter groups, but, incredibly, the front-line units received no replacement pilots whatsoever in January. The 30th was a particularly chastening day, as Heinz Knoke discovered to his cost.

One of the reasons he had returned to his *Gruppe* so soon after being so badly injured earlier in the month was because of the chronic pilot shortage; another was because Hitler had reduced the recuperation period allowed for pilots. A further reason, however, was that Knoke could not bear being confined in a large hospital with its pervading stench of disinfectant. He spent the first couple of days back at his base sitting in a deckchair wrapped in rugs. His legs and arms were not working very well, but he gradually started to regain strength and with it increased movement in his limbs. 'In time,' he jotted in his diary, 'I became accustomed to the never-ending headaches.'

On Sunday, 30 January, the day that Bob Johnson shot down his thirteenth enemy aircraft, orders arrived moving 5/JG11 to Arnhem in Holland. Still on crutches, Knoke hobbled to his Gustav and managed to clamber into the cockpit, then take off, fly and land back down at their new base. At 1.05 p.m. they were scrambled and, having gained height, were bounced by Fighter Command Spitfires, who drove them away from the bombers. 'We are taken completely by surprise,' wrote Knoke, 'and we cannot put up effective opposition against the Tommies.' Suddenly, it was every man for himself. Knoke did not even have a chance to fire, but found himself being pursued and hit in the engine. Yet again, his Gustav was in trouble, although on this occasion he was able to crash-land with his wheels up just a mile from Hilversum airfield. Needless to say, he should never have been flying in the first place. 'No. 4 Staffel has lost five killed, No. 6 has lost three and Headquarters has lost one,' he noted. 'I have lost from my own Staffel Sergeant Nowotny, who was posted to me only a few weeks ago.' It had been a slaughter.

The mood of increasing anxiety emanating from USAAF Headquarters in Washington filtered down to US Strategic Air Forces HQ and then on to Eighth Air Force. On 24 January, when Doolittle had recalled his bomber force for a second time, it had prompted a sharp rebuke from Spaatz. 'I wonder if you've got the guts to lead a big air force,' he told him. 'If you haven't, I'll get someone who has.'

Doolittle had struggled to keep his temper, even though

he accepted that they were all under a huge amount of pressure to get results and to fulfil the POINTBLANK directive as soon as possible. Calmly, he had explained that he had not wanted to endanger the lives of his men in what he considered an uncalculated risk. If the weather had completely closed in over East Anglia, as had been forecast, the losses could have been truly catastrophic, with bombers low on fuel circling blindly for airfields that were hidden by thick fog. Doolittle and Spaatz had been friends for a long time, but the Eighth Air Force commander was dismissed with a curt, 'That will be all.'

A few days later, however, Spaatz invited Doolittle on a tour of bomber units. They would be flying in *Boots*, Spaatz's personal B-17. After a visit to several bases on the first day, they stayed overnight and the following morning were assured that the weather would be good enough to continue their trip. As they walked out towards their waiting Fortress, the cloud was low, visibility poor and there was drizzle in the air.

Once airborne, they found the first base on their list, then the second but, as the visibility worsened, the third eluded them. The pilot took the plane lower and lower in his attempt to fly under the cloud base. 'Hedge-hopping in bad weather has killed hundreds of pilots before and since,' noted Doolittle, 'and I had lost many friends who had chosen to stay in visual contact with the ground.' Eventually, the pilot was forced to land in a field, side-slipping as he did so and coming to a bumpy halt only yards from a stone wall.

Spaatz clambered down looking slightly shaken by the experience. 'You were right, Jim,' he said, turning to Doolittle. 'I see what you mean about uncalculated risks.'

But time was marching on. It was now February. In April, the strategic air forces would be subordinated to the Supreme Allied Commander, General Eisenhower, for operation before D-Day. It was now even more imperative that the threat of the Luftwaffe be removed first. 'I have reviewed the problem of strategic bombing of our enemies,' Spaatz wrote to Arnold on 26 January, two days after his dressing down of Doolittle, 'and the thing that has struck me most is the critical time factor. We have very little time in which to finish the job.'

Spaatz's new position – and his direct access to Eisenhower – outweighed that of both Harris and Trafford Leigh-Mallory. The latter had been, mystifyingly, appointed commander of the Allied Expeditionary Air Force for OVERLORD. Together with Hap Arnold, Spaatz had been putting pressure on the British for a new directive, which was issued by Air Chief Marshal Portal on 17 February. The overall mission remained the same, but the emphasis was changed for both the USAAF and RAF Bomber Command. 'Primary objective, the German Air Force,' it ran. 'Depletion of German Air Force with primary importance upon German fighter force by all means available.'

Portal had agreed to the change mainly because he remained sceptical about the Americans' ability to achieve the aims of POINTBLANK on their own and because he believed that the time had come for Bomber Command to help in a more comprehensive and direct manner. None the less, this was based on a fundamental misunderstanding of the Eighth's growing strength and completely ignored the changes in fighter tactics, the arrival of the long-range Mustangs and the dramatically increasing dominance of the Eighth's fighter arm. For all Portal's undoubted skill, intelligence and usually sound judgement, he maintained a big blind spot when it came to long-range fighters.

The net result, though, was his insistence, against Harris's wishes, that Bomber Command now get directly involved in the 'depletion' of the Luftwaffe. On 14 January he had ordered Harris to send his bomber force to Schweinfurt as his first priority target; now, on 17 February, came this new directive. 'Overall reduction of German air combat strength in its factories, on the ground and in the air', was the aim, 'through mutually supporting attacks by both strategic air forces pursued with relentless determination against same target areas or systems so far as tactical conditions allow, in order to create the air situation most propitious for OVERLORD is immediate purpose of Bomber Offensive.'

In a nutshell, this was also the aim of the planned Operation ARGUMENT, for which Spaatz had been waiting to be given the green light since November. All that was needed now was a gap in the weather.

At the beginning of February, Hugh McGinty and his comrades were given leave. They had had a traumatic trip to Frankfurt on 29 January, under attack by an Me109. Bill Rau, the navigator, had been hit, and their oxygen supply shot out. Ernal Bridwell, the pilot, had put the Fortress into a steep dive of some 22,000 feet. McGinty, who had lost his parachute, felt convinced that his time had come, but Bridwell had managed to level them off and Bill Rau succeeded in plotting a course for home before dying in the arms of Matt Nathan from loss of blood.

Nathan too was badly wounded in the back and right shoulder.

Incredibly, they had been sent off again the next day, albeit in another ship and with a new navigator and bombardier. It had once more been a tough trip and, although the weather had then kept them grounded for a few days, they had been scheduled to fly again on the 4th. McGinty was struggling and knew he wasn't alone. 'The missions were beginning to wear us down and our morale was starting to deteriorate,' he wrote, yet this latest mission was only their tenth. 'We were starting to feel like twenty-year-olds going on forty.' Each group had a medical officer, a flight surgeon whose task was, in part, to look out for signs of combat fatigue and give a crew a rest before nerves became too frayed. On 5 February, McGinty and the others were told they were being sent off base for a few days.

Before they headed off, however, they had to bury Bill Rau. It was raining as they were driven out to the new American servicemen's cemetery at Madingley, on the edge of the university city of Cambridge, and it was still raining as they stood by the grave. Matty Nathan had been given a pass from hospital and they watched as a procession of some thirty caskets was brought out; Bill Rau was not the only one being buried that day.

The following day, McGinty and the others took a train to Blackpool. It continued to rain while they were there and one evening, after getting soaked, he was picked up by a middle-aged woman who insisted he come back to her house to dry off. Still painfully young and innocent, McGinty didn't realize he was being seduced. After stripping to his underwear, the woman took his clothes to dry, then returned wearing only a dressing gown. Horrified, he quickly made his excuses, grabbed his still-damp clothes and left. It wasn't the kind of rest he'd been after.

On the days when the Eighth did fly, they were starting to show their growing superiority. On Thursday, 10 February, the targets were split: the 3rd Division sent off 169 B-17s to Brunswick once again, while 81 B-24s of the 2nd Division were scheduled to attack the Luftwaffe air base at Gilze-Rijen in Holland. Accompanying the bombers to Brunswick were 466 fighters, among them Larry Goldstein and the crew of *Worry Wart*. That Thursday was Goldstein's twenty-second birthday. From the moment they crossed the French coast it seemed as though enemy fighters were swarming all over them; Goldstein reckoned he had never seen so many. There were plenty of Little Friends too, but the determination with which the German fighters pressed home their attacks shook up Goldstein.

Among them, once again climbing into the fray, was Heinz Knoke, still struggling with severe headaches and not yet fully recovered. He and his *Staffel* climbed to 25,000 feet above the Rhine and, while over Lake Dümmer, he saw the bombers of Eighth Air Force heading towards them, surrounded by hundreds of fighters. Knoke found it an awe-inspiring spectacle. 'Against them,' he noted later, 'we are forty aircraft. Yet even if we were only two, we should still have to engage the enemy.'

Picking up a group of Fortresses on the left flank, he sped towards them for a frontal attack, exactly as Galland had prescribed. Anticipating this, the leading Fortress altered course at the last moment and, unable to adjust in time, Knoke found himself swinging round with the entire *Gruppe* for a second attack with the forty Messerschmitts in a tight vic formation of three aircraft flying in an arrow-head. He told his pilots over the radio to keep calm and make every shot count. Looking around, he spotted Thunderbolts hovering above. Knoke glanced across at his old friend, Hans Raddatz, now tight off his wingtip; the two had flown together for over a year. Raddatz waved at him and then they closed in upon the enemy. Just as Knoke was about to fire, he saw a flash of light next to him and Raddatz's plane plummet downwards. Shocked, he continued towards his target, pressing down on the gun button and firing towards the cabin of the Fortress before pulling up and over at the last moment. His bullets and shells had hit their mark, however, as the Fortress reared up on its tail. Other bombers desperately tried to get out of the way as the stricken bomber's wing dropped and the Fortress began spiralling downwards.

Suddenly Knoke was alone and set upon by eight Mustangs of the 354th Fighter Group. Making a few sharp turns, he managed to get away and then on to the tail of one, but just as he was about to open fire he found himself surrounded by a pack of snapping Thunderbolts. Breaking away, he climbed in a corkscrew, a manoeuvre that had saved him many times before, then dived down for another attack on the American fighters. Again, he made no headway and for half an hour the cat-and-mouse continued until finally Knoke was able to hurtle down and attack another Fortress. Before he could check whether he had hit the bomber, he was attacked by more Thunderbolts.

One of the Mustang pilots that day was Dick Turner of the 354th FG. They had been bounced by a lone Me109 about fifteen minutes after crossing the coast, and Lieutenant George Barris had been hit in the pass and, rolling over, his plane had dived out of sight. Turner had followed the Messerschmitt, diving vertically and catching him at around 10,000 feet as he pulled out of his dive. Drawing close, he opened fire and saw the tracer hitting the cockpit and wing root. The Messerschmitt was yawing wildly as though the pilot had lost all control. Turner hurtled past and climbed back to rejoin the rest, but he never found them, so he circled the bombers, flying patrol around them until it was time to head for home.

Meanwhile, the bombers had hit Brunswick hard and were now making their way back too. Larry Goldstein had never been more relieved than when he finally touched back down. Miraculously, all the crew were safe, although their Fortress looked badly battered. 'Believe me,' Goldstein jotted in his diary that evening, 'I am not ashamed to say that I was scared today and never prayed harder to come through.' At least his nineteenth mission had been chalked up.

In Germany, Heinz Knoke landed back down a little over an hour after taking off and learned that Raddatz had not survived. 'He was the finest of comrades,' he wrote later. 'I cannot believe that he is in fact no more.'

The following day, the main target was Frankfurt. Dick Turner led his flight on to a group of Messerschmitt 109s and shot down the leader's wingman, obliterating the pilot and cockpit with a mass of concentrated .50-calibre slugs. Up there again was Heinz Knoke, who was caught up in yet another wild dogfight.

And then the weather closed in again and no further major raids took place for over a week. But at last, on 19 February, the meteorologists were forecasting better weather on its way. By this time, the American air chiefs were so determined to get on with the fight that they were prepared to take significant casualties. They had nearly a thousand bombers, almost as many fighters and a hundred P-51 long-range Mustangs. It would be tough on the crews, very tough, but the time had come to launch Operation ARGUMENT. What was about to unfold over the next seven days was the biggest, most concentrated air battle yet of the war.

It would become known as Big Week.

PART III

Big Week

CHAPTER 19

Saturday, 19 February 1944

SATURDAY, 19 FEBRUARY 1944 dawned dry but cold, with a biting wind and plenty of cloud. At around 8.30 a.m., Air Marshal Sir Arthur Harris turned in to the entrance of Bomber Command Headquarters in his Bentley sports saloon and sped towards No. 1 Site, a series of brick offices built in the 1930s. Pulling up outside, he headed straight to his office, which was on the first floor. He was given a folder of signals and memos that had come in overnight and then, after a quick perusal, he got back into his Bentley and drove to the Headquarters Operations Room in a deep underground bunker. It wasn't far and was easily walkable, but early during the First World War Harris had served as a soldier in Southern Africa and had walked the best part of 500 miles across the Kalahari Desert to fight the Germans. After that he decided to join the Royal Flying Corps instead and vowed never again to walk anywhere unless he had to. Stubborn, bullish and determined, Harris was someone who always knew his own mind.

He went down the steps into the 'Hole', as it was known, for 'High Mass' – the daily senior staff meeting at which daily operations were planned. His senior staff officers were all there, including Dr Magnus Spence, his Chief Meteorological Officer. The first item on the agenda, as always, was the weather. Spence reported that there would likely be cloud over central Germany, but patchy and unlikely to be a blanket ten-tenths covering. For some days, Harris had been intending to strike Leipzig, a major target on the ARGUMENT list and one that supported the new directive issued two days earlier. This, then, would be the night's mission.

The city was home to the large ATG Me109 assembly plant at Leipzig–Mockau, as well as two further assembly plants in the area. At Leipzig, ATG had been completing some 130 Me109s a month, but the Allies knew that expansion was planned and that final assembly of Ju88s and Ju188s had also begun there. The attack was scheduled to launch later that afternoon. It was to be a maximum effort. Harris now had around 900 heavy bombers in his command and over 1,000 aircraft of all types. Not all would be fit for flying, but most would, giving him in excess of 800 for the night's main operation.

Nor was Leipzig to be the only target. Harris had begun introducing new methods to confuse the enemy's air defence. Nearly fifty aircraft, mostly largely obsolescent Stirlings, would be sent to Kiel on mining operations as a diversion. Twelve Mosquitoes were to go on a light bombing mission to Berlin, while a further sixteen Oboe-carrying Mossies would attack Luftwaffe night-fighter airfields in Holland. A further dozen Mosquitoes were equipped with Serrate radar-detection devices to catch enemy night-fighters and confuse the Luftwaffe's radar systems. High Mass over, Harris returned to his office with the chain now in motion and orders being sent to group headquarters then to the bomber stations.

At RAF Bomber Command stations around the country the aircrews had already woken and had breakfast. Rusty Waughman tended to get up at about 7.30 a.m. if he had not been flying the previous night and none of them at 101 Squadron had done so for four days since the last trip to Berlin. Since being given a new engineer, the fortunes of Waughman and his crew had improved dramatically. There had been, inevitably, some hairy moments. Over Berlin on 28 January, for example, they had been attacked five times by night-fighters: three times by a single Ju88, once by a FW190 of Herrmann's *Wilde Sau* and then again by an aircraft they had been unable to identify. 'Office holed just behind head!' Waughman had scribbled in his diary. The mid-upper hatch had been blown off so that freezing air had hurtled through the Lancaster for much of the journey home. They'd all nearly frozen to death, but had survived and such experiences had taught them much and helped forge a strong team spirit and camaraderie.

They had all initially been NCOs and so had been able to mess together for the first couple of months. That had now changed, as in early February a decree had required all pilots and navigators to be commissioned. Waughman and Alec Cowan, his navigator, had been presented with cheques for £90 and told to go and buy themselves a new uniform. Given a few days' leave, Waughman had headed to London to be kitted out. He wasn't particularly pleased about it, despite the extra pay, because it meant he and

Cowan were now in the officers' mess, which separated them from the rest of the crew. He was still living in a Nissen hut, however, as Ludford Magna had only ever been built as a temporary airfield. 'It was very primitive. The only thing extra you had was a bit of carpet,' said Waughman. 'That was the only difference.'

Having showered – in cold water – shaved and dressed, Waughman walked the half mile to the mess hall for breakfast, then across the road, down Fanny Hands Lane, over a small stream and up to the C Flight Office. A glance at the noticeboard told him that night they were due to go on ops. Briefing for pilots and navigators was at 11 a.m. That gave him a couple of hours to head back to his Nissen hut, change his underwear to warmer silk long-johns for night flying, meet up with the crew and head to his Lancaster. There they met the ground crew. Fuelling the aircraft was already under way. Pre-flight checks were carried out and then he clambered on board and revved up the four Merlin engines with his flight engineer.

Back at the Flight Office, he learned that the pre-briefings for pilots and navigators had been pushed back to 5 p.m. instead. Orders were often chopped and changed. Missions could be scrubbed entirely. Getting oneself mentally prepared was made harder by the frequent changes, but Waughman was a phlegmatic fellow and tried, as far as possible, to take such challenges in his stride.

Some 170 miles away to the south at US Strategic Air Force Headquarters in Bushy Park, General Tooey Spaatz was taking direct control of Operation ARGUMENT. This might have been drawn up the previous November by the Combined Operational Planning Committee, but on his arrival as commander of US Strategic Air Forces Spaatz had picked it up and given it a far greater clarity of purpose. While he still believed air power alone could bring about the defeat of Germany, he had accepted that OVERLORD was going to happen and that, from April, his strategic air forces – and those of the RAF – would come under the direct authority of Eisenhower as Supreme Allied Commander. For now, POINTBLANK remained the priority, but come the spring it would be OVERLORD.

Yet for OVERLORD to be successful, that all-important criterion – air superiority over much of France and northern Europe – remained unchanged. Since the start of the year, Eighth Air Force had been chipping away at the Luftwaffe. Doolittle's and Kepner's new fighter tactics were bearing fruit and, with more long-range Mustangs on their way, the time was right for a much more concentrated and sustained assault on the German Air Force. No longer would bombers simply head to a target, drop their bombs and return; the bomber formations would also be used as bait to entice the German fighters into combat with the Allies' own increasingly large fighter force. Strategic air power had always been about bombers. Now, six months after the first deep-penetration bombing raids, that belief had been cast aside, because it had become widely agreed that even more important than the bombers were the fighters. Fighters piloted by men of superior skill and training. Fighter aircraft that had greater speed and agility than those of the enemy, and in greater numbers. Fighters that had greater endurance too, so that they could maraud deep into Germany, hammering the beleaguered enemy in the air and on the ground and destroying the enemy fighter force.

Spaatz had been embroiled in lengthy discussions with his subordinates but also with Leigh-Mallory, as commander of the Allied Expeditionary Air Force, over priorities and assets. Against the wishes of General Lewis H. Brereton, the Ninth Air Force commander, Spaatz had successfully ensured that P-51s would go to the Eighth, not the Ninth as had been originally – and illogically – agreed. In all, seven of the planned nine Mustang fighter groups would now go to the Eighth.

His next challenge had been to gain the support of the Ninth for his drive to defeat the Luftwaffe. At this, Leigh-Mallory had baulked, because he did not want his air forces consumed into a bigger strategic air battle over which he no longer had complete control. Until April, however, Spaatz wanted a concentrated and focused effort, and on 4 February, at a joint meeting with his commanders and also Leigh-Mallory and senior staff of the Allied Expeditionary Air Force, Spaatz pressed for a resolution. The Ninth, he told them, had a vital role in carrying out diversionary raids and strikes on Luftwaffe airfields in Holland. What's more, the Ninth's medium bombers and fighters had a key part to play in confusing the Luftwaffe's early-warning system. Spaatz also wanted the medium bombers of the Ninth to push beyond their 350-mile limit. If that meant operating without fighter escorts on occasion, then that was a risk they should be prepared to take. Spaatz was prepared for both Eighth and Ninth Air Forces to suffer casualties – even heavy losses – if that was what it took to grind down the Luftwaffe in bloody attrition. The pain now, he sincerely believed, would be more than worth the gain.

Still Leigh-Mallory prevaricated and appealed to Portal,

as did Spaatz. The British Chief of the Air Staff, however, sided – rightly – with Spaatz and Arnold, who had also waded in, and on 15 February Leigh-Mallory had been brought to heel. On direct orders from Portal, both the Ninth and the newly formed Second Tactical Air Force were now instructed to give priority support to the Eighth's operations above all other. With Leigh-Mallory brought into line, Spaatz only now needed to persuade Brereton, who resented the idea of being subordinate to the Eighth in any way.

Finally, earlier this same day, Saturday, 19 February, Spaatz met with Brereton, Doolittle and Anderson of VIII Bomber Command. And, admittedly under some duress, Brereton reluctantly accepted that the Ninth's IX Fighter Command would inform Kepner's headquarters of their daily availability and would accept the Eighth's daily 'primary' field orders. In other words, in all respects the Ninth's fighter force now had to supply direct support to the Eighth's efforts. Without the creation of Spaatz's new command and authority, pushed through with such vigor by Arnold, this level of cooperation would not have happened.

The final settlement of the Ninth's role had been concluded with serendipitous timing, for at around 3.30 p.m. the weathermen at Spaatz's headquarters, the central meteorological agency through which all forecasting was coordinated for the American air forces in England, reported that the weather looked to be improving at long last. They thought it likely that the pressure over the Baltic would move south-east across Europe with the resulting winds forcing the cloud to clear or, at worst, leaving scattered cloud. For Spaatz, that was good enough.

ARGUMENT was on, and over the next few days, by both night and day, the RAF and USAAF intended to pummel the Luftwaffe with intense round-the-clock air operations the like of which had never yet been seen. Alerts were sent out to the bases of the Eighth and Ninth.

Spaatz now had considerable air power under him. In many ways, the build-up of American air forces had been working up to this moment since the summer of 1942. The figures for Eighth Air Force alone were jaw-dropping: 132 airfields and enough supply and repair depots to cover an area of 9,700,000 square feet. There was housing for half a million personnel – equivalent to a city larger than pre-war Washington DC. Over a million man-months' worth of labour had been involved, with the movement of 16,400,000 cubic yards of soil and the laying of 46 million square yards of concrete and 262,000,000 bricks. There were, on this Saturday, 19 February 1944, some 944 B-17s, 348 B-24s and 707 combat-ready fighters. Every air base had stores crammed with bombs and ammunition, and fuel depots filled with all the high-octane fuel they could possibly need. These were huge resources and ones that would have made Göring, Milch and everyone in the Luftwaffe weep with envy.

Spaatz was confident everything was ready. He now needed to ensure that all the immense forces under his control pulled together, took the necessary risks they would undoubtedly have to take, and hammered the Luftwaffe hard. And he had to pray the weathermen were right.

At Bomber Command Headquarters that Saturday afternoon, further weather reports had been arriving. A

Mosquito had flown high over central Europe and at around 1 p.m. his report reached High Wycombe: 10/19 cloud over Leipzig, with predicted freezing cloud and the possibility of ice forming. A second reconnaissance Mosquito reported clear skies over Berlin but heavy cloud at Leipzig and strong winds. This was far from ideal but, with a take-off time pushed back to 11 p.m., it was hoped the situation would have improved. Spaatz's headquarters had also by now confirmed the start of ARGUMENT and that they, too, would be targeting Leipzig the following day. For once, the Combined Bomber Offensive would be working properly in tandem.

Pilots' and navigators' briefings were held at last at 5 p.m. At Graveley, Gordon Carter and his pilot, Julian Sale, attended along with those of sixteen other crews. At Ludford Magna, Rusty Waughman and his young navigator, Alec Cowan, were also attending theirs. All were carried out in strict secrecy: guards on the door, blacked-out windows, pilots and navigators unable to say a word at this stage to the rest of the crew. On large map boards, they were shown the route, which took them out over the North Sea then over the northern Dutch coast and towards Berlin, before turning south-east and then a final dog-leg south-west to the target. The return leg would take them almost due west, then north-west back over the North Sea. All aircraft would carry similar loads of one 2,000lb high-explosive bomb and 2 tons of incendiaries. The main briefing would be at 9.30 p.m., ninety minutes before take-off. For Waughman, Carter and the rest of the 823 heavy bomber crews who would be flying that night, the remaining hours until take-off were often hard to fill: crew supper, maybe some letter writing, and any other distraction. Waughman liked to read a book or a paper in the mess, or play cards and drink cups of tea or coffee. 'It was a sort of steady permanent feeling,' he said. 'You knew you were going on an operation and you knew what operations could do. You couldn't put it out of your mind, but you had to try to.'

At US Strategic Air Force Headquarters, Spaatz's plans for Operation ARGUMENT were already going slightly awry. The meteorologists at both Eighth and Ninth Air Forces HQs were not nearly as confident as those at USSTAF. Doolittle always naturally erred on the side of scepticism when it came to weather forecasting – he had been caught short too many times, so, although he was prepared to do as ordered, he couldn't help listening to the advice his own meteorology team were giving him. The truth was, weather forecasting in early 1944 always involved a lot of guesswork. There were a large number of weather stations on the British Isles, but it was further west, out at sea, that they were really needed, and there they were far fewer. The weather was fickle and, certainly, the skies had been solid over England that Saturday.

The second concern was over the air forces in Italy. As a courtesy to his old friend, Spaatz had also alerted Eaker that ARGUMENT was being launched and requested that Fifteenth Air Force bomb the aircraft assembly plants at Regensburg and Augsburg or the ball-bearing works at Stuttgart; for ARGUMENT to have the greatest effect, he wanted to smash the twelve key targets heavily and with multiple forces all at the same time. As a secondary target, he asked for the Fifteenth Air Force to carry out an area raid on Breslau. The aim was to overwhelm the German

Rusty Waughman in the cockpit of his Lancaster, and newly commissioned (*right*).

Below: The interior of a Lancaster looking back from the flight engineer's side of the cockpit and showing one of the huge wing spars that had to be clambered over. Crew comfort and safety was not a big consideration in its design.

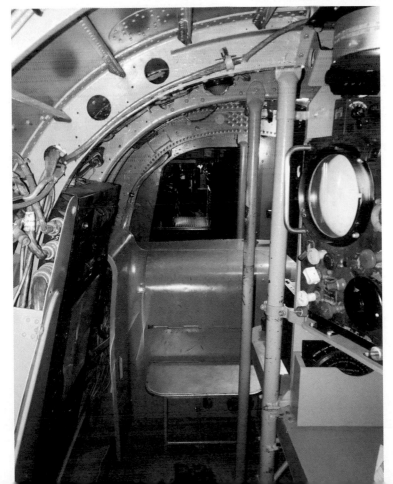

Conditions in the winter of 1943 and early 1944 were awful. Here (*right*), 101 Squadron crew cross 'Mudford' Magna.

Below: After a mission. Rusty Waughman — centre with cigarette — pours himself a welcome hot drink.

Nissen huts at Ridgewell in winter (*left*). Accommodation for air crew was often pretty basic (*below*) and the single stove barely enough to alleviate the cold and damp.

Below: Pilots of the 336th Fighter Squadron in their dispersal hut. Don Gentile is at the table on the left, while Jim Goodson is standing centre.

Reichsmarschall Hermann Göring (*below left*) rapidly losing his grip on the Luftwaffe by the second half of 1943. Instead, it was left to the younger men to try to keep the German Air Force going.

Dolfo Galland

Hajo Herrmann

Wim Johnen

Heinz Knoke

FW190

Me110
night-fighter

Above: Bill Lawley's battered B-17 showing the cannon-shell hole in the windscreen that decapitated his co-pilot.

Below: Ground engineers strip down a wrecked Flying Fortress.

Bottom left: A damaged B-17 falling out of formation, while a B-24 (*right*) explodes mid-air.

Flying a bombing mission was brutally tough: terrifying, often confusing, requiring enormous reserves of concentration and with the ever-present anxiety that random and extreme violence could strike at any moment.

Below: B-24s over the target.

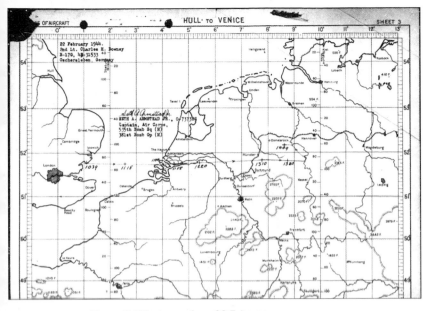

Above: Big Week map from 22 February.

Below: Post-raid photograph of the extensive damage caused at Regensburg.

Thorpe Abbotts, home to the 100th Bomb Group. The chow line (*top left*), crew accommodation (*top right*) and a Fortress coming in to land (*left*).

Most of the many bases of the Eighth have disappeared but remnants are not hard to find. Now covered by brambles are the old cinema at Ridgewell and Chaplain James Good Brown's office (*right*) and the old main runway (*below*).

defences; enemy fighters could not be everywhere at all times and so Fifteenth Air Force had a vital role in both causing damage and drawing German fighters away from the bombers of the Eighth.

This put Eaker in a difficult position. Strictly speaking, he only had administrative control over Major-General Nathan Twining's Fifteenth Air Force, not operational authority. Second, US Strategic Air Forces had already been called upon to provide support for US Fifth Army's operations at Anzio. Both Lieutenant-General Mark Clark, the Fifth Army commander, and Major-General John Cannon, commander of the Twelfth Tactical Air Force, had been given assurances that the Fifteenth would help on what was expected to be a critical day on the bridgehead around this coastal town south of Rome. What's more, Eaker's weathermen were also predicting heavy cloud and bad weather over much of Italy. As he pointed out, the Fifteenth lacked any H2X equipment and so would be unlikely to bomb the targets allocated to them accurately in any case.

Spaatz understood the conundrum facing Eaker, but POINTBLANK – and now ARGUMENT – had to take precedence. OVERLORD trumped operations in Italy and right now POINTBLANK trumped OVERLORD. He felt they should all stop worrying about the weather. He and Anderson had accepted that extraordinary risks now needed to be taken. The stakes were simply too high. It was better, Spaatz fervently believed, that they lost more aircrews now but pressed home their assault on the Luftwaffe, rather than preserve lives now only for more to be lost in the long run.

It was now late evening on the 19th and time was fast

running out. Spaatz appealed to Portal, who in turn appealed to Churchill. The Prime Minister, however, insisted the operations at Anzio should take priority, so Portal's hands were tied and, consequently, so too were Spaatz's. Later that night, Doolittle sent up weather planes to gauge whether there was any sign of the improvement predicted by the met men at Spaatz's HQ. They found none. The tension mounted. For the deep-penetration mission that was planned, crews would have to be up early to make the most of the winter daylight, and they would be taking off early, too, into potentially thick cloud that could easily then freeze on their aircraft as they struggled to climb up through 5,000 feet. Much now rested on the shoulders of Spaatz. Risks needed to be taken, but what if catastrophe awaited?

11 p.m. Across Bomber Command's airfields, crews were now being driven out to their waiting aircraft, looming monstrously against the night sky around the perimeters. Up at Leeming, the Canadians of 429 Squadron would be sending out sixteen Halifaxes, although Bill Byers and his crew were not among them. After flying to Berlin on the 14th, they had been given a week's leave. At Graveley, Gordon Carter and his pilot, Julian Sale, were both about to undertake their fifty-first mission. Carter was just beginning to get to the end of his tether. Anyone serving in the war, whether a soldier, sailor or airman, had a bank of courage that would, eventually, run empty without very careful management. For some, the bank was larger than it was for others. In the RAF, men like Rusty Waughman's first flight engineer were termed 'Lacking Moral Fibre' once their nerve went – a horrible label and one that

brought barely imaginable shame on those who were cat-
egorized thus. Anyone considered LMF was stripped of
rank and sacked immediately, as if they had a contagious
disease, and were taken off the station without delay for
fear of infecting morale.

Some who had clearly run dry desperately tried to keep
going. Friends would cover up for them as far as possible
and more of them than might be imagined were able somehow to get through their tours. Others would become
'flak-happy' – a condition that usually brought about
unpredictable behaviour and even rashness. Carter reckoned he hadn't quite reached the flak-happy stage, but
knew he wasn't far off. He had also found something of a
soulmate in Julian Sale – a sign that both men were becoming more introverted and detached from others around
them. They stuck together and even on crew leaves always
spent their time together in London. 'I doubt whether I
can convey the special relationship which united Julian
and me,' Carter wrote. 'We were determined to be A1 in all
we did and worked as hard at it on the ground as in the air.'
Sale had also been shot down over France and escaped,
and both were determined that, should it ever happen
again, they would be better prepared. They went on long
cross-country runs, practised breaking out of the airfield
without being seen, and even made light and loose cloth
packs containing civvy clothes they could change into if
forced to go on the run. Carter also squeezed in a lightweight mackintosh behind his Mae West and parachute
harness. This kind of escape and evasion kit could have got
them shot if caught on the ground – British airmen in
civilian clothing might well be assumed to be spies – but
that was something both men were willing to risk.

As they started up their engines at around 11.40 that night, the weather was once again rotten. They all knew the trip to Leipzig would be what they termed, with classic British understatement, 'a shaky do': a long flight along a route where the night-fighters were at their most concentrated. Their Halifax, TL-J, was painted matt black all over save for the RAF rondels and squadron markings. At 11.51 p.m. Sale hauled back on the control column and they were airborne and climbing slowly through the sleet and ice.

Some 120 miles to the north, at RAF Leconfield in Yorkshire, just to the north of the old East Riding market town of Beverley, the Australians of 466 Squadron, part of RAF 4 Group, were also taking off. In Flight Sergeant Jack Scott's crew the only Englishman was Flight Sergeant Ken Handley, the flight engineer and just twenty years old. Being the odd one out didn't bother Handley much – like most crews, they had gelled quickly and he got along well with all of them. They were a new crew; this was only their second flight, having had their baptism of fire four nights earlier on a long mission to Berlin. There had been a lot of flak over the target, but they had successfully dropped their bombs then turned for home. The return leg had been far more eventful, with plenty of night-fighters around, but Scott had taken evasive action a few times and they had successfully made it back to Leconfield after seven hours and thirty minutes in the air. 'Not so frightening as I had expected,' Handley had written in his diary after that first trip. 'A little fear at the bottom of it all. Tense last half hour when tank 4 iced up.'

Now, at just ten minutes to midnight, they were taking off again for another brutally long trip, fighting their way up through thick cloud and eventually emerging high over the North Sea. Also now over the North Sea were the Lancasters of 101 Squadron. Rusty Waughman and his crew had taken off from Ludford Magna at 11.44 p.m. Above the water, the crews tested their guns, then almost the moment they crossed over the Frisian Islands and the Dutch coast the flak opened up and they began to be aware of night-fighters.

From his Halifax, Gordon Carter looked down and saw the route ahead lit up by strings of flares fired by the Luftwaffe to illuminate the cloud below and so silhouette the bombers against it. Accompanying the bombers were RAF twin-engine Beaufighters whose task it was to hunt down the hunters. Carter never felt they made much difference and preferred to trust in Sale and his own navigational skills to get them out of trouble. Sitting at his plotting desk, he felt the Halifax being continually yawed from side to side and dipping downwards, then climbing; the trick was to avoid flying straight and level. Sale also took them higher – up to 23,000 feet, which was about as high as a Halifax could reach when fully laden. Onwards they droned, deeper into Germany and towards Leipzig.

Jack Scott's Australian crew were also pushing on towards the target. Sitting beside him was Ken Handley. After their last trip he had discovered their problem had not been icing but rather that he had forgotten to pump 230 gallons from tank 4 into tanks 1 and 3 after leaving the target. The ground crew had found a completely full tank the following morning, which meant they had made the entire trip to Berlin and back on just three tanks. No wonder they had landed with what seemed like no fuel at all. It was a mistake Handley would not make again.

Now they faced the same worrying number of night-fighters that was troubling Gordon Carter and crew. Flak opened up the moment they crossed the Dutch coast and twice they were picked up by searchlights. Scott took quick evasive action and managed to get them clear, but other bombers were already starting to fall from the sky as night-fighters made no fewer than fifty separate attacks on the bomber stream. Down below, the German ground controllers had not been fooled by the diversionary raid on Kiel and had sent only part of their fighter force there, which was why so many night-fighters had been waiting for the bombers as they flew over the coast. The bomber stream would find itself under attack all the way to the target.

Carter and his crew were still en route to Leipzig when, at 2.43 a.m., they were suddenly raked by cannon fire from a Ju88. It had stalked them from underneath using the *Schräge Musik* technique. The fuel-overload tank exploded, engulfing the plane in fire. They still had their bombs on board and there was absolutely no hope of the extinguishers being able to save them, so Sale at once ordered them to bail out. This was easier said than done in a burning bomber that was spiralling out of control. Carter was immediately pinned to the fuselage by the centrifugal forces, but managed to fight these, pull up the hatch and get out before the flames engulfed him. Relief coursed through him as he plunged down, then he pulled the rip-cord and his parachute ballooned. His first thought was that now he would not face the ignominy of having to ask to be taken off ops and the shame that would have come with it. Bailing out of a burning wreck meant there would be no stigma of LMF for him.

Any immediate thoughts of relief, however, were soon followed by the realization that he was drifting down from above most of the other bombers in the stream with the air around him about 50° below freezing and with no oxygen. It would be very easy for him to hit another aircraft or, even more probable, have his parachute blown in from the slipstream. And he had to worry about landing safely and whether he would then be able to avoid the Germans. It took him around twenty minutes to drift down, which gave him a lot of time to contemplate his future. By the time he finally passed through the thick layer of cloud he was only just conscious, but managed to summon the presence of mind to wrest his revolver from his pocket and throw it away. Now he could see the land rising towards him and saw he was over a wood with a path running through it. By tugging on the cords, he managed to land perfectly without so much as touching a single branch. Thick snow lay on the ground. Gathering his parachute, he hid it along with his Mae West and battledress in undergrowth and slipped into his civilian clothes, then he struck out along the path.

At group and command headquarters, staff were receiving the latest reports on the weather situation from fifteen navigators in each group who had been selected to provide updates as the bomber stream progressed. On aircraft equipped with GEE, H2S and Oboe, they had been transmitting their reports, which also included estimations of wind speed, to Bomber Command Headquarters. These reports were then forwarded to the Central Forecast Office – CFO – at Dunstable, near High Wycombe, where they were examined and plotted by upper air forecasters.

Their conclusions were relayed to Bomber Command HQ, who transmitted their updated reports back to the designated navigators' crews, who then forwarded the information to the rest of the force.

The reports showed winds significantly stronger than forecast. Rather than being pushed along by tail winds of 40 m.p.h., for which the force had been originally briefed, the winds were in fact as strong as 100 m.p.h. This was why Rusty Waughman and many others found themselves over the target far earlier than anticipated, and before the Pathfinders had been able to complete their marking, requiring the bombers to circle over Leipzig for around twenty minutes waiting for the moment to carry out their bomb runs. When every moment of the mission was fraught with risk, spending an extra twenty minutes, especially when right in the jaws of the lion, was torturous for the crews. Four aircraft collided and were lost as they circled.

Eventually, just before 4 a.m., white incendiaries from the Pathfinders began showering down from the sky. The targets were completely cloud-covered, but blind markers were dropped and then backed up by further 'Wanganui' – or Christmas tree – flares.* Waughman and his crew then began their bomb run. Searchlights were now coning aircraft through the cloud and lighting up much of the sky over the city, while the flak was heavy and the bomber was being jolted and jerked all over the place. Down below the bright light of the flares mixed with the orange glow of

---

* Wanganui was the first town in New Zealand to begin the custom of lighting a giant Christmas tree in the town square. New Zealander crews began calling Christmas tree flares 'Wanganui flares' and the name soon stuck.

explosions and flames beneath the cloud. At 4.08 a.m. they were over the target, flying at 23,000 feet and dropping their bombs on the markers.

As Waughman turned homewards, Jack Scott and his crew began their run. They were at 22,000 feet and fortunately most of the flak seemed to be exploding below them. From his position in the cockpit Ken Handley was able to look out of the blister in the Perspex and see the marker flares clearly below. He also spotted puffs of black smoke around them where the gunners on the ground were trying to blast out the flares.

As they neared the target, they were unable to open the bomb bays because they had iced up, so they quickly used the Bomb Door Emergency Operation, which meant pulling the pin on the emergency air control in the nose of the Halifax and holding the control mechanism down until the doors were fully open. Fortunately, this failsafe worked and at 4.18 a.m. their bombs dropped and they, too, were climbing and on their way home.

Rusty Waughman touched back down at Ludford Magna at 6.55 a.m. The squadron had got off comparatively lightly – just one had failed to return. For Ken Handley and his Australian crew, however, fuel was once again the issue, although on this occasion it was an overload pump that had packed in, leaving them short. As they flew back across the North Sea, it was touch and go whether they would make landfall, but they did so and called up Snetterton Heath, an American air base in Norfolk. As they were circling to land, they suddenly saw another Halifax coming in just ahead of them and only 50 feet below. With a wingspan of over 100 feet, that was all too close for comfort, especially at the end of a long and fraught flight. To make matters worse, their own hydraulics were shot, which meant they had to land with no brakes. Touching down, the big bomber kept running and Handley thought they would keep going off the runway and crash. Quick thinking by Jack Scott enabled him to wheel the Halifax by using the throttles to steer, but still they ran on, off the perimeter and over a slight ditch, which eventually brought them to a standstill.

Leipzig had none the less proved a bloody raid for Bomber Command. 'Pretty deadly trip,' noted Rusty Waughman. 'Lost 78 A/C.' Ken Handley noted the same figure in his diary, along with the three that did not return from 466 Squadron. That the number was so widely known so quickly was not brilliant for morale. And the losses were huge – 9.5 per cent of the force; of those, fifty-four had been shot down by night-fighters. Harris's stubborn insistence that sustained and coordinated night bombing alone was the best way to shorten the war was being disproved only too palpably. Only when the Luftwaffe was destroyed would his bombers be free of marauding night-fighters and therefore considerably more effective. And to win air superiority, the Allied strategic air forces needed to continue daylight bombing and employing the aggressive tactics of their increasingly superior day-fighters.

Even so, despite the losses, and despite the cloud, the best part of 800 heavy bombers had hit Leipzig, a major target. Furthermore, this raid had just been the start, because as the weary returning crews wolfed down their eggs and bacon and headed off to bed, the Eighth Air Force was readying to launch its own strike. And one of the main targets was Leipzig once again.

CHAPTER 20

Sunday,
20 February 1944

THE NIGHT OF 19/20 February had been a long one at US Strategic Air Forces Headquarters in south-west London. Starting ARGUMENT without the Fifteenth Air Force in Italy had been a blow, but then had come the doubts from Doolittle and Brereton. On top of that it had become increasingly clear that something was fundamentally wrong with the P-38 Lightning, which, although nothing like as effective as the Mustang against Me109s and FW190s, still had an important long-range role to play. Powered by twin Allison engines – which had also powered the P-51A – it was proving unsuited to the extreme cold and high moisture levels. On 17 February, staff at VIII Fighter Command had reported that as much as 40 per cent of its P-38 force of five fighter groups was currently affected by trouble with its Allison engines; not for nothing had the aircraft gained the name the 'Widow Maker'. In fact, the problem of icing was not just the preserve of the Luftwaffe or P-38 Lightning; overnight, Bill

Kepner also waded in, warning that if temperatures were as cold and cloudy as the Eighth's weathermen predicted, then icing could be expected not only to cut the P-38s' performance by half, but also to lower the performance of the Mustangs and Thunderbolts.

General Fred Anderson, commanding officer of VIII Bomber Command, was determined ARGUMENT should go ahead, however, and spent the entire night at his desk, by his phone, ready to counter the opinions of any of the nay-sayers. Hovering at the back of the minds of all the senior commanders and staff were the losses suffered every time their bombers had previously penetrated deep into Germany. Schweinfurt, Regensburg and, more recently, Oschersleben hung heavy on their collective conscience. After so carefully building up their air forces, was it sensible to risk everything when the weather was so notoriously fickle? Long months of cold, dark days and seemingly constant cloud, rain and fog had been enough to dent anyone's confidence.

Anderson was also concerned that his boss, General Spaatz, was starting to waver. Spaatz always let his subordinates express their points of view. What Anderson interpreted as a sign that Spaatz was having second thoughts, however, was, in reality, just his boss listening to other opinions.

The decision, when it came, was made early and was Spaatz's alone. On his shoulders was the terrifying thought that they might lose in the region of two hundred crews. The dangers were certainly considerable. On the other hand, Arnold had been urging more ruthlessness and for the strategic air forces to take greater risks. So, early in the morning of Sunday, 20 February, Spaatz made his decision. 'Let 'em go.'

The wake-up call was 3 a.m. for most of the bomber crews of the Eighth. 'Awakened very early today,' scribbled Larry Goldstein in his diary, 'and expected a long, rough mission, even long before briefing.'

As usual, the map on the wall at the end of the briefing room was covered, but there was also an extension to the right, which could mean only one thing: that their target was so far away it did not fit on to their normal wall map. That hardly eased nerves. Then Colonel William R. David, commander of the 388th, pulled back the curtain and there was a long strip of red tape running from England out over the North Sea to Denmark, then across the Baltic and back to eastern Germany and into Poland, until it finally stopped at Poznań, nearly 1,000 miles away.

'Men,' Colonel David said, 'your bomb is 5,000 lbs, gas load, naturally, maximum. Don't start your engines before you have to. You'll need all the gas you have.' They were to climb to 11,000 feet and cruise at that altitude, then over the Baltic climb again to 17,000 feet, which was to be their bombing height. 'If you lose an engine over or near the target,' he continued, 'check your gas and if you don't think you can make it, head for Sweden.' Their wing, he explained, was hitting Poznań, but the 13th Wing, who would be flying with them much of the way, would be hitting a target in Germany instead. Then came the worst part: they would be alone all the way back, the colonel told them; the rest of the Eighth would be bombing targets all over central and southern Germany. 'You'll have no fighter escort,' he said, 'so shoot at anything you see in the way of a fighter. Keep on the ball and good luck to all of you.'

At Tibenham, Jimmy Stewart, now a major, had turned in the previous night conscious that something was up. He had seen the ground crew busy fuelling and loading the B-24s, but the consensus was that nothing would come of it and that the mission would probably be scrubbed, because whatever the talk of improving weather, there was certainly no sign of it at Tibenham.

Stewart was also roused at 3 a.m., and after quickly shaving and dressing, and before heading to the mess for breakfast, was ordered to attend a pre-pre-briefing. With nine missions already under his belt, Stewart was considered an old hand. More than that, the commanders of the 2nd Division had come to regard him as a safe pair of hands and a man with sound judgement. While he and some of the other senior pilots waited, one of them, Bob Kiser, read out a letter from his wife, who was describing getting the nursery ready; the couple were expecting their first child in May. When the briefing officer arrived, they all stood to attention, then were seated again as the curtain was drawn back. Target: Brunswick, some 450 miles from Tibenham, with a component plant for the Ju88 as the primary and the factory at Neupetritor, on the edge of the city, as the secondary.

'We will put up thirty-five ships today,' they were told. 'Major Stewart and Lieutenant Conley will be Second Combat Wing lead ship, low. They will be in front of the 445th, 453rd and 389th.' Pathfinders would lead them in and they would have fighter escort from Thunderbolts, Lightnings and Mustangs. Afterwards, for breakfast there were real eggs, rather than powdered, and bacon, which always had a whiff of the condemned man's last meal about it.

Elsewhere, other crews were also getting ready. At Chelveston, Lieutenant Bill Lawley and his crew would be targeting aircraft factories and assembly plants at Leipzig and nearby Bernburg, the day's principal target, along with some 417 bombers from the 1st Division. As the curtain had been drawn back, Lawley had turned to his bombardier, Lieutenant Henry Mason, and said, 'Doesn't sound too bad, Henry.'

'Who knows?' Mason had replied. 'You never can tell about a strike into Germany.'

While the 1st Division were heading to Leipzig, the B-24s of the 2nd Division would be split up over five targets: Poznań, Brunswick, Gotha, Oschersleben and Helmstedt. For the Fortresses of the 3rd Division, some 314 in all, there were two further targets: Tutow and Rostock. Hitting multiple targets at once with over a thousand bombers was intended to cause widespread destruction and also to confuse the enemy air defence. The idea was for the main bomber force striking the Brunswick–Leipzig targets to appear on enemy radar screens first and attract the enemy fighter force, leaving the northern bombers with a clear run.

After starting engines as late as possible, just before taxiing, the Fortresses of the 388th BG took off and, after managing to cut their assembly time by half, headed off on their northern course. On board *Worry Wart*, Larry Goldstein's pilot, BJ Keirsted, and co-pilot, Ace Conklin, were using the lowest possible power settings and lowest r.p.m. in an effort to conserve fuel.

The B-24s of the 2nd Division were also airborne. On board *Tenovus*, Major Jimmy Stewart sat in the co-pilot's seat next to Lieutenant Bill Conley, the pilot. They took off at 9.08 a.m. and by 10.30 had completed assembly and were heading off on the 450-mile trip to Brunswick. Just then, Stewart saw a formation of B-17s out of position to their left, so quickly ordered their own group to climb and shift to the south of their planned route to avoid them, but already that meant a three-minute delay to the schedule. However, everyone adjusted without the need to break radio silence, including the all-important Pathfinders, and by the time they were approaching the Dutch coast the B-17s were little more than specks on the horizon.

The sky was a bright, deep blue. Above and away to their right, another combat box of bombers was trailing long white streaks of vapour. So too were their own ships as they crossed the coastline at some 17,000 feet. Ahead, flak began to open up, puffs of dark brown, initially above them, then too far below; but then the gunners below found their range and the bombers were heading straight for it, although it was neither heavy nor particularly threatening. Stewart thought about warning everyone, but then resisted the urge, while behind him Sergeant Wilson, the radio man, tapped him on the arm and made urgent signals: their radio frequency was being jammed. Stewart understood and, in any case, the boys all knew what to do. It was now nearly midday.

Winds were pushing them slightly off course, Lieutenant Steinhaurer, the navigator, reported, but they were able to adjust quickly, with only a minute lost.

'Good work, Manny,' said Conley.

*

The fighter boys had an early start too. At Leiston, Bud Anderson was woken while it was still dark and told to get ready. On went the long-johns, two pairs of socks, trousers, shirt, flight suit, GI shoes with fur-lined boots on top, and RAF-issue gloves that went halfway up his forearms. Dressed and ready, he headed to the mess in one of the station Jeeps, ate a peanut butter-and-marmalade sandwich, then heard the bombers heading off overhead. That meant the mission was definitely on.

Group briefing was in a large Nissen hut that could seat fifty pilots. As with the bomber crews, a curtain was drawn back from a large map and there they saw their destination: Leipzig. This was to be Anderson's fifth mission, and the rule of thumb was 'Do five, stay alive', so he was eager to get it under his belt. He paid attention to the reaction from his fellow pilots when the target was revealed. 'Some would groan when the target looked tough,' he noted, 'and some would grin. The guys who grinned were the ones I wanted with me.' The group operations officer then took over with more specific details about the targets, timings, the number of other groups involved, the rendezvous point with the bombers and the course back home. The pilots wrote the key stats and details on the back of their hands. Then came the weather brief and finally the synchronizing of watches.

Outside, light snow was falling over the Suffolk coast as they headed to their Mustangs. Take-off was in pairs, and in squadrons with one squadron strung out on the long main runway and the other two lined up on the secondary runways that criss-crossed the main one like a giant 'A'. A flare was fired, brakes were released, throttles gunned and they were away, flagged off in pairs, each squadron in order, eight seconds per pair, sixty-four seconds per squadron, and three and a half minutes at the most for the entire 357th Fighter Group to get themselves airborne.

They took off in radio silence, although they soon guessed that the enemy knew they were coming. On his first few missions, Anderson had already become familiar with a strange harmonic humming in his headset, a kind of *yuum-yuum-YUUM-yuum-yuum*, which he had discovered was the enemy radar beam tracking them. It was a reminder that, as they flew across seemingly empty skies, they were being watched. Anderson found it a bit of a distraction but, in any case, they wanted the Germans to come up and fight; that was half the point of being there.

As the Mustangs climbed high to 30,000 feet or more and cruised towards Germany, the 3rd Division were continuing on their northern route. Thick cloud covered the North Sea, but as the 388th BG neared Denmark, the skies cleared. Soon they spotted enemy fighters away to their left and saw another group under attack. Two Fortresses could be seen plunging down, then a little further on a third came under attack, although ten parachutes were spotted.

FW190s swept at them until they were out of the Baltic, but the attacks were not pressed home with the normal degree of fury. Their formation now changed course, climbed to 17,000 feet and gradually the clear skies gave way to increasingly thick cloud, which became a mounting concern.

In Italy, many of the Fifteenth Air Force's bomb groups were getting ready to bomb Regensburg after all. The problem facing Spaatz had been that General Henry Maitland

Wilson, the Supreme Allied Commander in the Mediterranean, had the authority to pull rank and demand the Fifteenth's bombers be used for supporting ground operations; however, General Eaker had got around the dual demands of the Anzio crisis and ARGUMENT by offering a part of his strategic bomber forces – supporting US V Corps at Anzio did not require all the Fifteenth's heavy bombers.

As a result, crews had been woken early from their tents and other roughly erected barracks for operations into Germany. Among those getting ready had been Lieutenant Robert 'Sully' Sullivan, a navigator in the 32nd Bomb Squadron, part of the 301st Bomb Group now based at Lucera, one of the hastily created airfields of the Foggia complex in central southern Italy.

Sullivan had joined the 301st in late December. 'January 1, 1944, finds me here in southern Italy,' he had jotted on the first page of his diary for the new year, 'trying to do my bit to end this damn war.' Life was basic: there were few paved tracks, even officers were expected to live in tents, and there was a lot of mud. No one had told Sullivan that Italy was going to be so wet and cold. One of the biggest problems had been boredom; for far too many days since his arrival, missions had been scrubbed due to bad weather and, even when they did go ahead, they were usually only within Italy itself and rarely very far.

'Miserable day,' Sullivan noted of the morning of Sunday, 20 February, 'and we never dreamed that we'd even get to the briefing room before the mission would be scrubbed!' They had been wrong.

They took off for their target, Regensburg, an hour later, climbed through the cloud and began their assembly at just 1,500 feet over the Adriatic. They were due to rendezvous with a fighter escort of Thunderbolts at 19,000 feet, but an hour later were still struggling through thick cloud when they were told to return to base, as the mission was being abandoned. 'Had a recall and was very happy,' Sullivan jotted, 'even tho' a mission over the Alps counts double for us.' So that was the end of the Fifteenth's efforts to join the day's attacks – not stymied by other priorities, but once again by the fickleness of the weather.

The heavies of the Eighth Air Force were continuing their missions, however. The 379th BG, with forty-seven B-17s, were en route to attack the aircraft assembly plant at Bernburg, some 40 miles to the north-west of Leipzig. This was Hugh McGinty's eleventh mission and from his position in the tail he could see the massed armadas climbing up through the largely clear skies. This was a good start, with not one crew lost to collision on take-off. None the less, it still took a good while to get so many bombers into formation. Each would climb up to 11,000 feet then begin flying a circuit in a rectangular pattern over their forming-up area. Each bomber group had an assembly plane, usually an old, beaten-up ship no longer suitable for combat. It would be painted in wild, bright colours – stripes, polka dots, anything to make it stand out, and each group's was painted differently. This would be the first plane off, followed by the group leader for the mission. The assembly plane and group leader would then circle over their allocated assembly area, with newly arriving bombers joining the circle, first in threes and then vics of three threes, which made up a squadron. Thirty-six aircraft – four squadrons of nine – made up a group. Usually some four or even six aircraft would fly as spares in case any dropped out due to technical glitches.

The bombers ran into enemy fighters as soon as they crossed the coast. One of the consequences of the time needed to form up was that it allowed the Luftwaffe's early-warning system to pick up the gathering raid and scramble aircraft to meet it. McGinty, from his tail position, saw their own escorts turning towards the enemy fighters with the result that, as they droned on, more and more swirling dogfights were breaking out. Despite the escorts, some enemy aircraft still managed to get close, but McGinty's group at least managed to drive them off. So far, he had not seen a single bomber going down.

As they headed east towards Berlin, enemy fighters appeared in greater numbers, but then suddenly the P-51s appeared. McGinty rather enjoyed watching the Mustangs tangling with the Me109s and FW190s. On more than one occasion he saw a German fighter barrelling through their formation with a Mustang on its tail. 'We had to be careful not to hit our little friends,' he noted. A great deal of lead was criss-crossing the sky.

From there until they reached the target, the flak was heavy, and as they began their bomb run McGinty saw that many stragglers, presumably already hit and damaged, were struggling to keep with the main group. Clusters of enemy fighters swarmed around these planes. McGinty saw several going down in flames but with parachutes opening as crew hurriedly bailed out of their stricken aircraft. Over the target, however, there were – as forecast by Spaatz's weathermen – clear skies and in *Blue*

Blazing Blizzard Matty Nathan, the bombardier, reckoned he had dropped their bombs pretty accurately.

Among those escorting the bombers to Leipzig were the P-47s of the 56th FG. For Bob Johnson, it was his only mission so far all month – he had missed the first couple of weeks due to an infected boil on his leg – but now, as they headed over Germany with big new 150-gallon drop tanks strung underneath them, he could only marvel at the sight of miles upon miles of bombers droning towards their targets, contrails streaking across the bright winter sky.

All was quiet for them until it was time to break off escort some 30 miles west of Hanover. Gabby Gabreski was leading the squadron, with Johnson commanding Blue Flight to his left. Lieutenant Justus Foster suddenly called out, 'Bandits, seven o'clock low.' They looked down and saw thirteen Me110s skimming along the tops of patchy cloud at about 15,000 feet. 'Everything,' noted Johnson, 'was shaping up for the perfect bounce.' This required a 180-degree turn to the left and a 7,000-foot dive. 'We really hit those 110s hard,' wrote Gabreski. The twin-engine fighters were split into two sections and Gabreski latched on to the second from the right of the rear group. 'He exploded when I was about fifty yards behind him,' he added, 'with his tail and wing separating from the rest of the plane, and went down spinning.' Beside him, Johnson had slid under him to come out on Gabreski's right, so that, by the time they came upon the 110s, eight Thunderbolts were in line abreast. All eight opened fire at pretty much the same time: thirty-two heavy machine guns pummelling the startled Messerschmitts before they could react. 'We hit the first bunch in true Thunderbolt fashion,' noted Johnson, 'ripped through their scattering ranks and began to chop up the second echelon.'

Pulling into a climbing turn, Gabreski glanced back and saw the sky littered with burning 110s and parachutes blooming. By his reckoning, only one had escaped and, seeing it hurriedly diving away, he sped after it, firing off a burst just as the Messerschmitt disappeared into cloud. Johnson had followed his squadron leader down and spotted two more enemy planes in a shallow dive, engines trailing smoke and hurrying for safety. He sped on after them, caught them and opened fire. 'They went down like wheat before a scythe,' he noted, 'One, two and two flaming fighters.' In just a few minutes of violent aerial combat, the group had claimed fourteen enemy planes for no loss.

As the 1st Division reached Leipzig, the new boys of the 357th in their Mustangs now successfully entered the fray. In his cockpit, Bud Anderson was feeling pretty chilly; the heater helped a bit, but not enough when 6 miles high. Already he had rubbed frost from the inside of the canopy and was glad of the layers of clothing. He had also taken to wearing a silk scarf, not to look flamboyant but so that he didn't chafe his neck from constantly swivelling his head around.

And he was doing just that – checking all around him – when he spotted a Focke-Wulf 190 some 4,000 feet below. Nosing over, he plunged down and came out 300 yards dead astern. Opening fire, he felt the Mustang vibrate from the burst of his four .50-calibres and some hits and smoke. The pilot now performed a split S, inverting his plane then diving down in a half-loop, and skidding violently as he did so. Then he did what all Germans did to get out of danger: he dived. Anderson followed, diving steeper and steeper until his air speed indicator was approaching 500 m.p.h. 'I was determined,' he wrote. 'I would go wherever he went, do whatever he did. I wanted a victory.' But then he noticed his canopy starting to open – the side and top pieces were pulling apart where the two were latched together. Suddenly, the clarity of his situation struck home. This was his fifth mission and he hadn't completed it yet. Aggression was a good thing in a fighter pilot, but not recklessness. At 11,000 feet, prudence won. He gave up the chase and instead climbed back to find the rest of the squadron. 'Thinking about it afterwards,' he noted, 'I decided I had come close to doing something unforgivably dumb.'

Now nearing Leipzig, away to the south-east, was Lieutenant William Lawley in a brand-new B-17. Lawley and the other nine in his crew had all been on leave and while they were away their ship had been assigned to another crew, who had failed to return, so, after having the first *Cabin in the Sky* taken off them on arrival in England, and the second now lost, his latest, brand-new Fortress was *Cabin in the Sky III*; they hadn't had time to have the name painted on the cowling yet.

They had been harried by enemy fighters much of the way, but the Thunderbolts had kept with them and now, as they neared Leipzig, Mustangs were hurtling about the sky. His own gunners had been busy, the .50-calibre machine guns hammering as enemy fighter planes sped past. The sky was criss-crossed with tracer, while up ahead it was peppered with dark puffs of flak. As they reached the IP and began their bomb run, the fighters started to leave them alone, but then the flak grew heavier and for the bomb run Lawley had to switch over to automatic pilot and fly straight and level. The flak, though, was definitely lighter than it might have been, because the anti-aircraft crews below were exhausted after a long night attacking the RAF. Despite the usual jolts, bumps and occasional clatter of shell blast, Lawley's crew reached the target without problem; even better, the sky was largely clear and their targets, the assembly plants of Leipzig–Mockau, were easily visible. Staring below at the white, snow-covered landscape, bombardier Henry Mason could see perfectly and, because of the snow, the target looked as monochrome as the aerial reconnaissance photographs they had been shown at the briefing. With the bomb bays open, he pressed the bomb release, fully expecting the lurch that came with the sudden loss of 2½ tons of bombs. But nothing happened. Mason closed the doors, then opened them again and tried once more to jettison the bombs. Again, nothing. Almost certainly, the bomb racks had frozen in place, but whatever the reason, they were now potentially in serious trouble. Ahead and around them, everyone else in the group was dropping their bomb loads and immediately accelerating away. Lawley opened the throttles in an effort to keep up, but their Fortress was rapidly starting to lag behind. Each time they opened the bomb-bay doors, the added drag combined with the weight of the bombs ensured they dropped ever further behind the rest of the squadron.

This was a nightmare situation for the crew because nothing was more vulnerable in a sky swarming with enemy fighters than a straggler with a belly full of bombs.

After opening the doors again, Lieutenant Mason hurried from his position in the nose, past the cockpit to the bomb bay and, despite the plane jolting from flak at 17,000 feet up, tried to kick the bombs free. But still he couldn't budge them. All on board were keenly aware that they were now dicing with death even more than usual. As they turned to follow the others, the distance between their lone ship and the rest of the group began slowly but surely, agonizingly, to widen. Up ahead, the rest of the 305th were turning for the home run, still in tight, defensive formation.

Suddenly, one of the crew called out a warning on the intercom that a *Schwarm* of Focke-Wulfs was diving on them from behind, although, blinded by the sun, Sergeant Alfred Wendt, the tail gunner, couldn't see them. The Fortress up ahead on their wing was hit and, in flames, the B-17 dropped out and began plummeting downwards. Flak now burst close by, knocking *Cabin in the Sky* as though it had been punched by a giant fist. Shrapnel hit one of the outer engines, which began to lick flames. Lawley immediately ordered Lieutenant Paul Murphy, his co-pilot, to apply the onboard extinguisher and shut it down. This, however, lost them even more power.

As the Fortress dropped further and further behind the rest, so more enemy fighters began to home in on the struggling bomber. The gunners were calling out and firing furiously as more than a dozen enemy aircraft converged from above and below, the German pilots sensing easy pickings. Then suddenly, up ahead, more FW190s appeared and, directly in front, one in particular was heading straight for them. Flashes appeared from its gun ports, then there was a huge crash and for a moment Lawley's vision went black.

He came to moments later to see Murphy's shattered body slumped forward, killed instantly by a 20mm cannon shell. There was a massive hole in the cockpit Perspex, and blood, gore and debris spattered the instruments and remaining windshield. Effectively blind, Lawley realized he had been hit by cannon splinters. His right arm had been peppered and so had his face. Another engine was on fire and the aircraft was falling in a sharp dive.

Somehow, despite his wounds, the ringing in his ears, the carnage around him and a bomb-laden Flying Fortress screaming in its death-dive, something deep inside Lawley told his brain to think clearly and rationally and not to panic. And so, after frantically wiping his face, he used his bloody right arm to pull Murphy back out of the way, while with his left he pulled the control column towards him and desperately tried to regain control of the aircraft. Perhaps the only benefit of the dive was the centrifugal forces that helped propel the bloody remains of his co-pilot backwards and off the second control column, but that wasn't going to help anyone if he couldn't pull out of the dive.

Lawley now called out to the crew to bail out. Up ahead in the nose, Henry Mason lifted the hatch to jump, while behind, navigator Lieutenant Henry Seraphine did the same, yet before either jumped Lawley suddenly managed to start regaining some control. The dying ship was actually emerging out of its dive. Henry Mason clambered up into the cockpit and went back to check on the crew. Only he and one other man had escaped injury and two crew members were so badly wounded there was no chance of them making the jump.

Levelling out, Lawley cleared the instrument panel and

windshield in front of him as best he could, then swiftly made a decision. Anyone who wanted to jump could do so, but he would stay with the ship and try to nurse it back, despite his wounds. The flight engineer decided to take his chances and, lowering himself out of the forward hatch, disappeared. For Lawley and the other seven men, however, the situation remained critical, because another engine was now on fire and the bombs remained stuck in the bomb bay. Freezing-cold air was blowing like a high-speed wind through the aircraft and Lawley himself was struggling badly. Of those left on board, only Lieutenant Mason was uninjured. The rest of the crew could barely function at all and their ship was trailing more than enough smoke for any enemy fighter for miles around to see on that clear winter's morning. The prospects of a safe return seemed slight to say the very least.

At just after 1 p.m., the B-24s of the 2nd Division were nearing their IP. Aboard *Tenovus*, Jimmy Stewart watched the Pathfinders pass south of Hanover, then they were on the bomb run and pilot Bill Conley switched over control to Lieutenant John Rankin, the bombardier. Flak started up again and their B-24 rocked and shuddered with the blast. A shell exploded uncomfortably near, shrapnel clattering against the cockpit, causing the ship to buck.

'Damn it!' exclaimed Conley, but now up ahead they saw red flares bursting and the burning lights floating down on parachutes.

'Uh-oh,' said Stewart. This, they knew, was the signal for the flak gunners below to stop firing in order to let the fighters attack unhindered. On cue, the flak stopped and suddenly their gunners were calling out the enemy fighters they could see sweeping in from above and below. Machine guns began hammering as they continued with the bomb run, but then Rankin called out, 'Bombs away!' and, as always, Conley took back control, the B-24 surging upwards and banking as it began the turn for home.

'Get 'em, Little Friends!' someone called out as Stewart looked out and saw P-38s tearing down towards the enemy fighters. Despite their arrival, the German pilots continued to press home their attacks. A Liberator started flaming and falling out of formation. Bob Kiser's ship, someone called out. The youngest pilot in Stewart's squadron. On they flew towards the rallying point and then, when all the survivors had joined them, Stewart ordered them to tighten up formation. With the Me109s and FW190s disappearing as quickly as they had arrived, they began the journey home: first an hour or so to Cologne, then a change of course and two more hours across Belgium and then over the Channel at Dunkirk.

Far to the north, the 388th BG had reached Poznań. The Focke-Wulfs had gone but had been replaced by twin-engine fighters. 'There were quite a few enemy fighters,' noted Larry Goldstein, 'but somehow they weren't too eager and did not pester us.' Perhaps the enemy pilots lacked experience, or maybe simply didn't want to risk pressing home their attacks: a bomb group of thirty-six Fortresses still had 468 .50-calibre machine guns between them, with nearly a million bullets.

Somewhere below, hidden by cloud, was the target, but it couldn't be seen and they had been told to hit it only in the clear. Much to the deep frustration of all, they had no option but to turn for Rostock, their secondary target. They had flown all that vast distance for nothing.

The Thunderbolts of the 4th FG had been given the job of withdrawal support for the B-17s returning from Leipzig and so had not even been briefed until midday. They had taken off shortly after, led by Captain Jim Goodson, and reached the Dutch coast at just before 1.50 p.m. and flying at 23,000 feet. Just as they rendezvoused with the bombers, they spotted five Me109s attacking the third box of B-17s with rockets and so the 334th Fighter Squadron was sent down after them. A little further on, above Malmedy in Belgium, a further eight Focke-Wulfs were spotted.

Captain Bee Beeson was flying Green 1 and leading his flight as they dived down, Green section following behind Blue and White sections. Beeson now spotted two more Focke-Wulfs at about seven o'clock in the sky and below the B-17s. Keeping his eyes glued on them, he watched them circling some 5,000 feet directly below and so dived straight upon them, but they were still circling and Beeson struggled to get on any of their tails. He was just diving down for a second attack when he spotted another P-47 closing in on one of the enemy planes, so Beeson waited for him to shoot down the last of the four Focke-Wulfs and then intended to go for the leader of the German *Schwarm* himself. However, the other P-47 overshot with his attack and the German leader and his wingman whipped around in a starboard turn. Swiftly reacting, Beeson now homed in on the wingman, who began to climb rather than following his leader, who was now diving out of the fray. Beeson followed, opening fire at 300 yards and closing to just 100. Strikes clattered around the cockpit and next moment the pilot jettisoned the canopy and bailed out. Always meticulous, Beeson then made sure he got footage of both the aircraft and pilot descending on his fine camera.

The northern formation of 1st Division bombers had hit Rostock and the heavies were now turning back for home, Goldie Goldstein and his crew on *Worry Wart* among them. Flak continued to pound and pepper the sky, but gradually it thinned. They all began to breathe just a little bit more easily.

Meanwhile, Bill Lawley was still at the helm of his badly damaged Fortress. They had managed to use the in-built extinguishers to put out the second engine fire and now, at a much lower altitude, Mason had been able finally to jettison the bomb load somewhere over open French countryside, so the immediate risk of the whole crate exploding into a million fragments appeared to have passed. But then some Me109s had begun circling. Despite their wounds, the gunners had let fly with everything they had, while Lawley, still using only his left hand, had taken evasive action and the enemy planes had sloped off; perhaps they had been short of fuel or decided the bomber was already finished. At any rate, *Cabin in the Sky* had been given a chance to try to make it home.

Lawley was struggling badly, however. He was losing blood and in severe pain, and was becoming exhausted from the strain of flying one-handed. It was difficult to see through the mess of the cockpit and blood was still streaming down his cheeks from the wounds to his face and head, while sub-freezing winds were howling through the shattered Perspex. He was feeling faint, but continually refused the pain relief offered by Mason, knowing that if he took morphine he would be unable to continue to fly, let alone land. Getting them back on the ground was the only hope his crew had of survival.

To make matters worse, Lieutenant Harry Seraphine, the navigator, had lost his maps when he had opened his escape hatch; they had all blown off his desk and out of the opening. He was now navigating from memory and estimated speed, but there was cloud cover below. Seraphine gave Lawley what he thought was the best heading and told him to stick on it. If they hit some flak, then he would quickly make adjustments. Sure enough, soon puffs of black smoke started peppering the sky around them and the B-17 shook and jerked as bits of shrapnel clattered against the damaged airframe. It was time for another bearing and then, suddenly, they were over the coast and out above the Channel.

Many of the Eighth's bombers were now reaching home. Hugh McGinty's crew made it back to Kimbolton in one piece, along with every other Fortress from the 379th BG, although there were twenty-two ships with damage of some kind, two dead and fourteen wounded. One of the 379th's Fortresses had suffered a similar fate to *Cabin in the Sky*. An Me109 had sprayed the ship of Lieutenant Paul Breeding. The co-pilot had been badly hit and died soon after, while Breeding was also wounded, but the top-turret gunner, navigator and waist gunner all came to his help. They pulled the co-pilot clear, then the navigator took the controls, flying high above the rest of the bombers while the two gunners administered first aid to Breeding. As they neared England, the navigator knew he would be unable to land the plane through the cloud, so after a vote they decided they should all bail out. Breeding, however, vetoed it and insisted he take back the controls. Incredibly, he managed to land the plane safely and only after taxiing off the runway did he finally pass out.

At Ridgewell, the chaplain, Captain James Good Brown, had spent much of the afternoon in his cubbyhole at the far end of the base's cinema. The hours always seemed interminable during a long raid. Eventually, though, it was time to head over to the control tower to watch the planes return. He had been dreading this moment all day, remembering all too clearly the devastating losses suffered over Oschersleben on 11 January. 'I guess we had feared the worst,' he noted. Now standing anxiously by the control tower, he noticed some of the other pilots and crew who had not flown that day looking nervous and fidgety. Some pilots had their crews on other ships. Then came a distant drone, getting louder and louder as the first aircraft appeared. Then another, and another. And one more, and so it continued. 'On this day,' noted Brown, 'the ships did not arrive in formation. They were strewn all over the sky. It seemed that they were going in all directions. I could not make head nor tail out of what was happening. The old days of sending out 18 planes were gone. We were now sending out 40 planes. Counting them became difficult.' It was clear, though, that they had had a good day and before long all but one – Kirch Cogswell's crew – had safely made it back. That seemed like little short of a miracle to those waiting on the ground.

Even better, two crews had completed their twenty-fifth missions – those of Lieutenants Butler and Tucker. As the first of them touched down, everyone shouted out, 'It's Butler!', then Tucker came in and buzzed the airfield in salute. Everyone rejoiced when a crew completed a tour, in part happy for them and in part because it showed there was hope and a chance of survival despite the appalling odds.

Bill Lawley's crew crossed the English coast near Dover. Lawley had been so weak he had passed out, but Mason was right behind him. 'Stay with us!' he said, shaking Lawley back to consciousness. Gripping the control column with his left hand once more, on he flew. One of the two still-running engines now ran out of fuel and spluttered to a halt, which meant they were flying at just 1,500 feet on only one engine. Feathering the prop on the stopped engine to reduce drag, Lawley began looking for an airfield on which to land. It needed to appear soon, because their last valiant engine was about to run out of fuel.

Now that they were back over England the lovely, clear, azure-blue skies of the continent had been replaced by cloud and drizzle. They were flying low, but visibility was far from good and the lower they came the harder it was to see any great distance. Then suddenly Lawley spotted an airfield away to his left, but with one engine feathered, another windmilling and a third smouldering and smoking, he lacked control and, furthermore, he was struggling with rapidly diminishing strength in his left hand. Unable to turn quickly enough, he missed it.

Lawley now gave the warning for a crash-landing, fully intending to come down in the first large, flat field he saw, but then up ahead, through the grey drizzle, he spotted some hangars. With his radio shattered, he was unable to call the airfield, so flashed the emergency signal instead. Bracing themselves, they descended slowly towards the airfield, Lawley desperately trying to keep her steady, and then, with a mighty jolt, they landed on the plane's belly, sliding and grinding across the grass, then over the runway and finally coming to a halt. By this time one of the engines was on fire again and, before they could stagger out of the broken aircraft, fire crews were speeding towards them. Miraculously, though – and it truly was something of a miracle – all apart from Murphy had survived. Lawley even managed to clamber out of the wreckage on his own. 'It was hair-raising and it was exhilarating,' he said later, 'and it was sad and most any other descriptive term . . . I ended up with two permanently crippled men on board. However, all did survive other than the co-pilot.'

Among the last to land back home that day were the bombers of the northern force. At Knettishall, Larry Goldstein and the crew of *Worry Wart* touched down after ten hours in the air, by which time they were flying pretty much on fumes alone. 'We returned to base just as it was getting dark,' jotted Goldstein in his diary. 'Sweated out the landing in a haze.' Everyone was utterly exhausted by the experience but, with twenty completed missions, Goldstein was now on the final stretch. Five more missions and he'd be heading home, his combat service done.

CHAPTER 21

Monday,
21 February 1944

As THE BOMBER CREWS of the Eighth were being debriefed, so Bomber Command was getting ready to send another six hundred RAF heavies to Germany. This time, the mission was to Stuttgart, another major POINTBLANK target not only because of the large Daimler-Benz aero-engine plant, but also as the site of an important Bosch factory producing dynamos, fuel-injection pumps and magnetos, and considered one of the principal aircraft-industry targets in Germany. The Licht-werk main Bosch factory where starters for aircraft engines were made was the primary focus for the night's raid. Another feint was planned: this time over 150 air-craft from twenty-four different squadrons would fly what was described by the planners as a training exercise across the North Sea. They would take off first and, it was hoped, draw the enemy night-fighters towards them and away from the main effort far to the south. In addition, some two dozen Mosquitoes were to attack airfields in Holland, while a further seven of these high-altitude, very fast twin-engine aircraft would fly a further diversionary raid on Munich.

Rusty Waughman and his crew at 101 Squadron were scheduled for what was going to be their second mission in two nights, one of twenty crews to fly from Ludford Magna. Rarely would a crew be expected to fly two nights in a row and especially two long trips deep into Germany; it was also unusual for American crews to fly twice in two days, but Operation ARGUMENT was an exceptional week of operations and what in Bomber Command parlance was known as a 'maximum effort'. For the most part, adrenalin tended to kick in and ensured pilots and crew reached the target without feeling excessively exhausted but, unlike American crews, British bombers had no co-pilot, so the onus on the single pilot to get his boys to the target and then home again was immense. If fatigue crept in, it tended to do so on the return leg, once the worst of the danger was over. Even to Stuttgart, the trip would take up to seven and a half hours – a long flight on the back of an even longer trip the previous evening, and made worse by lack of sleep in between.

On his return from Leipzig, Rusty Waughman had had to go to his debrief, then ate and was in bed by perhaps 8.30 a.m. By early afternoon he was up again for flight tests and briefings. The body clock of all the bomber crews was all over the place – normal days and nights one day, night operations the next.

Medical officers kept a close watch on all crews, but especially on pilots, and had the authority to give stimulants to pilots and aircrew. This might be a flask of coffee or a caffeine tablet; or it might be Benzedrine, an amphetamine developed in the United States in the late 1920s and known by the bomber crews as 'wakey-wakey' pills – it would be called 'speed' today. It could keep pilots awake for up to twenty-four hours, and it was clearly better for an exhausted pilot to take a Benzedrine tablet and consequently ensure the safe return of himself and his crew, than not to take one, fall asleep and crash into the North Sea, never to be seen again. However, the problems of taking amphetamines were numerous, because they were a short-term fix. Although they kept a man awake, they were not a cure for fatigue and, after taking them, pilots found it very difficult to get to sleep once back on the ground. Some pilots refused them, because often missions were scrubbed at the last minute and then they would be unable to sleep, which didn't help if they were expected to fly the following day. Benzedrine also gave its user sensations of well-being, which could reduce fear, which in turn could lead to recklessness. In one case, a Lancaster pilot on Benzedrine dived down and ordered his crew to ground-strafe targets on the return trip.

The British were aware of the dangers of amphetamine use and in fact, although it had been quite prevalent among aircrew since the start of the war, not until November 1942 had it been officially sanctioned by the Air Ministry, but only under medical supervision, and even then with a number of warnings. It was to be issued only 'in situations of stress where sleep was a threat to performance.' Flying long missions into enemy territory two nights in a row was precisely such an occasion.

Rusty Waughman took off at 11.40 p.m., dodging the flak off the Dutch coast. Beside Waughman, on the dicky seat on the right-hand side of the cockpit, was his engineer, Pilot Officer John 'Curly' Ormerod. He had joined the crew after their first engineer, Les Reeves, had been swiftly removed from the squadron and, as far as Waughman was concerned, he had been a vast improvement. Ormerod was a Lancastrian who had worked for Oldham Council before joining the RAF. In early January he had missed a mission from which the rest of his crew hadn't returned and so was a flight engineer without a crew, while Waughman had a crew without an engineer.

Thin cloud built up as they neared Stuttgart. 'Hazy cloud,' Waughman described it later in his diary. As they reached the bomb run, the flak swiftly grew heavier, although Waughman had seen much worse; Stuttgart was a piece of cake compared with the thousands of heavy guns defending Berlin, for example. What's more, his and his crew's growing experience made a difference; the learning curve was a steep one when making regular trips to the capital of the Third Reich. 'You learnt very quickly,' Waughman admitted. The technique of the flak gunners down below was to send up a box of shellfire – firing in such a way that shells burst in a wide area of the sky shaped like an imaginary box. The idea was that a bomber formation would fly directly into it and that some would inevitably be hit. Gun-laying radar helped the gunners on the ground by calculating height and speed, and predicting where a bomber would be by the time the shell reached a height of 4 or 5 miles, on a level with the bombers. Anti-aircraft fire was, however, an imprecise science, even with the help of predictive radars. Flak caused plenty of damage to airframes but rarely was anything shot down; in fact, by February 1944, on average 5,000 rounds of light flak and 3,500 rounds of heavy flak were needed to shoot down a single aircraft, which amounted to a 0.002 per cent chance of a heavy flak round destroying a bomber. Fighters, on the other hand, could knock a bomber out of the sky with a few bullets and cannon shells.

One of the reasons gun-laying radar wasn't especially effective was because pilots like Waughman were able to roughly predict the prediction. 'You knew it took forty-five seconds for the guns to be relayed,' said Waughman, 'and for the shell to burst. So you turned off forty-five degrees, flew for forty-two seconds, turned back ninety degrees, and then, with a bit of luck, the next burst would miss.'

As they flew over Stuttgart, jostled and jolted by flak, the bomb-aimer spotted the target, although it was partly shrouded by thin cloud and looked tiny from 22,000 feet up. Even so, they reckoned they bombed pretty accurately and, now lightened, climbed, turned and made their way back towards England and home. 'Long trip,' noted Waughman in his diary, 'but quiet.'

Waughman had been untroubled by night-fighters and, in fact, losses were slight – just seven Lancasters and two Halifaxes, which amounted to only 1.5 per cent of the attacking force. The lack of night-fighters was the main reason for the easy ride Bomber Command had that night, and in part that was because this time the Germans had been duped by the northern feint and their night-fighters had scrambled too late. By the time Wim Johnen and his *Gruppe* had reached Stuttgart, the attackers had gone. Johnen had looked down on the burning city, cursing the old crates they were still expected to fly. He had begun his Luftwaffe career as a night-fighter on an Me110 *Zerstörer* and was still flying one now.

The bombing had been a little scattered but had caused considerable damage to the city centre and the north-eastern and north-western suburbs, as the main Bosch factory stood on the river all too close to the city centre. A number of historic buildings had been destroyed or badly damaged, including the Landtag, the old parliament building, and the State Gallery, State Theatre and two churches. Although there were now a good number of air-raid shelters in the city, some 125 civilians were still killed and 510 injured – no small number, and casualties that stretched the city hospital and medical services.

It was the Lichtwerk that was hardest hit, however. The manager of the plant was 36-year-old Willi Hofmann, whose job was sufficiently important to have kept him away from military service. As he was discovering, however, civilian life could be every bit as dangerous as it was at the front. The Bosch factories had been targeted before – not least three times during the previous October and November – and had prompted Feldmarschall Erhard Milch to order the movement of vital machine tools and other equipment. He had even visited the factory. 'If the Bosch firm fails,' he told Hofmann and other senior staff, 'or if the German Wehrmacht fails because the Bosch firm has failed, heads will roll!'

Hofmann had been responsible for moving much key equipment, but none the less was staggered by the level of destruction. Nor had he appreciated just how powerful giant flames could be. 'You had to hold on tight,' he said, 'to avoid being dragged into the roaring flames by the tremendous air suction.' The old factory was largely ruined, its back broken by the bombs and the conflagration. As far as Hofmann was concerned, it had been hit by precision bombing, despite the strays that struck else-where in the city. 'No doubt about it,' he said.

On 21 February, at the headquarters of US Strategic Air Forces and Eighth and Ninth Air Forces, preparations were already well under way for Day Two of ARGU-MENT. The losses of the previous day had been light, all things considered – just 2.8 per cent – while at the same time reports were reaching them of astonishing acts of heroism. Bill Lawley, for example, would later be awarded the Congressional Medal of Honor for what he had done. Two others would be awarded posthumously to men in the same crew from the 351st Bomb Group. Rather like Lawley's ship, *Ten Horsepower* had been attacked frontally and the co-pilot decapitated and the pilot badly wounded, incapable of flying any further. Two other members of the crew, Lieutenant Walter Truemper and Sergeant Archie Mathies, then managed to fly the stricken Fortress back to England, where the rest of the crew bailed out. In an effort to save the wounded pilot, Truemper and Mathies then attempted to land the plane. Tragically, they crashed and all three were killed. Never before or again would three Medals of Honor be awarded for actions on the same day in the air war.

The action of Mathies and Truemper was symptomatic of the intense bond that existed within most crews. Few clambered into their planes each day out of patriotism. Rather, they did so for the age-old reason that most con-tinue fighting in a war: because they were in it together and because to let down a fellow crew member was simply unthinkable. 'We would never abandon a wounded man if the plane was still under control,' noted Hugh McGinty.

'We were mostly untrained in first aid. We were, on average, twenty years old.' Larry Goldstein agreed. His crew had bonded well from the outset. He never thought much about the enemy or the wider cause. 'It's just that we were doing a job,' he said. 'We were trained to fly in an airplane, to drop the bombs and go home.' He never thought of the bombs hitting civilians. As far as he was concerned, they were going after military targets. 'If the German government had built their factories close to a city or a town and it was residual damage, it wasn't our fault.'

Death and the prospect of dying hung heavily over all bomber crews, especially during this week of intense activity. Aircrew were all volunteers, but the reminders of what a short straw they'd drawn when they initially signed up were all around them. Empty beds in the Quonset hut where that morning there had been six men. Scenes of vivid and violent destruction in the air. Aircraft blown up, chopped in half, disintegrated. Body parts splattered over fuselages and windshields. Crew shot up and bleeding to death in front of their comrades. Larry Goldstein had lost one of his best pals on 30 December. He and Danny Letter had trained together, come to England together and, although on different crews, the enlisted men of both shared the same Nissen hut. Letter's Fortress, *Satan's Sister*, had collided with another aircraft on the bomb run. As Goldstein had looked out of his radio hatch he had seen his friend's Fortress sway back and forth, flip over and break in half. 'Our morale was at its lowest point,' he said, 'especially when we returned to our barracks and saw their empty beds.'

And then there were the shortening odds. If even 5 per cent of crew, on average, were being lost every mission, that meant 100 per cent losses in twenty missions. Usually, loss percentages were higher than that. By Operation ARGUMENT, an average crew was doing well to reach thirteen completed missions, which meant surviving twenty-five required a massive dose of luck. Skill and experience helped, but only went so far. BJ Keirsted, Larry Goldstein's pilot, repeatedly and emphatically told his crew they would make it through, and although it did boost their confidence, the others never felt the same degree of conviction.

Lieutenant Bob Hughes, of the 100th BG, was finally about to complete his tour but in November had lost one of his crew, Joe Boyle, during the mission to Gelsenkirchen. Hughes had, of course, written a letter of condolence to Boyle's mother, which had reached her just before Christmas. He received her reply in the middle of February and, while young men were able to a large degree to push the deaths of friends and colleagues to one side, it was much harder to reconcile oneself to the grief of parents, wives and loved ones. 'This all seems so unreal to me,' wrote Boyle's mother in her letter to Hughes, 'yet I know now that it is true.' To Hughes' wife, Elaine, she wrote, 'When I lost him I lost my whole world and it will take me quite some time to get used to living without him . . . That something like this was going to happen was the farthest from my mind. I kept planning for when he would be home.'

One reason why so many young men were able to get back into a bomber and head off into the fire was because to most of them death was so incomprehensible that they simply could not imagine it happening to them. Sometimes, however, that conviction was punctured and premonitions of imminent death took root. Such powerful feelings very often became self-fulfilling. One of Robbie Robinson's best pals, Earl Doggett, had been on Lieutenant Metcalf's crew, but shared the same Nissen hut as Robinson. One evening in early February the two had been returning to their hut when Doggett had told Robinson he felt certain he would die the next day. He had tears in his eyes. Robinson tried to talk sense into his friend. 'I get as scared as you,' he told him, 'but I am going to do everything I can to stay alive. I am not going to give up. Earl, if you really do expect to get killed, then you will because you will do something wrong. You don't have to give up. There is always a way.' Doggett, though, was convinced God wanted him to die. He couldn't shake it, no matter how hard Robinson tried to persuade him otherwise.

Robinson's crew had not been scheduled to fly the following day, but twenty-eight from the group took off and two crews did not return. One of those was Metcalf's. Apparently, the plane had gone down into the Channel on the return leg. They had simply disappeared. The next day, 3 February, Robinson and the rest of the Wright crew had been on a mission, but when they got back the six beds of the Metcalf crew on the other side of the hut had all been stripped, the blankets rolled up and their lockers cleared. It was as though they had never been there at all. 'I don't think I could have said anything without crying,' wrote Robinson. 'It was like losing a big part of our family all at once.' He couldn't stop thinking about Earl Doggett's premonition. Could it really have been possible that he had known? He couldn't believe it himself, but that was exactly what had happened.

Over the next few days, Robinson noticed everyone

getting a little twitchy; tempers quickly flared. They had had a tough mission on 29 January, when they had lost two engines and been cut adrift from the rest of the formation, but thankfully they'd made it back in one piece. They had had civilian photographs taken for fake IDs as part of their escape and evasion kit should they be shot down and bail out. It was another sobering reminder of the ever-present risks on a mission. The weather had cleared for their mission on the 11th and they had another close call when flak shards knocked out an engine and once again they found themselves on their own and with no fighter protection. Fortunately, they made it back across the Channel, but were forced to come down at the first airfield they saw in Kent.

Two days later, Robinson and his crew had been due for another mission but their pilot, Lieutenant George Wright, had arrived late. It wasn't the first time – in fact, it was becoming something of a habit – and Major Jimmy Stewart gave him a public tongue-lashing. Afterwards, they headed out to their plane, *Bullet Serenade*, and were on board with their engines running when a Jeep arrived with the operations officer and medical officer on board offering them an immediate week's furlough. It had been presented as a choice – after all, having leave meant it took longer to reach twenty-missions – but the arrival of a different crew told them the decision had already been made. In the air, Wright had repeatedly proved himself to be a first-class pilot with a cool head; but maybe the combination of a dressing down and seven days off base would get him back on track, and so they were sent to a camp in Blackpool, known as a 'Flak Home', for rest and recuperation.

*

More fighters were reaching England, including increasing numbers of Mustangs, which was good news for
the 4th Fighter Group, who were itching to ditch their
Thunderbolts and get themselves into this wonderful
new fighter. The first of their new Mustangs had reached
Debden on 13 February and they had taken possession
of several more since then. Don Blakeslee had con-
fessed to his boys his pledge to General Bill Kepner:
that they would be ready to fly operationally in them
twenty-four hours after their full complement had arrived
at the weekend. That had prompted a fair bit of teeth-
sucking. 'You can learn to fly 'em,' Blakeslee told them, 'on
the way to the target.' But in between sorties, the pilots
had been swapping Thunderbolts for Mustangs and taking them for a ride. 'The guys are working the new
Mustangs to death,' noted the group's diarist, 'Everyone
wants a ride.'

The weekend was still a long way off, however, and this
Monday Blakeslee led them in their Thunderbolts as they
escorted the bombers on Day Two of Operation ARGU-
MENT. The weather over Europe once more looked
promising, and the plan was to hit the enemy again after
what had been unquestionably a good day for the Eighth
Air Force that Sunday. Out of more than a thousand
bombers detailed to fly, only twenty-one had failed to
return. Subsequent reconnaissance showed considerable
damage. Four assembly plants in the Leipzig area had
been heavily hit, with substantial structural destruction
and significant damage to machine tools. For Spaatz and
Anderson, the losses were far lighter than they had dared
to hope and the results had been encouraging too. This
was no time to sit back. Main targets were to be aircraft

factories at Brunswick, Diepholz and a number of other aircraft storage parks.

Fifteenth Air Force in Italy were also due to take part in the day's operations, with primary attacks again planned for Regensburg. At Lucera, Lieutenant Sully Sullivan once more emerged from his tent to a day of heavy cloud and by 6 a.m. was at the 301st BG's briefing. The secondary target was Augsburg, but just in case the weather closed in, Plan B was an attack on the marshalling yards at Rome, which had nothing to do with ARGUMENT at all.

Just down the road was the 2nd Bomb Group, where Lieutenant Michael Sullivan was also being briefed. The 2nd BG had finally moved to Foggia in early December but, as for everyone else in the Fifteenth, actually reaching a target – any target – was proving difficult and when they did they were invariably battling weather as well as enemy fighters and flak. 'Failure to take off. Bad weather,' Sullivan wrote on 1 February. 'Whole group recalled from mission, reason unknown,' he scribbled the next day. 'Non-op,' on the 3rd. He did fly on 4 and 5 February, but again the weather was terrible, the wing formation separated and they came up against 'very aggressive' Messerschmitts and Focke-Wulfs. 'Strain of combat telling on all crew members,' he added. 'Tempers are short. Opposition tougher all the time. Raid tomorrow, weather bad.' So it had continued. On the 17th, they had taken off for a raid on the Anzio beachhead, but the strain on the navigator, Lieutenant Celestine 'Tony' Antonie, proved too great. 'Tony went nutz on route,' noted Sullivan, 'crazy as a loon. Too much combat strain.' And so the pilot of their Fortress, *The Second Was First*, Lieutenant Marshall McKew, had returned to base. Later, the colonel of the 2nd

BG, Lieutenant-Colonel Barthelmess, had threatened to bring charges against both Antonie and McKew. In the end, McKew had been let off with a roasting – pilots were too precious – and only Antonie had been suspended from duties and put up for a court martial, but the episode had not been good for team morale. Nor had the ongoing poor weather: planned raids had been scrubbed on the 18th, 19th and 20th, and no one was accepting odds on them flying again on the 21st. But, with the briefing over, they were told to get ready and then wait by their ships. Outside the briefing room, however, it was raining once again.

Flying his first combat mission this Monday, 21 February, from a far more clement England was 20-year-old Lieutenant James H. Keeffe from Sioux City, Iowa. Keeffe was co-pilot in Lieutenant Jimmy McArthur's crew, which had formed up while at Blythe Army Air Base near Phoenix, Arizona. How and why some were made pilots and others co-pilots was down to a number of factors, but in Keeffe's case he had fallen sick during his final training, lost a week, and so got placed in a low-flying-time group and was appointed a co-pilot. Sometimes this didn't sit well with those who had higher ambitions, but Keeffe had immediately recognized that McArthur was both a very good pilot and a nice guy, so he had no issue about playing second fiddle. In any case, he got on well with most of the crew, especially the bombardier, Lieutenant Raymond 'Moose' H. Moulton, and by the time they reached England in late November 1943 they had gelled nicely. The only personality clash as far as Keeffe was concerned had been with the navigator, Lieutenant Don Stevens. 'Right from square one I didn't like him,' wrote Keeffe, 'and my initial impression didn't change over time.' On the trip over, however, the crew was split in two and by the time they were reunited in Scotland Stevens was gone, ill with gonorrhea.

For several weeks they had been stuck at the B-24 United Kingdom Orientation Program, carrying out their transitional training and getting used to conditions very different from those in the Arizona desert. Then in early January they had been posted to the 566th Bomb Squadron, part of the 2nd Division's 389th Bomb Group, based at Hethel in Norfolk. There they had carried out a few familiarization flights and then the crew had been sent off on its first mission, although without Keeffe; a more experienced pilot had sat in his seat to check out Jimmy McArthur on this first flight. Thus, on this second day of Operation ARGUMENT, Keeffe was finally making his first combat flight, some eighty-five days after arriving in England.

Their primary target that day was Brunswick, with nearby Diepholz the secondary. After the main briefing and specialist briefings for the gunners, navigators and bombardiers, the crew reconvened and went over to a separate squadron building to pick up their parachutes, flying helmets and oxygen masks. The chaplain now came round, offering prayers and distributing Holy Communion to any who wanted it. Dropped off at their ship, each man went through his own personal checklist around the outside of the plane and on board. Gunners went to a shack next to the hardstand to pick up the barrels for their machine guns, which had been cleaned, oiled and stored there since the previous mission. In the bomb bays, the day's load was already stacked up in the bomb racks.

When everyone had been through their checks and collected all they needed, Jimmy McArthur called them together on the stand and gave them a short briefing. After that, they clambered aboard and took up their ten different stations. In the cockpit, Keeffe and McArthur went through ritual pre-flight checks prior to starting up the engines.

'Brakes?' asked McArthur.

'On,' replied Keeffe.

'Superchargers?'

'Off.'

'Cowl flaps?'

'Open.'

'Wing flaps?'

'Up.'

The list was long, but neither pilot nor co-pilot was prepared to rush. Every part of the procedure was done by synchronized clock. At start time, engines were run up and radios and all other vital equipment were checked. At their allotted taxi time, they moved off their hardstand and began to taxi around the perimeter, one of nine in the squadron, creeping forward nose to tail along the edge of the airfield. Green Very flares were fired from the control tower, and off went the assembly aircraft – at Hethel affectionately known as the 'Green Dragon' because of the wild green and yellow stripes across the wings and fuselage – and then the group leader.

The big bombers headed off down the runway at thirty-second intervals, so that it took the best part of twenty minutes for them all to take off. In their ship, McArthur ran up the engines, watching the r.p.m.s on each, while Keeffe set the wing flaps to 20 degrees to give them extra lift and checked that the auxiliary hydraulic pump was on and the auxiliary power unit off. Next, he switched the cowl flaps to 'Trail' and continued to work his way down the take-off list. Now they were off, the throttles opening wide and the beast thundering down the runway with Keeffe calling out the speed so McArthur could concentrate on looking ahead. At just under 100 m.p.h. the B-24 lifted and began to climb. Keeffe applied brakes to stop the wheels rotating, then retracted them into the wings. Next he set the superchargers to 'Climb', adjusted the r.p.m.s, raised the wing flaps and switched the booster and auxiliary hydraulic pumps to 'Off'. Gradually, they climbed up towards the assembly point. In theory, each plane would ascend safely in its own air space, but at all times, and especially when flying through cloud, they had to keep a close watch to make sure they didn't collide with each other. They all felt better once they had emerged into the clear, bright sky above.

The Thunderbolts of the 4th FG crossed the Dutch coast at around 12.50 p.m. and then rendezvoused with the B-17s of the 3rd Combat Wing at about 1.15. Blakeslee was flying with the 334th Fighter Squadron – Bee Beeson was not on the sheet this time – and led them off to investigate some contrails while the rest of the group stuck with the bombers. They found nothing, but then, on their return, bounced fifteen FW190s and shot down four of them without any loss of their own.

While the fighters were tussling, Larry Goldstein and

the crew of *Worry Wart* were among the 3rd Division Fortresses heading to Brunswick. When the curtain had been drawn back at the briefing, Goldstein had not been the only one to groan and immediately think of the hellish experience they had suffered on their last visit to the city eleven days earlier.

Among those escorting the bombers to Brunswick were the Mustang-flying 357th Fighter Group, although Bud Anderson was not one of them. As a flight leader, it was up to him when he flew and there were always seven or eight pilots available for the four aircraft needed in the flight, which meant nearly half his pilots missed out on every mission. Rather like Dick Turner, Anderson tended to fly more than the others, but who was going to fly and who was stood down was decided the night before. 'There was no way to know in advance what the mission would be,' he noted, 'what fate might hand you, and I always worried I might miss something special.' But he had decided to sit out the Brunswick ramrod and Al Boyle had taken his Mustang, a still new P-51B-5, which had had all the usual teething bugs of a new aircraft sorted out and *Old Crow* painted neatly below the exhaust stubs on the engine cowling.

Gordon Carter, having bailed out of his Pathfinder in the early hours of 20 February, was still tramping across northern Germany. He had walked much of the night, then briefly tried to get some sleep in the snow by covering himself in foliage. Realizing the absurdity of the idea, he hauled himself back up and continued on his way, his prime motivation being the large tankard of Dutch beer that he had promised he would give himself the moment he could.

Early in the morning he decided to have a shave. He had packed all sorts of things in his escape and evasion pack, including a Gillette razor, thinking that being unshaven would only attract attention. Scrambling down to the base of an archway over a stream, he was about to start shaving in the freezing-cold water when a young boy pedalled up the bridge and, stopping, looked down over the parapet. Carter froze and the boy moved on. Carter had a rough, icy scrape of his chin, then pushed on his way.

In the afternoon he reached some sort of fenced compound, cut his way through the fencing but, seeing warning signs that trespassers would be shot, quickly retreated. He then saw hundreds of American bombers flying over on their way to Brunswick and Diepholz. 'What a sight it was for an airman stranded five miles below,' he wrote, 'who couldn't get over the fact that they would be back home in a few hours' time.'

It wasn't just American bombers in the sky above, however, but also German fighters, most of which were already flying their second sorties of the day. Among them were Heinz Knoke's whole *Gruppe*, who were now airborne once more having swiftly rearmed, refuelled and taken off again. On this second flight of the day, Knoke and his pilots had been ordered to draw off the escorting fighters at any cost; the idea was to keep the American fighters engaged while others went for the bombers. The flaw in these new tactics was twofold, however: first, there were enough American fighters to deal with both bombing and fighting; and second, in a dogfight German fighters generally came off worse. 'That cost my squadron two more dead,' scribbled Knoke curtly in his diary.

Meanwhile, back at the airfields of Foggia, once again the missions were scrubbed. Instead, Michael Sullivan planned to watch a Mickey Rooney film at the airfield's makeshift cinema. 'This weather,' jotted his namesake, Sully Sullivan, in his diary, 'has sure been against us this month.' It sure had.

To the north, however, the bombers from the Eighth were still forging on towards their targets. From his position in the cockpit in the left-hand seat, Jim Keeffe now saw his first flak and to begin with he found it rather mesmerizing. 'They looked like vertical elongated columns,' he noted, 'with blackish-grey smoke at the base coming out in two puffs to the side.' After watching more flak bursts, he quickly realized that, if they could see it, there wouldn't be any damage because it had already done its work. If they could hear the burst then it was getting uncomfortably close; and if the debris and shrapnel rattled against the airframe then it really was too close.

He saw his first enemy fighter planes too, watching as they flew wide past them before turning and making their runs straight towards them. 'I watched as they queued up for their attack,' he wrote. 'They rolled over onto their backs and fired at us from upside down while going through our formation.' Suddenly, unusual-looking reddish balls began streaking towards them, zipping past down the outside of their plane. To his naked eye they looked to be the size of basketballs with black speckles in the middle. 'What in the world are those?' he thought to himself, then realized they were 20mm cannon shells.

Their first pass over, he saw about eight enemy fighters roll upright and bank to the left, then climb parallel with the formation. Machine guns from the bombers were hammering away at the German planes as they sped on ahead and re-formed to make another attacking pass. Once again, those bright stabs of tracer were speeding towards them in the cockpit and Keeffe found himself ducking involuntarily.

'Keeffe, are you hit?' McArthur asked him.

Rather sheepishly, Keeffe sat up again. Curiously, though, he didn't feel particularly frightened, which meant he was probably well cut out for the task in hand. They managed to drop their bombs on Diepholz, the secondary target, and then they headed for home.

The crew of *Worry Wart* landed back down safely and Larry Goldstein, for one, reckoned it had been a pretty easy trip, all things considered. The Little Friends – not least the P-51s of the 357th FG – watching their backs had helped. 'Our fighter support today was terrific,' he jotted in his diary that evening. 'It felt good to see our boys up there instead of Jerry.' In fact, he had not seen too much of the enemy at all and even the flak had seemed substantially lighter than on their last trip. To really put the icing on the cake, they had bombed well and, it had seemed to him, pretty accurately. 'So all in all,' he added, 'it was an easy mission.' What's more, he now had only four more to do until his tour was over and he could head home to Brooklyn.

The bombing of Brunswick had not, however, gone as well as hoped. The cloud over the target had meant they had used H2X and had not been accurate, with the bombs landing on the city rather than the aircraft factories. On the other hand, only sixteen bombers had been lost and a further seven written off, which amounted to just 2 per cent of the attacking force of 762 heavy bombers. Every bit as important as the bombing, however, was what had gone on in the air battle between the fighters, and in this the Allies were once again very much in the ascendancy with a score of thirty-three aircraft confirmed shot down on gun camera, against a loss of five of their own.

One of the pilots not returning, however, was Al Boyle of the 357th FG. He had been lost over Holland, along with Bud Anderson's brand-new Mustang, *Old Crow*. Anderson was upset about losing his new plane, and Boyle's best friend in the squadron, Lieutenant William 'OBee' O'Brien, waited up hours that night, out by the runway, watching for an aircraft that wasn't coming home. In fact, Boyle was safe, although he would lose a leg and spend the rest of the war in a POW camp. For Anderson, grouching about his plane was a studied pose and nothing more. 'By now,' he wrote, 'I was getting pretty good at blocking out unpleasant distractions. I was developing a thick hide.'

At Tibenham, Robbie Robinson and his crew had still been on leave when Operation ARGUMENT opened, so had missed the 445th BG's first mission of the week. Robinson was feeling pretty good after a seven-day furlough that had been all the better for having tracked down a cousin in Nottingham. 'Finding a family here in England,' he noted, 'was like finding a light at the end of a dark tunnel.' A major shock on their return, however, had been the news that their trusted B-24, *Bullet Serenade*, had gone down in flames with another crew. Robinson had taken this news very badly, as had all the crew. That ship had seen them through some tough missions yet had always got them home. That she was gone was like losing one of the crew. 'The bottom dropped out again,' wrote Robinson. 'I felt empty, like I had lost everything.'

That afternoon, Monday, 21 February, George Wright told them they would be flying the following day. After supper in the mess hall they returned to their hut and had settled down for the night when in walked Major Jimmy Stewart. After telling them to stay at ease, he went over to the pot-bellied stove, warmed his hands then his backside, then, after a brief glance around the hut, went over to a pile of rugs and lifted them to reveal a keg of beer that had been mysteriously 'liberated' before their furlough by Ken Dabbs, their tail gunner. He had never explained how he had got it, nor had any of them ever pressed him; instead they had all been quietly helping themselves, but, having been on leave for a week, there was still quite a lot left.

Stewart took Robinson's canteen from the shelf and helped himself. 'Well, this black English beer is pretty good,' he said, 'if you can't get anything else. Right?' Robinson smiled but no one dared speak. Then Stewart poured himself a refill and sat down. After a short while, he looked up at them and said, 'Fellers, someone stole a keg of beer from the officers' club a few days ago. Ah, you guys hear anything about that?'

The crew all shook their heads. No, they said, they'd not heard a thing about that. Stewart finished off his beer, then said, 'I thought not.' After putting the cup back on the shelf, he walked over to the keg, covered it once more with the rugs and, clearing his throat, said, 'I know that Lieutenant Wright's crew doesn't know anything about this. I'm certain they didn't have a thing to do with stealing a keg of beer.' He walked out without saying another word.

CHAPTER 22

Tuesday,
22 February 1944

Finally, on Tuesday, 22 February, Fifteenth Air Force in Italy was able to contribute to Operation ARGUMENT. Yet again, the planned main target was Regensburg and specifically the Prüfening plant. The Messerschmitt plant at Augsburg was a secondary target once more, as were various bridges and marshalling yards and also the airfield at Graz, in southern Austria, which, it was hoped, might draw off enemy fighters. 'Finally, our first trip in to Germany!' scribbled Sully Sullivan in his diary.

Nearly 300 of the Fifteenth's bombers would be joining ARGUMENT, making well over 1,000 heavies in all for the day. They would also be providing around 150 Lightnings and Thunderbolts. It was no small contribution and the first time German targets would be hit by night by the RAF and by day by the heavies of both the Fifteenth and Eighth Air Forces. Spaatz had always wanted ARGUMENT to be about grinding the Luftwaffe down through sheer weight of relentless numbers. It looked as though he was going to get his wish.

In England, much of the country was covered in misty low cloud and drizzle. At Kimbolton, none of the crews had believed there was the slightest chance of them flying that day. At the briefing, a collective groan went out when the curtain was drawn back to reveal their target as Halberstadt, almost all the way to Berlin. Hugh McGinty and the rest of his crew remembered what had happened last time they had gone there, on 11 January: sixty crews had not made it back.

By the time they reached their B-17, the weather had worsened and it seemed impossible they could still fly. Surely, McGinty thought, the mission would be scrubbed. But the green flare was fired into the sky and so they started their engines. McGinty always said a silent prayer before each mission, but this time he spoke it aloud, imploring God to help him find the courage. For some reason, he had a profound feeling of dread and intense fear about the mission ahead – much more so than usual. Soon it was their turn to take off into the murk. As they climbed, from his tail position McGinty saw one of the Fortresses crash, burst into flames and explode. It was not a good start.

The Liberators of the 445th BG were flying to Gotha, and Robbie Robinson and the Wright crew were in a new ship, No. 666, a somewhat ominous number. As they climbed and moved into formation, they passed through large banks of towering cumulus, then they were out across the Channel, testing their guns while Elvin Cross, the armourer, and one of the gunners removed the arming wires on the bombs.

As always, fighter escorts worked in rotation in order to manage fuel, as combat flying used a lot more than just cruising. Now, as the bombers neared the IP, the P-51s left and before more could arrive the Me109s were suddenly speeding past them like a shoal of sharks – above, below and alongside, with tracer from their cannons and machine guns flashing past. Machine guns hammered and American tracer criss-crossed towards them as they sped by.

Flak was now bursting up ahead, and beyond the target towered a huge front of cloud. Gotha lay a short distance away.

'We should be over our Initial Point,' called out George Wright, 'but the ships in front of us haven't opened their bomb bay doors.'

Robinson now felt stabbing heat under his armpit and noticed smoke coming from his sleeve. The air around them was 40°C below, but he had no choice but to pull off his heated glove, pull off his flak suit – a kind of heavy armour that covered his front and back – and feel inside his armpit. Already his right hand was starting to freeze, but his electric suit was short-circuiting and the only way he could sort it was by taking off the next layer – his silk glove – and exposing his bare hand. Quickly thrusting his hand under the armpit of the flight suit, he felt for the heating wires and twisted them together. Immediately he felt warmth start returning to the sleeve. 'Boy!' he wrote. 'It sure would have been cold if the heated suit had failed and not gone back to heating.' Had it not worked, he would have suffered frostbite or, worse, died of hypothermia.

Then Wright reported a recall order. He was furious. 'We are being recalled when we are almost over the target,' he called out in exasperation. 'For God's sake, we should drop some bombs!' They began turning in formation, but as they did so Robinson watched two bombers drop their loads. If two others were doing so, why couldn't they?

'Eleven o'clock. Fighters!' called out Lieutenant Wendell Wittman, the bombardier. 'Me109s coming in!' Once again, their machine guns blazed away as the 109s sped through the formation. Away to their left another flight of B-24s were dropping their bombs, which Robinson reported to Wright.

'We have been ordered to drop in the Channel,' replied Buckey, the radio man.

'What a waste of effort,' Robinson replied.

'It won't be a waste,' answered Wright. 'We will drop near the coastline and maybe hit some of the mines they have buried. We might even hit some other German defences.'

'Fighters coming in at six o'clock!' called out Dabbs. This time it was just a lone Me109 that roared through the formation then disappeared.

The raid was turning into a fiasco, with both the 2nd and 3rd Divisions recalled. When General Fred Anderson heard the news, he was furious, especially since no one had bothered to contact his headquarters to ask permission. As far as Anderson was concerned, once committed to the operation the bombers had to press on regardless. In any case, the priority was not so much the targets themselves but more the opportunity to draw enemy fighters into the air and then shoot them down. Not all turned back, however. The 379th BG, which included Hugh McGinty and his fellow crew, were part of the 41st Combat Wing, led that day by Brigadier-General Robert F. Travis, who had also led them on 11 January. It was left to Travis to decide whether to accept the recall. Since they were nearing the target, he decided to press on.

At the time, they were crossing 'Happy Valley' as the Ruhr was known, bristling with nearly three thousand anti-aircraft guns. Their formation was flying high, at some 28,000 feet, to try to avoid the worst, but soon shells were peppering the sky. McGinty curled himself into as tight a ball as he could as the Fortress jolted around the sky. It sounded to him as if they were flying through a hailstorm so thick he reckoned he could have almost walked on it.

At Wunstorf in northern Germany, Heinz Knoke and the pilots of JG11 were airborne just before 1 p.m., scrambled yet again to intercept large formations of American bombers. There were just five of them from the entire *Gruppe*; at full strength there should have been thirty-six and twelve in Knoke's 5 Staffel alone, but such had been the losses already that year that a mere five was the best they could manage from all three squadrons.

By chance, they intercepted the bombers directly over Hamelin, Knoke's home town, so he was able to look down at familiar hills from 25,000 feet. On his wing was Feld-webel Kreuger, who had joined his *Staffel* just two days before, and Knoke now led him down to attack a group of about thirty Flying Fortresses. On board his Gustav, Knoke had fitted a gun camera so that the Fighter Schools might then use the footage as part of their training. At the start of the war, Nazi Germany had been awash with movie and stills film; never had any armed forces been more filmed or photographed. Now, Allied fighters had gun cameras as standard while in Germany it was just another once-common article in desperately short supply.

Knoke was making good use of his gun camera as he swooped in for a textbook front attack; he opened fire and saw hits straight into the cockpit, then circled wide and came back for a second run, speeding towards the bomber until they almost collided, but, as Knoke knew, getting in close was how to cause the most damage and this time bullets and cannon shells tore across the wing and fuselage. Flames now erupted from the tail of the bomber, and Knoke thought about the gun camera and how devastating his handiwork would look.

Kreuger, meanwhile, had stuck admirably close by and was now opening fire at the Fortress on Knoke's left; moments later flames erupted all along the fuselage. Sweeping in a wide arc to the left, it then tottered and began diving in an uncontrollable spin directly towards Hamelin. Knoke watched as it plummeted and saw it land in the meadow beside the river, from where, as a 17-year-old, he had taken his first flight – that fifteen-minute joyride in an old transport plane during the air pageant at the edge of town. That had been in 1938. A lifetime ago.

Suddenly a second aircraft hurtled down out of the sky, also in flames, and crashed and exploded at the southern end of town in a timber yard that Knoke knew belonged to the Kaminski wagon-maker and repair shop. 'It was my wingman, the young corporal,' noted Knoke. 'This was his first mission.'

Knoke now dived down and swept low over his home town. The streets were utterly deserted, no doubt because of the air battle raging above, then he flew on back to Wunstorf, his fuel tanks showing empty after ninety minutes in the air.

Gabby Gabreski and the 56th FG boys were once more on escort duty that day. Over northern Holland, they dived down on a number of FW190s and Gabreski managed to shoot one down before climbing back up to continue their assigned escort duty. Flying on his wing was Lieutenant-Colonel Gil Meyers, commander of the 368th Fighter Group, which had just arrived in England. Meyers was flying with the 56th for experience and stuck dutifully to Gabreski, but during the tussle with the Focke-Wulfs they lost contact with the rest of the squadron and when it was time to turn back for home, the two did so alone.

As they were flying over Eindhoven in Holland, Gabreski spotted the airfield below and noticed what looked like a Dornier bomber parked beside a hut. It seemed the perfect opportunity to try out General Doolittle's new instructions about attacking aircraft on the ground as well as in the air.

Diving down, they swooped over the airfield low and fast, Gabreski spraying the Dornier and Meyers letting rip at a hangar. Light flak and small-arms fire was coming up at them, but they were over the airfield in a trice. Although Gabreski knew he had hit the Dornier, exactly how much damage he had caused wasn't clear, but he had no intention of sticking around. 'Ground strafing was a sure way of blowing off steam and it was a lot of fun,' he wrote later, 'but I couldn't see any point in pushing my luck.' Both made it home without a scratch and Gabreski was able to celebrate in the mess with the rest of his men in the 61st FS that night because that day they had scored their hundredth victory for the squadron. It was no small feat; in February alone they had so far accounted for forty-four enemy aircraft for no loss of their own. It was indicative of the increasing superiority the American fighter pilots had over their enemy.

The bombers of the Fifteenth Air Force were having mixed fortunes. Sully Sullivan and the crews of the 301st BG were battling the inevitable heavy cloud in southern Germany as well as furious attacks by the Luftwaffe. As navigator, it was Sullivan's job to direct them to the target, and despite the cloud they still managed to bomb the Prüfening plant, as did a number of others, hitting the main factory as well as causing damage to an assembly shop and several other buildings.

As they were turning for home, however, they came under heavy enemy fighter attack. These planes had been expected to have been drawn towards the Eighth's bombers attacking southern Germany first, before the heavies of the Fifteenth reached their target, but because the 2nd and 3rd Divisions had been recalled, the German fighters based in central and southern Germany were instead able to turn their full fury on the bombers of the Fifteenth. The damage was considerable. Sullivan had been at his gun position when a 20mm cannon shell burst through the nose and smashed his navigator's stool. 'Lucky I was at my gun,' he wrote, 'or I would have been a goner!' Both the radio man and tail gunner were wounded, and the radio room caught fire after their Fortress was raked by bullets and cannon shells. While one of the waist gunners managed to put out the flames, Sullivan hurried back to give the two wounded men first aid as best he could. They were in trouble, however, because as they crossed back over the Alps and into Italy they ran out of oxygen; the electrical system on the plane had been badly shot up too.

Meanwhile, on Hugh McGinty's aircraft, they somehow emerged through the flak over the Ruhr Valley only for him to see a B-17 on fire. Flames were billowing out of the bomb bay and radio hatch. The pilot pulled out of the formation so as not to endanger the rest and McGinty watched, mesmerized, as the crew tried to get the fires under control. An auxiliary fuel tank was discarded and soon after the flames disappeared altogether and the pilot began moving to rejoin the rest. A hundred yards off McGinty's ship's wingtip the B-17 suddenly blew up in a blinding flash of flame. Shocked, McGinty now saw two parachutes, one with only half a torso and another on fire.

On they flew, only to be attacked by successive waves of enemy fighters. Of the Little Friends, there was no sign. The Luftwaffe seemed to be everywhere: Me109s, Focke-Wulfs, Ju88s, Me110s, Me210s, all swarming around them like angry bees. The sky was now clear and McGinty's eyes were smarting from straining into the sun. He attempted to concentrate on maintaining the firing discipline he always tried to use, despite the mayhem outside. His twin .50-calibre machine guns had a fast rate of fire of around 800 r.p.m. Each box of ammo held five hundred rounds, so around forty-five seconds' worth of firing time. Long, sustained bursts of fire were not effective, however, and McGinty had learned to shoot short bursts of just a handful of rounds at a time and alternately with each of the brace of machine guns. The moment a fighter broke off, McGinty also stopped firing at him, even though as the enemy turned away he would often show the juicy target of his underside; McGinty knew German fighter pilots operated in fours and that if he was focused on trying to shoot down a plane that was no longer a direct threat, he would not see the other three fighters rolling in behind.

Halberstadt was overcast by the time the 1st Division's combat wing reached it, which was why the mission had been withdrawn. Once again, the weather had proved a fickle and difficult force to predict. 'We dropped our bombs,' noted Hugh McGinty, 'and could not be sure of the results. As we started a sweeping turn toward home, I could see a lot of smoke but not the target itself.' He hoped it was enough and that they wouldn't be ordered back again. Once more, as they cleared the target area, the flak thinned and out of the sky enemy fighters swooped in for the kill. Machine guns hammered, tracer criss-crossed the sky, a few ships fell, and then the fighters disappeared, only to be replaced by the intense flak of the Ruhr once again. At least he felt he could do something about fighters and try to defend their ship, but flak just had to be taken on the chin. He hated the feeling of helplessness. A hole the size of a bathtub appeared in the right wing, which was then reported over the intercom, but Ernal Bridwell, the pilot, told the others he didn't want to hear it.

Then they were through once more. And still flying.

Still in one piece. A group of FW190s now appeared parallel to their formation. The leader suddenly pulled clear, turned and barrel-rolled through the bomber formation, then rejoined his group before leading them all down for a mass attack. Once in range, the fighter leader was pummelled by machine-gun fire and blew up; the rest split-S'ed and headed for the clouds.

Hovering overhead since Koblenz had been the pilots of the 4th Fighter Group, led once more by Don Blakeslee and rendezvousing with just twenty-four 1st Division B-17s, although not those of Hugh McGinty and co. Sticking with them until just south of Brussels, they then headed for home and, although they chased after two Me109s, they managed to escape into cloud. It was then 3.35 p.m.

Not long after, the rest of the 1st Division was nearing the Dutch coast when yet more enemy fighters appeared. This time, they hit the Fortress of McGinty's great pal Willy McGinnis. The ship went down from 22,000 feet and exploded shortly before hitting the deck. Suddenly Spitfires appeared and tore into the enemy fighters. Their arrival gave the struggling B-17s the chance they needed to reach the coast; McGinty reckoned the English Channel had never looked so good. The remains of their combat wing tried to maintain close order, but there were too many stragglers trailing smoke, with their aircraft shot up and short of fuel. McGinty's crew reached Kimbolton safely, however, touching down and taxiing on to their hardstand, where they finally shut down the engines. McGinty could hardly believe he was still alive, that he had been spared one more time. His premonitions had, thankfully, not been self-fulfilling after all.

*

In Italy, Sully Sullivan and his crew also made it back to Lucera, where pilot Bill Epps managed to land safely despite the extensive damage to their Fortress. 'Tail gunner pretty bad off,' noted Sullivan. A good Catholic boy, he always prayed hard and even managed to get to mass in a makeshift chapel that had been created in a tent. 'The good Lord is looking out for me!!!!!!!' he wrote.

The crews of the 2nd BG had also returned to their base at Foggia. Half had been sent to Regensburg and the rest to Graz. Neither had hit their primary target due to the ten-tenths cloud; those heading to Regensburg had hit a railway marshalling yard at Ochling near Munich, while bombardier Michael Sullivan and his crew had given up on Graz and bombed Zagreb airfield instead. The 2nd BG had lost only one bomber but, much to Sullivan's dismay, it had been the crew of his good friend Airleigh Honeycutt, with whom he shared a hut.

It had not been a bad day for the Fifteenth, all things considered. After their Fortresses had hit their target in Regensburg so too had their Liberators, destroying two assembly buildings and badly damaging a third along with a number of workers' buildings. Some twenty-six enemy fighters had been brought down too.

The Wright crew also made it back safely to Tibenham. Robbie Robinson was frustrated and felt the entire mission had been a wasted effort. Nor was he pleased to find himself by turns almost frying and then freezing, so after the debrief he took himself off to find the quartermaster. There was a shortage of new electric suits, so he was given a kind of small clamp to join the wires together. For the time being, that would have to do.

It had been a dark day for the 381st BG and, after the euphoria of the 20th, Chaplain James Good Brown struggled to absorb the palpable sense of despair at Ridgewell when it became clear that six crews would not be returning. 'The end may be victory,' he noted, 'but there are many spots of darkness along the way. February 22, 1944, is one of these dark spots.' Brown had attended the debrief in the interrogation room. The crews had talked incessantly, describing the persistent German attacks. Ships had gone down in flames, others had been torn in half. One of Brown's best friends on the base had been lost in this way. 'A man who had been on the base a long time and had won the hearts of everyone,' wrote the chaplain. 'He was a smiling, kindly, honest, stalwart and steady citizen of society, a peach of a fellow.'

Back on the ground in Germany, Gordon Carter was still on the run. As daylight started to fade, he reached the River Weser near Nienburg. It was flowing far too fast and the water temperature was much too cold to risk trying to swim, so he thought he would attempt to cross by one of the town bridges once it became dark. At that moment, however, as he was contemplating his route, a group of schoolboys approached him and started chatting. They soon left him alone, but shortly afterwards he came across a German sailor shooting crows with a shotgun and the man beckoned him over. For a brief moment, Carter considered trying to take him on, but as he could speak reasonable German he decided instead to see if he could talk his way out of his predicament. It didn't work. Carter had no papers to show and so the sailor told him he was turning him in. At shotgun point, he escorted Carter to his house and called the local police. Carter couldn't fault his manners or those of his family. 'While waiting for the police to show up,' he noted, 'the lady of the house and her two teenage daughters gave me a glass of schnapps and invited me to return and visit them after the war.' Soon the police appeared, with the line, *'Für Sie ist der Krieg zu Ende.'* Gordon Carter's luck had run out. For him, the war was over.

CHAPTER 23

Thursday,
24 February 1944

'U.S. IN FIRST JOINT North–South Air Blow', ran the headline in *Stars & Stripes,* the US forces' newspaper, on Wednesday, 23 February. 'Heavies From Italy And Britain Plaster Bomb-Drunk Reich'. The Allied press had been reporting the attacks with increasing glee, and *Stars & Stripes* guessed that so far in the '60-hour' Allied assault some 11,000 tons must have been dropped. 'Even as flames were leaping from German targets north and south,' the lead article continued, 'Prime Minister Winston Churchill, in a report on the war to Parliament, was promising that in the coming spring and summer the scale of attacks will reach far beyond the dimensions of anything which has yet been employed or, indeed, imagined.'

The first few days of ARGUMENT had shocked the Luftwaffe's leadership. I Jagdkorps reported losing 28 fighters on the 20th and many more badly damaged; in all, 58 had to be written off. Some 65 per cent of the floor space at Messerschmitt's Heiterblick plant at Leipzig had been destroyed and 83 per cent at Leipzig–Mockau, and although most of the machine tools had been salvaged, the Luftwaffe could in no way function properly when its factories were being as badly hit as this. Dispersal of the aircraft industry was going to have to be sped up, but was neither very efficient nor good for economies of scale. On the 21st, a further 32 fighters had to be written off and 52 on the 23rd.

On the 22nd, Göring had summoned his senior commanders to an emergency meeting at Carinhall, his estate near Berlin, and told them of his growing concern. Schmid once again asked for unification of all German fighter defences; it was too split up, he argued. I Jagdkorps had three fighter divisions in northern and central Germany, but there was also II Jagdkorps with three fighter divisions still in the west, a further fighter division in the south and Luftflotte IV in Hungary. As Schmid pointed out, no one command had enough fighters to cope with the American daylight raids and each regional commander, understandably, was anxious to hold on to his fighters until the last minute rather than releasing them to other areas earlier. By the time they were finally being released to help other commands, it was too late and the bombers were on their way home. Although Luftflotte Reich had the power to overrule any of the regional commands, it could do so only with the Reichsmarschall's say-so, which caused a delay that, again, worked against a swift and coordinated response. Göring accepted Schmid's arguments and placed all fighters in southern Germany, Austria and Hungary under I Jagdkorps' control, but effective only from 1 April, so no immediate help. He did, however, also order the immediate transferral of another fighter *Gruppe* from the Eastern Front to bolster 1 Jagddivision.

Schmid called his own meeting on 23 February to work out how best to meet these new and intense attacks. It was obvious, he told those gathered, that the current assaults were designed to gain air supremacy as a prelude to an invasion. From now on, their fighters would have to do their utmost to defend the aircraft industry, which was clearly the Allies' priority. Each fighter division was to assign one *Gruppe* to attack the American fighter escorts, which was a reversal of Göring's earlier order to ignore the enemy fighters and just go for the bombers. He also posted these *Gruppen* to airfields in western Germany in an effort to distract and divert the American escorts before they reached the bombers' targets. At the same time, other units were ordered to retreat further into Germany because those still in the west were not having enough warning time to reach the kinds of altitudes needed to prevent them being bounced by Allied fighters.

All the while, the Luftwaffe's half-hearted 'mini Blitz' continued, which meant nights of air-raid alerts for many of the air bases in England. The Luftwaffe's bomber missions might not have been achieving much, but they were an undoubted nuisance. At Debden, there had been a 'semi-alert' at midnight and then a 'full alert' at five past. The all-clear had sounded at 1.20 a.m. No bombs had been dropped anywhere near the base – they never were. 'The American sporting spirit of the enlisted personnel,' ran the 334th squadron diary, 'is well illustrated by the fact that pools are being made up predicting the exact hour of the next full air-raid alert.'

However annoying it may have been for the aircrews to have air-raid alerts repeatedly waking them up, this was, of course, as nothing to the exhaustion, terror and trauma caused by the Allied bombing of Germany. What Margarete Dos was experiencing in Berlin was repeated in many German cities, and although Operation ARGUMENT was targeting aircraft factories, the bombers were still flying near or over other cities, air-raid sirens were going off across the Reich day and night, anti-aircraft guns were booming, and in target areas such as Regensburg, Leipzig and Brunswick, civilians were victims of those attacks. Normal life was constantly disrupted as civilians all over Germany, but especially in the western half, spent weary nights in air-raid shelters or found themselves having to stop their work and tramp down into shelters. It was demoralizing to say the least. So far in 1944, Cologne, for example, had had at least one air-raid alert every single day.

'You learned to live from one air raid to the next,' said Hugo Stehkämper, who was a 14-year-old boy living in Cologne. 'It became routine.' A lot of people moved out to the countryside, although there was precious little housing to spare and it was still winter. Stehkämper and his family preferred to stay put, fully aware they were risking their lives by doing so. 'You simply continued to live from day to day with a certain degree of indifference.' When the bombs started falling, however, he, like so many others, found himself gripped by a deathly, unshakeable fear that only ever passed when the all-clear sounded.

The city was crumbling, rubble lay everywhere, there was a chronic shortage of coal and particularly food. On paper, an adult was supposed to get nearly 2,000 calories a day, but the disruption and constant problems of supply meant this was rarely met. The SD – the Sicherheitsdienst, the SS intelligence agency – planted observers throughout the Reich to make reports on morale. 'After the attacks,' wrote one SD report, 'the population appeared completely exhausted and apathetic.'

Apathy and despair mixed with a hardening of many to the horrors they were witnessing. Another living in Cologne was Heribert Suntrop, who was fifteen and rapidly becoming inured to the death and carnage around him. The morning after one raid, he found the corpse of a British airman who had fallen without a parachute. He kicked the dead man with his boot. Another airman lay a bit further down the street, his body cut in half. 'Only the upper part was there, completely naked,' Suntrop recalled. 'And this sight left me completely cold as well.'

German civilians were given a much-needed respite on 23 February when poor weather put paid to a fourth consecutive day of operations, which meant the Allied aircrew, at any rate, could have a lie-in and catch up on rest. For the moment, ARGUMENT would have to pause, giving the beleaguered ground crews of the Eighth a chance to patch up the battered bomb groups. Although the number of destroyed bombers had been small, many more had been damaged, plenty of them beyond redemption. Some 223 bombers had returned with battle damage on the first day, for example, all of which required immediate attention. Eighth Air Force had been able to fly 1,017 heavies on 20 February, 914 the following day and just 603 on the 22nd. Through the super-human efforts of the ground crews, that number had risen again to 854 by Thursday, 24 February. These ground engineers might not have faced danger in the skies, but all aircrews were mindful of how much they owed them. Camaraderie among the ground crews was as intense as it was among the air-crews; all understood the necessity of working immensely long hours in freezing conditions to make aircraft as safe as humanly possible.

All through the night and the wet, washed-out daylight hours of Wednesday, 23 February, the ground crews worked their magic and by Thursday morning over 800 heavy bombers were ready to fly along with 947 fighters. What's more, the morning dawned cold and clear. Hugh McGinty could barely believe his eyes. 'Was this England?' he won-dered. 'We were almost glad to fly.' He, for one, felt rested and refreshed after a day's break, the terrors of the trip to Halberstadt pushed out of his mind. Then at the briefing the curtain was pulled back to reveal the target was Sch-weinfurt, prompting widespread groans and a dramatic deflation of spirits. Schweinfurt – a byword for the very worst of targets, and for McGinty's thirteenth mission too.

It was to be another maximum effort. This time, the B-24s of the 2nd Division were being sent to the Messer-schmitt factory at Gotha in eastern central Germany, which meant another long trip deep into the Reich. The 389th BG was detailed to lead the group, but because they now had only thirty B-24s available rather than the full complement with which they had begun the week, their formation included a section of fifteen ships upfront and a second section of fifteen behind. Jim Keeffe's squadron, the 566th, was in the second echelon.

They were ordered to fly in lower than usual, at 14,500 feet, which was reckoned still to be above the light flak but low enough to get a better and more accurate bombing pattern. They were to completely paste the Gotha works; each mission in this week of weeks needed to count hard.

Also joining the 2nd Division's strike on Gotha were the Liberators of the 445th from Tibenham, and Lieutenant Wright's crew were once again on the list. At the briefing, Robbie Robinson – who had put on his electric flight suit with special care and no small amount of anxiety that it might once again malfunction – had been horrified to discover they were heading back to Gotha. The numbers were getting noticeably smaller: just twenty-five heavies could be put into the air from the 445th that day. They were promised fine weather and a clear target. Robinson remained sceptical, however; they had been told the same before the last trip.

A better, less predictable route had been chosen, and it seemed to work because they encountered neither much flak nor any enemy fighters. There had also been snow over central Europe – from the cockpit, Keeffe saw nothing but a monochrome landscape below. He guessed 4 or 5 inches of snow had fallen; perhaps that had grounded the enemy fighters.

Also heading far into Germany were the Fortresses of the 1st Division. After the shock of learning they would be heading to Schweinfurt, by the time they took off Hugh McGinty had managed to regain some confidence, not least because climbing up to the assembly point would be done in the clear for pretty much the first time.

Meanwhile, the Fortresses of the 3rd Division were heading to Brunswick. Larry Goldstein and the crew of *Worry Wart* were among those on the list from the 388th BG, along with 303 other heavies scheduled to fly from the 3rd Division. When the curtain had been drawn back, Goldstein had not been the only one immediately to think of the hellish experience they had suffered eleven days earlier on their last visit to the city.

To the south, the Liberators of the 2nd Division were also having a fairly easy passage across Germany: the weathermen had got it right and they were flying in clear skies and, so far, had not been bothered by enemy fighters. Robbie Robinson wondered whether the Germans were asleep that day.

In Italy, the day had also dawned cold and clear, so a hundred Fortresses and a similar number of Liberators attacked the Steyr-Daimler-Puch aircraft factory at Steyr in Austria. Among those due to fly were bombardier Lieutenant Michael Sullivan and the McKew crew on *The Second Was First*. The target was the same that had been listed the previous day – the 2nd BG, including the McKew crew, had been sent off but had once again returned early due to 'impenetrable weather'. However, eighty-five Liberators had attacked Steyr and had themselves come under heavy attack from enemy fighters, including Ju88s firing rockets. Seventeen of the attacking force had been shot down, a staggering 20 per cent. Now, on the morning of Thursday, 24 February, the briefing officer told them about the losses and warned them they could expect similarly heavy attacks today. He then said that if anyone wanted to leave the room now, they could do so without recriminations. No one did.

Sullivan and the crew of *The Second Was First* were part of the 429th Bomb Squadron, which was leading the 2nd's effort, with the B-17s of the other three squadrons following and the group in turn forming up behind those of the 97th and 301st BGs. After assembling over Foggia, they flew north over the Adriatic. The crews were already talking about the Alps between Italy and Austria as 'Coffin Corner', and, with the Italian coast around Udine approaching, that was exactly where they were heading. After their briefing that morning, every man on board was keenly scanning the skies and watching for trouble.

The B-24s of 566th BS droned on over Nazi-occupied Europe, then eventually turned en masse, heading due east and readying themselves for their arrival at the IP and the inevitable flak that would follow. An error had occurred when the bombardier in the lead ship had suffered from anoxia – oxygen deficiency – and, as he passed out, opened his bomb bays and dropped their bombs early over Eisenach and on to a truck factory. Realizing their mistake, the lead aircraft in Keeffe's second section broke radio silence. 'You bombed the wrong target,' said the second section leader. 'We're going on.' This now made them the lead section for the entire 2nd Division.

The sky was crystal clear. It was a beautiful day. From that lower altitude, Keeffe saw the white blanket of snow below but also, as they reached the IP, he was able to see German fighter aircraft hurriedly taking off across the snow from their grass runways. 'I could see these multiple individual fighters taking off far below us,' he wrote, 'and they were blowing snow out behind them as they took off, just like a boat leaves a wake behind it.'

As the 445th BG Liberators reached the IP, once again the flak rose up. Several large bursts were worryingly close to Wright's ship, and then another exploded right in front of their number one and two engines. The number two began to smoke as Wright reported a loss of oil pressure. He was, he told the rest of the crew, going to shut it down and feather it, but try to keep up with the rest of the formation.

That, however, put too much strain on the number three engine. Already they began dropping back; and the number two was still smoking from the leaking oil passing over the hot supercharger. They flew over the target and, as the bombs left, the big B-24 seemed to jump into the air with a new spring in its step.

'That will help,' Wright said over the intercom. 'But we still can't keep up.' He was, he told them, now going to dive right down to the overcast skies away to the west, then try to make it back through the cloud all the way to the Channel. It sounded like a long shot.

'Fighters at three o'clock high,' Tyler now called out.

'We can't stay any longer,' said Wright. 'Here we go.'

'Fighters coming at three o'clock,' said Tyler again.

Dropping the left wing, they banked and dived. Robinson felt himself lifted mid-air and saw Cross and Tyler also suspended. The number two engine continued to smoke – worse, it seemed, now they were diving. Ears began to pop then stab with pain at the dramatic change in air pressure. The big bomber was screaming. Dabbs now called out, 'Two Fighters coming in on our tail. They're following us down. I can't identify them yet. They're coming right for us.'

From Wright: 'Are they ours? If they are, fire a flare.'

'I don't know,' replied Dabbs, 'but they're closing. I believe they're Me109s.'

They were now approaching the clouds and the race

was on. Buckey was complaining about his eardrums, but suddenly Wright was levelling out and thick white cloud enveloped them.

'Dabbs, do you see the fighters?' Wright asked.

No, he replied; they broke as the bomber entered the clouds. 'I think they thought we were going down,' Dabbs added.

'I thought so too,' Robinson replied.

Others were not so lucky, and aircraft were now falling in droves. There was no doubt that by flying in close formation the American bombers were defensively stronger, but that proximity could also work against them. At one point, an Me109 dived towards a B-24 firing until at almost point-blank range, its cannon shells ripping the nose to shreds and causing the bomber to start to fall earthwards. The Messerschmitt climbed up steeply, but as it did so the top-turret gunner in the stricken Liberator opened fire and his bullets tore into the enemy, so that suddenly both bomber and attacker were falling out of the sky. As the B-24 began spinning in a nose-dive, it smashed into another bomber below it, ripping off the unsuspecting Liberator's tail. Instead of immediately plunging downwards too, the front half continued flying, but vertically and straight into a third B-24, which also broke apart, and now large sections of two bombers were falling through the formation with everyone else taking evasive action and risking further collision as they did so.

The Messerschmitt factory at Gotha lay just outside the town. On Jim McArthur's ship, Jim Keeffe, in the co-pilot's seat, spotted it clearly: a large square divided diagonally into two triangles. The factory and its test airfield next door were on one triangle, while a major fighter base was on the other. Enemy aircraft were still taking off from both. They were scrambled too late to interrupt the bomb run of the lead section of the 389th BG, however, and Jimmy McArthur's ship had a good run in, dropped its bombs accurately, then climbed and turned for the home leg.

By now, however, those enemy fighters Keeffe had just seen taking off were rapidly climbing up to meet them and in no time single- and twin-engine fighters were making head-on passes at them, then circling back again in a pattern that deftly moved along with the bomber formations. As a new crew, they had been put on the inside of their formation, the left-hand ship in a vic of three behind and to the right of Captain Wood, the element leader, so they were in the safest place in a suddenly very unsafe part of the sky; Keeffe was grateful not to be on the outside of the formation or in the lead, or tail-end Charlie at the back. Again and again, the fighters hurtled towards their formation, machine guns and cannons blazing. 'It became pretty grim,' noted Keeffe, 'and airplanes began to go down.' The B-24 flying above and to the left caught a hail of cannon shells and immediately veered off then went into a spin. There was something unreal about watching such violence at close hand, but almost immediately to Keeffe's left, just 100 yards or so away and flying at the same level, another B-24 was in trouble. In no time, flames began pouring out of the windows and fuselage where the bomb bays had opened. He spotted a waist gunner standing at his station, flames all around him, clutching his arms to his head. Then he fell, his body on fire, while the bomber began to tilt downwards. Keeffe watched, aghast, then saw the nose wheel come down, which also enabled the forward hatch to be opened. One man now tried to get himself out, but got caught against the nose wheel, and then a moment later the entire aircraft blew up. 'I saw it explode,' wrote Keeffe, 'and then it was gone. It was behind us, all in a matter of seconds, ten young men dying in an exploding inferno.'

No sooner had Keeffe watched this horror than an FW190 slowly looped down and flew alongside them no more than 100 feet away, then throttled back so that they were flying in tandem. Keeffe was wondering what on earth the pilot was doing when he saw flames licking from the enemy fighter and, seconds later, the canopy popped up and spun away. The pilot now clambered on to his seat and then his parachute blossomed – in flames. It was open enough to yank the man clear of the fighter, but a second later he had been flung through the burning flames of the chute and pilot and burning debris fell downwards together. Keeffe was certain the German had not been wounded when he had bailed out, but now that young enemy pilot faced falling some 14,000 feet to his certain death. 'It was going to take him a minute plus to go down, and then there'd be a big thud and that would be the end of it,' he noted. 'What a way to go.'

Keeffe and his crew still had to get through their own bomb run, but they managed to drop their payload and lurch upwards to join the rest of the 389th, who had already delivered their bombs and were now weaving in a wide 'S' waiting for the last of the group to catch up. Just as the second section caught up with the first, another bomber on Keeffe's left began falling back out of formation and was immediately pounced upon by enemy fighters.

An engine exploded and fell away, then, as suddenly as they had arrived, the enemy were gone. Once more the skies were clear.

Not far away, the Fortresses of the 1st Division were having a fairly easy time of it for a change. Certainly, compared with the past few trips, Schweinfurt was proving a cakewalk for the boys of the 379th BG. Escorts dutifully accompanied them all the way, including the P-51s, whose pilots tussled repeatedly with the 109s and 190s so that enemy fighter attacks were pressed home with nothing like the severity of recent missions. 'Our losses were not nearly as high as we expected,' noted Hugh McGinty. 'We plastered the target with very good results.' In fact, the only hiccup for McGinty came shortly after they hit the target, when his electric suit short-circuited and he had to depend on the heated Norden bombsight cover to keep him from freezing.

Covering 1st Division's withdrawal were the 4th Fighter Group, which managed to rendezvous successfully near Koblenz on the Rhine at around 2 p.m. with the 4th Combat Wing of B-17s and 1st Combat Wing of 2nd Division's B-24s. No sooner had they arrived on the scene than four FW190s were seen attacking the Liberators head on. Don Gentile was flying Blue 1 in 336th FS and immediately led his section down in a hard starboard turn. As he neared, he saw the four Focke-Wulfs speeding straight towards them, tracer arcing across the sky. Just before they all collided, the German pilots broke and rolled down through the bomber formation. Gentile followed one of them through the bombers, whose gunners were blasting their machine guns for all they were worth. He could feel their propeller wash as he sped down, and also his own airframe shaking, but then he was through and up ahead was his 190. Closing in, he opened fire, saw the Focke-Wulf start to smoke, then the enemy fighter rolling over and falling like a lead weight from the sky.

The mass of close escorts without doubt made life difficult for the Reich's defenders, and Heinz Knoke and the fighter pilots of I Jagdkorps felt the strain that day. The shortage of fighter aircraft was less of a problem than the lack of pilots. Young, under-trained freshmen like Knoke's Feldwebel Kreuger did not really have a chance; they were still thinking about how to fly the aircraft as they were thrust into skies criss-crossed with lead. All too many were arriving and promptly being shot down. Attrition affected the veterans too. It was a miracle that Heinz Knoke was still flying despite having been shot down more times than he could count on one hand, but others did not share his apparent invincibility. That morning, he had heard that his friend August Geiger, a Knight's Cross-winning night-fighter ace, had been killed. Back in early 1940, Knoke and a group of aspiring pilots had all been taught to fly at the Military Academy by an inspiring instructor called van Diecken. Knoke realized sadly that he was now the sole survivor.

It was an altogether bleak day for him and the men of JG11, as a further six pilots had been killed at noon in another one-sided tussle with American fighters. 'Our little band grows smaller and smaller,' he wrote in his diary. 'Every man can work out for himself on the fingers of one hand when his own turn is due to come.'

*

Far to the south, across the Alps, the Fifteenth Air Force's bombers heading to Steyr were having a brutal time, and particularly so the 2nd Bomb Group, who were flying at the rear of the bomber formation. Although escorted by 150 Thunderbolts and Lightnings, only a handful of P-47s showed up, while the P-38s did not appear until the badly mauled formation was on the return leg. For an hour after midday, from the moment they crossed over into Austria to the moment they returned again, the formation was attacked by a Luftwaffe force of over a hundred fighters of varying types.

Fortunately for Michael Sullivan and the crew of *The Second Was First*, they were in the lead squadron; the rear two squadrons were particularly badly pummelled with wave after wave of Messerschmitts, Focke-Wulfs and even Ju88s attacking from the rear, with the sun behind them, rather than head-on. Enemy fighter groups would attack in turn, then head out of range, re-form, and attack once again. Suddenly, ships – and fighters – were falling, breaking up mid-air, plummeting in flames, parachutes swinging down slowly all over the mountains. Despite this, those that were able to press home their attack managed to hit a number of machine shops and assembly buildings, but their bombs also fell in a residential area.

Seventeen bombers were shot down that day, of which thirteen were from the 2nd BG, although the Luftwaffe had also paid a price, with over thirty shot down in all, including eleven by the P-38s. '49th Squadron annihilated in its entirety,' noted Sullivan, then added, 'The Luftwaffe must be destroyed.'

*

To the north-west, the Eighth Air Force's 2nd Division Liberators were heading home. Among those on the return leg were the Wright crew of 445th BG, whose B-24 was now running on engines one and four. In the pilot's seat, Wright was keeping them under the top of the cloud layer and at just 6,000 feet. For the time being, they were safe, but if the cloud disappeared they would be vulnerable again. Fortunately, however, the skies cleared just as they reached the coast after a tense and painfully slow journey back across Germany and western Europe. On they went, limping across the sea and eventually back to Tibenham. Two engines had got them home.

Back at base, everyone was surprised to see them. Others had reported them going down in flames with two Me109s on their tail. 'You were lucky to get back,' the debriefing officer told them. 'Thirteen other bombers went down behind you.' The 445th had taken a hammering that day.

For once, every one of the 379th BG's bombers that had left Kimbolton that morning returned safely to base. The ground personnel had lined up to watch them coming in and had begun cheering as one after the other landed safely, with just one crewman killed and another wounded.

Thirty miles away at Knettishall, the crew of *Worry Wart* also landed back in one piece, and Larry Goldstein, for one, reckoned it had been a pretty good trip, all things considered. He had not seen much of the enemy at all, and even the flak had seemed substantially lighter than the last time they had made the trip. They had bombed well and, it had seemed to him, pretty accurately. 'So all in all,' he added, 'it was an easy mission.' What's more, he now had only four more until his tour was over and he could head home to Brooklyn.

Jim Keeffe and the rest of the 389th, who had survived the carnage above Gotha, had also made it home without further trouble. Taxiing in to their hardstand, McArthur and Keeffe shut down the engines, gathered up their kit and clambered down from the bomber as its engines ticked and clicked while they cooled. Before they could head to the debrief, they had to note down the condition of the aircraft, how it had flown and write up any problems. Keeffe now realized his hands were shaking, something about which he felt acutely embarrassed, so he thrust them into his pockets in the hope that none of the others would notice.

Over three hundred holes were counted in their ship, yet, incredibly, 'Not one of us had been hit,' noted Keeffe, 'not one scratch!' But Keeffe couldn't stop his hands shaking. Before the debrief they were all offered a shot of whisky and he took several, hoping it would calm him down. Then came the debrief, a grim experience where they had to relive all they had seen. The 389th had lost seven aircraft that day, including one from their own squadron. Seven crews gone in one mission left a big hole in a bomb group.

All the crews in their section were given an immediate pass for five days. Keeffe decided to catch a train to London, where he hoped he would be able to enjoy himself. But he couldn't shift the thought that, if seven ships had gone down in one operation, the chances of finishing twenty-five missions seemed horribly unlikely. It was a question of simple mathematics. So far, he'd completed just two.

CHAPTER 24

Friday, 25 February 1944

THE ROUND-THE-CLOCK bombing continued during the night of 24/25 February, with RAF Bomber Command finally hitting Schweinfurt, following directly on from the Eighth's attack earlier that day. The suggestion that Bomber Command strike Schweinfurt had been pushed first by the Ministry of Economic Warfare in November, then championed by the planning men at the Air Ministry and not least Air Marshal Sir Norman Bottomley, the Deputy Chief of the Air Staff, who had written to Air Marshal Harris on 17 December specifically suggesting it as a priority target. Harris had replied three days later, giving a number of very sound reasons why it was not the best target for night ops. 'It is extremely small and difficult to find,' he wrote. 'It is heavily defended, including smoke-screens. In these circumstances it might need up to six or seven full scale attacks before a satisfactory result was secured.' If it was as important a target as was being claimed, then Harris felt it was definitely a target on which the Americans should focus.

Harris's arguments were entirely valid, but in January he had been overruled by Portal and ordered directly to send his bombers there. Now, during Operation ARGUMENT, the time had come, and while Harris might still be privately muttering about the prospect, he had taken the decision on the chin and was now determined to make as good a fist of it as possible. Following the Americans' earlier raid made sense and, furthermore, he now had more H2S-equipped aircraft than he had had in December when his exchange with Bottomley had taken place.

Some 734 aircraft were available for this first Bomber Command attack on Germany's main ball-bearing plant. As well as more H2S-carrying Pathfinders, another new tactic was to be introduced. The attacking force was to be split in two, with 392 bombers heading out earlier than the second attack group of 342 aircraft. The hope was to overwhelm the enemy night-fighter force as well as draw them towards the usual diversions, in this case 179 training aircraft sent over Kiel plus a number of Mosquitoes attacking night-fighter airfields.

Among those in the first wave was Flight Sergeant Ken Handley and his Australian crew, one of sixteen Halifaxes heading out from 466 Squadron. This was Handley's third trip and, although he always felt anxious and apprehensive beforehand, once they took off at 6.15 p.m. he found those nerves had disappeared. In his dicky seat next to the pilot, Jack Scott, Handley had a clear view of night-time Europe spread out beneath them. Far away, he saw the cones of searchlights criss-crossing, but otherwise their journey was untroubled: they avoided any flak and were not molested by night-fighters.

By 11 p.m. they were nearing the target. As they began their bomb run, searchlights swept the sky and Scott had to take evasive action to avoid being caught in their cones.

Flak was coming up, but most seemed to be below them – they were now at 22,500 feet. Back on their bomb run they soon spotted the target – the Pathfinders appeared to have laid down their markers well. 'No clouds obscured the target,' noted Handley later, 'and it was shown up by cones of searchlights and fighter flares. The ground markers, giving off their orange colours were spread over the target area.' The city was already burning by the time the Halifaxes of 466 Squadron arrived – and there was still another wave of bombers to come later that night.

Bombs away, they climbed to 25,000 feet. Soon after they were caught by searchlights, prompting Scott to dive dramatically and almost directly into a Lancaster below them, but, taking evasive action, he managed narrowly to avoid a catastrophic collision. Thereafter, it was plain sailing. 'We saw no searchlights or flak,' noted Handley, 'and let down over the French coast.' They touched back down at RAF Leconfield at 2.21 a.m. and went to their debrief, followed by the usual bacon and eggs then bed.

Two hours after the first raid, the second hit the target. How many bombs landed on the ball-bearing plant was not entirely clear, but losses were comparatively light – thirty-three in all, of which only eleven were shot down during the second wave.

As Ken Handley was climbing into his bed, American aircrews were being roused as staff toured the Nissen and Quonset huts calling out, 'Mission today!' Another maximum effort. Spaatz, Anderson and Doolittle were determined to press home the advantage and ensure the big week they had envisaged. The Eighth Air Force might suffer a large number of casualties, but it could and would recover; they did not believe the same could be said for the Luftwaffe.

At Tibenham, George Wright's crew was woken in the early hours of Friday, 25 February for their third mission in five days. Getting out of bed in the dark and cold was hard enough at the best of times, but even more so when just twenty-four hours earlier the men had done exactly the same and had headed out on a long mission from which 130 of them had not returned and from which they had been very lucky to come back safely themselves. This time, Robbie Robinson and the other enlisted men in Wright's crew got up and dressed without a word. 'All of us were like a bunch of automatic zombies,' wrote Robinson. 'We all walked together down the mud path to the mess hall, to the locker room where we got into our flight gear, then to briefing.'

Another at Tibenham now preparing for the day's mission was Major Jimmy Stewart. He had not flown since that first day of ARGUMENT but, like everyone, had felt keenly the losses suffered by the 445th and not least those thirteen crews over Gotha the previous day. As a squadron commander, it was his duty not only to read after-action reports but also to write yet more letters of condolence, not only one of the most unenviable aspects of command but one that reminded him all too starkly – as if any further reminder were needed – that flying bomber missions over enemy air space was a brutally dangerous occupation. Like most of those aircrew heading up into such uncertain skies, he too felt scared. He had known the previous evening that he would be leading the group today and during the night had woken and walked over to the window. He pulled up the blackout curtain and looked out over the dark, peaceful English country-side. 'My thoughts raced ahead to the morning,' he said, 'all the things I had to do, all the plans I must remember for an emergency. How could I have a clear mind if I was saturated with fear?'

Only seventeen bombers would be going from the 445th; it was all they could get into the air after the Gotha mission. The target, they learned, was Nuremberg. Jimmy Stewart would be the lead in the first flight, while Wright's crew were to fly in the second section. It would be a long trip. As far as Robinson could tell, Nuremberg was almost as far as Czechoslovakia. As if to really ram home the point, the briefing officer warned them to conserve every drop of fuel they could. Bomb bays were to be opened and shut quickly. The ball turret should be dropped down into position – it was operated hydraulically – only when absolutely necessary, otherwise it caused drag, which burned up more fuel. They would have enough fuel for ten hours, but the trip would take nine and a half. 'There will be very little margin for deviating from the planned path of your flight,' the briefing officer warned them. Robinson stared at the red ribbon across the map. The briefing officer continued: there would be thousands of flak guns beneath them, especially when they flew over the Ruhr. It was important those carrying cameras did not forget to switch them on.

At Knettishall, the 388th BG were also getting ready. 'No rest as the air blitz on German aircraft production continues,' noted Larry Goldstein in his diary that morning. 'Up and at them again today.' This time, the 3rd Division's Flying Fortresses were heading to Regensburg. Some 290 of them heading out on what was to be yet another long mission. In fact, Regensburg was to be hit doubly hard because the Fifteenth Air Force were going to join in – the first time bombers from both England and Italy would be attacking the same target on the same day – and bomb the city's Messerschmitt assembly plants too. For Goldstein, this would be mission number twenty-three.

For the men of the Fifteenth Air Force, the main target was once again the Prüfening aircraft factory at Regensburg. In all, the Fifteenth planned to send up some 180 bombers, of which around 100 would be directed to Regensburg, while four smaller groups would attack a diversionary target. Lieutenant Michael Sullivan and his crew were among eleven B-17s from the 2nd BG that would be heading to bomb the harbour at Zara in Yugoslavia. Sully Sullivan, however, and the Fortresses of the 301st BG were on the slate for attacking Regensburg. And after the previous day's encounter with the Luftwaffe, everyone was braced for a bumpy ride, despite talk of diversionary raids to draw the enemy away.

In neither England nor Italy, then, was there much enthusiasm from the bomber crews for the mission that day. Robbie Robinson wished it would be cancelled altogether. After the briefing, they headed for the truck that would take them to their waiting B-24s. 'My feet were walking in one direction with the crew,' he noted, 'my mind and body wanted to go back to the hut.' But he clambered up into the truck, as he knew he had to, and then found Jimmy Stewart jumping up too and sitting beside him.

'Sergeant,' he said, 'we are going to have a mighty fine flight today.'

'Yes, sir,' Robinson replied. 'It looks like we really are.' Neither of them believed it.

The 445th BG started taking off around 9.30 a.m., all with bomb bays full of 100lb fragmentation bombs. They were also carrying large amounts of Window, which they were to throw out manually from their waist-gunner positions as they crossed the enemy coastline. Sure enough, flak soon began bursting around them, so Robinson and Tyler began throwing out the tinfoil. Looking out, Robinson saw formations of B-24s and B-17s stretching for what seemed for ever. Depleted they might have been, but theirs was still a mighty armada. Suddenly the flak stopped and, although they had fighter escort, Robinson knew that any moment enemy fighters would show up. Then his foot started to freeze and once again he had to perform emergency repair work on the electric heating wires – a task he managed in the nick of time because enemy fighters were wheeling in for the attack. Robinson barely saw them as they streaked by, but then the Little Friends dived in after them and the 109s scattered after just one pass.

To the south, the bombers of the Fifteenth Air Force had reached Regensburg without much difficulty, largely thanks to closer escort from the fighters, although the Little Friends had been forced to turn back before nearing the target, which was beyond their range. Bombing was reasonably accurate and component and final assembly shops were hit – and would be hit again later by the bombers of the Eighth.

On the return leg, however, at around midday, the trouble started. As they were flying over Trieste on the north-east coast of Italy, they were attacked by more than two hundred fighters. The result was carnage. Sully Sullivan and his crew were among only two from the 32nd Bomb Squadron to make it back. 'Sad, sad day,' he wrote, 'for I lost one of my best friends – our pilot, Bill Epps!' Epps was flying with the 419th BS that day and was shot down, along with twelve other crews. Sullivan also saw his good friends Joe Baughman and Joe Chapas, part of David Paxton's crew, go down in flames just off the right wing of his own ship. 'Such things as I saw are really horrible,' he noted on his return. 'B-17s falling with tails shot away. Chutes all over the place and flaming planes in spirals. B-24s caught hell above. God grant there be no more days like this one!'

In all, twenty-one B-17s and fourteen B-24s were shot down this day, a terrible 25 per cent of the attacking bomber force. Spaatz had known he was going to have some tough days and Regensburg on this last Friday in February was certainly one of those for the Fifteenth Air Force.

While some two hundred enemy fighters had been sent up to meet the earlier attack by the Fifteenth, only fifty-nine were scrambled to meet the far larger effort by the Eighth. Among the latter were the fighters of JG11, who were ordered into the air as once more Division control reported enemy bombers approaching their air defence sector. Heinz Knoke could hardly believe it. It was relentless; being on standby all day, continually feeling tense, with nerves on edge and knowing that after every mission another portrait photograph was going to have to go up on the wall. Everyone looked haggard and strained. 'Concentrations in sector Dora-Dora!' came the repeated message and, despite the fatigue, despite the deep knot of dread and fear, they had to pull themselves up from their chairs, put away their game of skat and run to their Gustavs. 'No laxatives are needed,' jotted Knoke, 'to assist the sinking feeling Dora-Dora creates.'

Among those escorting the bombers to the target were once again the 4th Fighter Group, which, with drop tanks attached, had taken off from Debden and rendezvoused with the bombers over Sedan in eastern France. Bee Beeson was at Green 1, flying with the 334th FS as they approached the bomber box from the rear. One lone Fortress had fallen far back from the rest of the group and was now being attacked by two enemy fighters who were making passing sweeps at the stricken bomber. Beeson now led his section down, diving towards them, but before they reached them the Fortress slowly fell off to starboard and began to spiral down, while the two enemy fighters circled above it. Suddenly, they spotted the Thunderbolts heading towards them and, while one dived away, the other whipped into a turn, giving Beeson a 60-degree deflection shot that was hard even for someone of his marksmanship, and his bullets went wide. None the less, he had closed at around 500 m.p.h., which had given him enough speed to zoom up over the enemy and dive down once more. This time, the German dived for the deck, giving Beeson a chance to come in on his tail. He soon got behind him, but the German pilot was taking evasive action all the way down, so Beeson was finding it hard to get a clear shot. Then they both levelled out over a town and the German circled around it, then began following the course of a stream. At this point, Beeson's dogged pursuit paid off because he opened fire from 300 yards, closing to just 100. He saw his bullets hit and bits of the Focke-Wulf fall off. Beeson sped past, so did not see the enemy plane crash, but his wingman, following close behind, did. Climbing back up, they saw eight or nine parachutes floating down, probably from the Fortress they had tried in vain to rescue.

Don Gentile was also in action, leading his section down in a bounce on a gaggle of Focke-Wulfs. Picking out one, he opened fire at 400 yards, then again at 300, until at just 75 yards he saw his bullets hit home. Suddenly, oil was splattering his Thunderbolt and bits of aircraft were smacking into his own airframe. Gentile pulled up and watched the enemy fighter plunge down. 'Well,' he thought to himself, 'he definitely had it.'

The hammer blow taken by the bombers of the Fifteenth Air Force meant those of the Eighth were having a comparatively easy ride. The Liberators of the 2nd Division were now reaching their target. As Wright's crew arrived at the Initial Point, Buckey called out, 'Bomb bay doors coming open.' Robinson was now asked to switch on the K-20 camera. This was no casual request, because to do so he had to get a walk-around oxygen bottle, plug it on to his mask, disconnect his throat mike and headset and then his electric heated suit. He still had his flak armour on, so waddled over to the camera hatch and turned on the K-20, then returned and did the whole procedure again in reverse. 'Trying to get around in the ship while wearing flight gear,' he noted, 'was like a teddy bear in a bottle with lead weight.'

They were now approaching the target, a large airfield, with flak blasting all around them. Tyler and Robinson were throwing out Window as quickly as they could in an effort to confuse the gun-laying radar. The bomber was rocking, jolting and jerking, while outside white and black puffs dotted the sky as anti-aircraft shells exploded all around. Despite oxygen masks, the stench of cordite was choking. Outside, down below, the airfield appeared to be full of aircraft, all lined up in rows.

'For God sakes,' called out Wright, 'get those damned bomb bay doors closed.'

'Bombs away,' Lieutenant Wittman called out almost immediately. Robinson watched the bombs falling and saw rows of explosions all along the lines of parked aircraft. 'Bull's eye. Every bomb,' he called out. Bombs from the Fortresses also appeared to be hitting their mark.

Up ahead, no more than 20 yards in front, was Jimmy Stewart's plane, and suddenly it was hit by a direct burst of flak by the flight deck, behind the nose wheel. Wright moved up, underneath, and, sure enough, there was a large hole. A package fell out – a parachute pack – and hit one of their propellers then disappeared.

'He's staying there,' called out Wright. 'The ship hasn't lost any speed.' He tried contacting them on the radio but there was no answer; they were, however, supposed to be on radio silence.

Robinson now saw enemy planes swooping towards them.

'Fighters! Me109s. Ten o'clock!' he called out. 'Enemy fighters coming in!' He began counting over the intercom but then stopped. No one wanted to hear that more than sixteen were heading towards them. The first *Schwarm* took out two B-24s, which began flaming and falling. There were no parachutes. A B-17 was also falling; Robinson saw it hit the ground. Wright kept them tight in the formation; they all stayed close, just as Stewart liked it. Robinson and the other gunners hammered on until eventually the enemy planes melted away, only to be replaced by more flak. More Window was thrown out, although Robinson was increasingly convinced it was little more than a magnet and achieved quite the opposite of its intended goal.

The three squadrons of II/JG11 had joined up at 15,000 feet over Lüneburg Heath in northern Germany and had then climbed to 30,000. Heinz Knoke glanced down at his dials. Supercharger running smoothly. Revs, boost, oil and radiator temperatures all as they should be. Compass bearing, 360 degrees.

'On your left,' a ground controller crackled in Knoke's headset. 'Watch for heavy babies to your left.'

Knoke could see nothing. He felt tense and on edge. Carefully he scanned the skies looking for vapour trails, then suddenly there they were – at least 6,000 feet below and to the south heading eastwards.

'I see them,' said Major Specht, the *Gruppe* commander.

'Victor, victor,' came the acknowledgement from the control room at Division.

Knoke gazed at the bombers. It was hard to tell how many there were, but he guessed as many as six hundred, or even eight hundred with fighter escorts. A vast armada at any rate.

Fear departed as adrenalin surged through him. Specht dipped a wing and began his dive, with Knoke and the rest of the *Gruppe* following. As he dived, Knoke checked his guns and the sights. Both hands now grasped the moulded Bakelite grip on his control column. Finger and thumb on the twin cannon and machine-gun triggers. They were almost upon the bombers, but a glance behind showed him the Thunderbolts were coming down after them in turn and, as he was well aware, the American fighters could out-dive them.

Now they levelled out and swept through the lead bomber formation in a frontal attack. He pressed his gun buttons and felt the Messerschmitt judder as cannon shells and machine-gun bullets spat from his plane and punched fat holes across the wing of a Fortress. He cursed – he'd been aiming for the cockpit. Pulling back on the stick, he climbed up out of the fray, his *Staffel* following, and suddenly the Thunderbolts were upon them and they were swirling and turning, and Knoke was desperately trying to get himself into a firing position, but each time was forced to break because two, four, six, even ten Thunderbolts were bearing down on him. Fighters seemed to be everywhere in a massed melee, but the Messerschmitts were badly outnumbered.

Some P-38 Lightnings joined in too and Knoke had one in his sights. He fired as tracers hurtled over his canopy. Ducking instinctively, he looked up to see his hits on the Lightning. 'Good shooting!' he told himself, then pulled up in a steep corkscrew climb to grab a brief moment's breathing space. His friend Wenneckers pulled alongside and gestured towards four Lightnings below them. A dip of the left wingtip and then they were both diving down on them, the P-38s glistening in the sunlight. Knoke opened fire but was travelling too fast and overshot, only to discover a Lightning now on his tail in turn. He pushed the stick forward and over to his left and made a spiral dive to safety. His Messerschmitt screamed as he rapidly lost thousands of feet and he could feel the entire aircraft juddering and his ears popped with the rapid shift in air pressure. Rivets sprang free from the airframe and now he was throttling back and slowly but surely levelling out once more. He felt his chin forced into his chest and his vision black out. Then it cleared as a burning Lightning passed him, heading straight for the deck. Behind was Wenneckers.

'Congratulations,' said Knoke over the radio as his friend pulled up alongside.

'The bastard was after your hide,' Wenneckers replied.

They now headed for home where, much to Knoke's relief, they saw the others also coming in to land. 'This is one day we all come back,' he noted.

Meanwhile, Larry Goldstein and crew were having a fairly easy run. It was amazing how a target could prove to be a mission from hell on one occasion yet be a comparative piece of cake another time. The clear weather made a huge difference, as Hugh McGinty had discovered the previous day, and when the fighters turned up on cue, life was a lot easier on board the bombers. Goldstein and the crew of *Worry Wart* reached Regensburg without too much trouble, and dropped their bombs with the bombardier, Lieutenant Keith – whose last mission this was – able to see the target clearly and bomb accurately as a result. They all felt they had done a good job – in sharp contrast to the last mission. The flak grew progressively heavier and Goldstein 'sweated it out a bit' but once more they emerged unscathed.

Soon after, crews began landing back down at bases all over East Anglia and the English Midlands. And once again Wright's crew was one of them, making it back to Tibenham in one piece. The lead ship with Jimmy Stewart on board landed, but then broke in two at the nose-wheel compartment at the end of the runway; Wright, following in behind, had to take evasive action to avoid a collision. As soon as they came to a halt, Robinson leaped down from the waist window and ran to the broken plane. 'The tail of the ship was sticking up in the air and the nose was sticking up in the front,' he wrote. 'Just in front of the wing at the flight deck the airplane had cracked open like an egg.'

Jimmy Stewart stood by the edge of the left wing looking unperturbed. 'Sergeant,' he said as Robinson approached him, 'somebody sure could get hurt in one of those damned things.' Not a man on board had been seriously hurt – a miraculous escape.

Before heading to the debrief, Robinson and the rest of the Wright crew checked over their own ship as others came in to land on the secondary runways. 'There were flak holes everywhere you looked,' he noted. 'I didn't try to count them for I really didn't care any more. It looked like an axe maniac had been chopping it.' As he waited for the truck to pick them up, he was thankful to have completed his twelfth mission, then realized he wasn't even halfway through his tour.

On the other hand, Larry Goldstein was now within touching distance of completing his. Hugely relieved to get back to Knettishall in one piece, he was none the less utterly exhausted. He now had just two missions left, although freedom still seemed a long way off. 'These past few missions have been long, deep penetrations into the heart of Germany,' he mused in his diary that evening.

'Certainly could use a day off. As we say here, "23 Missions and no rest home yet!"'

Operation ARGUMENT was not finished yet, however, as that night RAF Bomber Command sent out 594 aircraft to Augsburg, for the first time in almost two years. The previous occasion had seen twelve new Lancasters set out on a low-level daylight operation that had been decimated; just five had made it home from the Augsburg raid of April 1942.

Once again, Ken Handley and his crew were on the list and took off at just after 9 p.m. on what was a refreshingly clear evening. However, no sooner had they got airborne than their intercom began acting up. The noise of the four engines was immense and clear communications between the crew absolutely essential. Flying Sergeant Max Pointon, the wireless operator, did his best to rectify the situation but was unable to get it to work and so, after dropping their bombs in the sea, they had no choice but to return to base. On landing, they discovered an oil leak in the cooler on the inner starboard, which could have caused all sorts of problems had they continued. 'Perhaps it was just as well we didn't go,' noted Handley. 'Better to play safe for the benefit of all concerned.'

Handley and his crew might have never reached Augsburg, but most of the force did, once again split into two separate streams. However ill-fated the last raid had been, this operation on what was to prove the last night of ARGUMENT was an outstanding success. The sky was clear, the markings of the Pathfinders accurate, the exhausted night-fighters few and the flak light. The heart of the old town was utterly ruined. A staggering 2,920 buildings were destroyed, another 5,000 badly damaged and as many as 90,000 people bombed out. There were 246 large and medium-sized fires and over 800 smaller ones. Some 760 people were killed and 2,500 injured. The Messerschmitt component factory was severely damaged, as were a number of buildings belonging to the MAN diesel plant. German news described this attack on the once beautiful medieval town as the latest example of 'terror' bombing.

Postscript

On Saturday, 26 February, the weather closed in once more and stayed that way for the rest of the month. Operation ARGUMENT was over. That this mighty week of aerial battle had ever had an official operational name would very soon be forgotten. It would come to be known simply as 'Big Week'. The week's effort prompted yet more excitement in the press on both sides of the Atlantic. *Stars & Stripes* pointed out that the Eighth Air Force alone had dropped more bombs in six days than it had over the course of its first year of operations. 'Since Jan. 1,' claimed an Eighth Air Force spokesman, 'strategic bombing of Germany by British and American forces has reduced the German two-engine fighter production by 80 per cent, single-engine fighter production by 60 per cent, and in addition, 25 per cent of bomber production has been destroyed. We believe we have fighter production down to the point where the Nazis can't keep up with the losses,' the spokesman continued. 'We can't help but feel that Germany has lost her last hope of maintaining a successful defense.'

On this last point, the spokesperson was quite right,

although he was wrong about the detail, because it was not so much the damage to the aircraft factories that really set the Luftwaffe back but more the catastrophic losses to their existing fighter defence. None the less, the damage caused on the ground through the week's bombing had been considerable. In all, some 70 per cent of the aircraft factory buildings targeted were destroyed. In Leipzig and the Messerschmitt works in southern Germany, around seven hundred Me109s had to be written off. Feldmarschall Erhard Milch's own survey showed that all night-fighter production of new types equipped with the latest Lichtenstein SN2 radar had been completely wiped out. Production of Ju88s was also halved by the attacks. Milch reported that production for March could be expected to be only 30–40 per cent of February's figures. The damage caused at Augsburg, Regensburg and Prüfening set back the entry of the Me262 jet, for which Galland and others had had such high hopes. Göring's response to this crisis was to head off on leave for three weeks – which actually, considering how useless he had been in recent months, was probably just as well.

And there was no denying the scale of the operation or that it had severely stretched the German defences. In total, some 3,300 bombers from the Eighth, over 500 from the Fifteenth Air Force and some 2,750 from Bomber Command had attacked the main German aircraft industry targets outlined in POINTBLANK. Together, they had dropped some 22,000 tons – 4,000 tons more than had been dropped on London by the Luftwaffe during the entire eight-month Blitz. The Americans lost 266 bombers in all, amounting to 2,600 aircrew, while the RAF lost 157 bombers and just over 1,000 aircrew killed, wounded or taken prisoner – a lot, undeniably, but still a small number compared with losses on the ground in Italy already that year and even better when considering that Spaatz and Anderson had been prepared to lose up to 200 bombers per day. Bomber Command's losses were 6.6 per cent and the Americans' 6 per cent, which rather put paid to Harris's arguments that massed bombing by night was the only way to go. The Americans had proved, conclusively, the value of bombing by day, but, more importantly, had demonstrated the ascendancy of the American fighter, and in this clash of arms the real weight of the victory should be judged. During Big Week, the Americans lost just 28 fighters, the Germans lost over 500: a ratio of 18:1.

The press departments of the USAAF and of both the Eighth and Fifteenth Air Forces did over-egg the damage caused to German industry, and historians ever since have not tired of pointing out that the Luftwaffe's aircraft production recovered soon enough. Many of the machine tools were salvaged and made to work again. In March, German factories would still produce an impressive 2,672 planes, and by July that had risen to a staggering 4,219. However, the gap between actual and planned production was still wide: there was a discrepancy of 1,103 aircraft in February, of almost 800 in April and still over 1,000 by June. The shortfall in the all-important production of Me109s and FW190s was 38.5 per cent in February. Big Week prompted yet another urgent reorganization of Luftwaffe production. Dispersal continued, often to new factories that had been built at vast cost and resources into the sides of mountains, while actual control was handed over from Milch to the Reich Armaments Minister, Albert Speer. Dispersal also required more manpower and a greater strain on the already bursting-at-the-seams Reichsbahn, the German railway network; it was a colossal inconvenience to the Germans at a time when they were also increasingly under pressure in all departments of their war effort.

The most marked impact of Big Week was unquestionably, however, the Luftwaffe's loss of aircraft and particularly pilots. The German Air Force had been struggling before Big Week, but the intensity of the air fighting had rammed a number of nails into its coffin. The loss of Heinz Knoke's wingman over Hamelin was symbolic of the terrible decline in which its fighter pilots found themselves. New pilots were lambs to the slaughter, arriving at their front-line squadrons with, on average, around 110 hours and often only 10–15 hours on front-line aircraft. That was simply nothing like enough before being flung into battle against a vastly superior enemy. Many never even made it that far; the number of accidents in training was extraordinarily high. On the other hand, the attrition on the old hands also took its toll. Somehow, Heinz Knoke seemed to get up again every time he was knocked down, but few had his apparent ability to defy death. In February 1944, total Luftwaffe losses of all types were 2,605 aircraft, of which 1,277 were to enemy action and, incredibly, 1,328 were to accidents and other causes. About 80 per cent of those were in the west. Actual – as opposed to on paper – monthly strength for February was, on average, 1,767, of which 62.7 per cent were lost and damaged. Such losses were utterly unsustainable and, inevitably, the numbers of experienced pilots were to be further chipped away while the number of new pilots, with ever decreasing amounts of training, would grow. In 1941 and 1942, German fighter pilots like Günther Rall and Bibi Hartmann had amassed huge personal scores on the Eastern Front because they were attacking inexperienced pilots of lesser skill who were flying inferior aircraft. By the end of Big Week, American pilots with greater skill and experience, flying superior aircraft, were now starting to slaughter increasing numbers of Luftwaffe pilots. How the tide had turned.

In early March, the Eighth Air Force turned on Berlin, with the 4th Fighter Group, led by Lieutenant-Colonel Don Blakeslee, among the hundred or so Mustangs escorting the bombers. Important aircraft component works were sited in and around the city and the psychological effect of sending fighter planes and bombers all the way to the capital of the Third Reich and back in broad daylight was significant. The raids also aimed to draw the German fighters up in a desperate act of defiance; from now on, bomber raids were no longer plotted to avoid enemy fighters but in the hope of running into them. The first two raids, on 3 and 4 March, were blighted by weather and were failures, but the next two, on 6 and 8 March, were more successful. The Luftwaffe managed only 200 fighters against 801 American fighters on the 6th and lost 66 aircraft and 34 pilots killed. American losses were heavy too – 69 bombers and 11 fighters. On the 8th, only 37 US bombers and 18 of the 861 escorting fighters were lost, while the Luftwaffe suffered 87 destroyed in the air and on the ground.

The weather then closed in once again, but whenever the Americans did strike, they did so with increasing numbers of fighter escorts and also rising numbers of Mustangs, as more and more fighter groups were being converted from Thunderbolts to this powerful new aircraft. An argument can be made that, in terms of decisive impact, the P-51 Mustang was the most important aircraft ever built. For its range, manoeuvrability and all-round performance, it must surely rank as the finest fighter aircraft of the entire war – and in a conflict that has been unrivalled in terms of the importance and scale of air power. The P-51B was excellent, but the next generation, the P-51D, arriving later that spring, was even better, with its bubble canopy, superb all-round vision and six.50-calibre machine guns.

During the crisis in the autumn of 1943, it had become increasingly obvious that fighters held the key to the Allies winning air superiority over western Europe before D-Day – fighters superior to those of the enemy, in larger numbers and with longer range, flown by pilots of greater skill and more experience, with superior tactics than their opponents. Although the Mustang first flew in December 1943, not until Big Week did those six categories of superiority so manifestly prove themselves. 'In numbers as well as in technical performance,' wrote General Beppo Schmid after Big Week, 'the daytime fighter units assigned to German air defence activity are inferior to the American fighter aircraft forces.' It was clear, he added, they were now fighting a hopeless battle they could not hope to win.

Over the weeks and months that followed, the German daylight fighter force continued to be worn down. Increasingly, they did not even bother to rise up to meet the enemy formations. When they did, they were hammered. On 16 March, for example, the 4th FG slaughtered the Me110s of ZG 76 – Zerstörergeschwader, or heavy destroyer wing, 76 – shooting down 21 of its 43 aircraft over Arnsberg. The

American fighter pilots also increasingly started shooting up anything that moved on the ground, as well as parked aircraft, in part to grind down the Luftwaffe even more but also to remind any German civilian who saw them of their utter superiority and the increasing weakness of the home defence. By 31 May 1944, just a week before D-Day, the combined actual strength of the Luftwaffe's day- and night-fighter force was 2,686. Against them were 16,956 Allied bombers and 25,416 fighters. The Luftwaffe would limp on, the Me262 would eventually appear over the skies and aerial battles would continue until the war's end, but air superiority had been emphatically gained.

In April, the formal transfer of control of the strategic air forces to General Eisenhower, the Supreme Allied Commander for the planned invasion, took place. The Ninth Air Force had already begun supporting specific pre-invasion tasks by the end of March, although Eisenhower did not send Spaatz a formal directive until 17 April, and even then his priority remained the 'destruction of German air combat strength'.

For Harris and Bomber Command, the so-called 'Battle of Berlin' finally ended on 30/31 March, not with an attack on the German capital, but with a disastrous raid on Nuremberg in which ninety-five bombers were lost. 'Wholesale slaughter,' noted Rusty Waughman in his diary. He reckoned he had seen at least sixteen bombers go down as the Lancasters and Halifaxes were mauled by German night-fighters. 'All of us were pretty tired and shaken!' he noted, although adding with phlegmatic understatement, 'Nevertheless, we must press on regardless!!!' It was Waughman's twelfth completed mission. Bill

Byers had also been on that trip, but had been fortunate enough to develop engine failure early on and so returned home. Ken Handley and crew had, however, endured the entire mission and, despite dodging rockets, fighter stalks and flak, had somehow made it back in one piece. 'Awe-inspiring at times,' he wrote in his diary, 'and most certainly frightening and tense.' Nuremberg would prove to be the costliest mission of the entire war for Bomber Command.

Nuremberg confirmed what was already crystal clear: that Harris's vision of massed bombing was not going to bring about the sudden and wholesale collapse of the Third Reich. A total of 1,047 bombers had been lost since the start of the battle on 18 November and, although his command had more bombers now than he had had then, such losses were unacceptable, particularly since they were not proving as decisive as he had hoped. Rescue was at hand, however, because now Bomber Command could get involved in the preparations for OVERLORD, and specifically the 'Transportation Plan'.

While Leigh-Mallory's Ninth and 2nd Tactical Air Forces would carry out an interdiction policy, hitting bridges and railway lines all across France and western Europe, the strategic air forces were to target larger railway centres, marshalling yards and depots. It was estimated that the Germans used as much as two-thirds of western Europe's railway capacity entirely for military matters; without it and the Reichsbahn the Nazi war effort would largely grind to a halt. Inevitably, Harris was deeply opposed to playing lackey to someone else's plan or to any diversion from his main stated aim of pulverizing German cities; however, his command was well equipped to support the Transportation Plan, not least because Bomber Command was becoming increasingly accurate. Allied air power was rapidly developing in all areas. Bomber Command had adopted area bombing in the first place because it was unable to attack with precision by night; the Americans had adopted daytime bombing to be more 'precise', but now, thanks to improved navigational aids, experience and tactics, the night bombers of Bomber Command were proving more accurate than those operating by day. Churchill also had grave concerns about the Transportation Plan, fearing it would cause huge loss of life of the very people they were about to try to liberate, but in the end Eisenhower held sway and Bomber Command proved more than up to the task, attacking their targets with accuracy, success and surprisingly little loss of life.

Meanwhile, Spaatz also implemented a plan to target key oil centres fuelling the Reich, from its one actual oil-field at Ploesti in Romania to the various synthetic-fuel plants dotted around Germany. By the end of May, this was really hurting the Luftwaffe. Training of new crews was cut even more, to save fuel and to allow enough fighter pilots to be processed to fly the numbers of aircraft being produced. By the end of May, training time had been cut to just 110–20 hours. Most were swiftly slaughtered.

If Big Week is taken as one single battle, then it was the largest of the war, yet today it is largely forgotten, as is the importance of the epic clashes that took place in the air during the autumn of 1943 and early months of 1944. For both sides, this was a pivotal moment in the air war and that third week of February was the point at which the Allied plans for D-Day were saved. By April, the skies over western Europe were largely clear and the Allies had the all-important air superiority they so needed. It deserves to be better known and to be woven more clearly into the D-Day narrative, rather than consigned to the general history of the war in the air, which in turn is so often viewed in isolation rather than in its more important wider context.

Many of those who flew in Big Week also took part in clashes that followed, over Berlin and beyond. Larry Goldstein did manage to make it to twenty-five completed missions, even though his last two were to Berlin, just about the worst target he could have been given. 'At last,' he wrote in his diary on the evening of Saturday, 4 March 1944, 'I have walked away from the plane on my 25th mission unscathed. <u>Thank God</u>!' He returned home to New York, got married and had children. He now lives in a retirement community to the north of Washington DC.

Jimmy Stewart continued flying. On 30 March, he was posted to the 453rd BG to become its operations officer, but he continued to fly until 1 July when he was promoted to lieutenant-colonel and became executive officer to Brigadier-General Ed Timberlake, commander of the 2nd Bomb Wing; he flew twenty official missions and a number more unofficially. Stewart was awarded two Distinguished Flying Crosses – the first for his leadership on 20 February 1944; he also received the Croix de Guerre and Air Medal with three Oak Leaf clusters. By the end of the war he was a full colonel and briefly commanded the 2nd Combat Wing. After the war, he returned to Hollywood and was Oscar-nominated for his career-defining performance in *It's a Wonderful Life*. Despite his return to the movies, he remained in the Air Force Reserve, served in Vietnam and rose to the rank of brigadier-general. He died in 1997, aged eighty-nine, having become one of the greatest film stars of the twentieth century and having never lost touch with his comrades from the war years – a period about which he rarely spoke, but of which he was justifiably proud.

Robbie Robinson survived his tour, making it home to his beloved wife, and together they raised children and lived a long, contented life. He died in 2011, aged eighty-nine.

Bill Lawley recovered from his wounds and returned to operational flying in May 1944. He was reassigned to the USA in June that year and was awarded his Medal of Honor in August. Remaining in the air force, he served for thirty years before retiring in 1972. He died in 1999. His Medal of Honor, flight jacket and dog-tags are all on display at the wonderful Mighty Eighth Museum outside Savannah, Georgia.

Bob Hughes of the 100th BG finished his tour on the last day of Big Week and headed back to the USA. Jim Keeffe was shot down over Berlin but bailed out, survived, and spent the rest of the war as a POW. He returned to the States after the war and eventually wrote his memoirs at the urging of his children.

Hugh McGinty finished his tour – extended for all bomber crews of the Eighth to thirty – at the end of May 1944 and eventually got back to the USA in July. He married, had children and many years later, in 1987, returned to Europe with his wife, Lois, to spend three weeks touring the German cities he had bombed all those years before. After going to Augsburg, Berlin, Frankfurt, Bremen and elsewhere, they went to England, intending to visit his old base at Kimbolton. They paused to see the beautiful American cemetery at Madingley, just outside Cambridge, and then drove on towards Kimbolton. At Bedford, however, they stopped. 'I was suddenly overcome by grief,' he wrote, 'and could go no further.'

The two Sullivans, T. Michael and Sully, also survived the war. As with many others, their wartime experiences remain vividly real through the immediacy and honesty of their jottings, written in their diaries at the time in those makeshift bases in southern Italy.

Bill Byers survived his tour too, married his English girlfriend and returned to Canada, before moving to California. He always thought about his brother a lot. 'I wonder what kind of life I would've had if he'd been here,' he told me seventy years later. 'He was my only brother and we were so close, you know.'

Gordon Carter was eventually liberated at the end of the war and returned to France to marry his French fiancée. Ken Handley also completed his tour and made it through the war. Their memoirs and diaries are now in the Imperial War Museum; they both appear to have had long, peaceful lives after the fighting was over.

For the German fighter boys, fortunes were mixed. Adolf Galland, Hajo Herrmann, Heinz Knoke and Wim Johnen all survived. Galland returned to operational flying in March 1945 when he took command of Jagdverband 44 of Me262 jets. Having survived the war, he became close friends with a number of his former adversaries, both British and American. He helped the Americans after the war as they began interviewing former commanders about all aspects of the Germans' military effort, advised the Argentinian Air Force and later ran his own business. He died in 1996.

Hajo Herrmann was captured by the Russians at the end of the war, spent ten years in a Gulag and then, on his return to Germany, became a highly successful lawyer; during his career he defended Holocaust deniers David Irving and Fred Leuchter, as well as Otto Ernst Remer, the head of the new-Nazi Socialist Reich Party. He married a celebrated soprano, had two children and lived to the age of ninety-seven. I interviewed him several times and it was always an intimidating experience. He wore a trim, silver goatee beard and at the heart of his pale, classically Aryan eyes were dark pupils that seemed to bore right into me. He was not a man who suffered fools, but he did eventually thaw a little and it was clear that behind those piercing eyes lay a mind that remained as keen and sharp as ever.

How Heinz Knoke survived the war is anyone's guess. He was shot down yet again on 29 April and, although he bailed out once more, suffered bad concussion. Nazi Germany being what it was, he was swiftly returned to the front line, however, and took command of III/JG1, flying over the Normandy front in August 1944. Having pulled back following the end of the campaign there, he was wounded yet again near Prague when his car struck a partisan-laid mine. Still on crutches in March 1945, he took command of Jever air base. After the war he dabbled in right-wing politics, joining the Socialist Reich Party, and then, once it was deemed illegal, became a local leader of the Liberal Democratic Party. Remaining in the Jever area, he also worked for the Jever Pilsener Brauhaus. After retiring in 1972, he went to university and studied for a degree in literature and philosophy. He died in 1993, still comparatively young at seventy-three, but by anyone's reckoning he had had fifty more years of life than had ever seemed possible during his wartime flying career.

Wim Johnen also made it through the war. He studied engineering at Munich University and later went on to work with Professor Willi Messerschmitt before setting up his own construction business. He retired to Lake Constance and continued to fly into his seventies. He died in February 2002.

Of the American fighters, Gabby Gabreski went on to become the top-scoring American ace of the ETO. He was due to return home after amassing three hundred combat hours, but on 20 July 1944 he decided to fly one more mission and damaged his Thunderbolt after flying too low on a strafing run. Forced to crash-land, he was taken prisoner and spent the rest of the war in a POW camp. After the war, he remained in the air force and served in Korea, amassing 6.5 kills against MiGs. He finally retired in 1967 and died in 1992, having fathered nine children, two of whom also joined the air force.

Bob Johnson left the 56th FG in June 1944, by which time he had become a top-scoring ace with twenty-seven victories and reached the rank of major. After the war, he became chief test pilot for Republic Aviation as well as remaining in the Air Force Reserve, then later he became an insurance executive. He died in 1998.

Bud Anderson ended up flying 116 combat missions on two tours and finished the war a triple ace with 16.25 victories to his name. Remaining in the air force, he became a leading test pilot and also served at the Pentagon, as well as taking command of the 355th Tactical Fighter Wing flying F-105s in Vietnam. After retiring from the air force he worked for McDonnell Aircraft Corporation as the manager of the Flight Test Facility and continued to fly and attend air shows – and still does. He lives close to his childhood home in northern California.

Dick Turner ended up with twelve victories to his name and, after finishing his tour in late 1944, returned to the US but remained in the air force and later served in Korea, rising to the rank of lieutenant-colonel. He died in 1986, aged just sixty-six.

Don Blakeslee was finally grounded in September 1944 having flown an incredible five hundred operational sorties and accumulated more than a thousand combat hours. No other single American fighter pilot flew more in the war. He stayed in the air force after the war, finally retiring in 1965 as a full colonel. During the war alone he won two Distinguished Service Crosses, eight Distinguished Flying Crosses, two Silver Stars and eight Air Medals, as well as a British DFC and French Croix de Guerre with Palm Leaf. He also served in the Korean War and picked up a further Distinguished Flying Cross and four more Air Medals. He was certainly one of the most remarkable fighter leaders who ever lived. Settling down in Florida, he died in 2008, aged ninety, an old warrior to the end.

At the beginning of April 1944, Bee Beeson was brought down by ground fire while flying low and was taken prisoner. At the end of the war, he finally made it back to Debden and was then posted back to the USA. Although he tried to get reassigned to the Pacific, he was instead posted to Sarasota Field in Florida, where he met his future wife. Marrying in January 1946, he soon after began feeling ill and was diagnosed with a brain tumour. He died in

February 1947, still tragically young at just twenty-five years old. Despite his curtailed wartime career, he was highly decorated and one of the leading aces of the ETO with twenty-two victories. He was also unquestionably one of the finest marksmen of all the Eighth's fighter pilots.

After his extraordinary tussle with the Focke-Wulfs over Compiègne in January 1944, Don Gentile and his wingman, John Godfrey, became two of the most celebrated Mustang fighter aces in the Eighth. Their fame quickly grew, so that Churchill called them 'Damon and Pythias' after the legendary Greek heroes. By mid-April, Gentile had become the leading ace of the ETO, but then crashed his P-51 while performing stunts over Debden for some assembled press reporters, which was embarrassing both for him and for the entire 4th FG. Blakeslee grounded him and, with 350 combat hours in his logbook, he was posted home to help sell war bonds. He recorded his memoirs for war correspondent Ira Wolfert in a promotional booklet called *One-Man Air Force*. After the war, he also stayed in the air force as a tactical and gunnery instructor, but was killed when he crashed his T-33 Shooting Star trainer in late January 1951.

Of the many air bases that once dotted eastern England – both USAAF and RAF – most have long since been carved up and returned to farmland. The remnants, however, are not hard to find and many have small museums that keep their wartime heritage alive. Debden is now an army base, but Halesworth, where the 56th FG were based, is still clearly etched on to the landscape, even though many of the wartime buildings have gone. At Thorpe Abbotts, the giant airfield itself is now fields, but the control tower has been restored. To the south, on the far side, the once vast encampment has largely gone, but cracked concrete tracks remain and in among the trees it is still possible to see remains of old Nissen huts, steadily being reclaimed by nature.

After the war, Chaplain James Good Brown wrote a highly moving and personal account of his wartime experiences with the 381st BG, based on his wartime jottings. Ridgewell is like many old Eighth Air Force air bases, but I was given a tour of the place on a cold October day – not dissimilar to those that plagued the Eighth's efforts in the autumn of 1943 – by Paul Bingley, a local resident who works in the aviation industry but whose passion is the heritage of the 381st. He took us to the old cinema, now surrounded by thick brambles and nettles and home to a collection of dust-covered old farm vehicles. At the far end, through a doorway, were the remains of the room where Chaplain Brown camped out and gave solace to so many of those frightened young men expected to take to the skies to bomb Germany. A bit further on, following another track of broken concrete, we emerged into a clearing that had once been the air base's makeshift baseball ground – a bat had been found in a hedge some time later.

Although derelict and overgrown, it didn't need a huge leap of imagination to picture what it must have been like all those years ago in early 1944. Half-close the eyes and it was almost possible to see the mighty Fortresses lined up and to picture the aircrew and ground personnel hurrying past on their bicycles. What battles had taken place in the skies back then and what sacrifices had been made. As my daughter skipped on ahead and ran down part of the old main runway, I thought again about how lucky we are.

Glossary

AFHRA	United States Air Force Historical Research Agency
CBO	Combined Bomber Offensive
CO	commanding officer
ETO	European Theatre/Theater of Operations
FW	Focke-Wulf
GAF	German Air Force
GSWW	Militärgeschichtliches Forschungsamt: *Germany and the Second World War*
IP	Initial Point
IWM	Imperial War Museum
JG	*Jagdgeschwader* – fighter group
Ju	Junkers
KG	*Kampfgeschwader* – bomber group
Me	Messerschmitt
NJG	*Nachtjagdgeschwader* – night-fighter group
ops	operations
RAF	Royal Air Force
ramrod	fighter escort mission on a bomber raid
RT	radio telephone
TNA	The National Archives, London
USAAF	United States Army Air Forces

German Aircraft Production

1943	Actual	Planned
October	2,349	2,521
November	2,111	2,786
December	1,734	2,975
1944		
January	2,445	2,962
February	2,015	3,118
March	2,672	3,426
April	3,034	3,819

Source: *GSWW*, Vol. VII, Table I.I.10

German Day-fighter Losses in First Third of 1944

Month	Total Losses (%)	Lost/ Damaged (%)	Monthly Average Actual Aircraft Strength
January	30.3	52.4	1,590
February	33.8	62.7	1,767
March	56.4	81.4	1,714
April	43.0	81.9	1,700

Source: *GSWW*, Vol. VII, Table I.I.11

Luftwaffe Aircraft Losses in First Third of 1944

Month	Enemy Action	Accidents, etc.	Total
January	786	980	1,766
February	1,277	1,328	2,605
March	1,209	1,403	2,612
April	1,759	1,860	3,619

Source: *GSWW*, Vol. VII, Table I.I.12

Timeline

1943

OCTOBER

Sunday, 3
Bill and George Byers on ops for first time

Monday, 4
Bill and George Byers on ops for second time

Friday, 8
US Eighth AF operations against Bremen

Sunday, 10
US Eighth AF operations against Münster
313 bombers dispatched, 236 reach target
Bob Johnson shoots down two to become ace
Heinz Knoke in action

Thursday, 14 – Black Thursday
US Eighth AF operations against Schweinfurt
229 bombers over target against 300+ enemy fighters
28% loss, 60 bombers lost, 594 killed
Bob Hughes flying for 100th BG with 95th BG

Thursday, 21
Dick Turner and 354th FG sail for Britain

Friday, 22
George and Bill Byers on ops – to Kassel

NOVEMBER

Monday, 1
Dick Turner and 354th FG reach Liverpool

Wednesday, 3
Gabby Gabreski in action
Bob Johnson sees burning pilot from 4th FG rescued, then on

mission over
Wilhelmshaven
Hugh McGinty and crew leave
New York
Bill Byers flying – George Byers
killed

Friday, 5
US Eighth AF operations
against Gelsenkirchen
synthetic-fuel plant
Bob Hughes flying – loses radio
operator Joe Boyle

Tuesday, 9
Hugh McGinty and crew reach
Glasgow and posted to 379th
BG at Kimbolton

Saturday, 13
Dick Turner and 354th FG move
to Boxted, now equipped
with P-51s

Wednesday, 17
Heinz Knoke meets Göring

Thursday, 18
Heinz Knoke in action

Friday, 19
Heinz Knoke in action

Tuesday, 23
Heinz Knoke reflects on lost
comrades

Thursday, 25
Jimmy Stewart arrives in

England in B-24 Liberator
with 703rd BS of 445th BG

Friday, 26
US Eighth AF operations to
Bremen
Goldie Goldstein's first mission

Saturday, 27
Gabby Gabreski and Bob
Johnson in action

Monday, 29
Hugh McGinty's first
mission – Bremen
The British and Americans
devise Operation
ARGUMENT to counter the
Luftwaffe threat through a
round-the-clock bombing
offensive, but it is postponed
by bad weather

DECEMBER

Wednesday, 1
Don Blakeslee at Boxted to teach
354th FG
Dick Turner in action for first time

Thursday, 2
Jimmy Stewart ordered to face
press in London

Sunday, 5
Gabby Gabreski and Bob
Johnson in action
Dick Turner in action

Saturday, 11
US Eighth AF ops against Emden
Bob Johnson, Gabby Gabreski
   and the 56th FG in big action

Sunday, 12
Bob Johnson in action over Berlin

Monday, 13
Jimmy Stewart on ops for first
   time – against Kiel

Friday, 24
Fighter relay system introduced
   for first time
Jimmy Stewart on ops
   against installations around
   Calais

Thursday, 30
Hugh McGinty flies 5th
   mission – Ludwigshafen

1944

JANUARY

Saturday, 1
A message to subordinates
   by USAAF C-in-C Hap
   Arnold calls for the
   destruction of the German
   Luftwaffe before Allied
   landings can begin
Don Blakeslee takes command
   of the 4th Fighter Group and
   leads them in action

Tuesday, 4
Goldie Goldstein on mission to
   Münster
Gabby Gabreski and Bob
   Johnson in action
Heinz Knoke shot down

Thursday, 6
Bob Johnson in action – tussles
   with Luftwaffe ace

Friday, 7
US Eighth AF operations to
   Ludwigshafen
First fighter relay system into
   Germany
Jimmy Stewart on ops against
   Ludwigshafen
Gabby Gabreski and Bob
   Johnson in action

Tuesday, 11
Jim Howard's big action
Gabby Gabreski in action
Dick Turner in action
Hugh McGinty's 6th Mission –
   Halberstadt Focke-Wulf factory
Bill Lawley on
   mission – Brunswick

Saturday, 15
Dick Turner promoted to
   captain and becomes

squadron commander of
356th FS

Thursday, 20
Bob Johnson gets 12th kill

Friday, 21
Baby Blitz begins

Thursday, 27
Wilhelm Johnen in action in
terrible weather

Saturday, 29
Hugh McGinty on eighth
mission – Frankfurt – loses
navigator

Sunday, 30
Bob Johnson gets 13th kill over
Bremen
Heinz Knoke back from hospital
and in action
Dick Turner gets fourth victory

FEBRUARY

Tuesday, 8
Bud Anderson's first mission

Thursday, 10
Heinz Knoke in action

Friday, 11
Dick Turner becomes an ace

Monday, 14
ARGUMENT is detailed
further
Big action for Don Gentile

Saturday, 19
First night-time ARGUMENT
operations
Better weather finally arrives
allowing the RAF to send up
its first 823-strong heavy
bomber force. The target is
Leipzig and 78 bombers are
lost.

Sunday, 20
Gordon Carter bails out
First daytime ARGUMENT
operations
US bombers and fighters strike
Germany – over
1,000 bombers and
660 fighters
12 industrial locations across
Germany are hit
21 US aircraft lost
Three Medals of Honor awarded
Sully Sullivan flying from Italy
with Fifteenth AF to
Regensburg but mission
scrubbed
Bob Johnson and Gabby
Gabreski flying over Leipzig
Heinz Knoke flying
Jimmy Stewart flying as deputy
leader of Combat Wing
against Gotha – 13 of
25 445th BG planes lost
Hugh McGinty – Mission 11
Bill Lawley mission – wins
Medal of Honor

Bud Anderson in action
Robbie Robinson on furlough
RAF Bomber Command also
   strike that night, with
   598 bombers attacking
   Stuttgart, and 156 aircraft on
   diversionary operations

Monday, 21
USAAF sends out 762 bombers
   with fighter escorts. The
   target is the Luftwaffe
   production centre at
   Brunswick
Sully Sullivan's mission
   scrubbed again
Heinz Knoke flying
James Keeffe first mission
Don Blakeslee leading the 4th FG

Tuesday, 22
Bad weather, but raids continue,
   although Nijmegen
   accidentally bombed and a
   number lost to accidents
Bombers from Ninth Air Force
   in Italy start attacks
Sully Sullivan on ops to
   Regensburg – two of his crew
   wounded
Hugh McGinty – Mission
   12 – Halberstadt
Heinz Knoke in action
Gabby Gabreski in action
Robbie Robinson flying
Don Blakeslee leading the
   4th FG

Wednesday, 23
Operations suspended due to
   poor weather

Thursday, 24
266 bombers of US Eighth Air
   Force hit Schweinfurt, Posen
   and Rostock
900 bombers then sent to attack
   a number of aircraft
   production centres, including
   Schweinfurt again
Bob Hughes in action
Hugh McGinty – Mission 13
Robbie Robinson flying
James Keeffe second
   mission
Don Gentile in action
734 bombers of RAF Bomber
   Command also attack
   Schweinfurt – 33
   are lost

Friday, 25
900 bombers of USAAF hit
   Regensburg, Augsburg and
   Forth
Bomber Command hits
   Augsburg with 594
   bombers.
Heinz Knoke in action – big
   action for him
Dick Turner in action
Jimmy Stewart as co-pilot and
   group commander on Robbie
   Robinson's crew

Notes

Prologue

8   'Bob, we have you . . .': Robert S. Johnson, AFHRA, p. 77
8   'To hell with . . .': ibid, p. 135
9   'It was a great and auspicious . . .': Johnson, *Thunderbolt!*, p. 147

Chapter 1   For the Love of Flying

19   'Remember, my friend . . .': cited in Francis Gabreski, *Gabby: A Fighter Pilot's Life*, p. 74
23   'He was a great believer . . .': James Goodson, *Tumult in the Clouds*, p. 63
23   'Tighten up! . . .': ibid, p. 64
24   'That evening, Blakeslee . . .': ibid, p. 65
24   'I told you the Jug . . .': ibid, p. 71
25   'We love fighting . . .': cited in Grover C. Hall Jr., *1,000 Destroyed*, p. 47
26   'In the RAF . . .': Hall, p. 55
27   'I can't remember . . .': Don Gentile, *One-Man Air Force*, as told to Ira Wolfert
27   'Your son bought . . .': ibid, p. 17
27   'Okay. You've learned a lesson . . .': ibid

28	'Flying an airplane . . .': ibid, p. 22
28	'Twenty-twenty is perfect . . .': ibid, p. 27
28–9	'All right, you're red hot . . .': ibid, p. 30

Chapter 2　Flying for the Reich

36	'Better wait until . . .': cited in Heinz Knoke, *I Flew for the Führer*, p. 36
40	'Attention all squadrons!': ibid, p. 119
41	'This is one time . . .': ibid, p. 120
42	'The Yanks do not leave . . .': ibid, p. 123
42	'It is all we can do . . .': ibid
43–4	'I am powerless . . .': ibid, p. 124

Chapter 3　Black Thursday

50	'. . . his bombers had destroyed . . .': cited in *GSWW*, Vol. VII, p. 66
52	'The Hundredth go off ops?': cited in Harry Crosby, *A Wing and a Prayer*, p. 171
53	'wonderful English dark bread.': Robert Hughes, *Schweinfurt 14 Oct 43*, Group History, www.100thbg.com
55	'Now we thought we knew . . .': cited in Robert Hughes: *Crew Information*, www.100thbg.com
56	'This air operation today . . .': cited in Martin W. Bowman, *On the Highways of the Skies*, p. 89
57–8	'We all knew . . .': J. Kemp McLaughlin, *The Mighty Eighth in WWII*, p. 97
58	'Gentlemen, may I have your . . .': Colonel Budd Peaslee, cited in Bowman, p. 90
60	'One quick glance . . .': McLaughlin, p. 102
61	'I did not relish . . .': ibid, p. 103
62	'A large formation approaching . . .': Bowman, p. 96
63	'My God, Mac . . .': ibid, p. 105
64	'Captain, I think we've had it.': ibid
65	'Okay, O'Grady . . .': ibid, p. 106
65	'Bombs away.': ibid, p. 107
65	'We've flown this far . . .': cited in Bowman, p. 101
66	'Move, Bob!': Hughes: *Schweinfurt*, www.100thbg.com
66	'Dick, I do not have . . .': ibid
67	'An hour and thirty-eight . . .': McLaughlin, p. 108

68   'From there on . . .': ibid
69   'A long, tough . . .': cited in Bowman, p. 105

Chapter 4   America's Bomber Men
71   'represent disaster': cited in James Parton, *Air Force Spoken Here*, p. 316
71   'We must show the enemy . . .': ibid
73   'Therefore it took all the hope . . .': James Good Brown, *The Mighty Men of the 381st*, p. 214
73   'How did you fare . . .': ibid, p. 213
74   'You ought to come . . .': cited in Parton, p. 29
84   'high-class spy': cited in Richard G. Davis, *Carl A. Spaatz and the Air War in Europe*, p. 41
85   'The Germans can't bomb at night . . .': ibid, p. 52

Chapter 5   Learning the Hard Way
89   'Whether it was some kind of telepathy . . .': Bill Byers, author interview
91   'They were so much alike . . .': Dick Meredith, author interview
93   'It appeared to be a good raid.': TNA AIR 27/1852
98   'I mention this because . . .': cited in Richard Overy, *The Bombing War*, p. 259
103–4 'We are bombing Germany . . .': cited in Marshal of the Air Force Sir Arthur Harris, *Bomber Offensive*, p. 116
105   'Well, they are sowing the wind.': ibid, p. 52

Chapter 6   The Defence of the Reich
107   'A wave of terror . . .': Adolf Galland, *The First and the Last*, p. 166
112   'This model is a tremendous . . .': cited in Raymond F. Toliver and Trevor J. Constable, *Fighter General*, p. 218
113   'The Führer sees it . . .': cited in David Irving, *The Rise and Fall of the Luftwaffe*, p. 232
114   'We have lost the war!': cited in ibid, p. 230
115   'I want bombers . . .': cited in *GSWW*, Vol. VII, p. 281
115   'bomber replacement': Irving, p. 23
115   'Not one swine . . .': cited in *GSWW*, Vol. VII, p. 281
116   'Never before and never again . . .': Galland, p. 169

116   'We were met . . .': ibid, p. 170, and in *GSWW*, Vol. VII, p. 282

117   'Oberst Peltz . . .': Galland, p. 171

117   'I was mistaken.': ibid

118   'A few days later . . .': AFHRA 5-3180-924, p. 12

119   'I functioned as adviser . . .': ibid

120   'His court favourites . . .': ibid, p. 15

121   'The defensive fire-power . . .': ibid, p. 21

124   'dragging' and 'remained a mystery . . .': cited in Richard Suchenwirth, *Command and Leadership in the German Air Force*, p. 274

126   'The Reichsmarschall is on the line.': cited in Hajo Herrmann, *Eagle's Wings*, p. 167

127   'How near to being . . .': Herrmann, p. 176

127   'Seldom in the history . . .': ibid, p. 177

Chapter 7   The Nub of the Matter

134   Luftwaffe losses from Charles Webster and Noble Frankland, *The Strategic Air Offensive Against Germany*, Vol. IV, Appendix 49

137   'progressive destruction and dislocation . . .': ibid, p. 158

138   'The German fighter force . . .': ibid, Vol. II, p. 24

138–9   'It is emphasized . . .': ibid, p. 157

140   'If we do not now strain . . .': cited in ibid, Vol. II, p. 31

141   'we may find that either . . .': cited in ibid, p. 34

Chapter 8   In the Bleak Midwinter

145   'It was really heavy . . .': Robert S. Johnson, AFHRA, p. 78

146   'Go away! . . .': Johnson, *Thunderbolt!*, p. 149

147   'Two hundred yards back . . .': ibid

148   'We have not got far . . .': Harris Papers, Folder H77

148   'There had been 553 . . .': Figures from AFHRA, Appendix II 'GAF Operations, Claims and Losses'

149   'Major Falck was a genial . . .': Wilhelm Johnen, *Duel Under the Stars*, p. 12

149–50 'In the old days . . .': cited in ibid, p. 69

150   'vastly superior': ibid, p. 88

152   'Here over Berlin . . .': ibid, p. 104

152   'At 1.08 this heavy . . .': ibid, p. 105
152   'We all knew . . .': ibid
153   'There's a "war" on . . .': cited in James Holland, *Twenty-One*, p. 3
158   'Skipper, I think you'd better land . . .': Bill Byers, author interview

Chapter 9   Mustang

161   'Rumor or not . . .': Richard E. Turner, *Mustang Pilot*, p. 21
166   'The point which strikes me . . .': https://todayshistoryles-son.wordpress.com/tag/ronald-harker/
167   'did not pretend to know . . .': cited in Bill Newton Dunn, *Big Wing*, pp. 189–90
170   'Attached are Mr. Lovett's . . .': 'Case History of Fighter Plane Range Extension Program', Part I & II, AFHRA 202.2–11
172   'Overlord hangs directly . . .': TNA AIR 8/1108
172–3   'Is it not true . . .': ibid
174   'Acceleration of production . . .': ibid
175   'It is becoming increasingly . . .': ibid
175   'We intend to continue . . .': ibid
175–6   'send every possible . . .': cited in James Parton, *Air Force Spoken Here*, p. 316
179   'Some malicious tongues . . .': Hajo Herrmann, *Eagle's Wings*, p. 199
179   'I found him to be interested . . .': ibid
180   'an infernal nuisance . . .': cited in Heinz Knoke, *I Flew for the Führer*, p. 125
181   'Göring makes a most peculiar . . .': ibid
181   'The inescapable fact . . .': ibid
181   'We need more aircraft . . .': ibid, p. 126
184   'It is axiomatic . . .': cited in Parton, p. 322
185   'Went to town . . .' Diary, 17/10/1943, in T. Michael Sullivan, 'Life in the Service', www.2ndbombgroup.org
185–6   'Ate a rotten supper . . .': ibid, 23/10/1943
186   'Impossible to see . . .': ibid, 24/10/1943
186   'Raid called off . . .': ibid, 7/11/1943
187   'It cut me deeply . . .': ibid
187   'I'm out of my teens . . .': ibid, 14/11/1943

496 NOTES

Chapter 10 New Arrivals

189 'exceptional': reports cited in papers of Squadron Leader G. H. F. Carter, DSO, IWM 96/41/1
190 'mild sort of . . .': ibid
191 'We were blinded . . .': ibid
192 'Navigator bailing out!': ibid
193 'Bomb doors open': ibid
194 'I think if I had stopped . . .': Bill Byers, author interview
196 'There was a shrill organ . . .': Hajo Herrmann, *Eagle's Wings*, p. 203
196–7 'It was cold and damp . . .': ibid, pp. 204–5
197 'I gave thanks to God.': ibid, p. 205
198 'I was impressed . . .': cited in Martin Bowman, *B-17 Combat Missions*, p. 60
198 'I must admit . . .': Larry Goldstein interview, National Museum of the Mighty Eighth Air Force
200 'I'm not interested . . .': ibid
200 'A loner, never seemed . . .': Larry Goldstein Diary
201 'Where are these guys?': Goldstein interview
202 'You're my third . . .': cited in Bowman, p . 62
202 'It was all very strange . . .': Goldstein Diary, 26/11/1943
202–3 'The two most welcome . . .': ibid
203 'I will have to work out . . .': ibid
203 'Lucky couldn't believe . . .': Hugh McGinty, *My Life, Book One: The War Years*, p. 5
204 'The ten-man crew . . .': ibid, p. 10
204 'I figured it would . . .': ibid, p. 13
209 'You're like a bird up there . . .': cited in Starr Smith, *Jimmy Stewart: Bomber Pilot*, p. 28
209 'It may sound corny . . .': ibid, p. 29
210 'I feel sure that God . . .': ibid, p. 72

Chapter 11 Fighter Boys

216 'I liked the idea of . . .': William R. Lawley interview, AFHRA, p. 3
218 'So this is going to be home.': John Harold Robinson, *A Reason To Live*, p. 159
222 'The comrades stare . . .': Heinz Knoke, *I Flew for the Führer*, p. 129

222   'He cannot get over . . .': ibid
223   'We regard life . . .': ibid, p. 130
223   'Fellows, do you not think . . .': ibid
223   'It makes me sick . . .': ibid
224   'He was all business . . .': Richard Turner, *Mustang Pilot*, p. 23
224   'In that case, son . . .': ibid, p. 24
225   'Every pilot who took off . . .': ibid, p. 25
226   'Fellas, I'll be riding with you.': Robinson, p. 171
227   'What are you doing now . . .': ibid
227   'Well, I suppose you fellas . . .': ibid, p. 172
229   'Which is exactly what . . .': Robert S. Johnson, AFHRA, p. 154
230   'Just like that . . .': ibid, p. 155
230–1 'Perfect! One short burst . . .': ibid

Chapter 12   Change at the Top

235   'The enemy has been sighted . . .': Margarete Dos, *Letters from Berlin*, p. 107
235   'Open up, open up! . . .': ibid, p. 111
236   'There are medical students . . .': ibid, p. 112
236   'No one spoke . . .': ibid, p. 113
245   'Foggia hard hit by bombs . . .': Hap Arnold, *American Air Power Comes of Age: General Henry 'Hap' Arnold's World War II Diaries*, ed. John W. Huston, Vol. 2, 9/12/1943
245   'Modern battle . . .': ibid, 11/12/1943
246   'As a result . . .': cited in Richard G. Davis, *Carl A. Spaatz and the Air War in Europe*, p. 274
246   'kicked upstairs': ibid
246   'I feel like a pitcher . . .': ibid, p. 275
246   'Believe war interest . . .': ibid; also James Parton, *Air Force Spoken Here*, p. 338
250   'My driver shook his head . . .': Heinz Knoke, *I Flew for the Führer*, p. 131
250   'Not a single man . . .': James Good Brown, *The Mighty Men of the 381st*, p. 239
251   'By now my pilots . . .': Richard E. Turner, *Mustang Pilot*, p. 29
252   'Anything you did . . .': Robert S. Johnson, AFHRA, p. 29

252   'The 56th was by now ...': Francis Gabreski, *Gabby: A Fighter Pilot's Life*, p. 123
252   'Fighter pilots are more likely ...': AFHRA 168.60005-78

Chapter 13   Berlin
254   'The Focke-Wulf company ...': *The Bomber's Baedeker 1944*, AHB
255   'We were all terrified': cited in Robert Matzen, *Mission*, p. 140
257   'Landed Blazing Bomber ...': cited in IWM 96/41/1
258   'My little short legs ...': Rusty Waughman, author interview
258   'So I asked him ...': ibid
259   'It wasn't treated ...': ibid
260   'He was a rogue ...': ibid
261   'Target pretty hot ...': Rusty Waughman Diary, 29/12/1943
261   'He just sat on the floor ...': Waughman, author interview
261–2 'You know, we can't ...': ibid
264   'I had become a victim ...': Hajo Herrmann, *Eagle's Wings*, p. 209
265   'It was a great joy ...': ibid, p. 201

Chapter 14   Spaatz and Doolittle Take Charge
269–70 'a) Aircraft factories ...': cited in Wesley F. Craven and James L. Cate (eds), *The Army Air Forces in World War II*, Vol. III, p. 8
272   'It is my belief ...': cited in Richard G. Davis, *Carl A. Spaatz and the Air War in Europe*, p. 300
272   'We're certainly sorry ...': General James H. Doolittle, *I Could Never Be So Lucky Again*, p. 350
272–3 'The British probably since ...': ibid
273   'miracles are confidently expected': ibid, p. 347
274   'Fighter aircraft are designed ...': ibid, p. 352
274   'The first duty ...' and subsequent conversation with Kepner: ibid, pp. 352–3
275   'There was no compromise ...': ibid, p. 353
276   'The most critical need ...': Davis, p. 298
278   'No other damage ...': Larry Goldstein Diary, 4/1/1944
278   'And wow! What a dive! ...': Robert S. Johnson, AFHRA

280   'And today was to have been . . .': Heinz Knoke, *I Flew for the Führer*, p. 138

280   'Today, war came close . . .': James Good Brown, *The Mighty Men of the 381st*, p. 280

281   'To stand there . . .': ibid, p. 281

281   'The body emerged . . .': ibid, p. 282

281–2   'One must see . . .': ibid, p. 283

283   'He was terrific . . .': Robert S. Johnson, *Thunderbolt!*, p. 160

283   'The bullets tore into . . .': ibid

283   'What are they doing?': cited in Robert Matzen, *Mission*, p. 189

284   'We know what we're doing . . .': ibid

284   'F Lead to Group . . .': ibid, p. 191

285   'The good judgement . . .': cited in Starr Smith, *Jimmy Stewart: Bomber Pilot*, p. 87

Chapter 15   Thirty Against One

287   'That put us in a better mood . . .': Hugh McGinty, *My Life, Book One: The War Years*

287   'The chaplain was a very . . .': ibid

294   'My God! There are Germans . . .': cited in Richard E. Turner, *Mustang Pilot*, p. 38

295   'shoot his ass off': ibid, p. 39

295   'Never mind, Dick . . .': ibid

295   'Here I was . . .': ibid, p. 40

296   'The startled Nazis . . .': McGinty, p. 24

297   'The last I saw of him . . .': ibid

299–300   'For sheer determination . . .': cited in Rebecca Grant, 'One-Man Air Force', *Air Force Magazine*, November 2010

300   'I seen my duty . . .': *Stars & Stripes*, 18/1/1944

Chapter 16   Dicing with Death

301   'I cannot understand . . .': cited in Richard G. Davis, *Carl A. Spaatz and the Air War in Europe*, p. 305

302   'The weather here . . .': cited in ibid, pp. 305–6

303   'Absolute pea-soup . . .': Wilhelm Johnen, *Duel Under the Stars*, p. 108

303   'Take it easy . . .': ibid, p. 109

305   'Herr Oberleutnant . . .': ibid, p. 112

305   'I almost felt like patting . . .': ibid, p. 113

306   'White Argus from Meteor . . .': ibid

307   'Go through that again . . .': ibid, p. 114

307   'Am putting out the shroud . . .': ibid, p. 115

309   'Keep going . . .': cited in Mark M. Spagnuolo, *Mustang Ace*, p. 160

310   'You can think . . .': Don Gentile, *One-Man Air Force*, as told to Ira Wolfert

312   'Right quick . . .': ibid

312   'Don, hold on . . .': ibid

313   'Help! Help! . . .': cited in Spagnuolo, p. 164

314   'And that's what happened . . .': Gentile

314   'It showed me . . .': ibid

Chapter 17   Little Friends

315–16   'I wanted that German . . .': Robert S. Johnson, AFHRA, p. 161

317   'After that, all we talked about . . .': Bud Anderson, *To Fly and Fight*, p. 15

318   'I thought that if I . . .': http://www.americanveteranscenter. org/2016/07/col-clarence-bud-anderson/

318   'Living close to the edge . . .': Anderson, p. 61

320   'The 357th was off to a very poor start.': ibid, p. 88

322   'I do what he does . . .': ibid, p. 91

322   'Mustang! Mustang! . . .': ibid

323   'Man, was my fighter leader . . .': ibid, p. 93

323   'That morning . . .': ibid

324   'No, sir. Most of these boys . . .': Grover C. Hall Jr., *1,000 Destroyed*, p. 80

324   'which every pilot should know': AFHRA 168.61-3

324   'No. 1 is free to look all around . . .': ibid

325   'When flying over enemy . . .': this and other citations all from AFHRA 2-2906-4

Chapter 18   Waiting for a Gap in the Weather

329   'The German people . . .': cited in *GSWW*, Vol. VII, pp. 287–8

330   'a crap machine . . .': cited in ibid, p. 417

333   'In time, I became accustomed . . .': Heinz Knoke, *I Flew for the Führer*, p. 138

333   'We are taken . . .': ibid

333   'No. 4 Staffel . . .': ibid, p. 139

333   'I wonder if you've got . . .': cited in General James H. Doolittle, *I Could Never Be So Lucky Again*, p. 355

334   'That will be all.': ibid

334   'Hedge-hopping in bad weather . . .': ibid, p. 356

334   'You were right, Jim . . .': ibid, p. 365

335   'I have reviewed . . .': Richard G. Davis, *Carl A. Spaatz and the Air War in Europe*, p. 306

335   'Primary objective . . .': Charles Webster and Noble Frankland, *The Strategic Air Offensive Against Germany*, Vol. IV, Appendix 8, p. 164

336   'Overall reduction . . .': ibid, p. 165

337   'The missions were beginning . . .': Hugh McGinty, *My Life, Book One: The War Years*, p. 34

338   'Against them we are forty . . .': Knoke, p. 139

340   'Believe me . . .': Larry Goldstein Diary, 10/2/1944

340   'He was the finest . . .': Knoke, p. 141

Chapter 19   Saturday, 19 February 1944

347   'Office holed . . .': Rusty Waughman Diary, 28/2/1944

348   'It was very primitive . . .': Rusty Waughman, author interview

354   'It was a sort of . . .': ibid

357   'I doubt whether I can convey . . .': papers of Squadron Leader G. H. F. Carter, DSO, IWM 96/41/1

358   'Not so frightening . . .': papers of Flight Sergeant Kenneth Handley, IWM 3198

364   'Pretty deadly trip . . .': Waughman Diary, 19/2/1944

Chapter 20   Sunday, 20 February 1944

367   'Let 'em go.': Wesley F. Craven and James L. Cate (eds), *The Army Air Forces in World War II*, Vol. III, p. 33

367   'Awakened very early today . . .': Goldstein Diary, 20/2/1944

367   'Men, your bomb is . . .': cited in Martin Bowman, *We Were Eagles*, Vol. II, p. 82

368   'We will put up thirty-five ships . . .': cited in Robert Matzen, *Mission*, p. 288

369   'Doesn't sound too bad . . .': cited in Wilbur H. Morrison, *The Incredible 305th*, p. 78

370   'Good work, Manny.': Matzen, p. 230

371   'Some would groan . . .': Bud Anderson, *To Fly and Fight*, p. 100

373   'January 1, 1944, finds me . . .': Robert L. Sullivan Diary, 1/1/1944

373   'Miserable day . . .': ibid, 20/2/1944

374   'Had a recall . . .': ibid

375   'We had to be careful . . .': Hugh McGinty, *My Life, Book One: The War Years*, p. 37

376   'Bandits, seven o'clock low.': Robert S. Johnson, *Thunderbolt!*, p. 163; and Francis Gabreski, *Gabby: A Fighter Pilot's Life*, p. 147

376   'Everything was shaping up . . .': Johnson, p. 163

376   'We really hit those 110s . . .': Gabreski, p. 147

376–7   'We hit the first bunch . . .': Johnson, p. 163

377   'They went down like wheat . . .': ibid, p. 164

378   'I was determined . . .': Anderson, p. 103

378   'Thinking about it afterwards . . .': ibid

382   'Damn it!': Matzen, p. 213

383   'Get 'em, Little Friends!': ibid

383   'There were quite a few . . .': Goldstein Diary, 20/2/1944

387   'I guess we had feared . . .': James Good Brown, *The Mighty Men of the 381st*, p. 322

387   'On this day . . .': ibid

389   'It was hair-raising . . .': William R. Lawley interview, AFHRA, p. 11

Chapter 21   Monday, 21 February 1944

392   '. . . in situations of stress . . .': cited in James Pugh, 'The Royal Air Force, Bomber Command and the use of Benzedrine Sulphate: an Examination of Policy and Practice During the Second World War', *Journal of Contemporary History*, 17 October 2016, p. 2

393   'You learnt very quickly . . .': Rusty Waughman, author interview

393–4   '. . . by February 1944 . . .': flak statistics from *GSWW*, Vol. VII, p. 227

394   'You knew it took forty-five . . .': Waughman, author interview

394   'Long trip . . .': Rusty Waughman Diary, 20/2/1944

395   'If the Bosch firm fails . . .': cited in Johannes Steinhoff et al., *Voices from the Third Reich*, p. 220

395   'You had to hold on . . .': ibid, p. 221

396–7   'We would never abandon . . .': Hugh McGinty, *My Life, Book One: The War Years*, p. 39

397   'It's just that we were doing a job . . .': Larry Goldstein interview, National Museum of the Mighty Eighth Air Force

397   'Our morale was . . .': Martin W. Bowman, 'My Friend Larry "Goldie" Goldstein', n.d.

398   'This all seems so unreal . . .': Robert Hughes, www.100thbg.com

399   'I get as scared as you . . .': John Harold Robinson, *A Reason To Live*, p. 265

399   'I don't think I could . . .': ibid, p. 270

401   'You can learn to fly . . .': Grover C. Hall Jr., *1,000 Destroyed*, p. 80

401   'The guys are working . . .': Frank E. Speer, *The Debden Warbirds*, p. 51

402   'Failure to take off . . .': T. Michael Sullivan Diary, 1–5/2/1944

402   'Tony went nutz . . .': ibid, 17/2/1944

403–4   'Right from square one . . .': James H. Keeffe III, *Two Gold Coins and a Prayer*, p. 48

405   'Brakes?': ibid, pp. 65–6

407   'There was no way . . .': Bud Anderson, *To Fly and Fight*, p. 93

408   'What a sight it was . . .': papers of Squadron Leader G. H. F. Carter, IWM, 96/41/1

409   'That cost my squadron . . .': Heinz Knoke, *I Flew for the Führer*, p. 141

409   'This weather has sure . . .': Robert L. Sullivan Diary, 21/2/1944

409   'They looked like vertical . . .': Keeffe, p. 60

409   'I watched as they . . .': ibid

410   'Keefe, are you hit?': ibid

410   'Our fighter support . . .': Larry Goldstein Diary, 21/2/1944
410   'So all in all . . .': ibid
411   'By now I was getting pretty good . . .': Anderson, p. 94
411   'Finding a family here . . .': Robinson, p. 285
412   'The bottom dropped out again . . .': ibid
412   'Well, this black English beer . . .': ibid, p. 288

Chapter 22   Tuesday, 22 February 1944

414   'Finally, our first . . .': Robert L. Sullivan Diary, 22/2/1944
416   'We should be over . . .': John Harold Robinson, *A Reason To Live*, p. 289
416   'Boy! It sure would . . .': ibid, p. 291
417   'We are being recalled . . .': ibid
417   'Eleven o'clock . . .': ibid
420   'It was my wingman . . .': Heinz Knoke, *I Flew for the Führer*, p. 142
421   'Ground strafing . . .': Francis Gabreski, *Gabby: A Fighter Pilot's Life*, p. 148
421–2   'Lucky I was at my gun . . .': Sullivan Diary, 22/2/1944
423   'We dropped our bombs . . .': Hugh McGinty, *My Life, Book One: The War Years*, p. 41
425   'Tail gunner pretty bad . . .': Sullivan Diary, 22/2/1944
426   'The end may be victory . . .': James Good Brown, *The Mighty Men of the 381st*, p. 329
426   'A man who had . . .': ibid, p. 330
427   'While waiting . . .': papers of Squadron Leader G. H. F. Carter, IWM 96/41/1

Chapter 23   Thursday, 24 February 1944

428   'U.S. in First Joint . . .': *Stars & Stripes*, 23/2/1944
430   'The American sporting . . .': AFHRA EO 13526
431   'You learned to live . . .': cited in Johannes Steinhoff et al., *Voices from the Third Reich*, p. 219
432   'After the attacks . . .': cited in Jeremy Noakes (ed.), *Nazism*, Vol. 4: *The Home Front in World War II*, doc. 1321, p. 567
432   'Only the upper part . . .': cited in Steinhoff et al., p. 213
433   'Was this England? . . .': Hugh McGinty, *My Life, Book One: The War Years*, p. 44

435   'impenetrable weather': T. Michael Sullivan Diary, 23/2/1944

436   'You bombed the wrong target . . .': James H. Keeffe III, *Two Gold Coins and a Prayer*, p. 74

436   'I could see these multiple . . .': ibid, p. 75

437–8   'That will help . . .': this episode is recounted in John Harold Robinson, *A Reason To Live*, pp. 296–8

439   'It became pretty grim . . .': Keeffe, p. 75

440   'I saw it explode . . .': ibid

440   'It was going to take . . .': ibid, p. 78

441   'Our losses were not nearly . . .': McGinty, p. 45

442   'Our little band . . .': Heinz Knoke, *I Flew for the Führer*, p. 143

443   '49th Squadron annihilated . . .': T. Michael Sullivan Diary, 24/2/1944

444   'You were lucky . . .': Robinson, p. 298

444   'So all in all . . .': ibid

445   'Not one of us . . .': Keeffe, p. 79

Chapter 24   Friday, 25 February 1944

446   'It is extremely small . . .': cited in Dudley Saward, *Bomber Harris*, p. 298

448   'No clouds obscured . . .': papers of Flight Sergeant Kenneth Handley, IWM 3198

448   'We saw no searchlights . . .': ibid

449   'All of us were like . . .': John Harold Robinson, *A Reason To Live*, p. 299

450   'My thoughts raced ahead . . .': cited in Robert Matzen, *Mission*, p. 243

450   'There will be very little margin . . .': Robinson, p. 300

450   'No rest as the air blitz . . .': Larry Goldstein Diary, 25/2/1944

451   'My feet were walking . . .': Robinson, p. 300

453   'Sad, sad day . . .': Robert L. Sullivan Diary, 25/2/1944

453   'Such things as I saw . . .': ibid

454   'No laxatives are needed . . .': Heinz Knoke, *I Flew for the Führer*, p. 144

455   'Well, he definitely . . .' Mark M. Spagnuolo, *Mustang Ace*, p. 172

455   'Bomb bay doors coming open.': Robinson, p. 302

455   'Trying to get around . . .': ibid
456   'For God sakes . . .': Robert S. Johnson, AFHRA, p. 78
456   'He's staying there . . .': Robinson, p. 303
457   'On your left . . .': this episode described in Knoke, pp. 144–6
460   'The tail of the ship . . .': Robinson, p. 304
460   'Sergeant, somebody sure could . . .': ibid
460   'There were flak holes . . .': ibid, p. 305
460–1   'These past few missions . . .': Goldstein Diary, 25/2/44
461   'Perhaps it was just as well . . .': Handley papers

Postscript

463   'Since Jan. 1 . . .': *Stars & Stripes*, 28/2/1944
468   'In numbers as well as . . .': Beppo Schmid, 'The Most Important Mistakes of the Luftwaffe as Seen from the Standpoint of the German Fighter Force', AFHRA
469   'destruction of German air combat . . .': cited in Alan J. Levine, *The Strategic Bombing of Germany, 1940–1945*, p. 128
469   'Wholesale slaughter . . .': Rusty Waughman Diary, 31/3/1944
470   'Awe-inspiring at times . . .': papers of Flight Sergeant Kenneth Handley, IWM 3198
472   'At last I have walked . . .': Larry Goldstein Diary, 4/3/1944
474   'I was suddenly . . .' Hugh McGinty, *My Life, Book One: The War Years*, p. 72
474   'I wonder what kind of life . . .': Bill Byers, author interview

Selected Sources

Personal Testimonies

Air Force Historical Research Agency, Maxwell AF Base, Alabama

Anderson, Frederick L.
Gabreski, Francis S.
Galland, Adolf
Hodges, James
Johnson, Robert S.
Kepner, William E.
Lawley Jr., William R.
Schmid, Josef
Spaatz, Carl A.

Author Interviews

Byers, Bill
Goldstein, Larry
Herrmann, Hajo
Munro, Les
Neumann, Julius
Waughman, Rusty

Imperial War Museum, London
Mayer, John

National Museum of the Mighty Eighth Air Force, Savannah, Georgia
Goldstein, Larry

National World War II Museum, New Orleans, Louisiana
Anderson, Bud
Shoens, Bob

Unpublished Memoirs, Diaries, etc.

Imperial War Museum, London
Carter, Gordon, *Memories of War*
Handley, Ken, Papers
Milch, Erhard, Papers

National Museum of the Mighty Eighth Air Force, Savannah, Georgia
Ankeny, Harry, Diary
Burgsteiner, Will D., Memoir
Davison, Ralph, *My Excursions from Podington*
Dolan, William, *Recollections of a Bombardier*
Emory, Frank N., Diary
Gentile, Don S., *One-Man Air Force*
Goldstein, Larry
Hanlyn, Calvin M., Diary
Herdic Jr., Carl W., Diary
Hivey, Eugene, Diary
Johnson, John R., *Hang the Expense*
Lewis, Daniel
McGinty, Hugh, *My Life, Book One: The War Years – A Tail Gunner Looks Back*
Sullivan, Robert L., Diary
Vaughn, Winfield C., Diary

Archives, Museums, etc.

Air Force Historical Research Agency, Maxwell AF Base, Alabama

Air Staff Post Hostilities Intelligence Requirements on GAF (German Air Force of Luftwaffe) Appendices I–VII

Bar, Oberstleutnant, *A Typical Fighter Mission in Defense of the Reich*

Bar, Oberstleutnant, and Galland, Adolf, *Fighter Tactics*

Eighth Air Force: Miscellaneous Reports, Aircrew Surveys, Tactics etc., A1756

Galland, Adolf, *The Birth, Life, and Death of the German Fighter Arm*

——, *Fighter Tactics*

Galland, Adolf, and Schmid, Josef, *The Most Important Mistakes of the Luftwaffe as Seen from the Standpoint of the German Fighter Force*

Interrogation of Generalleutnant Galland, Generalfeldmarschall Milch, Oberstleutnant Bar, Generalleutnant Hitschhold and Leutnant Neumann, *GAF Opinions of Allied Aircraft*

Kammhuber, Josef, *Problems in the Conduct of a Day and Night Defensive Air War*

Schmid, Josef, *Day and Night Aerial Warfare over the Reich*

——, *German Nightfighting*

——, *The Struggle for Air Supremacy over the Reich, 1 January 1944–31 March 1944*

Unit histories and war diaries: 4th Fighter Group; 56th Fighter Group; 354th Fighter Group; 357th Fighter Group; 100th Bomb Group; 364th Bomb Group; 379th Bomb Group; 388th Bomb Group; 389th Bomb Group; 445th Bomb Group

VIII Fighter Command, *Narrative of Operations*

——, *The Long Reach Deep Fighter Escort Tactics*

National Archives, London

Squadron Operational Record Books: 35 Squadron; 101 Squadron; 429 Squadron; 609 Squadron

General

Air Ministry, *The Rise and Fall of the German Air Force*, Public Record Office, 2001

Anon, *The Aircraft Book: The Definitive Visual History*, Dorling Kindersley, 2013

Archard, L. (ed.), *How to Fly a Second World War Heavy Bomber: Lancaster, Halifax, Stirling*, Amberley, 2014

Astor, Gerald, *The Mighty Eighth: The Air War in Europe As Told by the Men Who Fought It*, Berkley Caliber, 2015

Bekker, Cajus, *The Luftwaffe War Diaries: The German Air Force in World War II*, Corgi, 1972

Bishop, Patrick, *Bomber Boys: Fighting Back 1940–1945*, Harper Press, 2007

——, *Air Force Blue: The RAF in World War Two – Spearhead of Victory*, William Collins, 2017

Blake, Steve, *The Pioneer Mustang Group: The 354th Fighter Group in World War II*, Schiffer Military, 2008

Bowman, Martin, *USAAF Handbook 1939-1945*, Sutton, 2003

——, *B-17 Combat Missions: Fighters, Flak and Forts – First-hand Accounts of Mighty 8th Operations over Germany*, Metro Books, 2007

——, *On the Highways of the Skies: The 8th Air Force in World War II*, Schiller, 2008

——, *We're Here to Win the War For You: The US 8th Air Force at War*, Amberley, 2009

——, *We Were Eagles*, Volume One: *July 1942 to November 1943*, Amberley, 2014

——, *We Were Eagles*, Volume Two: *December 1943 to May 1944*, Amberley, 2014

Bruning, John R., *Bombs Away! The World War II Bombing Campaigns over Europe*, Zenith, 2011

Cooper, Alan, *Target Leipzig: The RAF's Disastrous Raid of 19/20 February 1944*, Pen & Sword, 2009

Corum, James S., *The Luftwaffe: Creating the Operational Air War, 1918–1940*, University Press of Kansas, 1997

Cotter, Jarrod, and Hammond, Maurice, *North American P-51 Mustang: Owners' Workshop Manual*, Haynes, 2016

Crane, Conrad C., *American Airpower Strategy in World War II: Bombs, Cities, Civilians, and Oil*, University Press of Kansas, 2016

Craven, Wesley Frank, and Cate, James Lea (eds), *The Army Air Forces in World War II*, Volume Two: *Europe: Torch to Pointblank, August 1942 to December 1943*, University of Chicago Press, 1949

——, *The Army Air Forces in World War II*, Volume Three: *Europe: Argument to V-E Day, January 1944 to May 1945*, University of Chicago Press, 1951

Davis Biddle, Tami, *Rhetoric and Reality in Air Warfare: The Evolution of British and American Ideas about Strategic Bombing, 1914–1945*, Princeton University Press, 2002

Earnshaw, James Douglas, *609 at War*, Vector, 2003

Eden, Paul (ed.), *The Encyclopedia of Aircraft of World War II*, Amber, 2017

Emerson, William R., *Operation Pointblank: A Tale of Bombers and Fighters*, United States Air Force Academy, 1962

Ethell, Jeffrey, and Price, Dr Alfred, *Target Berlin: Mission 250 – 6 March 1944*, Greenhill, 2002

Freeman, Roger A., *The Mighty Eighth: A History of the US 8th Army Air Force*, Macdonald, 1973

——, *Mighty Eighth War Diary*, Jane's, 1986

——, *Airfields of the Eighth Then and Now*, After the Battle, 1992

Gann, Ernest K., *Fate is the Hunter*, Weidenfeld & Nicolson, 2011

Graff, Cory, *P-51 Mustang: Seventy-Five Years of America's Most Famous Warbird*, Zenith, 2015

Gunston, Bill, *Illustrated Directory of Fighting Aircraft of World War II*, Salamander, 1988

Hall, David Ian, *Strategy for Victory: The Development of British Tactical Air Power, 1919–1943*, Praeger Security International, 2008

Hall Jr., Grover C., *1,000 Destroyed: The Life & Times of the 4th Fighter Group*, Brown Printing Co., 1946

Harris, Arthur, *Despatch on Operations: 23rd February 1942 to 8th May 1945*, Frank Cass, 1995

Hess, William N., *354th Fighter Group*, Osprey, 2002

Holland, James, *Heroes: The Greatest Generation and the Second World War*, Harper Perennial, 2007

——, *Dam Busters: The Race to Smash the German Dams*, Bantam Press, 2012

——, *The War in the West: Germany Ascendant, 1939–1941*, Bantam Press, 2015

——, *The War in the West: The Allies Strike Back, 1941–1943*, Bantam Press, 2017

Irons, Roy, *The Relentless Offensive*, Pen & Sword, 2009

Kay, Antony L., and Smith, J. R., *German Aircraft of the Second World War*, Putnam, 2002

Klein, Maury, *A Call to Arms: Mobilizing America for World War II*, Bloomsbury Press, 2013

Levine, Alan J., *The Strategic Bombing of Germany, 1940–1945*, Praeger, 1992

Mahoney, Kevin A., *Fifteenth Air Force Against the Axis: Combat Mission over Europe during World War II*, Scarecrow Press, 2013

——, *Bombing Europe: The Illustrated Exploits of the Fifteenth Air Force*, Zenith, 2015

Mahurin, Walker 'Bud', *Hitler's Fall Guys: An Examination of the Luftwaffe by One of America's Most Famous Aces*, Schiffer Military History, 1999

McFarland, Stephen L., and Philips Newton, Wesley, *To Command the Sky: The Battle for Air Superiority Over Germany, 1942–1945*, Smithsonian Institution Press, 1991

McLaren, David R., *Beware the Thunderbolt: The 56th Fighter Group in World War II*, Schiffer Military, 1994

Middlebrook, Martin, and Everitt, Chris, *The Bomber Command War Diaries*, Penguin, 1990

Miller, Donald L., *Eighth Air Force: The American Bomber Crews in Britain*, Aurum, 2008

Mombeek, Eric, *Defenders of the Reich: Jagdgeschwader 1*, Volume One: *1939–1942*, Classic Publications, 2000

Morrison, Wilbur H., *The Incredible 305th*, Belmont Tower Books, 1962

Murray, Williamson, *Luftwaffe: Strategy for Defeat 1933–1945*, Grafton, 1988

Nielsen, Andreas, *The German Air Force General Staff*, Arno Press, 1968

Noakes, Jeremy (ed.), *Nazism 1919–1945*, Volume 4: *The German Home Front in World War II*, University of Exeter Press, 2006

Overy, Richard, *The Bombing War: Europe 1939–1945*, Allen Lane, 2013

Pons, Gregory, *9th Air Force*, Histoire & Collections, 2008

Price, Alfred, *Instruments of Darkness: The History of Electronic Warfare*, Macdonald and Jane's, 1977

Rasmussen, Nicolas, *On Speed: From Benzedrine to Adderall*, New York University Press, 2008

Ries Jr., Karl, *Dora Kurfürst und Rote 13*, Volumes I–IV: *Flugzeuge der Luftwaffe 1933–1945*, Verlag Dieter Hoffmann, 1968

Rogers, Jeff, *Valor at Polebrook: The Last Flight of Ten Horsepower*, Ken Cook, 1998

Rumpf, Hans, *The Bombing of Germany*, Holt, Rinehart and Winston, 1963

Rust, Kenn C., *The 9th Air Force in World War II*, Aero, 1967

Scutts, Jerry, and Stanaway, John, *Aces of the Mighty Eighth*, Osprey, 2002

Speer, Frank E., *The Debden Warbirds: The 4th Fighter Group in World War II*, Schiffer, 2004

Spick, Mike, *Luftwaffe Fighter Aces: The Jagdflieger and Their Combat Tactics and Techniques*, Ivy Books, 1997

——, *Aces of the Reich: The Making of a Luftwaffe Fighter Pilot*, Greenhill, 2006

Steinhoff, Johannes, Pechel, Peter, and Showalter, Dennis, *Voices from the Third Reich: An Oral History*, Da Capo, 1994

Suchenwirth, Richard, *Command and Leadership in the German Air Force*, Arno Press, 1969

——, *Historical Turning Points in the German Air Force War Effort*, University Press of the Pacific, 2004

Szlagor, Tomasz, *P-47 Thunderbolt with the USAAF*, Kagero, 2013

Tooze, Adam, *The Wages of Destruction: The Making and Breaking of the Nazi Economy*, Penguin, 2007

Various, *World War II Day by Day*, Dorling Kindersley, 2001

Weal, John, *Jagdgeschwader 2 'Richthofen'*, Osprey, 2000

Webster, Charles, and Frankland, Noble, *The Strategic Air Offensive Against Germany 1939–1945*, Volume II: *Endeavour*, Naval & Military Press, 2006

——, *The Strategic Air Offensive Against Germany 1939–1945*, Volume IV: *Annexes and Appendices*, Naval & Military Press, 2006

Yenne, Bill, *Big Week: Six Days That Changed the Course of World War II*, Berkley Caliber, 2012

Zaloga, Steven J., *Operation Pointblank 1944: Defeating the Luftwaffe*, Osprey, 2011

Ziegler, Frank H., *The Story of 609 Squadron: Under the White Rose*, Crecy, 1993

Memoirs, Biographies, etc.

Anderson, Clarence E. 'Bud', *To Fly and Fight: Memoirs of a Triple Ace*, Pacifica Press, 1990

Anzanos, Andrew, *My Combat Diary With Eighth Air Force B-17s 390th Bomb Group*, Original Publication, 2004

Arnold, H. H., *Global Mission*, TAB Books, 1989

——, *American Air Power Comes of Age: General Henry H. 'Hap' Arnold's World War II Diaries*, ed. John W. Huston, Progressive Management Publications, 2017

Baker, David, *Adolf Galland: The Authorised Biography*, Windrow and Greene, 1996

Brereton, Lewis H., *The Brereton Diaries: The War in the Pacific, Middle East and Europe, 3 October 1941–8 May 1945*, William Morrow, 1946

Caine, Philip D., *Spitfires, Thunderbolts and Warm Beer: An American Fighter Pilot over Europe*, Potomac Books, 2005

Charlwood, Don, *No Moon Tonight*, Goodall, 2010

Clostermann, Pierre, *The Big Show: Some Experiences of a French Fighter Pilot in the R.A.F.*, Cassell, 2005

Crosby, Harry H., *A Wing and a Prayer: The Bloody 100th Bomb Group of the U.S. Eighth Air Force in Action over Europe in World War II*, iUniverse.com, 2000

Davis, Richard G., *Carl A. Spaatz and the Air War in Europe*, Center for Air Force History, 1993

Doolittle, James H. 'Jimmy', *I Could Never Be So Lucky Again*, Bantam Books, 1992

Dos, Margarete, and Lieff, Kerstin, *Letters from Berlin: A Story of War, Survival, and the Redeeming Power of Love and Friendship*, Lyon Press, 2013

Fischer, Wolfgang (ed.), *Luftwaffe Fighter Pilot*, trans. John Weal, Grub Street, 2010

Fleming, Samuel P., *Flying with the Hell's Angels*, Honoribus Press, 1991

Fortier, Norman 'Bud', *An Ace of the Eighth: An American Fighter Pilot's Air War in Europe*, Ballantine, 2003

Frankland, Noble, *History at War: The Campaigns of an Historian*, DLM, 1998

Franks, Norman, *Buck McNair: Canadian Spitfire Ace*, Grub Street, 2001

Gabreski, Francis, *Gabby: A Fighter Pilot's Life*, Orion, 1991

Galland, Adolf, *The First and the Last*, Buccaneer Books, 1990

Good Brown, James, *The Mighty Men of the 381st: Heroes All*, Publishers Press, 1984

Goodson, James, *Tumult in the Clouds*, Penguin, 2003

Harris, Sir Arthur, *Bomber Offensive*, Collins, 1947

Heaton, Colin D., and Lewis, Anne-Marie, *The German Aces Speak II*, Zenith Press, 2014

Herrmann, Hajo, *Eagle's Wings: The Autobiography of a Luftwaffe Pilot*, Airlife, 1991

Hinchliffe, Peter, *The Lent Papers*, Cerberus, 2003

Irving, David, *The Rise and Fall of the Luftwaffe: The Life of Erhard Milch*, Weidenfeld & Nicolson, 1973

——, *Göring: A Biography*, Macmillan, 1989

Johnen, Wilhelm, *Duel Under the Stars*, Crecy, 1994

Johnson, Johnnie, *Wing Leader*, Penguin, 1959

Johnson, Robert S., with Caidin, Martin, *Thunderbolt!: The Extraordinary Story of a World War II Ace*, Uncommon Valor Reprint, no date

Kaplan, Philip, *Two-Man Air Force: Don Gentile & John Godfrey World War Two Flying Aces*, Pen & Sword, 2006

——, and Currie, Jack, *Round the Clock: The Experience of the Allied Bomber Crews*, Cassell, 1993

Keeffe, James H. III, *Two Gold Coins and a Prayer: The Epic Journey of a World War II Bomber Pilot, Evader, and POW*, Appell Publishing, 2010

Kershaw, Ian, *Hitler: 1936–1945, Nemesis*, Penguin, 2000

Kesselring, Albert, *The Memoirs of Field Marshal Kesselring*, Greenhill, 2007

Knoke, Heinz, *I Flew for the Führer*, Cassell, 2003

Matzen, Robert, *Mission: Jimmy Stewart and the Fight for Europe*, GoodKnight Books, 2016

McLaughlin, J. Kemp, *The Mighty Eighth in WWII: A Memoir*, University Press of Kentucky, 2014

Melinsky, Hugh, *Forming the Pathfinders: The Career of Air Vice-Marshal Sydney Bufton*, History Press, 2010

Newton Dunn, Bill, *Big Wing: The Biography of Air Chief Marshal Sir Trafford Leigh-Mallory*, Airlife, 1992

Parton, James, *Air Force Spoken Here: General Ira Eaker & the Command of the Air*, Adler & Adler, 1986

Peden, Murray, *A Thousand Shall Fall: The True Story of a Canadian Bomber Pilot in World War Two*, Stoddart, 1988

Probert, Henry, *Bomber Harris: His Life and Times*, Greenhill, 2006

Propst, Robert, *The Diary of a Combat Pilot*, Carlton, 1967

Richards, Denis, *Portal of Hungerford: The Life of Marshal of the Royal Air Force Viscount Portal of Hungerford*, Heinemann, 1977

Robinson, John Harold, *A Reason to Live*, Castle Books, 1988

Saward, Dudley, *Bomber Harris*, Sphere, 1985

Schlange-Shoeningen, Hans, *The Morning After*, Victor Gollancz, 1948

Scholz, Günther, *In the Skies over Europe: The Memoirs of Luftwaffe Fighter Pilot Günther Scholz*, Schiffer, 2011

Smith Jr., Ben, *Chick's Crew: A Tale of the Eighth Air Force*, Yarborough Brothers, 1978

Smith, Dale O., *Screaming Eagle: Memoirs of a B-17 Group Commander*, Algonquin, 1990

Smith, Starr, *Jimmy Stewart: Bomber Pilot*, Zenith Press, 2005

Spagnuolo, Mark M., *Mustang Ace: The Story of Don S. Gentile*, Cerberus, 1986

Speer, Frank, *One Down, One Dead*, Xlibris, 2003

Tedder, Lord, *With Prejudice: The War Memoirs of Marshal of the Royal Air Force Lord Tedder*, Cassell, 1966

Toliver, Raymond F., and Constable, Trevor J., *Fighter General: The Life of Adolf Galland*, AmPress, 1990

Turner, Richard E., *Mustang Pilot*, New English Library, 1970

Magazines, Journals & Periodicals

Daneu, Karen, 'The P-51 Mustang as an Escort Fighter Development Beyond Drop Tanks to an Independent Air Force', Research Report, Air War College, Maxwell Air Force Base, Alabama

Giffard, Hermione S., 'The Development and Production of Turbojet Aero-Engines in Britain, Germany and the United States,

1936–1945', Dissertation for PhD at Imperial College, University of London, 2011

Grant, Rebecca, 'One-Man Air Force', *Air Force Magazine*, November 2010

Harvey, Arnold D., 'The Battle of Britain in 1940 and Big Week in 1944: A Comparative Perspective', *Air Power*, Spring 2012

Lande, David A., 'All the Winds of Doctrine: General Ira Eaker and the Implementation of Daylight Precision Bombing', Master of Arts thesis

Pugh, James, 'The Royal Air Force, Bomber Command and the use of Benzedrine Sulphate', *Journal of Contemporary History*, 17 October 2016

Stoddart, Paul, 'Spitfire to Berlin? Making Supermarine's Finest an Escort Fighter', *Air Enthusiast*, Autumn 2000

Stubbs, David, 'A Blind Spot? The RAF and Long-Range Fighters, 1936–1944', MPhil paper, RAF Cranwell

Online

Anon, *Defenders of Liberty: 2nd Bombardment Group/Wing1918–1993*, www.2ndbombgroup.org

Hughes, Robert L., *Black Thursday – 14 Oct 43*, www.100thbg.com

——, *Commendation Letter*, www.100thbg.com

——, *Crew Information*, www.100thbg.com

——, *DFC Transmittal Letter*, www.100thbg.com

——, *Important Dates*, www.100thbg.com

——, *Initial Aviation Cadet Record*, www.100thbg.com

——, *La Junta AAB – Class 43B*, www.100thbg.com

——, *Letters*, www.100thbg.com

——, *Missions and Events*, www.100thbg.com

——, *Ops Narrative – Bremen 26 Nov 43*, www.100thbg.com

——, *Promotion Record*, www.100thbg.com

——, *War Diary Part 1*, www.100thbg.com

Richards, Charles, *The Second Was First*, www.2ndbombgroup.org

Sullivan, T. Michael, *Echoes of the Army*, www.2ndbombgroup.org

Acknowledgements

I would like to thank a number of people who have helped with this book. In the United States, the staff at both the Air Force Historical Research Agency at Maxwell Air Force Base and those at the National Mighty Eighth Museum just outside Savannah have been unfailingly helpful. At Maxwell, especial thanks are due to Tammy Horton, while at the Mighty Eighth Museum, I am hugely grateful to Dr Vivian Rogers-Price and her team. At the National World War II Museum in New Orleans, thanks are due to Dr Rob Citino, Jeremy Collins and Seth Paridon in particular for their help. I'd also like to thank the staff of the Imperial War Museum and The National Archives at Kew in the UK and those at the military archives in Freiburg, Germany. Mike Faley of the 100th Bomb Group Foundation has been extremely helpful, pointing me in the direction of all manner of sources – thank you.

Many others have helped along the way. Paul Bingley gave

a wonderful tour of Ridgewell and has provided numerous documents as well. Captain Tony Dale kindly showed me around Debden. Martin Bowman, that great chronicler of the Eighth Air Force, has been incredibly generous with his time and sources, for which huge thanks.

I am also very grateful to the veterans who kindly gave me their time. Their numbers are sadly dwindling, but I feel very fortunate to have spent such time with the incredible Larry 'Goldie' Goldstein, Rusty Waughman and Bill Byers.

Friends and colleagues have also helped with advice, suggestions and direction-pointing. My deep thanks to Paul Beaver, Peter Caddick-Adams, Graham Cowie, Seb Cox, Conrad Crane, Nick Hartwell, Paul Stoddart, Adam Wheatley and Rowland White, but also to John Romain and Anna McDowell at the Aircraft Restoration Company and especially to Clive Denney and Steve Carter for the tour of Sally B. To Michelle Myers and Ingo Maerker in Freiburg, my grateful thanks, as ever. Thank you, too, to one of my oldest friends, James Petrie, to whom this book is dedicated – one of my very few old pals who actually shows any interest in this subject matter!

Enormous thanks are owed to Brenda Updegraff, who goes way beyond the normal bounds of a copy editor to provide real collaboration – thank you for your wonderful judgement, skill and forbearance. I am also, as always, indebted to all those at Bantam Press in London and Grove Atlantic in New York: Justina Batchelor, Morgan Entrekin, Larry Finlay, Tom Hill, Phil Lord, Darcy Nicholson, Deb Seager and Vivien Thompson, but most of all George Gibson and Bill Scott-Kerr. I couldn't hope for finer publishers. To Patrick Walsh, my enormous thanks, as ever.

My final thanks, as always, are to my long-suffering family, to whom I owe much. Watching Daisy clambering into a P-51 and then skipping down the old runway at Ridgewell will be among the enduring memories of writing this book.

Picture
Acknowledgements

Every effort has been made to trace copyright holders; those overlooked are invited to get in touch with the publishers.

p. xi–xiv Boeing B-17G Flying Fortress, Handley Page Halifax III, Avro Lancaster, Consolidated B-24 Liberator, Lockheed P-38 Lightning, Focke-Wulf 190 A-8, Junkers 88 G-1 Night-fighter, Messerschmitt 110F, Messerschmitt 210: Alamy

Plate section 1

Page 1
Cockpit of Boeing B-17: James Holland

Page 2
Top Waist gunner's station in B-17: James Holland
Bottom Prototype B-17: AFHRA

Page 3
Top Don Blakeslee briefing pilots of 4th Fighter Group: Getty Images
Bottom George and Bill Byers: Bill Byers

Page 4
Top (left) Fred Anderson, *(right)* Hap Arnold; *bottom* Bill Kepner and Carl Spaatz: AFHRA

Page 5
Middle right Duane Beeson; Gabby Gabreski: AFHRA

Page 6
Top Jim Howard; *bottom right* Hub Zemke: AFHRA

Page 7
Top right P-51B model: MustangsMustangs
Middle right Thunderbolt P-47 firing scheme: AFHRA
Inset Thunderbolt in flight: Alamy

Page 8
Top B-17s lined up for a mission: David R. Osborne
Middle (left) Ace Conklin, *(right)* Larry Goldstein; *bottom (left)* Kent Keith: Larry Goldstein

Plate section 2

Page 1
Top Rusty Waughman *(left)* in cockpit of Lancaster, *(right)* newly commissioned: Rusty Waughman
Bottom Interior of a Lancaster: James Holland

Page 2
All photos: Rusty Waughman

Page 3
Top Nissen huts: David R. Osborne
Middle Accommodation for air crew: Martin W. Bowman

Page 4
Top (left) Hermann Göring; *middle (left)* Hajo Herrmann; *bottom (left)* FW190, *(right)* ME110: James Holland
Middle centre Wim Johnen: Frontline Books

Page 5
Top (right) Bill Lawley's battered B-17: Bob Lister

Page 7
Top Big Week map: Paul Bingley

Page 8
Top (main) Thorpe Abbotts airfield today; *bottom (main)* Old main runway at Ridgewell today, *(inset)* Chaplain James Good Brown's former office at Ridgewell: James Holland
Inset (top left) The chow line at Thorpe Abbotts, *(top right)* Crew accommodation at Thorpe Abbotts, *(middle)* Flying Fortress coming in to land: Martin W. Bowman

Index

Achmer, Germany 180
AFCE *see* Automatic Flight Control
    Equipment
Ahrenholz, Lieutenant Augustus 62
airfields xv xvii, 47–8, 99, 102–3
Allison V-1710 jet engine 166
American Committee of Operation
    Analysts (COA) 49
amphetamines, use of 391–2
Anderson, Lieutenant Clarence 'Bud'
    xxvii, 317–23, 371–2, 377–8, 407,
    411, 476–7
Anderson, Major-General Frederick
    xxvii, 50, 52, 56, 70–1, 286, 293, 351,
    355, 366, 401, 417–18, 448–9, 465
Andersz, Tadeusz 19
Anglo-American Fifth Army 182
Anglo-French Purchasing Board 163
Anklam, Germany: Arado works 52, 73
anti-aircraft fire (flak) *xxii*, 101, 179,
    188, 195, 196, 267, 392, 393–4,
    400, 459
Antonie, Lieutenant Celestine 'Tony'
    402–3
ANVIL, Operation 269
Anzio, Italy 355, 356, 373, 402

ARGUMENT, Operation 276–7, 336,
    341, 346, 348–9, 352, 354–5, 366,
    373, 391, 396, 398, 401–2; 404,
    411, 414, 428, 431, 432, 447,
    461–2, 463
Arndt, Unteroffizier Alfred 40
Arnold, General Henry 'Hap' xxvii,
    49, 84; bombing philosophy 71–2,
    82, 86; and Eaker 71–2, 75, 140,
    172, 175, 239–41, 245–6; agrees
    need for fighter escorts 162–3,
    170–1, 175–6, 236–7;
    frustrations 171–3, 239–40, 241,
    255; and creation of Fifteenth Air
    Force 183, 237; and invasion of
    Italy 182; and Operation
    POINTBLANK 236, 240,
    245–46; wants single Allied
    Strategic Air Force Commander
    in London 173–5; shocked by
    conditions in Italy 245; makes
    five key points 269–70; and need
    for Pathfinders 276; angry at
    failure to hit targets 301–2; and
    Spaatz 302, 335, 351, 366–7; urges
    ruthlessness 366

Arnold, Colonel Milton 285
Arnold, Lt-Colonel Walter 'Pop' 210
Arnsberg, Germany 468
astro-navigation 191
Athlone Castle 160–1
Augsburg, Germany 402, 461–2;
    Messerschmitt factory 137, 354,
    414, 462, 464
Australian airmen 16, 234, 358–9,
    363, 447–8, 461, 470
Automatic Flight Control Equipment
    (AFCE) 64–5
Avro Lancaster bombers *xi*, 86,
    92, 97–8, 99, 104, 105, 142–3,
    151, 157, 188, 208, 234, 258,
    259–62, 306–7, 328, 347, 348,
    359, 461

B-17s *see* Boeing B-17 flying Fortress
    bombers
B-24s *see* Consolidated B24 Liberators
Badoglio, Marshal Pietro 182
Bär, Hauptmann 303, 304, 305, 308
BARBAROSSA, Operation 44
Barran, Methuselah 42–3, 222, 223
Barris, Lieutenant George 339–40
Barry, 'Nap' 192–3
Barthelmess, Lt-Colonel 402–3
Bates, Sergeant Ted 156
Battle of Britain (1940) 13, 21, 34, 35,
    85, 94, 95, 118, 125, 130–1, 141,
    155, 178, 181, 274, 327
Battle of the Atlantic 13–14, 160
Baughman, Joe 453
Beeson, Captain Duane 'Bee' xxvii,
    25–6, 311, 384–5, 406, 454,
    477–8
Benzedrine, use of 391–2
Berlin: raids on 96, 106, 141, 147–8,
    152, 159, 188–9, 194, 234, 255,
    257, 259–61, 265–8, 303, 346, 347,
    467; evacuation 107; Conference
    177, 179; defences 194–7, 267–8,
    303, 393–4
Bernburg, Germany 369, 374
Bingley, Paul 479
Blackett bombsight 102

Blakeslee, Lt-Colonel Don xxvii;
    personality 22, 23, 25, 223;
    background and training 22;
    joins Eagle squadrons 22–3;
    commands 4th Fighter Group
    24–5, 252, 309, 478; as instructor
    223–4, 325; loves Mustangs
    323–4, 401–2; missions 401–2,
    406, 424, 467, 477; postwar 477
blind-flying: Luftwaffe 125–6, 178,
    304; US Air Force 225, 243, 331
Blitz, the 85, 94, 95, 96, 98, 104–5, 141,
    327, 328–9, 464
Blue Blazing Blizzard 375–6
BMW jet engines 112, 120–1
Boeing Company: Boeing 247 80;
    Boeing 299 81; B-17G Flying
    Fortress bombers *xi*, *xxiv*, 1,
    81–2, 83, 86, 121, 136, 137, 139,
    142–3, 146, 186, 197–203, 204–5,
    207, 208, 275, 277, 280–2, 290,
    331, 234, 338, 352, 370, 374–6,
    378–82, 384, 402–3, 406, 415,
    422–3, 425, 434, 450–1,
    452–3, 456
BOLERO, Operation 76
Bomber Commands *see* Royal Air
    Force; United States Army Air
    Forces
bombsights 101–2; Blackett 102;
    Norden 81–2, 83, 94, 102, 441;
    Stabilized Automatic Bomb Sight
    (SABS) 102
Boots 334
'Boozer' radar-warning receiver 102
Bosch factories 137, 390, 395–6
Bottomley, Air Marshal Sir Norman
    141, 446
Bowman, Lt-Colonel Harold W. 300
Boxted, Essex 161–2, 223, 252, 287–8,
    289–90, 299, 320–1, 323
Boyle, Al 407, 411
Boyle, Sergeant Joe 55, 251, 398
Breeding, Lieutenant Paul 386–7
Bremen, raids on 42, 52, 73, 88, 202,
    205–6, 234, 255
Brereton, General Lewis H. 350, 351, 365

Breslau, Poland 354
Bridwell, Lieutenant Ernal 204, 288, 336
British Eighth Army 15, 182
Brown, Captain James Good 72–3, 250, 280–2, 387, 426, 479
Brunswick, raids on 286, 287, 299, 316, 331, 338, 340, 368, 369, 370, 401–2, 404, 407, 408, 410–11, 431, 434
Buckey (radio operator) 417, 438, 455
Bullet Serenade 217, 226–7, 400, 411–12
Bushy Park, London xvi, 18, 271, 348
Butler, Lieutenant 387–8
Butt Report 97, 98
Byers, George 89–93, 153, 154, 155, 156, 157, 158, 159
Byers, William 'Bill' xxix, 89–93, 153, 154, 156–9, 194, 228, 356, 469–70, 474

Cabin in the Sky 216, 297
Cabin in the Sky III 378–82, 385–6
Cairo Conference (1943) 239, 245
Calais 255, 303
Canadian pilots 16, 356; *see also* Byers, George *and* William; Royal Canadian Air Force
Cannon, Major-General 355
Carter, Squadron Leader Gordon xxix, 189–94, 203, 256, 353, 356–61, 407–8, 426–7, 474
Casablanca Conference (1943) 32, 136–7
CBO *see* Combined Bomber Offensive
Chamberlain, Neville 77
Chapas, Joe 453
Chelveston, RAF (Northamptonshire) 216, 369
Chennault, Captain Claire 79, 94
Chiang Kai-shek 79
Chipling, Squadron Leader Alban 157
Churchill, Winston 32, 97, 136, 137, 140, 147–8, 356, 428, 471, 478
Clark, Lieutenant-General Mark 182, 355
Clore, Lieutenant Cecil M. 280–1

Clough, Lieutenant 64
COA *see* American Committee of Operation Analysts
Cogswell, Kirch 387
Cologne, raids on 99, 126, 431–2
Combat Box formations, US xxiii
Combined Bomber Offensive (CBO) 69, 70, 138, 141, 172, 236, 237 239, 353
Combined Operational Planning Committee (COPC) 276, 348
Condor Legion 118, 124–5
Conklin, Lieutenant Clifford 'Ace' 198, 200, 369
Conley, Lieutenant William 'Bill' 282, 283, 368, 370, 382–3
Consolidated B-24 Liberators *xii*, 83, 136, 142, 146, 197, 207–8, 210, 216, 283–5, 338, 352, 368, 369, 370, 382–3, 415, 417, 425, 433, 436–8, 439, 444, 452, 453, 455, 456
Coventry (1940) 96, 105
Cowan, Alec 260, 347–8, 353
Croft-on-Tees, North Yorkshire 90
Cross, Elvin 416, 437
Curtiss-Wright Corporation: P-36 Hawks 163; P-40 Warhawks 163–4

Dabbs, Ken 412, 417, 437, 438
Daimler-Benz: factories 193, 390; jet engines 110, 121
David, Colonel William R. 367–8
Davis, David R. 207
Davis, Lieutenant Don 66
Debden, RAF (Essex) 21, 23–4, 26, 146, 314, 401, 430, 454, 478
Deelen, Holland 130
De Havilland Mosquitoes 101, 150, 157, 180, 346–7, 390–1
Delaney (military policeman) 146
Dickleburgh, Norfolk 48
Diepholz, Germany 402, 404, 408, 410
Dimmick, Allen 315, 316
Doggett, Earl 399
Dolenga, Hauptmann Werner 222
Dölling, Unteroffizier Rudolf 39, 222

Doolittle, Major-General Jimmy xxvii; background 242–3; develops instrument-only flying 243; leads raid on Japan 244; takes command of Eighth Air Force 242, 244, 246, 253, 271, 272–5; his new strategy 286, 290, 293, 300, 309, 316, 325, 349, 420, 448; and Arnold 301; recalls bombers 331, 333; and Spaatz 233–4, 351, 259; and Operation ARGUMENT 276–7, 354, 356, 365

Dos, Margarete xxix, 234–6, 265–6, 431

Douglas, Air Chief Marshal Sir Sholto 168

Douglas DC-3 80

Douhet, Giulio: *Command of the Air* 76–7, 94

Dowding, Air Chief Marshal Sir Hugh 77

Dresden, Germany 133

drop tanks 38, 166–7, 171, 174–5, 332

Dunstable, Bedfordshire: Central Forecast Office 361

Düren, Germany 145

Düsseldorf, raids on 147, 152, 153, 156, 158

Eaker, Lt-General Ira xxvii; background 74–5; as commander of Eighth Air Force 51–2, 57, 70–1, 73, 82, 136, 162; at Casablanca Conference 136–7; his 'Plan' to destroy German fighters 138–40, 142; and Schweinfurt raid 70–1, 72; and Spaatz 84; and Arnold 72, 172, 239–42; in need of aircraft 175–6, 197, 215, 240, 270, 271, 276; as commander-in-chief of Eighth and Ninth Air Forces 183, 274–5, 319; and Operation POINTBLANK 183–4, 245; replaced by Arnold 245–7, 272; and Operation ARGUMENT 354–5, 373

early-warning services/systems, German 128–30, 152

Eastern Front 31–2, 36, 104, 111, 125, 134, 177, 180, 266, 429; *see also* Soviet Union

Eder Dam, Germany 104

Edison, Sergeant 63

Eisenach, Germany 436

Eisenhower, General Dwight D. 182, 241, 271, 335, 349, 469, 471

Elliott, Dick 66–7

Emden, Germany 228

Epps, Bill 453

Essen, Germany: Krupp works 133

Fabius, Unteroffizier 303, 306

Falck, Major Wolfgang 149, 179

Fame's Favored Few 57–61, 67–9

Fawcett, Dick 158

Fest, Jonny 39, 223

Fieseler aircraft factory *see* Kassel

Fitzgerald, F. Scott: *The Great Gatsby* 168

flak *see* anti-aircraft fire

Flugmeldedienst 128–9

Flugwache 129

Focke-Wulf: factories 52, 254; FW 190s *xiii*, 24, 43, 120–1, 135–6, 140, 166, 169, 205, 231, 247, 282–3, 291, 292, 309–12, 315–16, 322–3, 372, 375, 377–8, 380, 406

Foggia airfields, Italy 183, 184, 186, 245, 373, 402, 409, 425, 436

Foley, Sergeant 67

Ford, Sergeant 63

Fortresses *see* Boeing B-17G Flying Fortress bombers

Foster, Lieutenant Justus 376

France 128, 163, 168, 184, 187, 191–2, 207–8, 255, 303, 357

Frankfurt am Main, raids on 91–2, 194, 255–6, 320, 336, 340

Freeman, Air Chief Marshal Sir Wilfrid 77

Freya radar 102, 122, 129

Führmann, Unteroffizier Erich 42, 221–2, 223

Gabreski, Major Francis 'Gabby' xxvii; background 17–21; missions 20, 145–6, 205, 228, 229, 230–3, 252, 278, 282, 376–7, 420–1; as POW 476; postwar 476

Galland, Generalmajor Adolf 'Dolfo' xxix, 36, 117–18; on bombing of Hamburg 107; has hopes for Me262 production 111–12, 112, 464; and Göring 116–17, 118, 119; appointed General der Jagdflieger 118–20, 121, 123, 125, 126, 130; and Herrmann's *Wilde Sau* 126, 127; increases day-fighter force 177; clashes with Göring 219–20, 247–8; concerned by pilots' lack of bad-weather training 302, 326; disagrees with Göring over tactics 332, 339; returns to flying 474; postwar 474

'GEE' (navigation system) 100, 190, 361

Geiger, August 442

Gelsenkirchen, Germany 398

Gentile, Captain Don xxvii, 26–9, 309–14, 441–2, 455, 478

George VI 256, 272

George, Harold 79

Gerhard, Dieter 37

German airforce *see* Luftwaffe

Giles, Lt-General Barney 170–1, 176, 293, 301

Giltner, Captain Joe 320

Gilze-Rijen airfield, Holland 149, 338

Ginn, 'Hydro' 8

Godfrey, John 478

Goebbels, Josef 114, 133

Goldstein, Sergeant Larry 'Goldie' xxvii; background 198–201; joins 388th BG 197–8, 201–2; missions 202–3, 234, 255, 277–8, 338, 340, 367, 369, 385, 389, 406–7, 410–11, 434–5, 444, 450–1, 459, 472; and loss of friends 397; postwar 472

GOMORRAH, Operation 104, 107–8

Goodfellow, Lieutenant John C. 185

Goodson, Captain Jim 23, 24, 309, 384

Göring, Reichsmarschall Hermann xxix, 114; shocked by Allied bombing raids 99, 107–8; and production of Me 262s 112, 114; breaks down 115–17; and Galland 116–17, 118–19, 219–20, 247–8; and Jeschonnek 124; and Herrmann's *Wilde Sau* 126, 127, 195, 196, 262; orders destruction of Allied bombers 177; and Schmid 178–9, 429; and Knoke 37, 180–1; at Insterburg air display 218–19; falls in with Hitler's strategy 328, 329; fooled by American raid 331–2; goes on leave 464

Gotha, Germany 369, 415, 433, 438–9, 449

Graveley, RAF (Cambridgeshire) 190, 193, 203, 353, 356

Graz, Austria 414, 425

Great Sampford, RAF (Essex) 23

Greece 125, 185

Greenham Common, RAF (Berkshire) 161

Grieg, Captain Nordhal 234

Grosvenor, William 'Bill' 2, 3, 4

Ground Position Indicators 188

Guernica, Spain 94

Halberstadt, Germany 286, 287, 293, 298, 415, 423, 433

Halesworth, RAF (Suffolk) 146, 478

Halifax bombers *see* Handley-Page Halifax III bombers

Halverson Provisional Detachment 208

Hamburg, raids on 104, 107–8, 114–15, 124, 127, 132, 133, 179–80, 267

Hamelin, Germany 35, 418–20, 466

Handley, Flight Sergeant Ken 358, 359, 363–4, 447–8, 461, 470, 474

Handley Page Halifax III bombers *xi*, 86, 89, 90–2, 151, 154–5, 156, 157, 189, 256–7, 356, 358, 363, 447

Hanover, Germany 88, 316, 376

Harding, Colonel Neil 'Chick' 52

Harker, Ron 166, 168–9
Harris, Air Marshal Sir Arthur xxix, 15, 45, 87, 96, 345; rebuilds Bomber Command 97–106; his 'Blue Books' 103; his bombing philosophy 72, 98–9, 132–3, 139–40, 141–2, 364; plans to bomb Berlin 141, 147–8; and Düsseldorf raid 153; launches 'Battle of Berlin' 159, 188–90, 194, 196, 234, 267, 469; meets Arnold and Doolittle 238, 272–3; and raid on Frankfurt 255; and cross-Channel invasion 268; and Spaatz 336; targets Leipzig 346, 364; introduces diversionary tactics 346; opposes Schweinfurt raid 446; massed bombing tactics fail 469, 470
Hartmann, Bibi 467
Hawker Tempests 173–4
Hawker Typhoons 173–4
Heinkel, Ernst 108, 150
Heinkel Flugzeugwerke, Rostock 137; He 111 113; He 177s 95, 328, 330; He 219 150
Helmstedt, Germany 369
Hemphill, Lieutenant George E. 205
Henschel factories, Kassel 88, 93
Herrmann, Oberst Hans-Joachim 'Hajo' xxix, 124–8, 179, 180, 195–7, 248, 261, 262–6, 330, 347, 475
Hethel, RAF (Norfolk) 404–6
High Wycombe, RAF (Buckinghamshire) 70, 103, 132, 153, 291, 353
Himmelbett radar system 122–3, 124, 128, 179–80
Himmler, Heinrich 218
Hitchcock, Major Tommy 168
Hitler, Adolf 44, 80; and Battle of Britain 13, 134; belief in technology and the Luftwaffe 33; judgement worsens 113, 131; clashes with Milch 113; vacillation 115, 329; and Göring 116–17; insists on offensive

action 149, 152, 174, 189, 327, 328; and Italy 182; his approach to leadership 195; at Insterburg air display 218–19; congratulates Herrmann 265; reduces pilot recuperation periods 332
Hofmann, Willi 395–6
Honeycutt, Airleigh 425
Hopkins, Harry 238
Horchdienst 128, 129, 157
Hornet, USS 244
Howard, Major Jim 294, 296–8, 299–300, 301
H2S (radar) 101, 147, 188, 190, 261, 271, 447
H2X (radar) 183, 271, 275–6, 302, 355, 410–11
Hubbard, Lloyd 323
Hughes, Elaine 398
Hughes, Captain Harry 60, 63, 67
Hughes, Lt Robert 'Bob' xxvii, 52–6, 61–2, 65–7, 69, 71, 255, 331, 398, 473

Ingmire, Sergeant Richard E. 281
Insterburg airfield, East Prussia 218–19
Iowa, USS 238
Irving, David 475
Italy/Italians 31, 32, 105, 181–7, 237–8, 245, 354, 372–4, 402–3, 409, 425, 435–6

Japan/Japanese 13, 79, 190; and Pearl Harbor 14, 18, 243; Doolittle Raid (1942) 243–4
Jena, Germany 234–6
Jeschonnek, General Hans 123–4, 126
Johnen, Oberleutnant Wilhelm 'Wim' xxix, 148–52, 181, 248, 267–8, 303–8, 330, 394, 474, 476
Johnson, Johnnie 167
Johnson, Ralph 9
Johnson, Lt Robert 'Bob' xxviii, 153, 323, 326; background 16–17, 21; missions 2–10, 17, 145–7, 205, 228–31, 252, 278, 282–3, 315, 316, 333, 376–7; becomes an ace 9, 42, 476; postwar 476

Jouanjean, Janine 192
Joyce, William (Lord Haw-Haw) 286
Junkers factories 293, 368; Ju 87
    Stukas 95; Ju 88s *xiii*, 4, 95, 113,
    140, 291, 297, 346, 360;
    Ju 188s 346
Junkers Motoren (Jumo) engines 112

Kammerer, Oberfeldwebel 308
Kammhuber, Oberst Josef 122, 123–4,
    126, 127, 128, 150, 179–80
Kamprath, Leutnant 305, 308
Kassel: raids on 88, 92–3, 106, 132,
    143, 147, 219; Fieseler factory 88,
    219; Henschel factories 88, 93
Keeffe, Lieutenant James H. 'Jim'
    xxviii, 403–6, 409–10, 433, 436,
    438–41, 445, 473
Keirsted, Lieutenant Belford J. 'BJ'
    197–8, 200, 201–2, 205, 369, 398
Keith, Lieutenant Kent 278, 459
Kepner, Major-General William 'Bill'
    xxviii, 74, 274–5, 293, 309, 316,
    323, 325, 349, 351, 365–6, 401
Kesselring, Feldmarschall Albert 182
Kiel, Germany 277, 280, 346, 360, 447;
    U-boat pens 55
Kimbolton, RAF (Cambridgeshire)
    203, 206, 286–7, 288–9, 298, 386,
    415, 424, 444, 474
Kindelberger, James Howard 'Dutch'
    164, 171
King, Admiral Ernest 84
Kiser, Bob 368, 383
Klopotek, Bob 225
Knettishall, RAF (Suffolk) 197, 201–2,
    389, 444, 450, 460
Knoke, Leutnant Heinz xxix, 35;
    marriage 35–6; missions 35,
    36–44; shot down 41–2, 131;
    and death of fellow airmen 43,
    221–3; 333, 340, 408–9, 419–20,
    442, 466; as leading ace 180, 248;
    not impressed by Göring 180–1;
    further missions 220–1, 230,
    249–50, 330; shot down again
    279–80; back flying 326, 332–3,

338–40, 408, 418–20, 453–4,
    457–9; shot down again 475;
    wounded by mine 475;
    postwar 475–6
Knoke, Ingrid 280
Knoke, Lilo 35–6, 249, 280
Körner, Paul 108
Kreidler, Captain Howard 217
Kreuger, Feldwebel 418–19, 442
Kruer, Ed 230
Krupp works, Essen 133
Kugel-Fischer ball-bearings factor *see*
    Schweinfurt
Kursk, Soviet Union 105

Lady Shamrock 282, 283–5
Lamb, Roger 'Sheep' 256–7
Lancaster bombers *see* Avro Lancaster
    bombers
Landry, Colonel Robert B. 145
Langley Field, Virginia: Air Corps
    Tactical School 78, 80
Lawley, Lieutenant William R. 'Bill'
    xxviii, 215–16, 297, 369, 378–82,
    385–6, 388–9, 396, 473
Leconfield, RAF (Yorkshire) 358, 448
Leeming, RAF (North Yorkshire)
    90–1, 92, 93, 153, 158–9,
    228, 356
Leigh-Mallory, Air Marshal Sir
    Trafford 167–8, 173–5, 335,
    350–1, 470
Leipzig, raids on 88, 346, 353, 358,
    360, 362–4, 369, 371, 376–80,
    401, 428–9, 431, 464
Leiston, RAF (Suffolk) 319–20, 371–2
LeMay, Brigadier-General Curtis 52, 145
Lemke, Hauptmann Wilhelm 249
Letter, Danny 397
Leuchter, Fred 475
Leverkusen, Germany 194
Liberators *see* Consolidated B-24
    Liberators
Lichtenstein radar 129, 150
Lightnings *see* Lockheed P-38
    Lightnings
Lindbergh, Charles 216

'Little Friends' 59
Lockheed P-38 Lightnings *xii*, 38, 170, 176, 186, 273, 287, 318, 365, 414, 443, 458
London 237, 257; 'Baby Blitz' 327, 330; *see also* Blitz, the
Lorient, France: U-boat pens 191–2
Lovett, Robert A. 162–3, 170, 171
Lucera airfield, Italy 373, 402, 425
Ludford Magna, RAF (Lincolnshire) 258–9, 347–8, 353–4, 359, 363, 391
Ludwigshafen, Germany 189, 255, 282
Luftflotte Reich 247, 331–2
Luftwaffe 10, 19, 20, 30–1, 33–5, 71–2, 85, 93–5, 96, 107–18, 119–22, 141–2, 148, 149–51, 152, 176–80, 247–8, 302–8, 327–30, 331–2, 428–30, 483; *Staffeln* 19, 122, 222; *Jagddivisionen* xviii–xix, xxii, 128; losses 133–4, 178, 222, 302, 418, 428, 463–4, 466, 467, 483, 484; *see also* Focke-Wulf; Heinkel; Herrmann, Hans-Joachim; Junkers; Knoke, Heinz; Messerschmitt
Lüneberg Heath, Germany 457

McArthur, Lieutenant Jimmy 403, 404–6, 410, 438–9, 445
McColpin, Carroll 'Red' 23
McGinley, Frank 186–7
McGinnis, Willy 424
McGinty, Sergeant Hugh 'Mac' xxviii, 396–7; background 203; missions 203–6, 255, 286–9, 290–2, 296, 297–8, 336–7; on leave 336, 337–8; further missions 374–6, 386–7, 415, 418, 422–4, 433, 434, 441, 459, 473; postwar 473–4
McKennon, Lieutenant 'Smoke' 68–9
McKew, Lieutenant Marshall 'Mac' 187, 402–3, 435
McLaughlin, Lieutenant J. Kemp xxviii, 57–61, 62–5, 67–9, 72
Madingley, Cambridgeshire: American cemetery 337, 474

Mahle (gunner) 304–5, 307
Mahurin, Major Walker 326
Malta 30, 125, 166, 173
'Mammut' radar 129
'Mandrel' (radar-jamming device) 102
Mannheim, Germany 189, 193–4; radar 196
Manston, Kent 232–3, 309
Marienburg, Germany: Focke-Wulf plant 52
Marseille, Hans-Joachim 110
Marshall, General George 84, 182, 238, 271
Martin Aircraft Company 80, 81
Mason, Lieutenant Henry 369, 379–80, 381, 382, 388
Mathies, Sergeant Archie 396
Mayer, Major Egon 121
Meredith, Dick 91, 159
Merlin engines 155, 166, 168
Messerschmitt, Willi 108, 111, 219, 476
Messerschmitt factories 137, 186, 414, 428, 438–9, 462, 464; Me 109s *xiv*, 4, 109, 110, 121, 135, 140, 146, 166, 169, 186, 205, 231–2, 247, 251, 278, 283, 290, 291, 294–5, 296, 297, 339–40, 346, 375, 416, 438, 456, 464; Me 110s *xiv*, 3, 4, 110–11, 149, 150, 205, 230, 291, 292, 294–5, 296, 297, 303–8, 376–7, 394; Me 210s *xiv*, 4, 111, 291; Me 262s 111–12, 113, 115, 219, 329, 464; Me 309s 109; Me 410s 111, 295–6, 316
Metcalf, Lieutenant 399
Meyers, Lt-Colonel Gil 420
Milch, Feldmarschall Erhard xxix, 108–10, 112, 113–16, 119, 123, 125, 218–19, 328, 329–30, 395, 464, 465
Miley, Captain Spike 28–9
Miller, Bob 200–1
Ministry of Aircraft Production, British 76, 175
Mitchell, William 'Billy' 77–8, 94
Möhne Dam 104
Mölders, Werner 118

'Monica' (tail-warning radar) 102
Moore, Sergeant John 156, 158
Mosquitoes see De Havilland Mosquitoes
Moulton, Lieutenant Raymond 'Moose' H. 403
Mülheim, Germany 126
Müller, Friedrich-Karl 'Tutti' 262
Munich: Beer Hall Putsch (1923) 178
Münster, raids on 1, 42, 49, 52, 69, 255, 277
Murphy, Lieutenant Paul 380-1
Murphy, Lieutenant Tom 55-6
Mussolini, Benito 32, 182
Mustangs see North American Mustangs

Nathan, Matt(y) 205, 336-7, 376
navigational systems 98, 133, 139; 'GEE' 100, 190, 361; see also radar systems
Neumann, Edu 127
Nine Little Yanks and a Jerk 52-3, 54-6, 65-6, 69
Nissen huts 217-18
Norden, Carl: bombsight 81-2, 83, 94, 102, 441
North African campaigns 15, 32, 75, 182, 184-5
North American Aviation 164-6, 171
North American P-51/P-51A/P-51B/ P-51D Mustangs xii, xxv, 144, 161-3, 165-73, 176, 184, 223, 224, 228, 273, 287-8, 289-90, 293-6, 299, 316-17, 319, 321-2, 324, 335-6, 341, 349-50, 375, 401, 407, 410, 416, 467-8
Nowotny, Sergeant 333
Nuremberg, Germany 450, 469-70

Oboe (radar) 100-1, 147, 183, 188, 190, 346, 361
O'Brien, Lieutenant William 'OBee' 411
O'Connor, Frank 294, 295
O'Grady, Lieutenant Ed 60, 64-5
Öhlschläger, Leutnant 36
Old Crow 407, 411

Ormerod, Pilot Officer John 'Curly' 392-3
Oschersleben, raid on 286, 287, 291-3, 296, 298, 299, 300, 366, 369
Osnabrück, Germany 255
Ott, Major George 63
OVERLORD, Operation 45, 140-2, 143, 172, 241, 269, 335, 336, 349, 355, 470

P-38 see Lockheed P-38 Lightnings
P-47 see Republic P-47 Thunderbolts
P-51/P-51A/P-51B/P-51D see North American P-51 Mustangs
Packard: Merlin engines 168-9, 170
panzer commanders 248, 249
Parchim airfield, Germany 302-3, 307-8
Park, Air Vice-Marshal Keith 178
Pathfinder Force (PFF) 101, 102, 148, 157, 188, 189, 190-4, 203, 255, 263, 276, 362, 368, 370, 447, 448, 461
Pattison, Wing Commander Jack 153, 158, 159
Patton, General George 273
Paxton, David 453
Pearl Harbor (1941) 14, 18, 243
Peaslee, Colonel Budd 60, 60-1, 62, 64, 65
Peenemünde research establishment, Germany 115, 124, 219
Peirse, Air Marshal Sir Richard 98
Peltz, Oberst Dietrich 116, 327-9, 330
Pentony, Flight Lieutenant 92
Pershore, RAF (Worcestershire) 90
PFF see Pathfinder Force
Philadelphia Story, The (film) 209
Piccadilly Lily 55
PINETREE, Operation 70
Piraeus, Greece 125
Ploesti, Romania 184, 471
Podington, RAF (Bedfordshire) 56-7, 68-9, 72
POINTBLANK, Operation 140, 147, 172, 182, 183, 236-7, 239-40, 245, 254, 268, 276, 334, 335, 349, 355, 390, 464

Pointon, Flying Sergeant Max 461
Poland 18, 54, 78, 118, 125, 367, 369, 383
Polish squadrons, RAF 18
Portal, Air Chief Marshal Sir Charles xxix, 97; and Eaker 75, 140; and resurgent German fighter force 140; and Arnold's demands for a combined aerial offensive 171–6; and invasion of Italy 182; coordinates Combined Bomber Offensive 239; objects to creation of new HQ 239; at Cairo Conference 239, 245; and Eaker's removal 245, 246; and establishment of USSTAF 271; issues change of objective for Bomber Command 335; overruled by Churchill 356; overrules Harris 446
Poznań, Poland 367, 369, 383
Prüfening plant *see* Regensburg

Queen Elizabeth 318
Queen Mary 201
Question Mark (Fokker aircraft) 83
Quonset huts 217

radar systems 128–30, 195, 226; Flugmeldedienst 128–9; Freya 102, 122, 129; gun-laying 393–4; *Himmelbett* 122–5, 128, 179–80; H2S 101, 147, 188, 190, 271, 361, 447; Horchdienst 128, 129, 157; H2X 183, 271, 275–6, 302, 355, 410–11; and jamming and detection devices 102, 346–7, *see also* 'Window'; Kammhuber Line 122, 123; Lichtenstein 129, 150; Mammut 129; Mannheim 196; Oboe 101, 147, 183, 188, 190, 346, 361; SN2 150, 151–2; Wassermann 95; Würzburg 122, 129, 196; Ypsilon/Y 151
Raddatz, Hans 339, 340
RAF *see* Royal Air Force
railway, German *see* Reichsbahn

Rall, Günther 467
Rankin, Lieutenant John 382–3
Rau, William 'Bill' 288–9, 336
Reeves, Les 260, 261, 393
Regensburg, raids on 50, 52, 56, 124, 170, 254, 366, 373–4, 402, 425, 431, 450–3, 459, 464; Prüfening factory 414, 421, 464
Reichsbahn (German railway) 88, 135, 265, 266, 466, 470
Reinhard, Obergefreiter Peter 38
Remer, Otto Ernst 475
Republic P-47 Thunderbolts *xiii*, 1–10, 24, 143, 146, 169, 170, 205–6, 223, 230–3, 273, 278, 283, 287, 309–14, 319, 376–7, 384, 401, 406, 414, 443, 458
Richards, Lieutenant 309, 310–11, 312
Ridgewell, RAF (Essex) 72, 250, 280–2, 387–8, 479
Robinson, Elizabeth 218
Robinson, Sergeant John 'Robbie' xxviii; arrives at Tibenham 217–18; and James Stewart 226–8, 412–13, 460; missions 255, 270, 399–400, 415–17, 425, 434, 435, 436–8, 449, 450, 451–2, 455–7, 460; and death of friends 399; postwar 473
Rolls-Royce engines 166, 168 and *n*, 170
Roosevelt, President Franklin D. 14–15, 32, 45, 80, 84, 136, 140, 238
Rostock, Germany 137, 369, 384, 385
Rotterdam, Netherlands 94
Royal Air Force 76–7, 122, 167–8, 242; Bomber Command/bombers 15, 31, 45, 70, 85–7, 88, 91, 93–4, 75–106, 123–4, 132, 137–8, 140, 147, 152, 153–4, 157, 194, 197, 239, 255, 335–6, 362, 390, 394, 446–7, 461, 464, 470–1; bases *xv*; losses 194, 234, 268, 364, 394, 461, 464–5, 469–70; *see also* Harris, Air Marshal Sir Arthur *and specific bombers*; squadrons: 101 Squadron 258–62, 347–8,

353–4, 359, 362–4, 391–4; 427
'Lion' Squadron 155; 429
Squadron 153, 155, 158–9, 356;
460 Squadron 234; 466 Squadron
358, 363, 461; Eagle Squadrons
(US) 21, 24, 26, 28; Fighter
Command 16, 75, 77, 138, 163–6,
167, 172–6; *see also* Battle of
Britain, Combined Bomber
Offensive, Pathfinders *and
specific fighters*
Royal Canadian Air Force 22, 26,
27–8, 190
Ruhr region, Germany 104, 114, 418, 423

Sale, Squadron Leader Julian 193,
256–7, 353, 356–7, 360
Satan's Sister 397
Saunders, Colonel/Saunders
Provisional Group 54
Schelp, Helmut 112
Schilling, Major David 2, 146, 325
Schmid, Generalmajor Josef 'Beppo'
xxix, 128, 176–7, 178–9, 195, 247,
331–2, 429, 468
Schmued, Edgar 164–5, 166, 169, 171
Schneider Cup air speed race (1925) 242
Schönert, Major Rudi 151
Schräge Musik 151–2, 360
Schweinfurt, raids on 49, 56, 73, 115,
124, 140, 170, 171, 176, 240, 366,
433, 434, 441, 446; Kugel-Fischer
ball-bearing factories 37, 49–51,
65–6, 70–2, 137
Scott, Flight Sergeant Jack 358, 359,
363, 364, 447
Second Was First, The 402, 435–6, 443
Seraphine, Lieutenant Henry 381, 386
Serrate radar-detection devices 346–7
Sharrard, Lieutenant Lloyd 217
Sicherheitsdienst (SD) 431–2
Sicily 31, 32, 105, 134, 181, 182–3,
185, 244
Smith, Les 315
Smith, Walter Bedell 271
Snetterton Heath, RAF (Norfolk)
363–4

SN2 radar 150, 151–2
Sorensen, Charles 197
Sorko, Leutnant 308
Sorpe Dam 104
Soviet Union 13, 31, 32, 33, 95, 107; and
Operation BARBAROSSA 44
Spaatz, Lt-General Carl 'Tooey'
xxviii, 45, 51; background 83–4;
and Eaker 75, 83, 84; takes
command of US Eighth Air
Force 84–6; at Casablanca
Conference (1943) 135; and
invasion of Italy 182; suggests
Doolittle takes command of
Eighth Air Force 176, 244, 273;
commands USSTAF 238, 245,
246, 270–2, 293, 302; on need
for more Pathfinder aircraft 276;
prioritizes arrival of aircraft 319;
clashes with Doolittle 333–4;
takes control of Operation
ARGUMENT 276, 335,
348–52, 354–6, 366, 401, 414–15,
448, 453; and Operation
POINTBLANK 355, 465,
469; targets key German oil
centres 471
Spanish Civil War 94, 118
Specht, Major 457
Speer, Albert 108, 109, 114, 196,
329, 465
Spence, Dr Magnus 346
Spitfires *see* Supermarine Spitfire
Mk IX
Spoden, Leutnant 308
Sprecht, Hauptmann 40
Stabilized Automatic Bomb Sight
(SABS) 102
Stacker, Jack 317, 318
Stalingrad (1943) 32, 107
Stanbridge Earls, nr Southampton 72
Stanford-Tuck, Bob 75
Stars & Stripes 428, 463
Stehkämper, Hugo 431
Steinhaurer, Lieutenant Manny 370
Stevens, Lieutenant Don 403–4
Stewart, Alex 210

Stewart, Major James 'Jimmy' xxviii;
    background 208–11; commands
    703rd Squadron 208, 210, 217;
    gives press conference 226;
    impresses his crew 226–7;
    missions 228, 255, 270, 282,
    283–5, 289, 368, 370, 382–3,
    449–50, 451–2, 456–7, 460, 472;
    gives Wright a tongue-lashing
    400; uncovers some stolen beer
    412–13; postwar 472–3
Steyr, Austria 435, 443
Stirling bombers 149, 152, 189, 346
Stockton, Norman 234
Strand, Larry 230
Strüning, Heini 149–50
Stumpff, General Hans-Jürgen 195, 331
Stuttgart, raids on 88, 137, 354, 390,
    391, 393–6
Sullivan, Lieutenant Robert 'Sully'
    xxviii, 373–4, 402, 409, 414, 421,
    425, 451, 453, 474
Sullivan, Lieutenant T. Michael xxviii,
    185–7, 402, 409, 425, 435, 443,
    451, 474
Sunflower Sue 217
Suntrop, Heribert 43
Supermarine Spitfire Mk IX xiii, 23, 118,
    120, 155, 166–7, 169, 173–5, 333

Talbot, Lieutenant John 292, 293
Tedder, Air Chief Marshal Sir
    Arthur 241
Tehran Conference (1943) 238–9
Ten Horsepower 396
Tenovus 370, 382–3
Terrill, Lt-Colonel Bob 210
Thelveton, Norfolk 48
Thomas, Flying Officer Tommy 191–3
Thorpe Abbotts, RAF (Norfolk) 47,
    48, 61–2, 72, 251, 255, 478–9
'Thousand Bomber Raids' 99, 100, 123
Thunderbolts see Republic P47
    Thunderbolts
Tibenham, RAF (Norfolk) 210–11,
    216–18, 285, 368–9, 411–13,
    425–6, 434, 444, 449–50, 460

Timberlake, Brigadier-General Ed 472
'Transportation Plan' 470–1
Travis, Brigadier-General Robert F. 418
Trenchard, Marshal of the Air Force
    Sir Hugh 'Boom' 77, 94
Truemper, Lieutenant Walter 396
Tucker, Lieutenant 387–8
Tunisia 14, 179, 184–5
Turner, Captain Dick xxviii; on
    Athlone Castle 160–1; posted
    to Boxted and P51Bs 161–2, 176;
    instructed by Blakeslee 223–4,
    325; missions 225–6, 251–2,
    287–8, 289–90, 293–6, 316–17,
    339–40, 407, 477; postwar 477
Tutow, Germany 369
Twente, Holland 43
Twining, Major-General Nathan 355
Tyler (bomber crew member) 437,
    452, 455

U-boats 14, 55, 191–2, 201, 228, 248,
    249, 254, 270; Type XXI 33
Udet, Ernst 118
United States Army Air Corps 78–82,
    84, 164, 207
United States Army Air Forces
    (USAAF) 16–17, 84, 86–7, 183,
    242, 244, 270, 333; Halveson
    Provisional Detachment 208;
    Eighth Air Force 15–16, 37, 45,
    50, 52, 57, 59–60, 69, 70, 71, 75,
    85, 86–7, 88, 136, 145, 171, 176,
    183, 207, 237–8, 239–40, 242,
    253, 269, 271, 275, 282, 288, 324,
    333–4, 338, 350, 351, 352, 354,
    367–8, 432, 467; bases xvi–xvii;
    headquarters 18; VIII Bomber
    Command 9, 50, 52, 72, 75, 168,
    197, 271, 335–6, 354, 366; losses
    9, 51, 69, 71, 79, 136, 140, 203,
    240, 270, 299, 366, 387, 396,
    397–9, 445, 448, 464, 467; 92nd
    BG 56–7, 58–61, 67–9; 93rd BG
    282, 284; 95th BG 62, 65–7;
    100th BG 9–10, 47, 48–9, 52,
    55–6, 62–5, 69, 251, 255, 331, 398;

305th BG 69, 73, 216, 297–8, 378–82, 385–6, 388–9; 306th BG 69; 351st BG 396; 379th BG 69, 203–6, 286–7, 288–9, 290–3, 298, 336–7, 374–6, 386–7, 415, 418, 422–4, 433, 441, 444; 381st BG 72, 250, 280–2, 426, 479; 384th BG 69; 388th BG 197–8, 201–2, 367, 369, 383–4, 389, 406–7, 434–5, 444, 450–1, 459; 389th BG 205, 283–5, 368, 404, 433, 438–41, 445; 390th BG 62; 401st BG 297–8, 300; 445th BG 215, 216, 226–8, 255, 282, 283–5, 289, 216–18, 368, 370, 382–3, 411, 415–17, 425, 434, 436–8, 444, 449, 450, 451–2, *see also* 703rd BS; 453rd BG 368; 326th BS 57; 351st BS 55; 364th BS 216; 407th BS 57; 524th BS 203–6; 563rd BS 197–8; 566th BS 404, 433, 436, 440; 701st BS 158; 703rd BS 208, 210–11, 399–400, 415–17, 425, 434, 436–8, 444, 449, 450, 455–6, 460; **VIII Fighter Command** 16, 19, 29, 138, 165, 170, 252, 300, 315, 324, 365–6; losses 316, 467; 4th Fighter Group 21–2, 23, 24, 26, 145–7, 223, 252, 309–14, 323, 384, 401, 406, 454–5, 478; 56th FG (61st, 62nd, 63rd Fighter Squadrons) 1–10, 16, 17, 18, 19–20, 39, 145–7, 205, 228–33, 252, 278, 282–3, 315, 316, 326, 376–7, 420–1; 328th FG 318; 354th FG 160–3, 176, 223–6, 228, 287–8, 289–90, 293–6, 316–17, 319, 320, 323, 340; 357th FG 317, 318, 319–23, 372, 377–8, 407, 410, 411; 334th FS 311, 384, 406, 430, 454–5; 336th FS (133 Squadron) 22–4, 28–9, 309–14, 441–2, 455; 356th FS 251–2, 294–7, 299–300; 363rd FS 318, 320; **Ninth Air Force** 163, 171, 176, 183, 237–8, 239, 309, 319, 350, 352, 354, 470; **Twelfth Air Force** 182, 183, 244, 355; **Fifteenth Air Force** 183, 184, 187, 237, 238, 269, 277, 355, 365, 373, 402, 414, 425, 443, 452; 2nd BG 184–7, 402–3, 414, 425, 435, 443, 452–3; 97th BG 436; 301st BG 373, 402, 421–2, 425, 436, 451, 453; 32nd BS 453; 419th BS 453; 429th BS 185–7, 425, 435–6, 443, 451

United States Strategic Air Forces (USSTAF) 237–8, 271, 293, 354, 365, 396

Upper Street, Norfolk 48

V1s and V2s 33, 115, 329
Van Horn, Sergeant 64

Walker, Kenneth 79
'Wanganui flares' 362–3 *and n*
Warsaw, Poland 94
Washington Conference (1943) 137
Wassermann radar 129
Waterman, Lieutenant 146
Waughman, Flight Lt Russell 'Rusty' xxix, 257–62, 347–8, 353–4, 359, 362, 364, 391, 392–4
Weigel, William 'Bill' 291–2
Weise, Generaloberst Hubert 123, 176, 177, 179
Wendt, Sergeant Alfred 380
Wenneckers (pilot) 458–9
Westby, Norman 189
Wiener Neustadt, Austria 186, 187
Wilde Sau ('Wild Boar') nightfighters 124, 125–8, 180, 194–5, 196, 261, 262, 265, 267, 347
Wilhelmshaven, Germany 146
Willow Run, Michigan: aircraft factory 197
Wilson, General Henry Maitland 372–3
Wilson, Sergeant (radio) 370
'Window' (radar jamming strips) 102, 105, 128, 147, 150, 179, 455–6, 457
Winning Your Wings (recruitment film) 209
Wittering, RAF (Cambridgeshire) 19
Wittmann, Lieutenant 456

Wolfert, Ira 478
Wood, Captain 439
World War, First 34, 44, 83, 89, 184, 209, 210
Worry Wart 202, 255, 277–8, 338, 369, 385, 389, 406–7, 410, 434–5, 459
Wright, Lieutenant George 217, 399, 400, 412, 413, 415–16, 417, 425, 434, 436–8, 444, 449, 450, 455–7, 460
Wunstorf, Germany 418
Würzburg radar 122–3, 129, 196
Wycombe Abbey, Buckinghamshire 70, 271, 272

'Yoxford Boys' 319–20
Ypsilon/Y navigation system 151

Z for Zebra 154, 157–8
Zahme Sau (Tame Boar) 128, 151, 157, 180, 267–8, 306
Zankey, Paul 258, 259
Zara, Yugoslavia 451
Zemke, Colonel Hubert 'Hub' 2, 19, 145, 252, 325–6
Zemke's 56th Fighter Group 2, 8, 252
ZITADELLE, Operation 31, 32

THE BATTLE OF BRITAIN
Five months that changed history: May–October 1940

'If Hitler fails to invade or destroy Britain, he has lost the war,' Churchill said in the summer of 1940. He was right. The Battle of Britain was a crucial turning point in the history of the Second World War. Had Britain's defences collapsed, Hitler would have dominated all of Europe and been able to turn his full attention east to the Soviet Union.

The German invasion of France and the Low Countries in May 1940 was unlike any the world had ever seen. It hit with a force and aggression that no one could counter and in just a few short weeks, all in their way crumbled under the force of the Nazi hammer blow. With France facing defeat and with British forces pressed back to the Channel, there were few who believed Britain could possibly survive. Soon, it seemed, Hitler would have all of Europe at his feet. But thanks to a sophisticated defensive system and the combined efforts of the RAF and the Royal Navy, as well as the mounting sense of collective defiance led by a new Prime Minister, Britain was not ready to roll over just yet.

From clashes between coastal convoys and *Schnellboote* in the Channel to astonishing last stands in Flanders, and from the slaughter by the U-boats in the icy Atlantic to the dramatic aerial battles over England, *The Battle of Britain* tells this most epic of stories from all sides, drawing on extensive new research from around the world. In so doing, it paints a complete picture of that extraordinary summer – a time in which the fate of the world truly hung by a thread.

'Holland is excellent on telling detail ... This is a notable account of an epic human experience, told with the informality and enthusiasm that distinguish Holland's work ... Holland tells it with authority and exuberant panache' Max Hastings, *Sunday Times*

'Ambitious and comprehensive ... the pace never flags as the narrative ranges effortlessly from the cockpit of the Spitfire to the gallery of the House of Commons' Saul David, *Daily Telegraph*

THE WAR IN
A NEW

Volume I: Germany Ascendant 1939–1941

So much has been written about the monumental conflict that was the Second World War, but never like this. Drawing on new research from around the world, acclaimed historian James Holland presents an entirely fresh look at the war that changed our world.

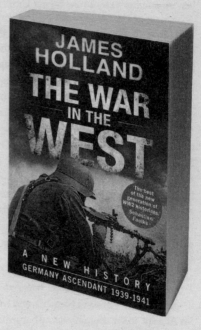

From the horror of the Blitzkrieg and Dunkirk to the heroism of the Battle of Britain and the colossal folly that was Operation Barbarossa, Holland relates the dramatic story of the war from all sides like never before, weaving together the experiences of the people who fought, planned, plotted, or just lived through the momentous events of 1939 to 1941. By challenging the conventional wisdom at every step, he has created a genuinely thrilling and epic narrative which redefines and enhances our understanding of one of the most significant cataclysms in history.

'The best of the new generation of WW2 historians'
Sebastian Faulks

THE WEST
HISTORY

Volume II: The Allies Fight Back 1941–1943

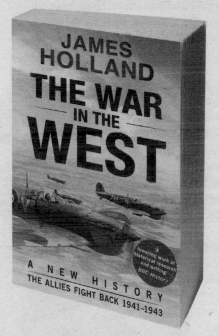

Tobruk, Leningrad, the Siege of Malta, the Odessa Massacre, the 1000 Bomber raids of Cologne and Hamburg, the Battle of the Atlantic, Operation Chariot – the Second World War is populated by some of the most notorious and familiar stories of the recent past.

But as we discover in this second part of James Holland's epic history, there are different ways of looking at those pivotal moments which offer a broader, more penetrating perspective than ever before, challenging what we think we know about the conflict that shaped our world.

From the battlefronts on land, in the air and at sea, to the factories and the shipyards, and the fields and streets of Britain, Holland reveals the true story of the war as the tide begins to turn: across the Atlantic Ocean, the Mediterranean and the deserts of North Africa, while on mainland Europe the Allies unleash a fearsome bombing campaign against Nazi Germany. Told from all sides, and incorporating startling new research, this is a truly ground-breaking and perceptive re-evaluation of an extraordinary and unprecedented cataclysm.

DAM BUSTERS

The Race to Smash the Dams 1943

The night of May 16th, 1943. Nineteen specially adapted Lancaster bombers take off from RAF Scampton in Lincolnshire, each with a huge 9,000lb cylindrical bomb strapped underneath it. Their mission: to destroy three dams deep within the German heartland, which provide the lifeblood to the industries supplying the Third Reich's war machine.

From the outset it was an almost impossible task, a suicide mission: to fly low and at night in formation over many miles of enemy-occupied territory at the very limit of the Lancasters' capacity, and drop a new weapon, that had never been tried operationally, on some of the most heavily defended targets in Germany.

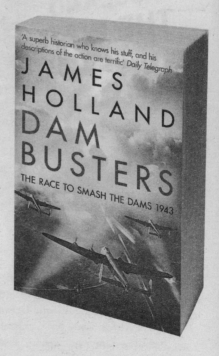

More than that, the entire operation had to be put together in less than ten weeks. When visionary aviation engineer Barnes Wallis's concept of the bouncing bomb was green lighted, he hadn't even drawn up his plans for the weapon that was to smash the dams. What followed was an incredible race against time, which became one of the most successful and game-changing bombing raids of all time.

'Holland tells the story with gusto and pace . . . He has truly and brilliantly plugged an enormous gap'
Mail on Sunday

BURMA '44

The Battle That Turned Britain's War in the East

In February 1944, a ragtag collection of clerks, doctors and muleteers, a few York-shiremen and a handful of tank crews defeated a huge and sophisticated contingent of the fearsome and previously unvanquished Japanese infantry on their march towards the prize of India.

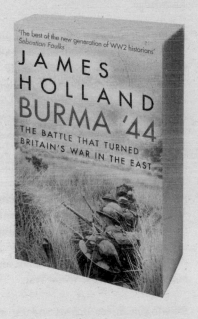

What became known as the Battle of the Admin Box was the first decisive victory for the Allies but, more significantly, it demonstrated how the Japanese could be defeated. Lessons learned in this otherwise insignificant corner of the Far East would underpin the campaign in Burma as General Slim's Fourteenth Army turned the tide of the war in the east.

Burma '44 is a tale of the triumph of human grit and heroism in what remains one of the most significant yet undervalued conflicts of World War Two.

'Up there with Rorke's Drift . . . in rescuing the Battle of the Admin Box from oblivion, Holland has performed a signal service for all the men who fought – and died – in its defence' *Daily Telegraph*

'It is the voices of the fighting men that lift this book above the level of a simple battle narrative. Holland has a good ear for the telling reminiscences that authenticate the dialogue of so many war films of the time' *The Times*

NORMANDY '44

D-Day & the Battle for France
A New History

D-Day and the 76 days of bitter fighting in Normandy that followed have come to be seen as a defining episode in the Second World War. Its story has endlessly been retold in books, films, television series, documentaries, and comic books. It is entirely familiar and yet it remains a narrative burdened by both myth and assumed knowledge.

In this new history, James Holland presents a broader overview, one which challenges much of what we think we know about D-Day and the Normandy campaign. The sheer size and scale of the Allies' war machine ultimately dominates the strategic, operational and tactical limitations of the German forces. Air power plays a more dominant role and the mechanics and operational level of war on land, sea and in the air are laid bare. This was a brutal campaign, and the shocking violence and carnage of the conflict is revealed in disturbing and unflinching detail. In terms of daily casualties, the numbers were worse than any one battle during the First World War.

Drawing on unseen archives and testimonies from around the world and introducing a cast of eye-witnesses which includes foot soldiers, tank men, fighter pilots and bomber crews, sailors, civilians, resistors and those directing the action. *Normandy '44* is rich in fresh and revealing analysis but firmly rooted in the real drama of men and women at war. It is an epic tale and this telling will profoundly recalibrate our understanding of its true place in the tide of human history.

COMING IN SUMMER 2019